American History
A CONCISE DOCUMENTS COLLECTION
Volume 2: Since 1865

D0166794

American History
A CONCISE DOCUMENTS COLLECTION
Volume 2: Since 1865

Douglas Bukowski

Bedford/St. Martin's
Boston/New York

For Bedford/St. Martin's
History Editor: Katherine E. Kurzman
Production Editor: Harold Chester
Production Supervisor: Dennis J. Conroy
Marketing Manager: Charles Cavaliere
Art Director: Lucy Krikorian
Text Design: Paul Agresti
Cover Art: Mid-Town, New York by Guy Wiggins. Courtesy of Owen Gallery, New York.
Composition: ComCom
Printing and Binding: Haddon Craftsmen, Inc.

President: Charles H. Christensen
Editorial Director: Joan E. Feinberg
Director of Editing, Design, and Production: Marcia Cohen
Managing Editor: Erica T. Appel

Library of Congress Catalog Card Number: 98-89220

Manufactured in the United States of America.

4 3 2 1 0 9
f e d c b a

For information, write: Bedford/St. Martin's, 75 Arlington Street, Boston, MA 02116 (617-426-7440)

ISBN: 0-312-19668-7

Acknowledgments

PREFACE

American History: A Concise Documents Collection, Volume 2 brings together over 90 primary source excerpts organized to parallel the chapters of *America: A Concise History, Volume 2* by Henretta, Brody, and Dumenil. This collection of documents echoes the earlier, longer edition designed to accompany *America's History,* Third Edition, the full-length textbook by Henretta, Brownlee, Brody, Ware, and Johnson. Both the text and the source collection have been reduced in size by about 40 percent from their forerunners, yielding trimmer, focused volumes for courses where either less reading or simply less textbook reading is desired. The resulting package of core-text-plus-reader places less of a burden on syllabi as well as on student pocketbooks.

The *Documents Collection* follows the chapter organization of *America* to provide a streamlined set of sources chosen specifically to mirror the themes of the texts, in the order in which they are presented. In each chapter an average of five to seven sources are included, each preceded by a headnote to establish context and followed by critical thinking questions. These questions are numbered and can be assigned by instructors wishing to test students on the readings. Finally, "Further Questions" appear at the end of each chapter, encouraging students to analyze the sources as a group, reflecting on the themes emphasized in each text chapter.

As a representative collection of our political, social, economic, and cultural history, the documents reflect the diverse and balanced approach of the Henretta textbooks. Ranging from a quarter page to eight full pages in length, they present first-person accounts from the past that show a maturing country, moving from Reconstruction through the present day. Senate testimony, biography, presidential speeches, government resolutions, and advertisements show a complex and textured past that today's students will connect with. Together with the textbook they accompany, these documents are meant to support a sophisticated and nuanced study of the American past.

CONTENTS

CHAPTER 24
Modern Times: The 1920s

CHAPTER 25
The Great Depression

CHAPTER 26
The New Deal, 1933–1939

CHAPTER 27
The World at War, 1939–1945

CHAPTER 32
The Lean Years: 1969–1980

CHAPTER 33
A New Domestic and World Order, 1981 to the Present

CHAPTER 16

Reconstruction 1865–1877

Carl Schurz, Report on Conditions in the South (1865)

By December 1865, when Congress was gathering in Washington for a new session, President Andrew Johnson had declared that all the Confederate states but Texas had met his requirements for restoration. Newly elected senators and representatives from the former Confederacy were arriving to take seats in Congress.

But Johnson's efforts to restore the South stalled. Congress exercised its constitutional authority to deny seats to delegations from the South and launched an investigation into conditions there. In response to a Senate resolution requesting "information in relation to the States of the Union lately in rebellion," Johnson responded with more wish than reality: "In 'that portion of the Union lately in rebellion' the aspect of affairs is more promising than, in view of all the circumstances, could well have been expected. The people throughout the entire south evince a laudable desire to renew their allegiance to the government, and to repair the devastations of war by a prompt and cheerful return to peaceful pursuits. An abiding faith is entertained that their actions will conform to their professions, and that, in acknowledging the supremacy of the Constitution and the laws of the United States, their loyalty will be unreservedly given to the government, whose leniency they cannot fail to appreciate, and whose fostering care will soon restore them to a condition of prosperity."

Johnson's message to the Senate was accompanied by a report from Major General Carl Schurz (see Chapter 13, "A German Immigrant"). Among the subjects Schurz considered were the level of white acceptance of defeat and emancipation and the condition of former slaves and southern Unionists. Since he had chosen Schurz for the task, Johnson did not expect to read a report that plainly contradicted him.

Sɪʀ: . . . You informed me that your "policy of reconstruction" was merely experimental, and that you would change it if the experiment did not lead to satisfactory results. To aid you in forming your conclusions upon this point I understood to be the object of my mission, . . .

CONDITION OF THINGS IMMEDIATELY AFTER THE CLOSE OF THE WAR

In the development of the popular spirit in the south since the close of the war two well-marked periods can be distinguished. The first commences with the sudden collapse of the confederacy and the dispersion of its armies, and the second with the first proclamation indicating the "reconstruction policy" of the government. . . . When the news of Lee's and Johnston's surrenders burst upon the southern country the general consternation was extreme. People held their breath, indulging in the wildest apprehensions as to what was now to come. . . . Prominent Unionists told me that persons who for four years had scorned to recognize them on the street approached them with smiling faces and both hands extended. Men of standing in the political world expressed serious doubts as to whether the rebel States would ever again occupy their position as States in the Union, or be governed as conquered provinces. The public mind was so despondent that if readmission at some future time under whatever conditions had been promised, it would then have been looked upon as a favor. The most uncompromising rebels prepared for leaving the country. The masses remained in a state of fearful expectancy. . . .

Such was, according to the accounts I received, the character of that first period. The worst apprehensions were gradually relieved as day after day went by without bringing the disasters and inflictions which had been vaguely anticipated, until at last the appearance of the North Carolina proclamation substituted new hopes for them. The development of this second period I was called upon to observe on the spot, and it forms the main subject of this report.

RETURNING LOYALTY

. . . [T]he white people at large being, under certain conditions, charged with taking the preliminaries of "reconstruction" into their hands, the success of the experiment depends upon the spirit and attitude of those who either attached themselves to the secession cause from the beginning, or, entertaining originally opposite views, at least followed its fortunes from the time that their States had declared their separation from the Union. . . .

I may group the southern people into four classes, each of which exercises an influence upon the development of things in that section:

1. Those who, although having yielded submission to the national government only when obliged to do so, have a clear perception of the irreversible changes produced by the war, and honestly endeavor to accommodate themselves to the new order of things. Many of them are not free from traditional prejudice but open to conviction, and may be expected to act in good faith whatever they do. This class is composed, in its majority, of persons of mature age—planters, merchants, and professional men; some of them are active in the reconstruction movement, but boldness and energy are, with a few individual exceptions, not among their distinguishing qualities.

2. Those whose principal object is to have the States without delay restored to their position and influence in the Union and the people of the

States to the absolute control of their home concerns. They are ready, in order to attain that object, to make any ostensible concession that will not prevent them from arranging things to suit their taste as soon as that object is attained. This class comprises a considerable number, probably a large majority, of the professional politicians who are extremely active in the reconstruction movement. They are loud in their praise of the President's reconstruction policy, and clamorous for the withdrawal of the federal troops and the abolition of the Freedmen's Bureau.

3. The incorrigibles, who still indulge in the swagger which was so customary before and during the war, and still hope for a time when the southern confederacy will achieve its independence. This class consists mostly of young men, and comprises the loiterers of the towns and the idlers of the country. They persecute Union men and negroes whenever they can do so with impunity, insist clamorously upon their "rights," and are extremely impatient of the presence of the federal soldiers. A good many of them have taken the oaths of allegiance and amnesty, and associated themselves with the second class in their political operations. This element is by no means unimportant; it is strong in numbers, deals in brave talk, addresses itself directly and incessantly to the passions and prejudices of the masses, and commands the admiration of the women.

4. The multitude of people who have no definite ideas about the circumstances under which they live and about the course they have to follow; whose intellects are weak, but whose prejudices and impulses are strong, and who are apt to be carried along by those who know how to appeal to the latter. . . .

FEELING TOWARDS THE SOLDIERS AND THE PEOPLE OF THE NORTH

. . . [U]pon the whole, the soldier of the Union is still looked upon as a stranger, an intruder—as the "Yankee," "the enemy." . . .

It is by no means surprising that prejudices and resentments, which for years were so assiduously cultivated and so violently inflamed, should not have been turned into affection by a defeat; nor are they likely to disappear as long as the southern people continue to brood over their losses and misfortunes. They will gradually subside when those who entertain them cut resolutely loose from the past and embark in a career of new activity on a common field with those whom they have so long considered their enemies. . . . [A]s long as these feelings exist in their present strength, they will hinder the growth of that reliable kind of loyalty which springs from the heart and clings to the country in good and evil fortune.

SITUATION OF UNIONISTS

. . . It struck me soon after my arrival in the south that the known Unionists—I mean those who during the war had been to a certain extent identified with the national cause—were not in communion with the leading social and political circles; and the further my observations extended the clearer it became to me that their existence in the south was of a rather precarious nature. . . . Even Governor [William L.] Sharkey, in the course of a conversation I had with him in the presence of Major General Osterhaus, admitted that, if our troops were then withdrawn, the lives of northern men in Mississippi would not be safe. . . . [General Osterhaus said]: "There is no doubt whatever that the state of affairs would be intolerable for all Union men, all recent immigrants from the north, and all negroes, the moment the protection of the United States troops were withdrawn." . . .

NEGRO INSURRECTIONS AND ANARCHY

. . . [I do] not deem a negro insurrection probable as long as the freedmen were assured of the direct protection of the national government. Whenever they are in trouble, they raise their eyes up to that power, and although they may suffer, yet, as long as that power is visibly present, they continue to hope. But when State authority in the south is fully restored, the federal forces withdrawn, and the Freedmen's Bureau abolished, the colored man will find himself turned over to the mercies of those whom he does not trust. If then an attempt is made to strip him again of those rights which he justly thought he possessed, he will be apt to feel that he can hope for no redress unless he procure it himself. If ever the negro is capable of rising, he will rise then. . . .

There is probably at the present moment no country in the civilized world which contains such an accumulation of anarchical elements as the south. The strife of the antagonistic tendencies here described is aggravated by the passions inflamed and the general impoverishment brought about by a long and exhaustive war, and the south will have to suffer the evils of anarchical disorder until means are found to effect a final settlement of the labor question in accordance with the logic of the great revolution.

THE TRUE PROBLEM — DIFFICULTIES AND REMEDIES

In seeking remedies for such disorders, we ought to keep in view, above all, the nature of the problem which is to be solved. As to what is commonly termed "reconstruction," it is not only the political machinery of the States and their constitutional relations to the general government, but the whole organism of southern society that must be reconstructed, or rather constructed anew, so as to bring it in harmony with the rest of American society. The difficulties of this task are not to be considered overcome when the people of the south take the oath of allegiance and elect governors and legislatures and members of Congress, and militia captains. That this would be done had become certain as soon as the surrenders of the southern armies had made further resistance impossible, and nothing in the world was left, even to the most uncompromising rebel, but to submit or to emigrate. It was also natural that they should avail themselves of every chance offered them to resume control of their home affairs and to regain their influence in the Union. But this can hardly be called the first step towards the solution of the true problem, and it is a fair question to ask, whether the hasty gratification of their desire to resume such control would not create new embarrassments.

The true nature of the difficulties of the situation is this: The general government of the republic has, by proclaiming the emancipation of the slaves, commenced a great social revolution in the south, but has, as yet, not completed it. Only the negative part of it is accomplished. The slaves are emancipated in point of form, but free labor has not yet been put in the place of slavery in point of fact. And now, in the midst of this critical period of transition, the power which originated the revolution is expected to turn over its whole future development to another power which from the beginning was hostile to it and has never yet entered into its spirit, leaving the class in whose favor it was made completely without power to protect itself and to take an influential part in that development. The history of the world will be searched in vain for a proceeding similar to this which did not lead either to a rapid and violent reaction, or to the most serious trouble and civil disorder. It cannot be said that the conduct of the southern people since the close of the war has exhibited such extraordinary wisdom and self-abnegation as to make them an exception to the rule.

In my despatches from the south I repeatedly expressed the opinion that the people were not yet in a frame of mind to legislate calmly and understandingly upon the subject of free negro labor. And this I reported to be the opinion of some of our most prominent military commanders and other observing men. It is, indeed, difficult to imagine circumstances more unfavorable for the development of a calm and unprejudiced public opinion than those under which the southern people are at present laboring. The war has not only defeated their political aspirations, but it has broken up their whole social organization. . . .

In which direction will these people be most apt to turn their eyes? Leaving the prejudice of race out of the question, from early youth they have been acquainted with but one system of labor, and with that one system they have been in the habit of identifying all their interests. They know of no way to help themselves but the one they are accustomed to. . . .

It is certain that every success of free negro labor will augment the number of its friends, and disarm some of the prejudices and assumptions of its opponents. I am convinced one good harvest made by unadulterated free labor in the south would have a far better effect than all the oaths that have been taken, and all the ordinances that have as yet been passed by southern conventions. But how can such a result be attained? The facts enumerated in this report, as well as the news we receive from the south from day to day, must make it evident to every unbiased observer that unadulterated free labor cannot be had at present, unless the national government holds its protective and controlling hand over it. . . . One reason why the southern people are so slow in accommodating themselves to the new order of things is, that they confidently expect soon to be permitted to regulate matters according to their own notions. Every concession made to them by the government has been taken as an encouragement to persevere in this hope, and, unfortunately for them, this hope is nourished by influences from other parts of the country. Hence their anxiety to have their State governments restored *at once,* to have the troops withdrawn, and the Freedmen's Bureau abolished, although a good many discerning men know well that, in view of the lawless spirit still prevailing, it would be far better for them to have the general order of society firmly maintained by the federal power until things have arrived at a final settlement. Had, from the beginning, the conviction been forced upon them that the adulteration of the new order of things by the admixture of elements belonging to the system of slavery would under no circumstances be permitted, a much larger number would have launched their energies into the new channel, and, seeing that they could do "no better," faithfully co-operated with the government. It is hope which fixes them in their perverse notions. That hope nourished or fully gratified, they will persevere in the same direction. That hope destroyed, a great many will, by the force of necessity, at once accommodate themselves to the logic of the change. If, therefore, the national government firmly and unequivocally announces its policy not to give up the control of the free-labor reform until it is finally accomplished, the progress of that reform will undoubtedly be far more rapid and far less difficult than it will be if the attitude of the government is such as to permit contrary hopes to be indulged in. . . .

IMMIGRATION [AND CAPITAL]

[The south would benefit] from immigration of northern people and Europeans. . . . The south needs capital. But capital is notoriously timid and averse to risk. . . . Capitalists will be apt to consider—and they are by no means wrong in doing so—that no safe investments can be made in the south as long as southern society is liable to be convulsed by anarchical disorders. No greater encouragement can, therefore, be given to capital to transfer itself to the south than the assurance that the government will continue to control the development of the new social system in the late rebel States until such dangers are averted by a final settlement of things upon a thorough free-labor basis.

How long the national government should continue that control depends upon contingencies. It ought to cease as soon as its objects are attained; and its objects will be attained sooner and with less difficulty if nobody is permitted to indulge in the delusion that it will cease *before* they are attained. This is one of the cases in which a determined policy can accomplish much, while a half-way policy is liable to spoil things already accomplished. . . .

NEGRO SUFFRAGE

It would seem that the interference of the national authority in the home concerns of the southern States would be rendered less necessary, and the whole problem of political and social reconstruction be much simplified, if, while the masses lately arrayed against the government are permitted to vote, the large majority of those who were always loyal, and are naturally anxious to see the free labor problem successfully solved, were not excluded from all influence upon legislation. In all questions concerning the Union, the national debt, and the future social organization of the south, the feelings of the colored man are naturally in sympathy with the views and aims of the national government. While the southern white fought against the Union, the negro did all he could to aid it; while the southern white sees in the national government his conqueror, the negro sees in it his protector; while the white owes to the national debt his defeat, the negro owes to it his deliverance; while the white considers himself robbed and ruined by the emancipation of the slaves, the negro finds in it the assurance of future prosperity and happiness. In all the important issues the negro would be led by natural impulse to forward the ends of the government, and by making his influence, as part of the voting body, tell upon the legislation of the States, render the interference of the national authority less necessary.

As the most difficult of the pending questions are intimately connected with the status of the negro in southern society, it is obvious that a correct solution can be more easily obtained if he has a voice in the matter. In the right to vote he would find the best permanent protection against oppressive class-legislation, as well as against individual persecution. The relations between the white and black races, even if improved by the gradual wearing off of the present animosities, are likely to remain long under the troubling influence of prejudice. It is a notorious fact that the rights of a man of some political power are far less exposed to violation than those of one who is, in matters of public interest, completely subject to the will of others. . . .

In discussing the matter of negro suffrage I deemed it my duty to confine myself strictly to the practical aspects of the subject. I have, therefore, not touched its moral merits nor discussed the question whether the national government is competent to enlarge the elective franchise in the States lately in rebellion by its own act; I deem it proper, however, to offer a few remarks on the assertion frequently put forth, that the franchise is likely to be extended to the colored man by the voluntary action of the southern whites themselves. My observation leads me to a contrary opinion. Aside from a very few enlightened men, I found but one class of people in favor of the enfranchisement of the blacks: it was the class of Unionists who found themselves politically ostracised and looked upon the enfranchisement of the loyal negroes as the salvation of the whole loyal element. But their numbers and influence are sadly insufficient to secure such a result. The masses are strongly opposed to colored suffrage; anybody that dares to advocate it is stigmatized as a dangerous fanatic; nor do I deem it probable that in the ordinary course of things prejudices will wear off to such an extent as to make it a popular measure. . . .

DEPORTATION OF THE FREEDMEN

. . . [T]he true problem remains, not how to remove the colored man from his present field of labor, but how to make him, where he is, a true freeman and an intelligent and useful citizen. The means are simple: protection by the government until his political and social status enables him to protect himself, offering to his legitimate ambition the stimulant of a perfectly fair chance in life, and granting to him the rights which in every just organization of society are coupled with corresponding duties.

CONCLUSION

I may sum up all I have said in a few words. If nothing were necessary but to restore the machinery of government in the States lately in rebellion in point of form, the movements made to that end by the people of the south might be considered satisfactory. But if it is required that the southern people should also accommodate themselves to the results of the war in point of spirit, those movements fall far short of what must be insisted upon. . . .

Questions

1. Is Schurz optimistic or pessimistic about the likelihood of substantive reconstruction in the South? Explain.

2. Why do southern views of Union soldiers matter?
3. Why does Schurz support suffrage for the former slaves?

The Mississippi Black Codes (1865)

As Carl Schurz reported, after the Civil War whites in the South sought a system of race relations in which African-Americans would be in a clearly subordinate position and would constitute a readily accessible and controllable work force.

Immediately after the war, southern whites wrote or revised vagrancy laws and the old slave codes as a means of establishing the system of race relations they wanted. Below are the Black Codes passed by the Mississippi legislature, one of the South's most famous attempts to codify race relations.

The Mississippi codes gave blacks rights they had not had before and clearly acknowledged that chattel slavery was dead. The codes recognized the right of African-Americans to own property, though not in incorporated towns or cities. (Before the Civil War there were black property owners in the state and even a few black slaveholders, but their legal standing was unclear.) The 1865 codes also recognized marriages between blacks as legal.

1. CIVIL RIGHTS OF FREEDMEN IN MISSISSIPPI

. . . That all freedmen, free negroes, and mulattoes may sue and be sued . . . may acquire personal property . . . and may dispose of the same in the same manner and to the same extent that white persons may: [but no] freedman, free negro, or mulatto . . . [shall] rent or lease any lands or tenements except in incorporated cities or towns, in which places the corporate authorities shall control the same. . . .

All freedmen, free negroes, or mulattoes who do now and have herebefore lived and cohabited together as husband and wife shall be taken and held in law as legally married, and the issue shall be taken and held as legitimate for all purposes; that it shall not be lawful for any freedman, free negro, or mulatto to intermarry with any white person; nor for any white person to intermarry with any freedman, free negro, or mulatto; and any person who shall so intermarry, shall be deemed guilty of felony, and on conviction thereof shall be confined in the State penitentiary for life; and those shall be deemed freedmen, free negroes, and mulattoes who are of pure negro blood, and those descended from a negro to the third generation, inclusive, though one ancestor in each generation may have been a white person. . . .

[F]reedmen, free negroes, and mulattoes are now by law competent witnesses . . . in civil cases [and in criminal cases where they are the victims]. . . .

All contracts for labor made with freedmen, free negroes, and mulattoes for a longer period than one month shall be in writing, and in duplicate. . . . and said contracts shall be taken and held as entire contracts, and if the laborer shall quit the service of the employer before the expiration of his term of service, without good cause, he shall forfeit his wages for that year up to the time of quitting.

. . . Every civil officer shall, and every person may, arrest and carry back to his or her legal employer any freedman, free negro, or mulatto who shall have quit the service of his or her employer before the expiration of his or her term of service without good cause; and said officer and person shall be entitled to receive for arresting and carrying back every deserting employe aforesaid the sum of five dollars. . . .

. . . If any person shall persuade or attempt to persuade, entice, or cause any freedman, free negro, or mulatto to desert from the legal employment of any person before the expiration of his or her term of service, or shall knowingly employ any such deserting freedman, free negro, or mulatto, or shall knowingly give or sell to any such deserting freedman, free negro, or mulatto, any food, raiment, or other thing, he or she shall be guilty of a misdemeanor. . . .

2. MISSISSIPPI APPRENTICE LAW

. . . It shall be the duty of all sheriffs, justices of the peace, and other civil officers of the several counties in this State, to report to the probate courts of their respective counties semi-annually, at the January and July terms of said courts, all freedmen, free negroes, and mulattoes, under the age of eighteen, in their respective counties, beats or districts, who are orphans, or whose parent or parents have not the means or who refuse to provide for and support said minors; . . . the clerk of said court to apprentice said minors to some competent and suitable person, on such terms as the court may direct, having a particular care to the interest of said minor: *Provided,* that the former owner of said minors shall have the preference when, in the opinion of the court, he or she shall be a suitable person for that purpose. . . .

. . . In the management and control of said apprentice, said master or mistress shall have the power to inflict such moderate corporal chastisement as a father or guardian is allowed to inflict on his or her child or ward at common law: *Provided,* that in no case shall cruel or inhuman punishment be inflicted. . . .

3. MISSISSIPPI VAGRANT LAW

. . . That all rogues and vagabonds, idle and dissipated persons, beggars, jugglers, or persons practicing unlawful games or plays, runaways, common drunkards, common night-walkers, pilferers, lewd, wanton, or lascivious persons, in speech or behavior, common railers and brawlers, persons who neglect their calling or employment, misspend what they earn, or do not provide for the support of themselves or their families, or dependents, and all other idle and disorderly persons, including all who neglect all lawful business, habitually misspend their time by frequenting houses of ill-fame, gaming-houses, or tippling shops, shall be deemed and considered vagrants, under the provisions of this act, and upon conviction thereof shall be fined not exceeding one hundred dollars . . . and be imprisoned at the discretion of the court, not exceeding ten days.

. . . All freedmen, free negroes and mulattoes in this State, over the age of eighteen years, found on the second Monday in January, 1866, or thereafter, with no lawful employment or business, or found unlawfully assembling themselves together, either in the day or night time, and all white persons so assembling themselves with freedmen, free negroes or mulattoes, or usually associating with freedmen, free negroes or mulattoes, on terms of equality, or living in adultery or fornication with a freed woman, free negro or mulatto, shall be deemed vagrants, and on conviction thereof shall be fined in a sum not exceeding, in the case of a freedman, free negro or mulatto, fifty dollars, and a white man two hundred dollars, and imprisoned at the discretion of the court, the free negro not exceeding ten days, and the white man not exceeding six months. . . .

4. PENAL LAWS OF MISSISSIPPI

. . . That no freedman, free negro or mulatto, not in the military service of the United States government, and not licensed so to do by the board of police of his or her county, shall keep or carry fire-arms of any kind, or any ammunition, dirk or bowie knife. . . .

. . . Any freedman, free negro, or mulatto committing riots, routs, affrays, trespasses, malicious mischief, cruel treatment to animals, seditious speeches, insulting gestures, language, or acts, or assaults on any person, disturbance of the peace, exercising the function of a minister of the Gospel without a license from some regularly organized church, vending spirituous or intoxicating liquors, or committing any other misdemeanor, the punishment of which is not specifically provided for by law, shall, upon conviction thereof in the county court, be fined not less than ten dollars, and not more than one hundred dollars, and may be imprisoned at the discretion of the court, not exceeding thirty days. . . .

. . . If any freedman, free negro, or mulatto, convicted of any of the misdemeanors provided against in this act, shall fail or refuse for the space of five days, after conviction, to pay the fine and costs imposed, such person shall be hired out by the sheriff or other officer, at public outcry, to any white person who will pay said fine and all costs, and take said convict for the shortest time.

Questions

1. What is the significance of tracing black heritage back three generations?
2. What abuses are inherent in the apprentice law?
3. What civil liberties do the vagrancy and penal provisions violate?

Thaddeus Stevens on Black Suffrage and Land Redistribution (1867)

The Radical Republicans, including Congressman Thaddeus Stevens (1792–1868), believed that besides the vote, freedmen would need an economic basis for establishing their newly defined lives (see text p. 428). Below are excerpts from remarks made by Stevens and from a bill in which he proposed a drastic altering of southern society.

ON BLACK SUFFRAGE

Unless the rebel States, before admission, should be made republican in spirit, and placed under the guardianship of loyal men, all our blood and treasure will have been spent in vain. I waive now the question of punishment which, if we are wise, will still be inflicted by moderate confiscations. . . . Impartial suffrage, both in electing the delegates and ratifying their proceedings, is now the fixed rule. There is more reason why colored voters should be admitted in the rebel States than in the Territories. In the States they form the great mass of the loyal men. Possibly with their aid loyal governments may be established in most of those States. Without it all are sure to be ruled by traitors; and loyal men, black and white, will be oppressed, exiled, or murdered. There are several good reasons for the passage of this bill. In the first place, it is just. I am now confining my argument to negro suffrage in the rebel States. Have not loyal blacks quite as good a right to choose rulers and make laws as rebel whites? In the second place, it is a necessity in order to protect the loyal white men in the seceded States. The white Union men are in a great minority in each of those States. With them the blacks would act in a body; and it is believed that in each of said States, except one, the two united would form a majority, control the States, and protect themselves. Now they are the victims of daily murder. . . .

Another good reason is, it would insure the ascendency of the Union party. . . . I believe . . . that on the continued ascendency of that party depends the safety of this great nation. If impartial suffrage is excluded in the rebel States, then every one of them is sure to send a solid rebel representative delegation to Congress, and cast a solid rebel electoral vote. They, with their kindred Copperheads of the North, would always elect the President and control Congress. While slavery sat upon her defiant throne, and insulted and intimidated the trembling North, the South frequently divided on questions of policy between Whigs and Democrats, and gave victory alternately to the sections. Now, you must divide them between loyalists, without regard to color, and disloyalists, or you will be the perpetual vassals of the free-trade, irritated, revengeful South. . . . I am for negro suffrage in every rebel State. If it be just, it should not be denied; if it be necessary, it should be adopted; if it be a punishment to traitors, they deserve it.

BILL ON LAND REDISTRIBUTION

Whereas it is due to justice, as an example to future times, that some proper punishment should be inflicted on the people who constituted the "confederate States of America," both because they, declaring an unjust war against the United States for the purpose of destroying republican liberty and permanently establishing slavery, as well as for the cruel and barbarous manner in which they conducted said war, in violation of all the laws of civilized warfare, and also to compel them to make some compensation for the damages and expenditures caused by said war: Therefore,

Be it enacted by the Senate and House of Representatives of the United States of America in Congress assembled, That all the public lands belonging to the ten States that formed the government of the so-called "confederate States of America" shall be forfeited by said States and become forthwith vested in the United States. . . .

That out of the lands thus seized and confiscated the slaves who have been liberated by the operations of the war and the amendment to the Constitution or otherwise, who resided in said "confederate States" on the 4th day of March, A.D. 1861, or since, shall have distributed to them as follows, namely: to each male person who is the head of a family, forty acres; to each adult male, whether the head of a family or not, forty acres; to each widow who is the head of a family, forty acres—to be held by them in fee-simple, but to be inalienable for the next ten years after they become seized thereof. . . .

That out of the balance of the property thus seized and confiscated there shall be raised, in the manner hereinafter provided, a sum equal to fifty dollars, for each homestead, to be applied by the trustees hereinafter mentioned toward the erection of buildings on the said homesteads for the use of said slaves; and the further sum of $500,000,000, which shall be appropriated as follows, to wit: $200,000,000 shall be invested in United States six per cent securities; and the interest thereof shall be semi-annually added to the pensions allowed by law to pensioners who have become so by reason of the late war; $300,000,000, or so much thereof as may be needed, shall be appropriated to pay damages done to loyal citizens by the civil or military operations of the government lately called the "confederate States of America." . . .

That in order that just discrimination may be made, the property of no one shall be seized whose whole estate on the 4th day of March, A.D. 1865, was not worth more than $5,000, to be valued by the said commission, unless he shall have voluntarily become an officer or employé in the military or civil service of the "confederate States of America," or in the civil or military service of some one of said States. . . .

Questions

1. Why does Stevens endorse black suffrage?
2. How does he justify land redistribution?
3. What does the legislation propose to do? What would make northerners—otherwise hostile to former Confederates—uncomfortable with its passage?

Thomas Nast, The Rise and Fall of Northern Support for Reconstruction (1868, 1874)

Evidence of broad northern support for the Republican program could be found in many places other than the ballot box. Illustrations from Harper's Weekly, *for example, "This Is a White Man's Government," reflected popular attitudes in the North during the late 1860s.*

However, northern support for Reconstruction began to erode as early as 1868. For various reasons Republican state governments in the South got a very bad reputation in the North. Also, northern willingness to use force to keep Republican governments in office in the South, even when threatened by violence, intimidation, and fraud, was exhausted by 1874, the year the second Harper's Weekly *illustration shown here appeared.*

Both cartoons are by the renowned Thomas Nast. The first is packed with allusions. Depicted from left to right are an Irish immigrant; the former Confederate general and Ku Klux Klan leader Nathan Bedford Forrest; and an unscrupulous businessman. Together, the three figures are crushing an African-American Civil War veteran; note his Union jacket and cap, as well as the saber and American flag. In addition there are references to the 1863 Draft Riot; Forrest's involvement in an 1864 massacre of black soldiers at Fort Pillow; and a burning southern school.

The second Nast cartoon shows something else entirely—how much and how quickly public attitudes had changed.

Questions

1. How does the first cartoon play on emotions? on prejudice?
2. How does the depiction of white politicians in the second cartoon convey Nast's view of Reconstruction?
3. As cultural documents, what do these cartoons say about the prevailing attitudes toward non-WASPs?

COLORED RULE IN A RECONSTRUCTED (?) STATE.—[See Page 242.]

(THE MEMBERS CALL EACH OTHER THIEVES, LIARS, RASCALS, AND COWARDS.)

COLUMBIA. "You are Aping the lowest Whites. If you disgrace your Race in this way you had better take Back Seats."

Albion W. Tourgee, *A Fool's Errand. By One of the Fools* (1879)

An Ohio native, Albion Winegar Tourgee (1838–1905) was working as a schoolteacher in New York at the onset of the Civil War. In April 1861, Tourgee joined the 27th New York Regiment and was wounded at the first Battle of Bull Run. He returned to the army in July 1862 as a lieutenant in the 105th Ohio Regiment. Captured in 1863 at Murfeesboro, Tourgee returned to Ohio through a prisoner exchange. He rejoined his regiment to fight at Chickamauga, Lookout Mountain, and Missionary Ridge. Twice charged with insubordination, Tourgee resigned his commission in December 1863 and studied law in Ohio.

By the fall of 1865 he had relocated as a "carpetbagger" (see text p. 432) to Greensboro, North Carolina. In 1868, thanks to the electoral rule imposed under radical Reconstruction, Tourgee won election to the state superior court. He served there for six years, finding ample opportunity to defend the rights of freedmen and denounce the atrocities of the Ku Klux Klan.

When his tenure on the court ended, Tourgee was appointed by President Grant as pension agent at Raleigh; the former judge continued his battle with the Klan and with Redeemer Democrats (see text pp. 436–37). By the summer of 1879, Tourgee had had enough and moved north with his family; eventually they settled in Mayville, New York.

In this selection from his novel A Fool's Errand, *Tourgee describes his experiences during Reconstruction through the character of Colonel Comfort Servosse, "the Fool."*

It was in the winter of 1868–69 . . . when it was said that already Reconstruction had been an approved success, [and] the traces of the war been blotted out . . . a little company of colored men came to the Fool one day; and one of them, who acted as spokesman said,—

"What's dis we hear, Mars Kunnel [Master Colonel], bout de Klux?"

"The what?" he asked.

"De Klux—de Ku-Kluckers dey calls demselves."

"Oh! The Ku-Klux, Ku-Klux-Klan . . . you mean."

"Yes: dem folks what rides about at night a-pesterin' pore colored people, an' pretendin' tu be jes from hell, or some of de battle-fields ob ole Virginny."

"Oh, that's all gammon [humbug]! There is nothing in the world in it,— nothing at all. . . ."

"You don't think dey's ghostses, nor nothin' ob dat sort?" asked another.

"Think! I know they are not."

"So do I," growled one of their number who had not spoken before, in a tone . . . that . . . drew the eyes of the Fool upon him at once.

"So your mind's made up on that point too, is it Bob?" he asked laughingly.

"I know dey's not ghosts, Kunnel. I wish ter God dey was!" was the reply.

"Why, what do you mean, Bob?" asked the colonel in surprise.

"Will you jes help me take off my shirt, Jim?" said Bob . . . as he turned to one of those with him. . . .

"What d'ye tink ob dat, Kunnel?"

"My God!" exclaimed the Fool, starting back in surprise and horror. "What does this mean, Bob?"

"Seen de Kluckers, sah," was the grimly-laconic answer.

The sight which presented itself to the Fool's eyes was truly terrible. . . . The whole back was livid and swollen, bruised as if it had been brayed in a mortar. Apparently, after having cut the flesh with closely-laid welts and furrows, sloping downward from the left side towards the right, with the peculiar skill . . . which could only be obtained through the abundant opportunity for severe . . . flagellation which prevailed under . . . slavery, the operator had changed his position, and scientifically cross-checked the whole. . . . "Nobody but an ole oberseer ebber dun dat, Kunnel." . . . When his clothing had been resumed, he sat down and poured into the wondering ears of the Fool this story:—

BOB'S EXPERIENCE.

"Yer see, I'se a blacksmith at Burke's Cross-Roads. I've been thar ever sence a few days arter I heer ob de surrender. I rented an ole house dar, an' put up a sort of shop . . . an' went to work. . . .

"Long a while back—p'raps five er six month—I refused ter du some work fer Michael Anson or his boy, 'cause they'd run up quite a score at de shop, an' allers put me off when I wanted pay. . . . Folks said I waz gettin' too smart fer a nigger, an' sech like; but I kep' right on; tole em I waz a free man . . . an' I didn't propose ter do any man's work fer noffin'. Most everybody hed somefin' ter say about it; but it didn't seem ter hurt my trade very much. . . . When ther come an election, I sed my say, did my own votin', an' tole de other colored people dey waz free, an' hed a right ter du de same. Thet's bad doctrine up in our country. . . . Dey don't mind 'bout . . . our votin', so long ez we votes ez day tell us. Dat' dare idea uv liberty fer a nigger.

"Well, here a few weeks ago, I foun' a board stuck up on my shop one mornin', wid dese words on it:—

"'BOB MARTIN,—You're gettin' too dam smart! The white folks round Burke's Cross-Roads don't want any sech smart niggers round thar. You'd better git, er you'll hev a call from the

'K.K.K.'"

... [Y]esterday ... my ole 'ooman ... tuk part ob de chillen into bed wid her; an' de rest crawled in wid me. ... I kinder remember hearin' de dog bark, but I didn't mind it; an', de fust ting I knew, de do' was bust in. ... Dar was 'bout tirty of 'em standin' dar in de moonlight, all dressed in black gowns thet come down to ther boots, an' some sort of high hat on, dat come down ober der faces. ... Den dey tied me tu a tree, an' done what you've seen. Dey tuk my wife an' oldes' gal out of de house, tore de close right about off 'em, an' abused 'em shockin' afore my eyes. After tarin' tings up a heap in de house, dey rode off, tellin' me dey reckoned I's larn to be 'spectful to white folks herearter. ...

"Why have you not complained of this outrage to the authorities?" ... asked [the Fool] after a moment.

"I tole Squire Haskins an' Judge Thompson what I hev tole you," answered Bob.

"And what did they say?"

"Dat dey couldn't do noffin' unless I could sw'ar to the parties." ...

There was a moment's silence. Then the colored man asked,—

"Isn't dere no one else, Kunnel, dat could do any ting? Can't de President or Congress do somefin'? De gov'ment sot us free, an' it 'pears like it oughtn't to let our old masters impose on us in no sech way now. ... We ain't cowards. We showed dat in de wah. I'se seen darkeys go whar de white troops wa'n't anxious to foller 'em, mor'n once."

"Where was that, Bob?"

"Wal, at Fo't Wagner, for one."

"How did you know about that?"

"How did I know 'bout dat? Bress yer soul, Kunnel, I was dar!"

Questions

1. What is the Fool's initial assessment of Reconstruction? What makes him change his mind?
2. How does the KKK seek to terrorize the black population?
3. Why would Tourgee portray himself fictionally the way he does?

Charles Sumner, "Republicanism vs. Grantism" (1872)

Charles Sumner had come to the United States Senate during the first wave of antislavery's political insurgency across the North (see Chapter 14, "The Crime against Kansas"). Throughout the Civil War and Reconstruction, Sumner was among the most vehement and politically powerful radical Republicans. But during the Grant administration Sumner frequently opposed the president, as when he denounced Grant's efforts to acquire Santo Domingo (the present-day Dominican Republic) as a territory of the United States.

Grant loyalists retaliated in 1872 by deposing Sumner as chairman of the Foreign Relations Committee. With a remarkable number of former radical Republicans, Sumner cast his lot with the Liberal Republicans who opposed Grant's reelection by supporting the Democratic candidate, Horace Greeley. This break in party ranks—specifically the defection of radicals to the Liberal Republican platform of sectional reconciliation—marked the beginning of the end of Reconstruction. Here Sumner takes to the floor of the Senate to denounce "Grantism."

Mr. President,—I have no hesitation in declaring myself a member of the Republican Party, and one of the straitest of the sect. I doubt if any Senator can point to earlier or more constant service in its behalf. I began at the beginning, and from that early day have never failed to sustain its candidates and to advance its principles. . . .

Turning back to its birth, I recall a speech of my own at a State Convention in Massachusetts, as early as September 7, 1854, where I vindicated its principles and announced its name in these words: "as *Republicans* we go forth to encounter the *Oligarches* of Slavery." . . . The Republican Party was necessary and permanent, and always on an ascending plane. For such a party there was no death, but higher life and nobler aims; and this was the party to which I gave my vows. But, alas, how changed! Once country was the object, and not a man; once principle was inscribed on the victorious banners, and not a name only.

THE REPUBLICAN PARTY SEIZED BY THE PRESIDENT

It is not difficult to indicate when this disastrous change . . . became not merely manifest, but painfully conspicuous . . . suddenly and without any warning through the public press or any expression from public opinion, the President elected by the Republican Party precipitated upon the country an ill-considered and ill-omened scheme for the annexation of a portion of the island of San Domingo. . . .

PRESIDENTIAL PRETENSIONS

... [t]he Presidential office has been used to advance his own family on a scale of nepotism dwarfing everything of the kind in our history ... and ... all these assumptions have matured in a *personal government,* semi-military in character and breathing the military spirit,—being a species of Caesarism or *personalism,* abhorrent to republican institutions. ... [T]he chosen head of the Republic is known chiefly for Presidential pretensions, utterly indefensible in character, derogatory to the country, and of evil influence, making personal objects a primary pursuit, so that ... he is a bad example, through whom republican institutions suffer and the people learn to do wrong. ...

PERSONAL GOVERNMENT UNREPUBLICAN

Personal Government is autocratic. It is the One-Man Power elevated above all else, and is therefore in direct conflict with republican government, whose consummate form is tripartite ... each independent and coequal. ...

A government of laws and not of men is the object of republican government; nay, more, it is the distinctive essence without which it becomes a tyranny. Therefore personal government in all its forms, and especially when it seeks to sway the action of any other branch or overturn its constitutional negative, is hostile to the first principles of republican institutions, and an unquestionable outrage. That our President has offended in this way is unhappily too apparent.

THE PRESIDENT AS CIVILIAN

To comprehend the personal government that has been installed over us we must know its author. His picture is the necessary frontispiece,—not as soldier, let it be borne in mind, but as civilian. ...

To appreciate his peculiar character as a civilian it is important to know his triumphs as a soldier, for the one is the natural complement of the other. The successful soldier is rarely changed to the successful civilian. There seems to be an incompatibility between the two. ... One always a soldier cannot late in life become a statesman. ... Washington and Jackson were civilians as well as soldiers. ...

THE GREAT PRESIDENTIAL QUARRELER

Any presentment of the President would be imperfect which did not show how this ungovernable personality breaks forth in quarrel, making him the great Presidential quarreler of our history. ... With the arrogance of arms he resents any impediment in his path,—as when, in the spring of 1870, without allusion to himself, I felt it my duty to oppose his San Domingo contrivance. . . .

DUTY OF THE REPUBLICAN PARTY

And now the question of Duty is distinctly presented to the Republican Party. . . . Do the Presidential pretensions merit the sanction of the party? Can Republicans, without departing from all obligations, whether of party or patriotism, recognize our ambitious Caesar as a proper representative? . . . Therefore with unspeakable interest will the country watch the National Convention at Philadelphia. It may be an assembly (and such is my hope) where ideas and principles are above all personal pretensions, and the unity of the party is symbolized in the candidate; or it may add another to Presidential rings, being an expansion of the military ring at the Executive Mansion, the senatorial ring in the [Senate] Chamber, and the political ring in the customhouses of New York and New Orleans. A National Convention which is a Republican ring cannot represent the Republican Party. . . . I wait the determination of the National Convention. . . . Not without anxiety do I wait, but with the earnest hope that the Convention will bring the Republican Party into ancient harmony, saving it especially from the suicidal folly of an issue on the personal pretensions of one man.

Questions

1. What are Sumner's harshest charges against President Grant?
2. In demeaning the political abilities of the "successful soldier," what is Sumner ignoring in Grant's rise to power?
3. What does Sumner fear will come to dominate the Republican presidential convention?

Connections Questions

1. Using the Mississippi Black Codes as a measure, how accurate is Carl Schurz's report ("Report on Conditions") on conditions in the South?
2. How do the two cartoons by Thomas Nast engage a reader? To what extent, if any, does the message conveyed differ from that in a written source?
3. Imagine yourself a member of Congress in the 1860s. Would you vote for Thaddeus Stevens's bill ("Thaddeus Stevens on Black Suffrage") after reading the report by Carl Schurz ("Report on Conditions")? Why or why not?

CHAPTER 17

The American West

Hamlin Garland, "Our First Winter on the Prairie" (1920)

During the first ten years of his life, the novelist Hamlin Garland (1860–1940) lived in Wisconsin, Iowa, and the Dakota Territory. Garland's father was a farmer who seemed intent on proving the validity of Frederick Jackson Turner's frontier thesis (see text p. 590). But for a boy on the Great Plains, historical forces mattered less than getting used to life in "this wide, sunny, windy country."

For a few days my brother and I had little to do other than to keep the cattle from straying, and we used our leisure in becoming acquainted with the region round about.

It burned deep into our memories, this wide, sunny, windy country. The sky so big, and the horizon line so low and so far away, made this new world of the plain more majestic than the world of the Coulee.—The grasses and many of the flowers were also new to us. On the uplands the herbage was short and dry and the plants stiff and woody, but in the swales the wild oat shook its quivers of barbed and twisted arrows, and the crow's foot, tall and sere, bowed softly under the feet of the wind, while everywhere, in the lowlands as well as on the ridges, the bleaching white antlers of by-gone herbivora lay scattered, testifying to "the herds of deer and buffalo" which once fed there. We were just a few years too late to see them.

To the south the sections were nearly all settled upon, for in that direction lay the county town, but to the north and on into Minnesota rolled the unplowed sod, the feeding ground of the cattle, the home of foxes and wolves, and to the west, just beyond the highest ridges, we loved to think the bison might still be seen.

The cabin on this rented farm was a mere shanty, a shell of pine boards, which needed re-enforcing to make it habitable and one day my father said, "Well, Hamlin, I guess you'll have to run the plow-team this fall. I must help neighbor Button wall up the house and I can't afford to hire another man."

This seemed a fine commission for a lad of ten, and I drove my horses into the field that first morning with a manly pride which added an inch to my stature. I took my initial "round" at a "land" which stretched from one side of the quarter section to the other, in confident mood. I was grown up!

But alas! my sense of elation did not last long. To guide a team for a few minutes as an experiment was one thing—to plow all day like a hired hand was another. It was not a chore, it was a job. It meant moving to and fro hour after hour, day after day, with no one to talk to but the horses. It meant trudging eight or nine miles in the forenoon and as many more in the afternoon, with less than an hour off at noon. It meant dragging the heavy implement around the corners, and it meant also many ship-wrecks, for the thick, wet stubble matted with wild buckwheat often rolled up between the coulter and the standard and threw the share completely out of the ground, making it necessary for me to halt the team and jerk the heavy plow backward for a new start.

Although strong and active I was rather short, even for a ten-year-old, and to reach the plow handles I was obliged to lift my hands above my shoulders; and so with the guiding lines crossed over my back and my worn straw hat bobbing just above the cross-brace I must have made a comical figure. At any rate nothing like it had been seen in the neighborhood and the people on the road to town looking across the field, laughed and called to me, and neighbor Button said to my father in my hearing, "That chap's too young to run a plow," a judgment which pleased and flattered me greatly. . . .

The flies were savage, especially in the middle of the day, and the horses, tortured by their lances, drove badly, twisting and turning in their despairing rage. Their tails were continually getting over the lines, and in stopping to kick their tormentors from their bellies they often got astride the traces, and in other ways made trouble for me. Only in the early morning or when the sun sank low at night were they able to move quietly along their ways.

The soil was the kind my father had been seeking, a smooth dark sandy loam, which made it possible for a lad to do the work of a man. Often the share would go the entire "round" without striking a root or a pebble as big as a walnut, the steel running steadily with a crisp crunching ripping sound which I rather liked to hear. In truth work would have been quite tolerable had it not been so long drawn out. Ten hours of it even on a fine day made about twice too many for a boy.

Meanwhile I cheered myself in every imaginable way. I whistled. I sang. I studied the clouds. I gnawed the beautiful red skin from the seed vessels which hung upon the wild rose bushes, and I counted the prairie chickens as they began to come together in winter flocks running through the stubble in search of food. I stopped now and again to examine the lizards unhoused by the share, tormenting them to make them sweat their milky drops (they were curiously repulsive to me), and I measured the little granaries of wheat which the mice and gophers had deposited deep under the ground, storehouses which the plow had violated. My eyes dwelt enviously upon the sailing hawk, and on the passing of ducks. The occasional shadowy figure of a prairie wolf made me wish for Uncle David and his rifle.

On certain days nothing could cheer me. When the bitter wind blew from the north, and the sky was filled with wild geese racing southward, with swiftly-hurrying clouds, winter seemed about to spring upon me. The horses' tails streamed in the wind. Flurries of snow covered me with clinging flakes, and the mud "gummed" my boots and trouser legs, clogging my steps. At such times I suffered from cold and loneliness—all sense of being a man evaporated. I was just a little boy, longing for the leisure of boyhood.

Day after day, through the month of October and deep into November, I followed that team, turning over two acres of stubble each day. I would not believe this without proof, but it is true! At last it grew so cold that in the early morning everything was white with frost and I was obliged to put one hand in my pocket to keep it warm, while holding the plow with the other, but I didn't mind this so much, for it hinted at the close of autumn. I've no doubt facing the wind in this way was excellent discipline, but I didn't think it necessary then and my heart was sometimes bitter and rebellious.

The soldier did not intend to be severe. As he had always been an early riser and a busy toiler it seemed perfectly natural and good discipline, that his sons should also plow and husk corn at ten years of age. He often told of beginning life as a "bound boy" at nine, and these stories helped me to perform my own tasks without whining. I feared to voice my weakness.

At last there came a morning when by striking my heel upon the ground I convinced the boss that the soil was frozen too deep for the mold-board to break. "All right," he said, "you may lay off this afternoon."

Oh, those beautiful hours of respite! With time to play or read I usually read, devouring anything I could lay my hands upon. Newspapers, whether old or new, or pasted on the wall or piled up in the attic,—anything in print was wonderful to me. One enthralling book, borrowed from neighbor Button, was *The Female Spy,* a Tale of the Rebellion. Another treasure was a story called *Cast Ashore,* but this volume unfortunately was badly torn and fifty pages were missing so that I never knew, and do not know to this day, how those indomitable shipwrecked seamen reached their English homes. I dimly recall that one man carried a pet monkey on his back and that they all lived on "Bustards."

Finally the day came when the ground rang like iron under the feet of the horses, and a bitter wind, raw and gusty, swept out of the northwest, bearing gray veils of sleet. Winter had come! Work in the furrow had ended. The plow was brought in, cleaned and greased to prevent its rusting, and while the horses munched their hay in well-earned holiday, father and I helped farmer Button husk the last of his corn. . . .

The school-house which was to be the center of our social life stood on the bare prairie about a mile to the southwest and like thousands of other similar buildings in the west, had not a leaf to shade it in summer nor a branch to break the winds of savage winter. "There's been a good deal of talk about setting out a wind-break," neighbor Button explained to us, "but nothing has as yet been done." It was merely a square pine box painted a glaring white on the outside and a desolate drab within; at least drab was the original color, but the benches were mainly so greasy and hacked that original intentions were obscured. It had two doors on the eastern end and three windows on each side.

A long square stove (standing on slender legs in a puddle of bricks), a wooden chair, and a rude table in one corner, for the use of the teacher, completed the movable furniture. The walls were roughly plastered and the windows had no curtains.

It was a barren temple of the arts even to the residents of Dry Run, and Harriet and I, stealing across the prairie one Sunday morning to look in, came away vaguely depressed. We were fond of school and never missed a day if we could help it, but this neighborhood center seemed so small and bleak and poor.

With what fear, what excitement we approached the door on that first day, I can only faintly indicate. All the scholars were strange to me except Albert and Cyrus Button, and I was prepared for rough treatment. However, the experience was not so harsh as I had feared. True, Rangely Field did throw me down and wash my face in snow, and Jack Sweet tripped me up once or twice, but I bore these indignities with such grace and could command, and soon made a place for myself among the boys. . . .

I cannot recover much of that first winter of school. It was not an experience to remember for its charm. Not one line of grace, not one touch of color relieved the room's bare walls or softened its harsh windows. Perhaps this very barrenness gave to the poetry in our readers an appeal that seems magical. . . .

This winter was made memorable also by a "revival" which came over the district with sudden fury. It began late in the winter—fortunately, for it ended all dancing and merry-making for the time. It silenced Daddy Fairbanks' fiddle and subdued my mother's glorious voice to a wail. A cloud of puritanical gloom settled upon almost every household. Youth and love became furtive and hypocritic.

The evangelist, one of the old-fashioned shouting, hysterical, ungrammatical, gasping sort, took charge of the services, and in his exhortations phrases descriptive of lakes of burning brimstone and ages of endless torment abounded. Some of the figures of speech and violent gestures of the man still linger in my mind, but I will not set them down on paper. They are too dreadful to perpetuate. At times he roared with such power that he could have been heard for half a mile.

And yet we went, night by night, mother, father, Jessie, all of us. It was our theater. Some of the roughest characters in the neighborhood rose and professed repentance, for a season, even old Barton, the profanest man in the township, experienced a "change of heart."

We all enjoyed the singing, and joined most lustily in the tunes. Even little Jessie learned to sing *Heavenly Wings, There is a Fountain filled with Blood,* and *Old Hundred.*

As I peer back into that crowded little school-room, smothering hot and reeking with lamp smoke, and recall the half-lit, familiar faces of the congregation, it all has the quality of a vision, something experienced in another world. The preacher, leaping, sweating, roaring till the windows rattle, the mothers with sleeping babes in their arms, the sweet, strained faces of the girls, the immobile wondering men, are spectral shadows, figures encountered in the phantasmagoria of disordered sleep.

Questions

1. How did the weather shape life in the Dakota Territory?
2. What did Garland's life as a ten-year-old entail?
3. Was Garland's schooling adequate? Why or why not?

Helen Hunt Jackson, *A Century of Dishonor* (1881)

Born in Amherst, Massachusetts, Helen Hunt Jackson came out of the same New England moral climate that nurtured the abolitionist and feminist movements of the mid-nineteenth century. But this childhood friend of Emily Dickinson showed no interest in reform causes until her second marriage and move to Colorado in 1875. Ironically, it was during a trip to Boston in 1879 when Jackson heard the Ponca chief Standing Bear talk on the plight of the Plains Indians.

The incident served as a kind of conversion experience, and Jackson immediately went about making herself an expert on the history of government–Indian relations. Within two years, she published A Century of Dishonor. *Not all readers were pleased with Jackson's condemning the government for its mistreatment of its indigenous population. Because the book was "written in good English" by an author "intensely in earnest," Theodore Roosevelt feared it was "capable of doing great harm."*

In 1869 President Grant appointed a commission of nine men, representing the influence and philanthropy of six leading States, to visit the different Indian reservations, and to "examine all matters appertaining to Indian affairs."

In the report of this commission are such paragraphs as the following: "To assert that 'the Indian will not work' is as true as it would be to say that the white man will not work.

"Why should the Indian be expected to plant corn, fence lands, build houses, or do anything but get food from day to day, when experience has taught him that the product of his labor will be seized by the white man to-morrow? The most industrious white man would become a drone under similar circumstances. Nevertheless, many of the Indians" (the commissioners might more forcibly have said 130,000 of the Indians) "are already at work, and furnish ample refutation of the assertion that 'the Indian will not work.' There is no escape from the inexorable logic of facts.

"The history of the Government connections with the Indians is a shameful record of broken treaties and unfulfilled promises. The history of the border white man's connection with the Indians is a sickening record of murder, outrage, robbery, and wrongs committed by the former, as the rule, and occasional savage outbreaks and unspeakably barbarous deeds of retaliation by the latter, as the exception.

"Taught by the Government that they had rights entitled to respect, when those rights have been assailed by the rapacity of the white man, the arm which should have been raised to protect them has ever been ready to sustain the aggressor.

"The testimony of some of the highest military officers of the United States is on record to the effect that, in our Indian wars, almost without exception, the first aggressions have been made by the white man; and the assertion is supported by every civilian of reputation who has studied the subject. In addition to the class of robbers and outlaws who find impunity in their nefarious pursuits on the frontiers, there is a large class of professedly reputable men who use every means in their power to bring on Indian wars for the sake of the profit to be realized from the presence of troops and the expenditure of Government funds in their midst. They proclaim death to the Indians at all times in words and publications, making no distinction between the innocent and the guilty. They irate the lowest class of men to the perpetration of the darkest deeds against their victims, and as judges and jurymen shield them from the justice due to their crimes. Every crime committed by a white man against an Indian is concealed or palliated. Every offence committed by an Indian against a white man is borne on the wings of the post or the telegraph to the remotest corner of the land, clothed with all the horrors which the reality or imagination can throw around it. Against such influences as these the people of the United States need to be warned."

To assume that it would be easy, or by any one sudden stroke of legislative policy possible, to undo the mischief and hurt of the long past, set the Indian policy of the country right for the future, and make the Indians at once safe and happy, is the blunder of a hasty and uninformed judgment. The notion which seems to be growing more prevalent, that simply to make all Indians at once citizens of the United States would be a sovereign and instantaneous panacea for all their ills and all the Government's perplexities, is a very inconsiderate one. To administer complete citizenship of a sudden, all round, to all Indians, barbarous and civilized alike, would be as grotesque a blunder as to dose them all round with any one medicine, irrespective of the symptoms and needs of their diseases. It would kill more than it would cure. Nevertheless, it is true, as was well stated by one of the superintendents of Indian Affairs in 1857, that, "so long as they are not citizens of the United States, their rights of property must remain insecure against invasion. The doors of the federal tribunals being barred against them while wards and dependents, they can only partially exercise the rights of free government, or give to those who make, execute, and construe the few laws they are allowed to enact, dignity sufficient to make them respectable. While they continue individually to gather the crumbs that fall from the table of the United States, idleness, improvidence, and indebtedness will be the rule, and industry, thrift, and freedom from debt the exception. The utter absence of individual title to particular lands deprives every one among them of the chief incentive to labor and exertion—the very mainspring on which the prosperity of a people depends."

All judicious plans and measures for their safety and salvation must embody provisions for their becoming citizens as fast as they are fit, and must protect them till then in every right and particular in which our laws protect other "persons" who are not citizens.

There is a disposition in a certain class of minds to be impatient with any protestation against wrong which is unaccompanied or unprepared with a quick and exact scheme of remedy. This is illogical. When pioneers in a new country find a tract of poisonous and swampy wilderness to be reclaimed, they do not withhold their hands from fire and axe till they see clearly which way roads should run, where good water will spring, and what crops will best grow on the redeemed land. They first clear the swamp. So with this poisonous and baffling part of the domain of our national affairs—let us first "clear the swamp."

However great perplexity and difficulty there may be in the details of any and every plan possible for doing at this late day anything like justice to the Indian, however hard it may be for good statesmen and good men to agree upon the things that ought to be done, there certainly is, or ought to be, no perplexity whatever, no difficulty whatever, in agreeing upon certain things that ought not to be done, and which must cease to be done before the first steps can be taken toward righting the wrongs, curing the ills, and wiping out the disgrace to us of the present condition of our Indians.

Cheating, robbing, breaking promises—these three are clearly things which must cease to be done. One more thing, also, and that is the refusal of the protection of the law to the Indian's rights of property, "of life, liberty, and the pursuit of happiness."

When these four things have ceased to be done, time, statesmanship, philanthropy, and Christianity can slowly and surely do the rest. Till these four things have ceased to be done, statesmanship and philanthropy alike must work in vain, and even Christianity can reap but small harvest.

Questions

1. Why did official reports critical of U.S. government policy toward native Americans not have a greater effect on the public?
2. What was the importance of granting citizenship to Indians? What problems does Jackson think that will entail?
3. What was Jackson's prescription for improved relations?

The Chinese Exclusion Act (1882)

Immigration has always left Americans uneasy, in part because of the fear that newcomers will not assimilate. Chinese immigrants provoked extreme anxiety on the West Coast with their different language, customs, and dress. They also competed for jobs: Chinese laborers composed 80 percent of the Central Pacific Railroad's labor force. When journalist Henry George complained about "utter heathens," he found a ready audience. Congress answered nativist pleas with the passage of the Chinese Exclusion Act in 1882.

Whereas, in the opinion of the Government of the United States the coming of Chinese laborers to this country endangers the good order of certain localities within the territory thereof: Therefore,

Be it enacted by the Senate and House of Representatives of the United States of America in Congress assembled, That from and after the expiration of ninety days next after the passage of this act, and until the expiration of ten years next after the passage of this act, the coming of Chinese laborers to the United States be, and the same is hereby, suspended; and during such suspension it shall not be lawful for any Chinese laborer to come, or, having so come after the expiration of said ninety days, to remain within the United States. . . .

SEC. 4. That for the purpose of properly identifying Chinese laborers who were in the United States on the seventeenth day of November, eighteen hundred and eighty, or who shall have come into the same before the expiration of ninety days next after the passage of this act, and in order to furnish them with the proper evidence of their right to go from and come to the United States of their free will and accord, as provided by the treaty between the United States and China dated November seventeenth, eighteen hundred and eighty, the collector of customs of the district from which any such Chinese laborer shall depart from the United States shall, in person or by deputy, go on board each vessel having on board any such Chinese laborer and cleared or about to sail from his district for a foreign port, and on such vessel make a list of all such Chinese laborers, which shall be entered in registry-books to be kept for that purpose, in which shall be stated the name, age, occupation, last place of residence, physical marks or peculiarities, and all facts necessary for the identification of each of such Chinese laborers, which books shall be safely kept in the custom-house; and every such Chinese laborer so departing from the United States shall be entitled to, and shall receive, free of any charge or cost upon application therefor, from the collector or his deputy, at the time such list is taken, a certificate, signed by the collector or his deputy and attested by his seal of office, in such form as the Secretary of the Treasury shall prescribe, which certificate shall contain a statement of the name, age, occupation, last place of residence, personal description, and facts of identification of the Chinese laborer to whom the certificate is issued, corresponding with the said list and registry in all particulars. . . .

SEC. 14. That hereafter no State court or court of the United States shall admit Chinese to citizenship; and all laws in conflict with this act are hereby repealed.

Questions

1. What does the omission of specific reasons for barring the Chinese indicate about the motivations of Congress?
2. How did sections 4 and 14 affect Chinese immigrants?
3. What does the act suggest about the relationship between the United States and China?

John Muir, "Hetch Hetchy Valley" (1917)

John Muir came to the United States with his family from Scotland as an eleven-year-old in 1849; Muir's interest in nature was nurtured by the family's settling in rural Wisconsin. As a young man, Muir made walking trips through the Midwest and Canada before embarking on a thousand-mile trek to the Gulf of Mexico.

Muir's passionate love of nature led to his founding of the Sierra Club in 1892 and his support for the creation of Yosemite National Park. Muir (1838–1914) was less a conservationist than a preservationist who wanted nature saved for its own sake. When San Francisco moved in 1913 to improve its water supply system, the plan called for damming the Hetch Hetchy Valley in Yosemite. Muir's eloquent defense of the valley could not save it.

Yosemite is so wonderful that we are apt to regard it as an exceptional creation, the only valley of its kind in the world; but Nature is not so poor as to have only one of anything. Several other yosemites have been discovered in the Sierra that occupy the same relative positions on the range and were formed by the same forces in the same kind of granite. One of these, the Hetch Hetchy Valley, is in the Yosemite National Park, about twenty miles from Yosemite, and is easily accessible to all sorts of travelers by a road and trail that leaves the Big Oak Flat road at Bronson Meadows a few miles below Crane Flat, and to mountaineers by way of Yosemite Creek basin and the head of the middle fork of the Tuolumne.

It is said to have been discovered by Joseph Screech, a hunter, in 1850, a year before the discovery of the great Yosemite. After my first visit to it in the autumn of 1871, I have always called it the "Tuolumne Yosemite," for it is a wonderfully exact counterpart of the Merced Yosemite, not only in its sublime rocks and waterfalls but in the gardens, groves and meadows of its flowery park-like floor. The floor of Yosemite is about four thousand feet above the sea; the Hetch Hetchy floor about thirty-seven hundred feet. And as the Merced River flows through Yosemite, so does the Tuolumne through Hetch Hetchy. The walls of both are of gray granite, rise abruptly from the floor, are sculptured in the same style and in both every rock is a glacier monument.

Standing boldly out from the south wall is a strikingly picturesque rock called by the Indians, Kolana, the outermost of a group twenty-three hundred feet high, corresponding with the Cathedral Rocks of Yosemite both in relative position and form. On the opposite side of the Valley, facing Kolana, there is a counterpart of El Capitan that rises sheer and plain to a height of eighteen hundred feet, and over its massive brow flows a stream which makes the most graceful fall I have ever seen. From the edge of the cliff to the top of an earthquake talus it is perfectly free in the air for a thousand feet before it is broken into cascades among talus boulders. It is in all its glory in June, when the snow is melting fast, but fades and vanishes toward the end of summer. The only fall I know with which it may fairly be compared is the Yosemite Bridal Veil; but it excels even that favorite fall both in height and airy-fairy beauty and behavior. Lowlanders are apt to suppose that mountain streams in their wild career over cliffs lose control of themselves and tumble in a noisy chaos of mist and spray. On the contrary, on no part of their travels are they more harmonious and self-controlled. Imagine yourself in Hetch Hetchy on a sunny day in June, standing waist-deep in grass and flowers (as I have often stood), while the great pines sway dreamily with scarcely perceptible motion. . . .

It appears, therefore, that Hetch Hetchy Valley, far from being a plain, common, rock-bound meadow, as many who have not seen it seem to suppose, is a grand landscape garden, one of Nature's rarest and most precious mountain temples. As in Yosemite, the sublime rocks of its walls seem to glow with life, whether leaning back in repose or standing erect in thoughtful attitudes, giving welcome to storms and calms alike, their brows in the sky, their feet set in the groves and gay flowery meadows, while birds, bees, and butterflies help the river and waterfalls to stir all the air into music—things frail and fleeting and types of permanence meeting here and blending, just as they do in Yosemite, to draw her lovers into close and confiding communion with her.

Sad to say, this most precious and sublime feature of the Yosemite National Park, one of the greatest of all our natural resources for the uplifting joy and peace and health of the people, is in danger of being dammed and made into a reservoir to help supply San Francisco with water and light, thus flooding it from wall to wall and burying its gardens and groves one or two hundred feet deep. This grossly destructive commercial scheme has long been planned and urged (though water as pure and abundant can be got from sources outside of the people's park, in a dozen different places), because of the comparative cheapness of the dam and of the territory which it is sought to divert from the great uses to which it was dedicated in the Act of 1890 establishing the Yosemite National Park.

The making of gardens and parks goes on with civilization all over the world, and they increase both in size and number as their value is recognized. Everybody needs beauty as well as bread, places to play in and pray in, where Nature may heal and cheer and give strength to body and soul alike. This natural beauty-hunger is made manifest in the little windowsill gardens of the poor, though perhaps only a geranium slip in a broken cup, as well as in the carefully tended rose and lily gardens of the rich, the thousands of spacious city parks and botanical gardens, and in our magnificent national parks—the Yellowstone, Yosemite, Sequoia, etc.—Nature's sublime wonderlands, the admiration and joy of the world. Nevertheless, like anything else worthwhile, from the very beginning, however well guarded, they have always been subject to attack by despoiling gain-seekers and mischief-makers of every degree from Satan to Senators, eagerly trying to make everything immediately and selfishly commercial, with schemes disguised in smug-smiling philanthropy, industriously, shampiously crying, "Conservation, conservation, panutilization," that man and beast may be fed and the dear Nation made great. Thus long ago a few enterprising merchants utilized the Jerusalem temple as a place of business instead of a place of prayer, changing money, buying and selling cattle and sheep and doves; and earlier still, the first forest reservation, including only one tree, was likewise despoiled. Ever since the establishment of the Yosemite National Park, strife has been going on around its borders and I suppose this will go on as part of the universal battle between right and wrong, however much its boundaries may be shorn, or its wild beauty destroyed. . . .

These temple destroyers, devotees of ravaging commercialism, seem to have a perfect contempt for Nature, and, instead of lifting their eyes to the God of the mountains, lift them to the Almighty Dollar.

Dam Hetch Hetchy! As well dam for watertanks the people's cathedrals and churches, for no holier temple has ever been consecrated by the heart of man.

Questions

1. What does Muir find important about Hetch Hetchy?
2. What is the connection between the Temple of Solomon (the "Jerusalem temple") and the valley?
3. How—if at all—does Muir's failure to address the immediate concerns of San Franciscans affect the thrust of his argument?

"Farmer Green's Reaper" (1874)

Farmers believed in the virtues of hard work and perseverance, which had worked for their fathers and were supposed to for everyone else. It was that kind of belief that led Hamlin Garland's family and countless others to continue farming. The changes wrought by commercial agriculture caught many farmers unprepared, as shown in this 1874 Granger story on Farmer Green's reaper.

The sad history of Farmer Green (a veritable character, although we introduce him here by a fictitious name) should be a lesson and a warning to all his brethren.

Farmer Green was a resident of Iowa, and was reputed to be a sensible and prosperous man. He was far on in life, and had cleared his farm of debt, had stocked it with many things needful to his business, and was generally counted a prosperous man. His snug farm was his pride and boast, and he looked forward to the time when he should be able to add to it by the purchase of a desirable section of land adjoining it.

It was the early summer, and Farmer Green was rejoicing in the magnificent crop of wheat that was springing up on his land, and giving the promise of a handsome return for his care and labor. Day after day he watched the superb growth, and counted over in his mind the number of bushels of golden grain it would yield when the summer sun had warmed it into maturity. Many were the plans he laid for the use of the proceeds of that glorious crop. The goodwife's wants should be all supplied this year, and none of the children should be forced to put up with the deprivations that had fallen to their lot when he was still struggling to clear the farm from its encumbrance of debt.

One day, as he stood watching the bright field of green that spread out before him, and imagining what he would do when the grain was harvested and the money received for it, he was accosted by a stranger who came driving down the road from the village.

"A beautiful crop of wheat you've got there," said the stranger, as he drew rein before the farm gate.

"Yes," said Farmer Green, "I reckon it will turn out pretty well."

"A fine farm you have, too," said the stranger, glancing admiringly around him.

"Yes," said the farmer, pleased with the compliment to his place. "There's none better in the neighborhood."

"Paid for yet?" asked the stranger.

"Every dollar, thank God," said the owner, heartily. "It's clear at last, and I hope to keep it so."

"That's right," said the stranger. "Never contract a debt you're not sure of paying, and the farm will remain yours. That's a mighty nice crop of wheat," he added, as if speaking to himself. "I never saw anything look prettier. It will be ready for cutting soon. How do you cut it? By hand?"

"Yes," replied the farmer. "We've no reapers in this part of the country, and we farm in the oldfashioned way."

"That's a pity," said the stranger. "A reaper would work beautifully on this land. Why it would be no trouble at all to get your wheat in with a good reaper."

"That's true," said Farmer Green.

"You ought to have a reaper to cut it with," said the stranger.

"Can't afford it; haven't got the money to spare," said the farmer.

"See here, now," said the stranger, in a more confidential tone. "I'm selling a patent reaper—a first-class machine, and dirt-cheap at the money asked for it. You'd better let me sell you one."

"It's no use to talk about it, my friend. I haven't the money to spare."

"I don't want your money now," said the man, temptingly. "I'll sell you one at a bargain, and wait till it has paid for itself."

And with that the agent produced pencil and paper, and went into a calculation, showing the farmer how much it would cost him to cut his crop that year, and how much the reaper would save him, as well as a calculation of the amount of grain he could cut for other farmers in the vicinity.

"So you see," added the agent, persuasively, "before the time of payment comes around you will have saved and earned enough to pay for the reaper, and will still have a fine machine capable of doing more work, equally profitable, next season."

Farmer Green's better judgment bade him refuse the terms thus offered, liberal as they seemed. He knew the evil consequences of running into debt, and his conscience bade him put the temptation behind him. He wanted a reaper, however; he had always wanted one; and here was an opportunity of purchasing one upon terms which would enable him to pay for it out of its actual earnings. There was not a reaper in the county, and he felt confident that he would be able to keep it busy on his neighbors' farms, all through the season, after he had cut his own crop.

The agent was a smooth tongued, plausible fellow, and he plied the farmer with every argument he was master of. The result was that the farmer bought the reaper. He had not the money to pay for it, but he gave what is called in Iowa "an iron-clad note" for it. In plainer English, he gave his note accompanied with a statement of property. By the laws of Iowa such a note is equivalent to a mortgage. And so, in order to purchase the reaper, the farmer had imperilled his property, and had placed the safety of his home upon the turn of a chance.

The machine arrived in due time, and was found to be all the agent had claimed for it. It was a capital reaper, and a very handsome machine withal. Farmer Green could not help feeling a little downhearted as he remembered the risk he had incurred in order to obtain it; but he consoled himself with the hope that he would be able to make it pay for itself. When the harvest came around, the machine proved itself a good worker. Farmer Green soon had his crop cut and stacked, and then began to look about him for engagements for cutting his neighbors' grain. Some were willing to make the trial, and a few jobs of this kind enabled him to earn something with his reaper. But the work was less in amount than he had looked forward to, for the agent who had sold him the reaper had found other customers in the vicinity, and the demand for Farmer Green's machine was very much less than he had anticipated. The reaper stood idle under its shed during the better portion of the harvest season, and the farmer was doomed to a severe disappointment.

When the crop was sold there was another disappointment. There had been a heavy decline in the price of wheat, and the farmer did not receive as much as he had expected for his grain. All this while the day upon which the note must be paid was drawing near, and the farmer's chances of meeting it were rapidly diminishing. And still another blow fell upon him. Just after the harvest his wife fell sick, and her illness was long and expensive.

Upon the appointed day, the agent of the Reaper Company presented the note of Farmer Green, and demanded its payment. With a sad heart the farmer related his troubles to him, and told him he was unable to meet his note. He had not the money. The agent's face grew very long as he listened to the woful tale, and after considerable hesitation, he said he was very sorry; that Farmer Green should have made allowance for all these risks, in making the purchase. However, the mischief was done, and there was nothing but to accept the situation. If the farmer could not pay, he supposed the time would have to be extended, but it would be necessary to charge him a fair rate of interest. Farmer Green said that that was only just. He had done his best to meet the note, but failing to do so, he was willing to pay for his failure. What, he inquired, would be a fair rate of interest?

"Twenty per cent. per annum," replied the agent, gravely.

Farmer Green's heart sank, and he said in a despairing tone, that the rate was too high.

"For ordinary interest, perhaps," replied the agent; "but, you see, we assume a serious risk in this case. I'd rather have the money down than one hundred per cent. interest. But you haven't got it. We take the risk of your failing entirely to pay us, and it is only fair that we should be paid for this risk as well as for the delay we are put to."

There was no help for it, and Farmer Green was obliged to pay the extortionate demand. He had placed himself at the mercy of the Reaper Company, and he must do their bidding. He hoped that a succession of good crops would enable him to pay the interest and take up the note; but, alas for him, this hope was destined to disappointment also. He paid the interest once or twice, but the burden was too heavy for him, and at last, in sheer despair, he mortgaged the farm, paid the note, and got rid of the Reaper Company. But he had only shifted his burdens. The mortgage proved as troublesome as the note had been, and instead of being able to decrease it, he was obliged to increase it as time passed on. By the first false step he had placed the farm of which he was so proud in danger. He had voluntarily incurred a useless debt, and the rest of his bad luck was simply the logical consequence of a reckless and foolish act. He ran behind steadily, and at length his difficulties increased to such an extent that in order to rid himself of the debts he had no hope of paying in any other way, he sold his farm, discharged the mortgage, and bidding adieu to his old home and friends, went farther West, to a section where lands were cheaper, and there began life anew at the time he had once hoped to enjoy some rest from his labors.

And yet, Farmer Green, with all his shrewdness, never attributed his misfortunes to their true cause. He never admitted, even to himself, that his great error had been in contracting a useless debt, and assuming an obligation he had no certainty of meeting. He never believed that it was the reaper that ruined him, yet such was the case. Had he put by the temptation held out to him by the Reaper agent, there would have been no burden resting upon him, and his short crop, and other misfortunes, would not have driven him to the expedients he was obliged to resort to. "Out of debt, out of danger" is a true maxim; the wisdom and force of which only those who have passed through the agony and humiliation of such a slavery can appreciate.

There are debts enough that the farmer cannot help assuming; burdens that fall upon him through no fault of his. They are heavy enough, God knows, and they should teach him to assume none from which he can possibly escape.

Improved machinery is useful where it is honestly made, but even the best is worth less than the farmer ordinarily pays for it. He is charged too high, and his hard earnings, instead of constituting a fund for the rearing of his children and the protection of his old age, go to make up the colossal fortunes of the manufacturers and dealers in such machinery. A reform is needed, and it is near at hand.

Questions

1. How does this story convey the defensiveness of midwestern farmers in the 1870s?
2. Who is the salesman made to resemble in his tempting offer to Farmer Green?
3. How sound was the Grange's advice on debt and the use of farm machinery?

Connections Questions

1. Using the Garland and the Jackson readings as background, consider how conditions on the Great Plains might have affected settlers' attitudes toward native Americans.

2. What other readings show state or federal government acting as Congress did with the Chinese Exclusion Act? How is the motivation similar in the various instances?

3. Imagine yourself as John Muir. How would you appeal to the people of San Francisco in defending Hetch Hetchy?

CHAPTER 18

Capital and Labor in the Age of Enterprise 1877–1900

Philip Danforth Armour, Testimony before the U.S. Senate (1889)

Meat packing was one of the giant industries to emerge in the late nine-teenth century. The great Union Stock Yards in Chicago opened on Christmas Day 1865. The yards grew quickly thanks to Chicago's position as a rail cen-ter and proximity to pork and cattle producers. More than 10.2 million cattle and hogs were slaughtered in 1919, a year when the yards employed 46,000 people.

The leading meat packers were much respected for their ability to make money but little loved for their reluctance to share it. One of the leading pack-ers was Philip Danforth Armour, a New England native and onetime gold prospector. Armour once boasted, "Through the wages I disburse and the provisions I supply, I give more people food than any man living." Armour was humbler in 1889, when he appeared before a Senate committee to testify on price fixing. The following is an excerpt from Armour's testimony.

The depression in prices and the present state of the cattle market are due to overproduction, especially of grass fed cattle, the marketing of immature animals, which are too thin for the block (this has affected all corn fed cattle except the choicest) and the enforced competition of farmers raising cattle on the higher priced and highly improved farms of Illinois, Iowa, Missouri, Kansas, and Nebraska with the ranchers of the west and southwest who had thousands of this character of inferior cattle upon public lands or lands of lit-tle value. The gradual absorption of the ranges by actual settlers and over-production of range cattle have greatly overcrowded the remaining range country, and consequently lessened the quantity of range grass and impaired its nutritive quality. As a natural result grass fed range cattle have deteriorated in weight and value, and the southwestern steers now coming in weigh 10 to 20 pounds less than the steers of a similar character did six years ago. Grass fed southwestern steers are not as good as they were then and cannot be ex-pected to command the same prices.

Many other causes have transpired since to depress this branch of the cat-tle business and to cause the over marketing of cattle, among which may be mentioned the thinning of large ranches; drought and short pasture, severe winters and a necessity on the part of the cattle corporations and owners for the realization of quick profits to meet the payments of guaranteed dividends or of interest or mortgages. I am fully convinced that the farmers of Illinois, Iowa, Missouri, Kansas, and Nebraska have suffered serious losses in cattle values because of the effect upon the cattle market of such over shipments.

It is but a question of time when the Argentine Republic will prove a formidable competitor to American beef in foreign countries and probably in this, and in this contingency the action of Congress and the states in discrediting American beef products abroad by agitation and legislation may prove to be of a most harmful character; for unless we can market our surplus products abroad, cattle men must expect low prices and poor markets. Another evidence of our overproduction, and one which shows that cattle raisers themselves recognize it as the true cause of depressed markets, is the large number of young cows and heifers which are being sent to the slaughter pens and the large number of young heifers that are annually being spayed. When ranches and farms are so thinned out as to make the supply of cattle nearer the demand, and when we can market our surplus abroad, we may expect to see steady and proper cattle values; for it is a well established rule of trade that a surplus of any commodity in a market will reduce the value of the whole production of that commodity.

The dressed beef men, as they are called, are in no way responsible for the fixing of the price which the consumer pays for his meat. They sell only at wholesale. They are jobbers, so to speak, of meats. They neither attempt nor desire to enter the retailers' field. The margin between the wholesale price which we sell at and the retail price which the consumer pays in the market can be very readily ascertained.

The dressed beef business is protected by no patent. The methods in slaughtering the animal and preparing its product for the market are well known, and open to any one who wishes to engage in it. Armour and Company have wholesale beef markets and agencies throughout the country. Through the press and otherwise we advertise the products we have for sale, and the prices, and keep our beef and products constantly before the public. To these markets everybody is invited. Our prices are quoted to every enquirer, and any person can readily see for himself whether we are charging or receiving exorbitant prices or not.

There has never been any combination or agreement of any kind between the firm of Armour and Company, of which I am a member, and any other party or parties, to fix the price which we should pay for live cattle, or to control this price which should be paid therefor; nor has there been any attempt on the part of this firm, in connection with others engaged in the dressed beef business, or with other purchasers of cattle, to control or depress the market for cattle.

The firm of Armour and Company is not in any combination with other parties in the dressed beef business, or the shippers of beef in the carcass, to fix the price at which beef carcasses shall be sold.

We do arrange price lists for cut meats and canned meats, from time to time, with others producing these commodities. This is done according to the state of the market, according to supply and demand, and is absolutely necessary to protect dealers in those articles from the sudden and violent declines in prices which otherwise would follow an oversupply. In no case are the prices quoted exorbitant, nor would it be possible to make them exorbitant and maintain them for any length of time. The almost unlimited supply of such cattle, and the limited demand which the market affords for these articles, make the exacting of large prices impossible.

Questions

1. According to Armour, what forces control the price of cattle?
2. Why does Armour portray meat packers simply as wholesalers?
3. Does Armour make his case effectively? Why or why not?

Rocco Corresca, "The Biography of a Bootblack" (1902)

Not all immigrants came to the United States as part of families intent on becoming Americans. Many were like the young Rocco Corresca, whose 1902 account appears here. Corresca came to New York with a companion who may or may not have been his brother. Corresca intended to save enough money to buy a farm in Italy, but his success as a bootblack convinced him that his future lay in the United States.

When I was a very small boy I lived in Italy in a large house with many other small boys, who were all dressed alike and were taken care of by some nuns. It was a good place, situated on the side of the mountain, where grapes were growing and melons and oranges and plums.

They taught us our letters and how to pray and say the catechism, and we worked in the fields during the middle of the day. We always had enough to eat and good beds to sleep in at night, and sometimes there were feast days, when we marched about wearing flowers.

Those were good times and they lasted till I was nearly eight years of age. Then an old man came and said he was my grandfather. He showed some papers and cried over me and said that the money had come at last and now he could take me to his beautiful home. He seemed very glad to see me and after they looked at his papers he took me away and we went to the big city— Naples. He kept talking about his beautiful house, but when we got there it was a dark cellar that he lived in and I did not like it at all. Very rich people were on the first floor. They had carriages and servants and music and plenty of good things to eat, but we were down below in the cellar and had nothing. There were four other boys in the cellar and the old man said they were all my brothers. All were larger than I and they beat me at first till one day Francisco said that they should not beat me any more, and then Paulo, who was the largest of all, fought him till Francisco drew a knife and gave him a cut. Then Paulo, too, got a knife and said that he would kill Francisco, but the old man knocked them both down with a stick and took their knives away and gave them beatings.

Each morning we boys all went out to beg and we begged all day near the churches and at night near the theatres, running to the carriages and opening the doors and then getting in the way of the people so that they had to give us money or walk over us. The old man often watched us and at night he took all the money, except when we could hide something. . . .

It was very hard in the winter time for we had no shoes and we shivered a great deal. The old man said that we were no good, that we were ruining him, that we did not bring in enough money. He told me that I was fat and that people would not give money to fat beggars. He beat me, too, because I didn't like to steal, as I had heard it was wrong.

"Ah!" said he, "that is what they taught you at that place, is it? To disobey your grandfather that fought with Garibaldi! That is a fine religion!"

The others all stole as well as begged, but I didn't like it and Francisco didn't like it either.

Then the old man said to me: "If you don't want to be a thief you can be a cripple. That is an easy life and they make a great deal of money."

I was frightened then, and that night I heard him talking to one of the men that came to see him. He asked how much he would charge to make me a good cripple like those that crawl about the church. They had a dispute, but at last they agreed and the man said that I should be made so that people would shudder and give me plenty of money.

I was much frightened, but I did not make a sound and in the morning I went out to beg with Francisco. I said to him: "I am going to run away. I don't believe Tony is my grandfather. I don't believe that he fought for Garibaldi, and I don't want to be a cripple, no matter how much money the people may give."

"Where will you go?" Francisco asked me.

"I don't know," I said; "somewhere."

He thought awhile and then he said: "I will go, too."

So we ran away out of the city and begged from the country people as we went along. . . .

Now and then I had heard things about America—that it was a far off country where everybody was rich and that Italians went there and made plenty of money, so that they could return to Italy and live in pleasure ever after. One day I met a young man who pulled out a handful of gold and told me he had made that in America in a few days. . . .

The young man took us to a big ship and got us work away down where the fires are. We had to carry coal to the place where it could be thrown on the fires. Francisco and I were very sick from the great heat at first and lay on the coal for a long time, but they threw water on us and made us get up. We could not stand on our feet well, for everything was going around and we had no strength. We said that we wished we had stayed in Italy no matter how much gold there was in America. We could not eat for three days and could not do much work. Then we got better and sometimes we went up above and looked about. There was no land anywhere and we were much surprised. How could the people tell where to go when there was no land to steer by?

We were so long on the water that we began to think we should never get to America or that, perhaps, there was not any such place, but at last we saw land and came up to New York. . . .

We came to Brooklyn to a wooden house in Adams Street that was full of Italians from Naples. Bartolo had a room on the floor and there were fifteen men in the room, all boarding with Bartolo. He did the cooking on a stove in the middle of the room and there were beds all around the sides, one bed above another. It was very hot in the room, but we were soon asleep, for we were very tired.

The next morning, early, Bartolo told us to go out and pick rags and get bottles. He gave us bags and hooks and showed us the ash barrels. On the streets where the fine houses are the people are very careless and put out good things, like mattresses and umbrellas, clothes, hats and boots. We brought all these to Bartolo and he made them new again and sold them on the sidewalk; but mostly we brought rags and bones. The rags we had to wash in the back yard and then we hung them to dry on lines under the ceiling in our room. The bones we kept under the beds till Bartolo could find a man to buy them.

Most of the men in our room worked at digging the sewer. Bartolo got them the work and they paid him about one quarter of their wages. Then he charged them for board and he bought the clothes for them, too. So they got little money after all.

Bartolo was always saying that the rent of the room was so high that he could not make anything, but he was really making plenty. He was what they call a padrone and is now a very rich man. The men that were living with him had just come to the country and could not speak English. They had all been sent by the young man we met in Italy. Bartolo told us all that we must work for him and that if we did not the police would come and put us in prison.

He gave us very little money, and our clothes were some of those that were found on the street. Still we had enough to eat and we had meat quite often, which we never had in Italy. Bartolo got it from the butcher—the meat that he could not sell to the other people—but it was quite good meat. Bartolo cooked it in the pan while we all sat on our beds in the evening. Then he cut it into small bits and passed the pan around, saying:

"See what I do for you and yet you are not glad. I am too kind a man, that is why I am so poor."

We were with Bartolo nearly a year, but some of our countrymen who had been in the place a long time said that Bartolo had no right to us and we could get work for a dollar and a half a day, which, when you make it *lire* (reckoned in the Italian currency) is very much. So we went away one day to Newark and got work on the street. Bartolo came after us and made a great noise, but the boss said that if he did not go away soon the police would have him. Then he went, saying that there was no justice in this country.

We paid a man five dollars each for getting us the work and we were with the boss for six months. He was Irish, but a good man and he gave us our money every Saturday night. We lived much better than with Bartolo, and when the work was done we each had nearly $200 saved. Plenty of the men spoke English and they taught us, and we taught them to read and write. That was at night, for we had a lamp in our room, and there were only five other men who lived in that room with us.

We got up at half-past five o'clock every morning and made coffee on the stove and had a breakfast of bread and cheese, onions, garlic and red herrings. We went to work at seven o'clock and in the middle of the day we had soup and bread in a place where we got it for two cents a plate. In the evenings we had a good dinner with meat of some kind and potatoes. We got from the butcher the meat that other people would not buy because they said it was old, but they don't know what is good. We paid four or five cents a pound for it and it was the best, tho I have heard of people paying sixteen cents a pound.

When the Newark boss told us that there was no more work Francisco and I talked about what we would do and we went back to Brooklyn to a saloon near Hamilton Ferry, where we got a job cleaning it out and slept in a little room upstairs. There was a bootblack named Michael on the corner and when I had time I helped him and learned the business. Francisco cooked the lunch in the saloon and he, too, worked for the bootblack and we were soon able to make the best polish.

Then we thought we would go into business and we got a basement on Hamilton avenue, near the Ferry, and put four chairs in it. We paid $75 for the chairs and all the other things. We had tables and looking glasses there and curtains. We took the papers that have the pictures in and made the place high toned. Outside we had a big sign that said:

THE BEST SHINE FOR TEN CENTS.

. . . We remembered the priest, the friend of Ciguciano, and what he had said to us about religion, and as soon as we came to the country we began to go to the Italian church. The priest we found here was a good man, but he asked the people for money for the church. The Italians did not like to give because they said it looked like buying religion. The priest says it is different here from Italy because all the churches there are what they call endowed, while here all they have is what the people give. Of course I and Francisco understand that, but the Italians who cannot read and write shake their hands and say that it is wrong for a priest to want money.

We had said that when we saved $1,000 each we would go back to Italy and buy a farm, but now that the time is coming we are so busy and making so much money that we think we will stay. We have opened another parlor near South Ferry, in New York. We have to pay $30 a month rent, but the business is very good. The boys in this place charge sixty cents a day because there is so much work.

At first we did not know much of this country, but by and by we learned. There are here plenty of Protestants who are heretics, but they have a religion, too. Many of the finest churches are Protestant, but they have no saints and no altars, which seems strange.

These people are without a king such as ours in Italy. It is what they call a Republic, as Garibaldi wanted, and every year in the fall the people vote. They wanted us to vote last fall, but we did not. A man came and said that he would get us made Americans for fifty cents and then we could get two dollars for our votes. I talked to some of our people and they told me that we should have to put a paper in a box telling who we wanted to govern us.

I went with five men to the court and when they asked me how long I had been in the country I told them two years. Afterward my countrymen said I was a fool and would never learn politics. "You should have said you were five years here and then we would swear to it," was what they told me.

There are two kinds of people that vote here, Republicans and Democrats. I went to a Republican meeting and the man said that the Republicans want a Republic and the Democrats are against it. He said that Democrats are for a king whose name is Bryan and who is an Irishman. There are some good Irishmen, but many of them insult Italians. They call us Dagoes. So I will be a Republican.

I like this country now and I don't see why we should have a king. Garibaldi didn't want a king and he was the greatest man that ever lived.

I and Francisco are to be Americans in three years. The court gave us papers and said we must wait and we must be able to read some things and tell who the ruler of the country is.

There are plenty of rich Italians here, men who a few years ago had nothing and now have so much money that they could not count all their dollars in a week. The richest ones go away from the other Italians and live with the Americans.

We have joined a club and have much pleasure in the evenings. The club has rooms down in Sacket Street and we meet many people and are learning new things all the time. We were very ignorant when we came here, but now we have learned much. . . .

Questions

1. What conditions did Corresca endure in Italy?
2. What arrangement did Bartolo make with the men he housed?
3. What were some of the similarities and differences between Corresca's old and new lives?

Anonymous (A Black Domestic), "More Slavery at the South"

More than one-fourth of the non-farm work force in 1900 consisted of women, most of whom worked out of necessity (see text p. 486). Outside of teaching, social work, and nursing, women did not expect to enjoy a professional career (or equal pay), and a majority worked in factories or as domestics. This reading details the work of an African-American woman. Although caring for white children gave her a degree of social status, she found her life "just as bad as, if not worse than, it was during the days of slavery."

I am a negro woman, and I was born and reared in the South. I am now past forty years of age and am the mother of three children. My husband died nearly fifteen years ago, after we had been married about five years. For more than thirty years—or since I was ten years old—I have been a servant in one capacity or another in white families in a thriving Southern city, which has at present a population of more than 50,000. In my early years I was at first what might be called a "house-girl," or better, a "house-boy." I used to answer the doorbell, sweep the yard, go on errands, and do odd jobs. Later on I became a chambermaid. . . . Still later I was graduated into a cook, in which position I served at different times for nearly eight years in all. During the last ten years I have been a nurse. I have worked for only four different families during all these thirty years. But, belonging to the servant class, which is the majority class among my race at the South, and associating only with servants, I have been able to become intimately acquainted not only with the lives of hundreds of household servants, but also with the lives of their employers. I can, therefore, speak with authority on the so-called servant question; and what I say is said out of an experience which covers many years.

To begin with, then, I should say that more than two-thirds of the negroes of the town where I live are menial servants of one kind or another, and besides that more than two-thirds of the negro women here, whether married or single, are compelled to work for a living,—as nurses, cooks, washerwomen, chambermaids, seamstresses, hucksters [peddlers], janitresses, and the like. I will say, also, that the condition of this vast host of poor colored people is just as bad as, if not worse than, it was during the days of slavery. Though today we are enjoying nominal freedom, we are literally slaves. And, not to generalize, I will give you a sketch of the work I have to do—and I'm only one of many.

I frequently work from fourteen to sixteen hours a day. I am compelled by my contract, which is oral only, to sleep in the house. I am allowed to go home to my own children, the oldest of whom is a girl of 18 years, only once in two weeks, every other Sunday afternoon—even then I'm not permitted to stay all night. I not only have to nurse a little white child, now eleven months old, but I have to act as playmate or "handy-andy," not to say governess, to three other children in the home, the oldest of whom is only nine years of age. I wash and dress the baby two or three times each day; I give it its meals, mainly from a bottle; I have to put it to bed each night; and, in addition, I have to get up and attend to its every call between midnight and morning. If the baby falls to sleep during the day, as it has been trained to do every day about eleven o'clock, I am not permitted to rest. It's "Mammy, do this," or "Mammy, do that," or "Mammy, do the other," from my mistress, all the time. So it is not strange to see "Mammy" watering the lawn in front with the garden hose, sweeping the sidewalk, mopping the porch and halls, dusting around the house, helping the cook, or darning stockings. Not only so, but I have to put the other three children to bed each night as well as the baby, and I have to wash them and dress them each morning. I don't know what it is to go to church; I don't know what it is to go to a lecture or entertainment or anything of the kind; I live a treadmill life; and I see my own children only when they happen to see me on the streets when I am out with the children, or when my children come to the "yard" to see me, which isn't often, because my white folks don't like to see their servants' children hanging around their premises. You might as well say that I'm on duty all the time—from sunrise to sunrise, every day in the week. I am the slave, body and soul, of this family. And what do I get for this work—this lifetime bondage? The pitiful sum of ten dollars a month! And what am I expected to do with these ten dollars? With this money I'm expected to pay my house rent, which is four dollars per month, for a little house of two rooms, just big enough to turn round in; and I'm expected also to feed and clothe myself and three children. For two years my oldest child, it is true, has helped a little toward our support by taking in a little washing at home. She does the washing and ironing of two white families, with a total of five persons; one of these families pays her $1.00 per week, and the other 75 cents per week, and my daughter has to furnish her own soap and starch and wood. For six months my youngest child, a girl about thirteen years old, has been nursing, and she receives $1.50 per week but has no night work. When I think of the low rate of wages we poor colored people receive, and when I hear so much said about our unreliability, our untrustworthiness, and even our vices, I recall the story of the private soldier in a certain army who, once upon a time, being upbraided by the commanding officer because the heels of his shoes were not polished, is said to have replied: "Captain, do you expect all the virtues for $13 per month?" . . .

Nor does this low rate of pay tend to make us efficient servants. The most that can be said of us negro household servants in the South—and I speak as one of them—is that we are to the extent of our ability willing and faithful slaves. We do not cook according to scientific principles because we do not know anything about scientific principles. Most of our cooking is done by guesswork or by memory. We cook well when our "hand" is in, as we say, and when anything about the dinner goes wrong, we simply say, "I lost my hand today!" We don't know anything about scientific food for babies, nor anything about what science says must be done for infants at certain periods of their growth or when certain symptoms of disease appear; but somehow we "raise" more of the children than we kill, and, for the most part, they are lusty chaps—all of them. But the point is, we do not go to cooking-schools nor to nurse-training schools, and so it cannot be expected that we should make as efficient servants without such training as we should make were such training provided. And yet with our cooking and nursing, such as it is, the white folks seem to be satisfied—perfectly satisfied. I sometimes wonder if this satisfaction is the outgrowth of the knowledge that more highly trained servants would be able to demand better pay! . . .

You hear a good deal nowadays about the "service pan." The "service pan" is the general term applied to "left-over" food, which in many a Southern home is freely placed at the disposal of the cook, or, whether so placed or not, it is usually disposed of by the cook. In my town, I know, and I guess in many other towns also, every night when the cook starts for her home she takes with her a pan or a plate of cold victuals. The same thing is true on Sunday afternoon after dinner—and most cooks have nearly every Sunday afternoon off. Well, I'll be frank with you, if it were not for the service pan, I don't know what the majority of our Southern colored families would do. The service pan is the mainstay in many a home. Good cooks in the South receive on an average $8 per month. Porters, butlers, coachmen, janitors, "office boys" and the like, receive on an average $16 per month. Few and far between are the colored men in the South who receive $1 or more per day. Some mechanics do; as, for example, carpenters, brick masons, wheelwrights, blacksmiths, and the like. The vast majority of negroes in my town are serving in menial capacities in homes, stores and offices. Now taking it for granted, for the sake of illustration, that the husband receives $16 per month and the wife $8. That would be $24 between the two. The chances are that they will have anywhere from five to thirteen children between them. Now, how far will $24 go toward housing and feeding and clothing ten or twelve persons for thirty days? And, I tell you, with all of us poor people the service pan is a great institution; it is a great help to us, as we wag along the weary way of life. And then most of the white folks expect their cooks to avail themselves of these perquisites; they allow it; they expect it. I do not deny that the cooks find opportunity to hide away at times, along with the cold "grub," a little sugar, a little flour, a little meal, or a little piece of soap; but I indignantly deny that we are thieves. We don't steal; we just "take" things—they are a part of the oral contract, expressed or implied. We understand it, and most of the white folks understand it. Others may denounce the service pan, and say that it is used only to support idle negroes, but many a time, when I was a cook, and had the responsibility of rearing my three children upon my lone shoulders, many a time I have had occasion to bless the Lord for the service pan! . . .

Questions

1. How does domestic work humiliate women such as the narrator?
2. What paradox does the narrator experience in working for white families?
3. What is the service pan? Why is it important to African-American workers?

Frederick Winslow Taylor, *The Principles of Scientific Management* (1911)

Frederick Winslow Taylor (1856–1915) combined the American love of machines with a passion for improving production systems. Taylor believed so deeply in the ideal of efficiency that he designed his own tennis racquet and golf putter. Trained as an engineer, he began to implement his notion of "scientific management" in the 1890s. Taylor argued that productivity could be improved through better-designed machines and work habits along with a pay formula based on piecework.

There were skeptics, and in 1912, Taylor went before a special committee of the House of Representatives to defend what he called "this great mental revolution." However, critics persisted in charging that scientific management dehumanized work by emphasizing machines and productivity.

To return now to our pig-iron handlers at the Bethlehem Steel Company. If Schmidt had been allowed to attack the pile of 47 tons of pig iron without the guidance or direction of a man who understood the art, or science, of handling pig iron, in his desire to earn his high wages he would probably have tired himself out by 11 or 12 o'clock in the day. He would have kept so steadily at work that his muscles would not have the proper periods of rest absolutely needed for recuperation, and he would have been completely exhausted early in the day. By having a man, however, who understood this law, stand over him and direct his work, day after day, until he acquired the habit of resting at proper intervals, he was able to work at an even gait all day long without unduly tiring himself.

Now one of the very first requirements for a man who is fit to handle pig iron as a regular occupation is that he shall be so stupid and so phlegmatic that he more nearly resembles in his mental make-up the ox than any other type. The man who is mentally alert and intelligent is for this very reason entirely unsuited to what would, for him, be the grinding monotony of work of this character. Therefore the workman who is best suited to handling pig iron is unable to understand the real science of doing this class of work. He is so stupid that the word "percentage" has no meaning to him, and he must consequently be trained by a man more intelligent than himself into the habit of working in accordance with the laws of this science before he can be successful.

The writer trusts that it is now clear that even in the case of the most elementary form of labor that is known, there is a science, and that when the man best suited to this class of work has been carefully selected, when the science of doing the work has been developed, and when the carefully selected man has been trained to work in accordance with this science, the results obtained must of necessity be overwhelmingly greater than those which are possible under the plan of "initiative and incentive."

Let us, however, again turn to the case of these pig-iron handlers, and see whether, under the ordinary type of management, it would not have been possible to obtain practically the same results.

The writer has put the problem before many good managers, and asked them whether, under premium work, piece work, or any of the ordinary plans of management, they would be likely even to approximate 47 tons per man per day, and not a man has suggested that an output of over 18 to 25 tons could be attained by any of the ordinary expedients. It will be remembered that the Bethlehem men were loading only 12½ tons per man.

To go into the matter in more detail, however: As to the scientific selection of the men, it is a fact that in this gang of 75 pig-iron handlers only about one man in eight was physically capable of handling 47½ tons per day. With the very best of intentions, the other seven out of eight men were physically unable to work at this pace. Now the one man in eight who was able to do this work was in no sense superior to the other men who were working on the gang. He merely happened to be a man of the type of the ox,—no rare specimen of humanity, difficult to find and therefore very highly prized. On the contrary, he was a man so stupid that he was unfitted to do most kinds of laboring work, even. The selection of the man, then, does not involve finding some extraordinary individual, but merely picking out from among very ordinary men the few who are especially suited to this type of work. Although in this particular gang only one man in eight was suited to doing the work, we had not the slightest difficulty in getting all the men who were needed— some of them from inside of the works and others from the neighboring country—who were exactly suited to the job. . . .

With most readers great sympathy will be aroused because seven out of eight of these pig-iron handlers were thrown out of a job. This sympathy is entirely wasted, because almost all of them were immediately given other jobs with the Bethlehem Steel Company. And indeed it should be understood that the removal of these men from pig-iron handling, for which they were unfit, was really a kindness to themselves, because it was the first step toward finding them work for which they were peculiarly fitted, and at which, after receiving proper training, they could permanently and legitimately earn higher wages.

Although the reader may be convinced that there is a certain science back of the handling of pig iron, still it is more than likely that he is still skeptical as to the existence of a science for doing other kinds of laboring. One of the important objects of this paper is to convince its readers that every single act of every workman can be reduced to a science. With the hope of fully convincing the reader of this fact, therefore, the writer proposes to give several more simple illustrations from among the thousands which are at hand.

For example, the average man would question whether there is much of any science in the work of shoveling. Yet there is but little doubt, if any intelligent reader of this paper were deliberately to set out to find what may be called the foundation of the science of shoveling, that with perhaps 15 to 20 hours of thought and analysis he would be almost sure to have arrived at the essence of this science. On the other hand, so completely are the rule-of-thumb ideas still dominant that the writer has never met a single shovel contractor to whom it had ever even occurred that there was such a thing as the science of shoveling. This science is so elementary as to be almost self-evident.

For a first class shoveler there is a given shovel load at which he will do his biggest day's work. What is this shovel load? Will a first-class man do more work per day with a shovel load of 5 pounds, 10 pounds, 15 pounds, 20, 25, 30, or 40 pounds? Now this is a question which can be answered only through carefully made experiments. By first selecting two or three first-class shovelers, and paying them extra wages for doing trustworthy work, and then gradually varying the shovel load and having all the conditions accompanying the work carefully observed for several weeks by men who were used to experimenting, it was found that a first-class man would do his biggest day's work with a shovel load of about 21 pounds. For instance, that this man would shovel a larger tonnage per day with a 21-pound load than with a 24-pound load or than with an 18-pound load on his shovel. It is, of course, evident that no shoveler can always take a load of exactly 21 pounds on his shovel, but nevertheless, although his load may vary 3 or 4 pounds one way or the other, either below or above the 21 pounds, he will do his biggest day's work when his average for the day is about 21 pounds.

The writer does not wish it to be understood that this is the whole of the art or science of shoveling. There are many other elements, which together go to make up this science. But he wishes to indicate the important effect which this one piece of scientific knowledge has upon the work of shoveling. . . .

Questions

1. How does Taylor show his biases? How does he try to hide them?
2. Who is likely to benefit from and who is likely to be hurt by scientific management?
3. Given the need of business to turn a profit, what—if any—are the alternatives to scientific management?

Terence V. Powderly, "The Army of Unemployed" (1887)

The Knights of Labor, founded in 1869, offered some promise to workers concerned with finding a way to protect their interests. Though not a union in the modern sense—the Knights stressed education over organization— their membership reached 700,000 by 1885.

In the following selection, Terence V. Powderly (1849–1924), the Knights' Grand Master Workman, struggles to offer a solution to the labor problems of the 1880s.

The Cincinnati riots, that occurred less than one year ago, were not brought about through the agitation of the labor-leader. If the demand for "the removal of unjust technicalities, delays and discriminations in the administration of justice," had been listened to when first made by the Knights of Labor, Cincinnati would have been spared sorrow and disgrace, and her "prominent citizens" would not have had to lead a mob, in order to open the eyes of the country to the manner in which her courts were throttled, and virtue and truth were trampled upon in her temples of justice. That the army of the discontented is gathering fresh recruits day by day, is true; and if this army should become so large, that, driven to desperation, it should one day arise in its wrath, and grapple with its real or fancied enemy, the responsibility for that act must fall upon the heads of those who could have averted the blow, but who turned a deaf ear to the supplication of suffering humanity, and gave the screw of oppression an extra turn, because they had the power. . . .

It may be said that many of the employees of the manufacturing establishments are minors, and consequently cannot perform as great an amount of labor as a corresponding number of adults. That argument might have had some weight years ago, but now it is fruitless. The age and strength of the workman are no longer regarded as factors in the field of production; it is the skill of the operator in managing a labor-saving machine that is held to be the most essential. It is true that a child can operate a machine as successfully as a man, and that muscle is no longer a requisite in accomplishing results. It is also true that less time is required to perform a given amount of labor than heretofore. This being the case, the plea for shorter hours is not unreasonable. Benjamin Franklin said, one hundred years ago, that "if the workers of the world would labor but four hours each day, they could produce enough in that length of time to supply the wants of mankind." While it is true that the means of supplying the wants of man have increased as if by magic, yet man has acquired no new wants; he is merely enabled to gratify his needs more fully. If it were true in Franklin's time that four hours of toil each day would prove sufficient to minister to the necessities of the world's inhabitants, the argument certainly has lost none of its force since then. At that time, it took the sailing-vessel three months to cross the ocean; the stage-coach made its thirty or forty miles a day; the electric wire was not dreamed of; and the letter that traveled but little faster than the stage-coach was the quickest medium of communication.

It required six days' labor at the hands of the machinist, with hammer, chisel and file to perfect a certain piece of machinery at the beginning of this century. The machinist of the present day can finish a better job in six hours, with the aid of a labor-saving machine. In a yarn-mill in Philadelphia, the proprietor says that improved machinery has caused a displacement of fifty per cent. of the former employees within five years, and that one person, with the aid of improved machinery, can perform the work that it took upward of one hundred carders and spinners to do with the tools and implements in use at the beginning of this century. In Massachusetts, it has been estimated that 318,768 men, women and children do, with improved machinery, the work that it would require 1,912,468 men to perform, if improved machinery were not in use. To insure safety on a passenger-train, it is no longer necessary to have a brakeman at each end of the car; the automatic airbrake does the work, while one brakeman can shout, "All right here!" for the whole train. The employee that has had a limb cut off in a collision, must beg for bread or turn the crank of a hand-organ, and gather his pennies under the legend, "Please assist a poor soldier, who lost his leg at Gettysburg." He is no longer stationed, flag in hand, at the switch; the automatic lever directs the course of the train, and renders the one-legged switchman unnecessary. . . .

A great many remedies are recommended for the ills that I speak of. Let me deal with what seems to be the most unimportant,—the reduction of the hours of labor to eight a day. Men, women and children are working from ten to eighteen hours a day, and two million men have nothing to do. If four men, following a given occupation, at which they work ten hours a day, would rest from their labors two hours each day, the two hours taken from the labor of each, if added together, would give the tramp that stands looking on, an opportunity of stepping into a position at eight hours a day. It is said that a vast majority of those who are idle would not work, if they had work to do. That statement is untrue; but let us admit that five hundred thousand of the two million idle men would not work, and we still have a million and a half who are anxious and willing to work. If but six million of the seventeen million producers will abstain from working ten, fifteen, and eighteen hours a day, and work but eight, the one million and a half of idle men that are willing to work, can again take their places in the ranks of the world's producers. Need it be said, that a million and a half of new hats will be needed; that a corresponding number of pairs of shoes, suits of clothing, and a hundred other things will be required; that the wants of these men and their families will be supplied; that shelves will be emptied of their goods, and that the money expended will again go into circulation. It would entail hardship on some branches of business, to require men employed in them to work eight hours a day. Miners and those working by contract could not very well adopt the eight-hour plan, without lengthening their hours of labor. Before giving the matter a second thought, many of these men look upon the eight-hour agitation as of no consequence to them. If a mechanic is thrown out of employment, and cannot find anything to do at his trade, he turns toward the first place where an opportunity for work is presented. If he is re-enforced by two million idle men, the number that apply at the mouth of the mine, or seek to secure contracts at lower figures, becomes quite large; and the miner and contract-man grumble, because so many men are crowding in upon them in quest of work. Every new applicant for work in the mine makes it possible for the boss to let his contract to a lower bidder; therefore, it is clearly to the interest of the miner to assist in reducing the hours of labor in the shop, mill and factory, to the end that the idle millions may be gathered in from the streets to self-sustaining positions.

The eight-hour system, to be of value to the masses, must be put in operation all over the country; for the manufacturers of one State cannot successfully compete with those of other States, if they run their establishments but eight hours, while others operate theirs ten or twelve hours a day. The movement should be national, and should have the hearty co-operation of all men. . . .

Questions

1. What problems does Powderly identify as affecting the working class?
2. What are his solutions?
3. How does he characterize businessmen?

Connections Questions

1. How would someone like Rocco Carresca or the African-American nurse critique the arguments of Frederick Winslow Taylor?
2. Are the views of Terence Powderly relevant to the lives of Rocco Carresca and the African-American nurse? Why or why not?
3. As a whole, do the documents in this section suggest an optimistic view of America's industrial future? Explain your answer.

CHAPTER 19

The Politics of Late Nineteenth-Century America

William Graham Sumner, "The Forgotten Man" (1883)

Social Darwinism invoked science to argue that society should not go out of its way to help the poor or check the abuses of robber barons. Its proponents tried to apply Charles Darwin's theory of natural selection to society, as well as to plants and animals. The most prominent American Social Darwinist was the Yale professor William Graham Sumner (1840–1910), who warned, "if we do not like the survival of the fittest, we have only one possible alternative, and that is the survival of the unfittest." The lecture on which this essay is based was an 1883 address by Sumner to the Brooklyn Historical Society.

Now who is the Forgotten Man? He is the simple, honest laborer, ready to earn his living by productive work. We pass him by because he is independent, self-supporting, and asks no favors. He does not appeal to the emotions or excite the sentiments. He only wants to make a contract and fulfill it, with respect on both sides and favor on neither side. He must get his living out of the capital of the country. The larger the capital is, the better living he can get. Every particle of capital which is wasted on the vicious, the idle, and the shiftless is so much taken from the capital available to reward the independent and productive laborer. But we stand with our backs to the independent and productive laborer all the time. We do not remember him because he makes no clamor; but I appeal to you whether he is not the man who ought to be remembered first of all, and whether, on any sound social theory, we ought not to protect him against the burdens of the good-for-nothing. In these last years I have read hundreds of articles and heard scores of sermons and speeches which were really glorifications of the good-for-nothing, as if these were the charge of society, recommended by right reason to its care and protection. We are addressed all the time as if those who were respectable were to blame because some are not so, and as if there were an obligation on the part of those who have done their duty towards those who have not done their duty. Every man is bound to take care of himself and his family and to do his share in the work of society. It is totally false that one who has done so is bound to bear the care and charge of those who are wretched because they have not done so. The silly popular notion is that the beggars live at the expense of the rich, but the truth is that those who eat and produce not, live at the expense of those who labor and produce. The next time that you are tempted to subscribe a dollar to a charity, I do not tell you not to do it, because after you have fairly considered the matter, you may think it right to do it, but I ask you to stop and remember the Forgotten Man and understand that if you put your dollar in the savings bank it will go to swell the capital of the country which is available for division amongst those who, while they earn it, will reproduce it with increase.

Let us now go on to another class of cases. There are a great many schemes brought forward for "improving the condition of the working classes." I have shown already that a free man cannot take a favor. One who takes a favor or submits to patronage demeans himself. He falls under obligation. He cannot be free and he cannot assert a station of equality with the man who confers the favor on him. The only exception is where there are exceptional bonds of affection or friendship, that is, where the sentimental relation supersedes the free relation. Therefore, in a country which is a free democracy, all propositions to do something for the working classes have an air of patronage and superiority which is impertinent and out of place. No one can do anything for anybody else unless he has a surplus of energy to dispose of after taking care of himself. In the United States, the working classes, technically so called, are the strongest classes. It is they who have a surplus to dispose of if anybody has. Why should anybody else offer to take care of them or to serve them? They can get whatever they think worth having and, at any rate, if they are free men in a free state, it is ignominious and unbecoming to introduce fashions of patronage and favoritism here. A man who, by superior education and experience of business, is in a position to advise a struggling man of the wages class, is certainly held to do so and will, I believe, always be willing and glad to do so; but this sort of activity lies in the range of private and personal relations. . . .

Let us take another class of cases. So far we have said nothing about the abuse of legislation. We all seem to be under the delusion that the rich pay the taxes. Taxes are not thrown upon the consumers with any such directness and completeness as is sometimes assumed; but that, in ordinary states of the market, taxes on houses fall, for the most part, on the tenants and that taxes on commodities fall, for the most part, on the consumers, is beyond question. Now the state and municipality go to great expense to support policemen and sheriffs and judicial officers, to protect people against themselves, that is, against the results of their own folly, vice, and recklessness. Who pays for it? Undoubtedly the people who have not been guilty of folly, vice, or recklessness. Out of nothing comes nothing. We cannot collect taxes from people who produce nothing and save nothing. The people who have something to tax must be those who have produced and saved.

When you see a drunkard in the gutter, you are disgusted, but you pity him. When a policeman comes and picks him up you are satisfied. You say that "society" has interfered to save the drunkard from perishing. Society is a fine word, and it saves us the trouble of thinking to say that society acts. The truth is that the policeman is paid by somebody, and when we talk about society we forget who it is that pays. It is the Forgotten Man again. It is the industrious

workman going home from a hard day's work, whom you pass without noticing, who is mulcted of a percentage of his day's earnings to hire a policeman
to save the drunkard from himself. All the public expenditure to prevent vice
has the same effect. Vice is its own curse. If we let nature alone, she cures vice
by the most frightful penalties. It may shock you to hear me say it, but when
you get over the shock, it will do you good to think of it: a drunkard in the gutter is just where he ought to be. Nature is working away at him to get him out
of the way, just as she sets up her processes of dissolution to remove whatever
is a failure in its line. Gambling and less mentionable vices all cure themselves
by the ruin and dissolution of their victims. Nine-tenths of our measures for
preventing vice are really protective towards it, because they ward off the
penalty. "Ward off," I say, and that is the usual way of looking at it; but is the
penalty really annihilated? By no means. It is turned into police and court ex-
penses and spread over those who have resisted vice. It is the Forgotten Man
again who has been subjected to the penalty while our minds were full of the
drunkards, spendthrifts, gamblers, and other victims of dissipation. Who is,
then, the Forgotten Man? He is the clean, quiet, virtuous, domestic citizen,
who pays his debts and his taxes and is never heard of out of his little circle.
Yet who is there in the society of a civilized state who deserves to be remembered and considered by the legislator and statesman before this man? . . .

Questions

1. Why does Sumner oppose all attempts to help the weak?
2. What would be the ultimate cost to a society that allowed nature to elimi-
nate vice through people's destruction, as Sumner proposes?
3. How might Social Darwinism have affected organized religion of the time?

Frances E. Willard,
Woman and Temperance (1876)

The reform movements of the late 1800s brought women out of the home and into the larger community. Abolition and temperance touched on politics, which in turn led to the call for suffrage and women's right to shape responses to the issues that affected them. Frances E. Willard (1839–1898), the founder of the Woman's Christian Temperance Union, emerged as a symbol of the change in status women experienced after the Civil War. The following selection is excerpted from Willard's first major temperance speech, delivered in 1876.

Vice is the tiger, with keen eyes, alert ears, and cat-like tread, while virtue is the slow-paced, complacent, easy-going elephant, whose greatest danger lies in its ponderous weight and consciousness of power. So the great question narrows down to one of two(?) methods. It is not, when we look carefully into the conditions of the problem, How shall we develop more virtue in the community to offset the tropical growth of vice by which we find ourselves environed? but rather, How the tremendous force we have may best be brought to bear, how we may unlimber the huge cannon now pointing into vacancy, and direct their full charge at short range upon our nimble, wily, vigilant foe?

As bearing upon a consideration of that question, I lay down this proposition: All pure and Christian sentiment concerning any line of conduct which vitally affects humanity will, sooner or later, crystallize into law. But the keystone of law can only be firm and secure when it is held in place by the arch of that keystone, which is public sentiment. . . .

There is a class whose instinct of self-preservation must forever be opposed to a stimulant which nerves, with dangerous strength, arms already so much stronger than their own, and so maddens the brain God meant to guide those arms, that they strike down the wives men love, and the little children for whom, when sober, they would die. The wife, largely dependent for the support of herself and little ones upon the brain which strong drink paralyzes, the arm it masters, and the skill it renders futile, will, in the nature of the case, prove herself unfriendly to the actual or potential source of so much misery. But besides this primal instinct of self-preservation, we have, in the same class of which I speak, another far more high and sacred—I mean the instinct of a mother's love, a wife's devotion, a sister's faithfulness, a daughter's loyalty. And now I ask you to consider earnestly the fact that none of these blessed rays of light and power from woman's heart, are as yet brought to bear upon the rum-shop at the focus of power. They are, I know, the sweet and pleasant sunshine of our homes; they are the beams which light the larger home of social life and send their gentle radiance out even into the great and busy world. But I know, and as the knowledge has grown clearer, my heart was thrilled with gratitude and hope too deep for words, that in a republic all these now divergent beams of light can, through that magic lens, that powerful sunglass which we name the ballot, be made to converge upon the rum-shop in a blaze of light that shall reveal its full abominations, and a white flame of heat which, . . . shall burn this cancerous excrescence from America's fair form. Yes, for there is nothing in the universe so sure, so strong, as love; and love shall do all this—the love of maid for sweetheart, wife for husband, of a sister for her brother, of a mother for her son. And I call upon you who are here to-day, good men and brave—you who have welcomed us to other fields in the great fight of the angel against the dragon in society—I call upon you thus to match force with force, to set over against the liquor-dealer's avarice our instinct of self-preservation; and to match the drinker's love of liquor with our love of him! When you can centre all this power in that small bit of paper which falls

"As silently as snow-flakes fall upon the sod,
But executes a freeman's will as lightnings do the will of God,"

the rum power will be as much doomed as was the slave power when you gave the ballot to the slaves.

In our argument it has been claimed that by the changeless instincts of her nature and through the most sacred relationships of which that nature has been rendered capable, God has indicated woman, who is the born conservator of home, to be the Nemesis of home's arch enemy, King Alcohol. And further, that in a republic, this power of hers may be most effectively exercised by giving her a voice in the decision by which the rum-shop door shall be opened or closed beside her home.

This position is strongly supported by evidence. About the year 1850 petitions were extensively circulated in Cincinnati (later the fiercest battle ground of the woman's crusade), asking that the liquor traffic be put under the ban of law. Bishop Simpson—one of the noblest and most discerning minds of his century—was deeply interested in this movement. It was decided to ask for the names of women as well as those of men, and it was found that the former signed the petition more readily and in much larger numbers than the latter. Another fact was ascertained which rebuts the hackneyed assertion that women of the lower class will not be on the temperance side in this great war. For it was found—as might, indeed, have been most reasonably predicted—that the ignorant, the poor (many of them wives, mothers, and daughters of intemperate men), were among the most eager to sign the petition. . . .

HE WILL LEAD US OUT BY WAY OF THE BALLOT.
"We have never prayed more earnestly over the one than we will over the other. One was the Wilderness, the other is the Promised Land."

A Presbyterian lady, rigidly conservative, said: "For my part, I never wanted to vote until our gentlemen passed a prohibition ordinance so as to get us to stop visiting saloons, and a month later repealed it and chose a saloon-keeper for mayor."

Said a grand-daughter of Jonathan Edwards, a woman with no toleration toward the Suffrage Movement, a woman crowned with the glory of gray hairs—a central figure in her native town—

AND AS SHE SPOKE THE COURAGE AND FAITH OF THE
PURITANS THRILLED HER VOICE—

"If, with the ballot in our hands, we can, as I firmly believe, put down this awful traffic, I am ready to lead the women of my town to the polls, as I have often led them to the rum shops."

We must not forget that for every woman who joins the Temperance Unions now springing up all through the land, there are at least a score who sympathize but do not join. Home influence and cares prevent them, ignorance of our aims and methods, lack of consecration to Christian work—a thousand reasons, sufficient in their estimation, though not in ours, hold them away from us. And yet they have this Temperance cause warmly at heart; the logic of events has shown them that there is but one side on which a woman may safely stand in this great battle, and on that side they would indubitably range themselves in the quick, decisive battle of election day, nor would they give their voice a second time in favor of the man who had once betrayed his pledge to enforce the most stringent law for the protection of their homes. There are many noble women, too, who, though they do not think as do the Temperance Unions about the deep things of religion, and are not as yet decided in their total abstinence sentiments, nor ready for the blessed work of prayer, are nevertheless decided in their views of Woman Suffrage, and ready to vote a Temperance ticket side by side with us. And there are the drunkard's wife and daughters, who from very shame will not come with us, or who dare not, yet who could freely vote with us upon this question; for the folded ballot tells no tales.

Among other cumulative proofs in this argument from experience, let us consider, briefly, the attitude of the Catholic Church toward the Temperance Reform. It is friendly, at least. Father Matthew's spirit lives to-day in many a faithful parish priest. In our procession on the Centennial Fourth of July, the banners of Catholic Total Abstinence Societies were often the only reminders that the Republic has any temperance people within its borders, as they were the only offset to brewers' wagons and distillers' casks, while among the monuments of our cause, by which this memorable year is signalized, their fountain in Fairmount Park—standing in the midst of eighty drinking places licensed by our Government—is chief. Catholic women would vote with Protestant women upon this issue for the protection of their homes.

Again, among the sixty thousand churches of America, with their eight million members, two-thirds are women. Thus, only one-third of this trustworthy and thoughtful class has any voice in the laws by which, between the church and the public school, the rum shop nestles in this Christian land. Surely all this must change before the Government shall be upon His shoulders "Who shall one day reign King of nations as He now reigns King of saints."

Furthermore, four-fifths of the teachers in this land are women, whose thoughtful judgment, expressed with the authority of which I speak, would greatly help forward the victory of our cause. And, finally, by those who fear the effect of the foreign element in our country, let it be remembered that we have sixty native for every one woman who is foreign born, for it is men who emigrate in largest number to our shores. . . .

Questions

1. How does Willard describe vice?
2. To what extent is her argument based on a kind of political feminism?
3. How do Catholics—not normally sympathetic to the temperance movement—fare with Willard? Why does she treat them this way?

Luna Kellie, "Stand Up for Nebraska" (1894)

The Populist movement (see text p. 514) helped disprove the stereotype of the American farmer as rural reactionary. The party's 1892 platform—with its call for farm relief, an income tax, and greater government involvement in the economy—would not be fully realized until the advent of the New Deal forty years later. And, as Eleanor Roosevelt and Frances Perkins furthered reform in the 1930s, so had women Populists a generation earlier. The following selection is a speech by the Nebraska Populist Luna Kellie.

There are those who think the work of the Nebraska Farmers' Alliance is ended; that while the bankers of the state keep up their organization with the avowed purpose of "better influencing legislation" in their behalf, while the merchants, manufacturers, lawyers, doctors, men of every trade or profession, find it to their interest to keep up organizations to aid each other and look after their political welfare, the agriculturalists of the state and nation have no interest in common sufficient for the existence of an organization, but should leave their financial and political business for office seeking politicians to look after. It grieves us to think how little has been accomplished by the Alliance compared with all that is necessary to be done before the farmers of the state obtain anything like justice. At times we grow weary and discouraged when we realize that the work of the Alliance is hardly begun, and that after the weary years of toil of the best men and women of the state we have hardly taken a step on the road to industrial freedom. We know that although we may not arrive there *our children* will enter into the promised land, and we can make their trials fewer and lighter, even if we live not to see the full light of freedom for mankind. We work in the knowledge that our labor of education is not in vain, some one, sometime, will arise and call the Alliance blessed. Meanwhile to us who have learned "to labor and to wait" there come sometimes sweet glimpses of the land beyond, and it seems so near, the road so short, that we can not have long to wait to enter and possess the land. . . .

It does not seem as if that would be hard to do, nor that the road to the promised land of freedom need be long; yet there is a shorter one given by a noted guide hundreds of years ago. But they say, he was visionary, and his way impracticable. It was simply "Do unto others as ye would they should do unto you." The Christian way closely followed at the ballot box would soon right every legalized injustice, and yet the majority of the voters pretend to be his followers. Had they been so in deed and in truth how different would be the condition of our country. We have annually seen the greater part of the wealth produced in the state legislated out of the hands of the rightful owners and into the pockets of those who are allowed to eat, although they *will not* work.

The condition of the farmers of the state has changed greatly in the last three years.

Then the abolishment of high rates of interest on money and reduction of freight rates was all the average Alliance member desired. Thousands of farmers who would have preserved their homes if they could have obtained that relief at that time have now had the mortgage cleared off their farms by the sheriff and are today without a home, and they now demand that *occupancy and use shall be the sole title of land.*

So with the transportation question. While a slight reduction would have satisfied three years ago, the people now know that they have the constitutional right to take the railroads, under right of eminent domain and run them at cost in the interest of *all the people;* and never again will any party arouse any enthusiasm among them who advocate less.

Of course the renter does not care greatly for anything which does not free him from the servitude of giving one third or one half his labor for the *chance* to work on the earth. The farmers comprising this organization are the wealthier class of the farmers of the state, and doubtless most of them own land and a home; but if we do unto others as we would they should do unto us we must look out for the interest of our neighbors, who are mostly renters. This is now a state of renters, and the politicians will find they have a new factor to deal with, and that the rapidly increasing number of renters is proportioned very like that of the stay at home vote. And it is reasonable that any man should stay at home unless he sees some hope of benefiting himself by going to the polls. A renter does not care greatly for transportation charges. He who owns the land owns the man who works it, and as soon as freight rates go down the prices rise [and] the renter is raised in proportion. So also he regards the money question. If the value of his products is increased by increasing money volume the rent is raised in proportion so as barely to allow him to exist to produce more. He has no hope of education for his children, or of giving them a better chance in life than he has until he is permitted to go upon the unoccupied land of the state and make for himself a home while adding yearly to the state's productive capacity and wealth. It will soon be necessary for any organization political or social that wishes the renters' allegiance, to advocate occupancy and use as the sole title to land. And if they desire the allegiance of those who, owing to an insufficient money volume, have become debtors, they must advocate a sufficient medium of exchange so that no usury interest will be exacted for its use. The Alliance must not ask if an idea is popular, but rather is it right? If right advocate it, agitate it, write it, speak it, vote it. We can make it popular. If we wish the farmers to join and keep up this society we must convince them each and every one that it will benefit him individually. We should take a decided step forward in co-operative work. We can compel the building of a co-operative road to the Gulf. We can get an agent to contract the crops of the state at foreign markets for better prices. We can by ordering machinery, flour, coal, etc., in large quantities get greatly reduced prices, and we ought to place ourselves on a level with the Grange . . . in these respects, then each member can soon receive a benefit and a new impetus be given.

Some think the People's party has taken the place of the Alliance. It has to some extent, but cannot entirely.

Leaving our business co-operation which a political organization will not touch, the Alliance has an educational work to perform which no political party can do. Politicians are notoriously cowardly, and not over truthful, especially the law-interpreting class which make speeches for them, and the people will not put faith in them or be taught by them.

A farmer can teach his brother farmers much better the principles of political economy and what he needs to better his condition than the most silvery-tongued office-seeking lawyer that ever lived in any party. There is a large class (yearly becoming larger) who put no faith in political organizations of any class, as regards benefiting the toilers. They think as soon as the party attains power politicians will crowd to the front who care only for the "spoils of office," and the wishes of the voters will be ignored. The Alliance must make it its future work to educate this class to demand the Referendum and direct legislation. It is an excellent time to show the folly of placing one-sixth of the legislative power in the hands of a corrupt governor and president.

If this is to become a government by the people, they must have the right to initiate new laws and not have important questions tabled by a committee appointed by some scoundrel in the shape of a speaker. No power higher than the vote or veto of the people can exist in a free country. The Nebraska farmers and toilers whose productive labor has made the state all it is, whose labor will make it all it ever will become, should stand up for Nebraska by showing what wealth has been produced from her fertile soil and the vast amount paid by her each year to foreigners for the privilege of using the highways of our own state, and as interest money borrowed to replace that legislated from the pockets of our farmers.

Had the farmers of Nebraska obtained justice ten years ago not a dollar of foreign capital would now be drawing interest in the state. That is the sole reason why the loan agents oppose every effort to increase the price of Nebraska's products.

Stand up for Nebraska! from the hand of her God
She came forth, bright and pure as her own golden rod.
Sweet peas and wild roses perfumed all the air.

Her maker pronounced her both fertile and fair.
Not a boodler or pauper disgraced the state then;
Stand up for Nebraska and cleanse her again. . . .

Questions

1. What problems does Kellie cite?
2. What successes does she claim for the Nebraska Populists?
3. What does the speech reveal about the attachment Kellie and her audience feel toward their state?

Ida B. Wells, "Lynching at the Curve"

Violence was not an abstract concept for an African-American like Ida B. Wells, who was born a slave in 1862. She worked as a teacher before becoming part owner of a Memphis newspaper in 1889. The lynching Wells describes here persuaded her to leave Memphis for Chicago. She took part in suffrage and other reform activities there until her death in 1931.

While I was thus carrying on the work of my newspaper, happy in the thought that our influence was helpful and that I was doing the work I loved and had proved that I could make a living out of it, there came the lynching in Memphis which changed the whole course of my life. I was on one of my trips away from home. I was busily engaged in Natchez when word came of the lynching of three men in Memphis. It came just as I had demonstrated that I could make a living by my newspaper and need never tie myself down to school teaching.

Thomas Moss, Calvin McDowell, and Henry Stewart owned and operated a grocery store in a thickly populated suburb. Moss was a letter carrier and could only be at the store at night. Everybody in town knew and loved Tommie. An exemplary young man, he was married and the father of one little girl, Maurine, whose godmother I was. He and his wife Betty were the best friends I had in town. And he believed, with me, that we should defend the cause of right and fight wrong wherever we saw it.

He delivered mail at the office of the *Free Speech,* and whatever Tommie knew in the way of news we got first. He owned his little home, and having saved his money he went into the grocery business with the same ambition that a young white man would have had. He was the president of the company. His partners ran the business in the daytime.

They had located their grocery in the district known as the "Curve" because the streetcar line curved sharply at that point. There was already a grocery owned and operated by a white man who hitherto had had a monopoly on the trade of this thickly populated colored suburb. Thomas's grocery changed all that, and he and his associates were made to feel that they were not welcome by the white grocer. The district being mostly colored and many of the residents belonging either to Thomas's church or to his lodge, he was not worried by the white grocer's hostility.

One day some colored and white boys quarreled over a game of marbles and the colored boys got the better of the fight which followed. The father of the white boys whipped the victorious colored boy, whose father and friends pitched in to avenge the grown white man's flogging of a colored boy. The colored men won the fight, whereupon the white father and grocery keeper swore out a warrant for the arrest of the colored victors. Of course the colored grocery keepers had been drawn into the dispute. But the case was dismissed with nominal fines. Then the challenge was issued that the vanquished whites were coming on Saturday night to clean out the People's Grocery Company.

Knowing this, the owners of the company consulted a lawyer and were told that as they were outside the city limits and beyond police protection, they would be justified in protecting themselves if attacked. Accordingly the grocery company armed several men and stationed them in the rear of the story on that fatal Saturday night, not to attack but to repel a threatened attack. And Saturday night was the time when men of both races congregated in their respective groceries.

About ten o'clock that night, when Thomas was posting his books for the week and Calvin McDowell and his clerk were waiting on customers preparatory to closing, shots rang out in the back room of the store. The men stationed there had seen several white men stealing through the rear door and fired on them without a moment's pause. Three of these men were wounded, and others fled and gave the alarm.

Sunday morning's paper came out with lurid headlines telling how officers of the law had been wounded while in the discharge of their duties, hunting up criminals whom they had been told were harbored in the People's Grocery Company, this being "a low dive in which drinking and gambling were carried on: a resort of thieves and thugs." So ran the description in the leading white journals of Memphis of this successful effort of decent black men to carry on a legitimate business. The same newspaper told of the arrest and jailing of the proprietor of the store and many of the colored people. They predicted that it would go hard with the ringleaders if these "officers" should die. The tale of how the peaceful homes of that suburb were raided on that quiet Sunday morning by police pretending to be looking for others who were implicated in what the papers had called a conspiracy, has been often told. Over a hundred colored men were dragged from their homes and put in jail on suspicion.

All day long on that fateful Sunday white men were permitted in the jail to look over the imprisoned black men. Frenzied descriptions and hearsays were detailed in the papers, which fed the fires of sensationalism. Groups of white men gathered on the street corners and meeting places to discuss the awful crime of Negroes shooting white men.

There had been no lynchings in Memphis since the Civil War, but the colored people felt that anything might happen during the excitement. Many of them were in business there. Several times they had elected a member of their race to represent them in the legislature in Nashville. And a Negro, Lymus Wallace, had been elected several times as a member of the city council and we had had representation on the school board several times. Mr. Fred Savage was then our representative on the board of education.

The manhood which these Negroes represented went to the county jail and kept watch Sunday night. This they did also on Monday night, guarding the jail to see that nothing happened to the colored men during this time of race prejudice, while it was thought that the wounded white men would die. On Tuesday following, the newspapers which had fanned the flame of race prejudice announced that the wounded men were out of danger and would recover. The colored men who had guarded the jail for two nights felt that the crisis was past and that they need not guard the jail the third night.

While they slept a body of picked men was admitted to the jail, which was a modern Bastille. This mob took out of their cells Thomas Moss, Calvin Mc-Dowell, and Henry Stewart, the three officials of the People's Grocery Company. They were loaded on a switch engine of the railroad which ran back of the jail, carried a mile north of the city limits, and horribly shot to death. One of the morning papers held back its edition in order to supply its readers with the details of that lynching.

From its columns was gleaned the above information, together with details which told that "It is said that Tom Moss begged for his life for the sake of his wife and child and his unborn baby"; that when asked if he had anything to say, told them to "tell my people to go West—there is no justice for them here"; that Calvin McDowell got hold of one of the guns of the lynchers and because they could not loosen his grip a shot was fired into his closed fist. When the three bodies were found, the fingers of McDowell's right hand had been shot to pieces and his eyes were gouged out. This proved that the one who wrote that news report was either an eyewitness or got the facts from someone who was.

Questions

1. How and why does the lynching take place?
2. Why would public officials allow a lynching, which by its very nature represents a challenge to authority?

3. The lynching served a particular purpose for the supporters of Jim Crow in Memphis. How did it affect the black community?

W. E. B. Du Bois, *The Souls of Black Folk* (1903)

Unlike Booker T. Washington, W. E. B. Du Bois never experienced slavery. Du Bois was born in Great Barrington, Massachusetts, in 1868, and was educated at Fisk and Harvard, where he earned a Ph.D. As the selection here indicates, Du Bois could not accept Washington's toleration of segregation (see text p. 526). His call for social equality led him to participate in the founding of the NAACP. Du Bois spent his last years in Ghana, where he died in 1963.

Du Bois's critique of Washington appears in The Souls of Black Folk, *first published in 1903.*

Easily the most striking thing in the history of the American Negro since 1876 is the ascendancy of Mr. Booker T. Washington. It began at the time when war memories and ideals were rapidly passing; a day of astonishing commercial development was dawning; a sense of doubt and hesitation overtook the freedmen's sons,—then it was that his leading began. Mr. Washington came, with a simple definite programme, at the psychological moment when the nation was a little ashamed of having bestowed so much sentiment on Negroes, and was concentrating its energies on Dollars. His programme of industrial education, conciliation of the South, and submission and silence as to civil and political rights, was not wholly original; the Free Negroes from 1830 up to wartime had striven to build industrial schools, and the American Missionary Association had from the first taught various trades; and Price and others had sought a way of honorable alliance with the best of the Southerners. But Mr. Washington first indissolubly linked these things; he put enthusiasm, unlimited energy, and perfect faith into this programme, and changed it from a by-path into a veritable Way of Life. And the tale of the methods by which he did this is a fascinating study of human life.

It startled the nation to hear a Negro advocating such a programme after many decades of bitter complaint; it startled and won the applause of the South; it interested and won the admiration of the North; and after a confused murmur of protest, it silenced if it did not convert the Negroes themselves.

To gain the sympathy and coöperation of the various elements comprising the white South was Mr. Washington's first task; and this, at the time Tuskegee was founded, seemed, for a black man, well-nigh impossible. And yet ten

years later it was done in the word spoken at Atlanta: "In all things purely social we can be as separate as the five fingers, and yet one as the hand in all
things essential to mutual progress." This "Atlanta Compromise" is by all odds
the most notable thing in Mr. Washington's career. The South interpreted it
in different ways: The radicals received it as a complete surrender of the demand for civil and political equality; the conservatives, as a generously conceived working basis for mutual understanding. So both approved it, and today its author is certainly the most distinguished Southerner since Jefferson
Davis, and the one with the largest personal following.

Next to this achievement comes Mr. Washington's work in gaining place
and consideration in the North. Others less shrewd and tactful had formerly
essayed to sit on these two stools and had fallen between them; but as Mr.
Washington knew the heart of the South from birth and training, so by sin-
gular insight he intuitively grasped the spirit of the age which was dominat-
ing the North. And so thoroughly did he learn the speech and thought of triumphant commercialism, and the ideals of material prosperity, that the
picture of a lone black boy poring over a French grammar amid the weeds and
dirt of a neglected home soon seemed to him the acme of absurdities. One
wonders what Socrates and St. Francis of Assisi would say to this.

And yet this very singleness of vision and thorough oneness with his age is
a mark of the successful man. It is as though Nature must needs make men
narrow in order to give them force. So Mr. Washington's cult has gained un-
questioning followers, his work has wonderfully prospered, his friends are
legion, and his enemies are confounded. To-day he stands as the one recognized spokesman of his ten million fellows, and one of the most notable figures in a nation of seventy millions. One hesitates, therefore, to criticise a life
which, beginning with so little, has done so much. And yet the time is come
when one may speak in all sincerity and utter courtesy of the mistakes and
shortcomings of Mr. Washington's career, as well as of his triumphs, without
being thought captious or envious, and without forgetting that it is easier to
do ill than well in the world.

The criticism that has hitherto met Mr. Washington has not always been of
this broad character. In the South especially has he had to walk warily to
avoid the harshest judgments,—and naturally so, for he is dealing with the one
subject of deepest sensitiveness to that section. Twice—once when at the
Chicago celebration of the Spanish-American War he alluded to the color-
prejudice that is "eating away the vitals of the South," and once when he
dined with President Roosevelt—has the resulting Southern criticism been violent enough to threaten seriously his popularity. In the North the feeling has
several times forced itself into words, that Mr. Washington's counsels of submission overlooked certain elements of true manhood, and that his educational programme was unnecessarily narrow. Usually, however, such criticism
has not found open expression, although, too, the spiritual sons of the Aboli-

tionists have not been prepared to acknowledge that the schools founded before Tuskegee, by men of broad ideals and self-sacrificing spirit, were wholly
failures or worthy of ridicule. While, then, criticism has not failed to follow
Mr. Washington, yet the prevailing public opinion of the land has been but too
willing to deliver the solution of a wearisome problem into his hands, and say,
"If that is all you and your race ask, take it." . . .

Mr. Washington represents in Negro thought the old attitude of adjustment and submission; but adjustment at such a peculiar time as to make his
programme unique. This is an age of unusual economic development, and Mr.
Washington's programme naturally takes an economic cast, becoming a gospel
of Work and Money to such an extent as apparently almost completely to
overshadow the higher aims of life. Moreover, this is an age when the more
advanced races are coming in closer contact with the less developed races, and
the race-feeling is therefore intensified; and Mr. Washington's programme
practically accepts the alleged inferiority of the Negro races. Again, in our own
land, the reaction from the sentiment of war time has given impetus to race-
prejudice against Negroes, and Mr. Washington withdraws many of the high
demands of Negroes as men and American citizens. In other periods of intensified prejudice all the Negro's tendency to self-assertion has been called
forth; at this period a policy of submission is advocated. In the history of
nearly all other races and peoples the doctrine preached at such crises has
been that manly self-respect is worth more than lands and houses, and that a
people who voluntarily surrender such respect, or cease striving for it, are not
worth civilizing.

In answer to this, it has been claimed that the Negro can survive only
through submission. Mr. Washington distinctly asks that black people give up,
at least for the present, three things,—

First, political power,

Second, insistence on civil rights,

Third, higher education of Negro youth,—

and concentrate all their energies on industrial education, the accumulation
of wealth, and the conciliation of the South. This policy has been courageously
and insistently advocated for over fifteen years, and has been triumphant for
perhaps ten years. As a result of this tender of the palm-branch, what has been
the return? In these years there have occurred:

1. The disfranchisement of the Negro.

2. The legal creation of a distinct status of civil inferiority for the Negro.

3. The steady withdrawal of aid from institutions for the higher training of
the Negro.

These movements are not, to be sure, direct results of Mr. Washington's
teachings; but his propaganda has, without a shadow of doubt, helped their
speedier accomplishment. The question then comes: Is it possible, and probable, that nine millions of men can make effective progress in economic lines

if they are deprived of political rights, made a servile caste, and allowed only the most meagre chance for developing their exceptional men? If history and reason give any distinct answer to these questions, it is an emphatic *No*. And Mr. Washington thus faces the triple paradox of his career:

1. He is striving nobly to make Negro artisans business men and property-owners; but it is utterly impossible, under modern competitive methods, for workingmen and property-owners to defend their rights and exist without the right of suffrage.

2. He insists on thrift and self-respect, but at the same time counsels a silent submission to civic inferiority such as is bound to sap the manhood of any race in the long run.

3. He advocates common-school and industrial training, and depreciates institutions of higher learning; but neither the Negro common-schools, nor Tuskegee itself, could remain open a day were it not for teachers trained in Negro colleges, or trained by their graduates.

This triple paradox in Mr. Washington's position is the object of criticism by two classes of colored Americans. One class is spiritually descended from Toussaint the Savior, through Gabriel, Vesey, and Turner, and they represent the attitude of revolt and revenge; they hate the white South blindly and distrust the white race generally, and so far as they agree on definite action, think that the Negro's only hope lies in emigration beyond the borders of the United States. And yet, by the irony of fate, nothing has more effectually made this programme seem hopeless than the recent course of the United States toward weaker and darker peoples in the West Indies, Hawaii, and the Philippines,—for where in the world may we go and be safe from lying and brute force?

The other class of Negroes who cannot agree with Mr. Washington has hitherto said little aloud. They deprecate the sight of scattered counsels, of internal disagreement; and especially they dislike making their just criticism of a useful and earnest man an excuse for a general discharge of venom from small-minded opponents. Nevertheless, the questions involved are so fundamental and serious that it is difficult to see how men like the Grimkes, Kelly Miller, J. W. E. Bowen, and other representatives of this group, can much longer be silent. Such men feel in conscience bound to ask of this nation three things:

1. The right to vote.

2. Civic equality.

3. The education of youth according to ability.

. . . This group of men honor Mr. Washington for his attitude of conciliation toward the white South; they accept the "Atlanta Compromise" in its broadest interpretation; they recognize, with him, many signs of promise, many men of high purpose and fair judgment, in this section; they know that no easy task has been laid upon a region already tottering under heavy burdens. But, nevertheless, they insist that the way to truth and right lies in straightforward honesty, not in indiscriminate flattery; in praising those of the South who do well and criticising uncompromisingly those who do ill; in taking advantage of the opportunities at hand and urging their fellows to do the same, but at the same time in remembering that only a firm adherence to their higher ideals and aspirations will ever keep those ideals within the realm of possibility. They do not expect that the free right to vote, to enjoy civic rights, and to be educated, will come in a moment; they do not expect to see the bias and prejudices of years disappear at the blast of a trumpet; but they are absolutely certain that the way for a people to gain their reasonable rights is not by voluntarily throwing them away and insisting that they do not want them; that the way for a people to gain respect is not by continually belittling and ridiculing themselves; that, on the contrary, Negroes must insist continually, in season and out of season, that voting is necessary to modern manhood, that color discrimination is barbarism, and that black boys need education as well as white boys. . . .

The South ought to be led, by candid and honest criticism, to assert her better self and do her full duty to the race she has cruelly wronged and is still wronging. The North—her co-partner in guilt—cannot salve her conscience by plastering it with gold. We cannot settle this problem by diplomacy and suaveness, by "policy" alone. If worse come to worst, can the moral fibre of this country survive the slow throttling and murder of nine millions of men?

The black men of America have a duty to perform, a duty stern and delicate,—a forward movement to oppose a part of the work of their greatest leader. So far as Mr. Washington preaches Thrift, Patience, and Industrial Training for the masses, we must hold up his hands and strive with him, rejoicing in his honors and glorying in the strength of this Joshua called of God and of man to lead the headless host. But so far as Mr. Washington apologizes for injustice, North or South, does not rightly value the privilege and duty of voting, belittles the emasculating effects of caste distinctions, and opposes the higher training and ambition of our brighter minds,—so far as he, the South, or the Nation, does this,—we must unceasingly and firmly oppose them. By every civilized and peaceful method we must strive for the rights which the world accords to men, clinging unwaveringly to those great words which the sons of the Fathers would fain forget: "We hold these truths to be self-evident: That all men are created equal; that they are endowed by their Creator with certain unalienable rights; that among these are life, liberty, and the pursuit of happiness."

Questions

1. Which aspects of Washington's philosophy does Du Bois criticize?
2. Who does Du Bois expect to lead the opposition to Washington's ideas?
3. What role does Du Bois envision for blacks in American society?

Connections Questions

1. William Graham Sumner and Frances Willard were contemporaries, and both would have considered themselves practicing Christians. Why did they differ so greatly on society's proper response to the dangers of alcohol?

2. Would Luna Kellie be comfortable with Frances Willard's style of politics? Why or why not?

3. How might Ida B. Wells respond to the arguments of William Graham Sumner?

CHAPTER 20

The Rise
of the City

Frederic C. Howe, the "City Beautiful" (1905)

*Like countless other Americans, Frederic C. Howe (1867–1940) moved
from small town to big city. Howe was born in Meadville, Pennsylvania. He
attended Johns Hopkins and eventually (if, as he says in his autobiography,
reluctantly) became a lawyer. Rather than practice in a small town, Howe decided on Cleveland. There he served as an adviser to Mayor Tom Johnson
(1901–1909). The experience helped convince Howe that city life was full of
promise. In the following selection from* The City: The Hope of Democracy
(1905), Howe considers the importance of the city beautiful movement.

One of the most significant evidences of the gain we are making appears
in the beautification of our cities. This interest is general. In Washington,
New York, Boston, Cleveland, San Francisco, and Chicago public and private
movements have been organized for the unified treatment of the city's architecture, while hundreds of other communities are aiming to make their cities
more presentable through parks, cleaner streets and higher ideas of municipal art.

This indicates that the public is learning to act in an organized way. Heretofore we have lacked a city sense. In consequence, collective action has been
impossible. It also indicates a new attitude towards the city, a belief in its life,
outward form and appearance, its architectural expression, its parks, schools,
and playgrounds. A determination has come to make the city a more beautiful as well as a more wholesome place of living. All this is foreign to the business man's ideal of merely getting his money's worth out of government. The
belief in the city as a home, as an object of public-spirited endeavor, has superseded the earlier commercial ideals that characterized our thought.

The great cities of every age have probably passed through a similar evolution. First business, commerce, and wealth, then culture, beauty, and civic
activity. It was so with Athens, which became great as a commercial centre before it was adorned by the hands of Pericles and Phidias. Rome became mistress of the Mediterranean before she enriched her streets and public places
with the spoils of foreign conquest. The mediæval Italian cities of Florence,
Venice, and Milan were the creations of organized democracy, as well as the
centres of the world's trade with the East. In these cities it was freedom that
gave birth to a local patriotism that inspired democracy to its highest achievements in the realm of art, literature, and architecture. And it is probable that,
next to religion, democracy and the sense of a free city have been the greatest inspirations to art in the history of mankind. . . .

The splendid projects now on foot in America are an evidence that modern democracy is not satisfied with the commonplace. Just as the monumen-

tal cathedrals which everywhere dot Europe are the expression of the ideals and aspirations of mankind, so in America, democracy is coming to demand and appreciate fitting monuments for the realization of its life, and splendid parks and structures as the embodiment of its ideals. The twentieth century offers high promise of the ultimate possibilities of democracy in generous expenditure for public purposes. . . .

Probably no other city in America has projected as well as assured the carrying out of the systematic beautification of the city on so splendid a scale as has the city of Cleveland. This is the more remarkable inasmuch as no American city, with the possible exception of Chicago, is so essentially democratic in its instincts. Nowhere have the movements centring about municipal ownership, taxation, and the great industrial issues found more ready response at the hands of the voters than in this great industrial centre on the southern shore of Lake Erie. Cleveland is a commercial city *par excellence*. It has been termed the Sheffield of America. It is a centre second only to Pittsburg[h] in the iron, steel, coal, and coke trade. One-third of its population is foreign-born. But despite this fact, as well as the newness of its life, it has shown a willingness to expend many millions of dollars in the development of the artistic side of its existence.

The city is fortunate in the fact that all its public buildings are to be constructed at the same time. A uniform plan of procedure was thus possible. The Federal Building, County Courthouse, City Hall, and Public Library, as well as several other semi-public structures, are all to be built. Under ordinary circumstances and with the subterranean political and commercial forces at work in a city, isolated construction would doubtless have been the result. But public-spirited men have brought about a harmony of action among the many political agencies which had to be satisfied, and achieved a result not far from ideal in its possibilities. Through the aid of state legislation a Board of Supervising Architects was appointed, endowed with a final veto upon the location, plans, and style of architecture of all the public buildings. Despite some local jealousies, the city called to its aid Daniel H. Burnham, of Chicago, the supervising architect of the Chicago Exposition; John M. Carrere, supervising architect of the Pan-American Exposition of Buffalo, and Arnold W. Brunner, of New York, the architect of the new Federal Building in Cleveland. The members of this commission were employed by the city at generous salaries and given absolute freedom in the working out of a ground plan for the arrangement and development of the scheme. The commission is also entrusted with the problem of improving the public square, the approaches to the sites of the public buildings, and the development of the lake front.

This is the most significant forward step taken in America in the matter of municipal art. It is comparable to the designs of Napoleon III, who remade Paris, with the aid of Baron Haussmann, or to the prescience of Jefferson, who called a distinguished architect to the aid of the new government in the laying out of the national capital on its present scale.

The commission thus appointed was at work for more than two years, and has presented the results of its labors in a completed plan for the arrangement of the public buildings. The design has met with such enthusiastic approval that its consummation is now assured. The total expenditure involved approximates $14,000,000 for public purposes, with from three to five millions more for a terminal railway station, music-hall, museum, and the like. It involves the clearing of a large area of land laying between the business portion of the city and Lake Erie, and the utilization of this space as a site for the public buildings, parkage, a splendid mall, and the development of a lakefront park sixty acres in extent into a splendid terminal railway station, which is to be the gateway to the city. . . .

Questions

1. For Howe, the city has a symbolic function "foreign to the business man's ideal of merely getting his money's worth out of government." What is that function?
2. How does Cleveland go about creating a city beautiful?
3. Why should museums and lakefront parks matter to the poor and working class of the cities?

Josiah Strong, The Dangers of Cities (1886)

Americans accepted the city if for no other reason than that it generated prosperity. By the second half of the nineteenth century, there was a large urban middle class, confident in its success and yet worried over the future of city life. The Reverend Josiah Strong (1847–1916) addressed some of those concerns (see text p. 529) in Our Country, *first printed in 1886. Strong did not simply want to sit by as nature ran its course in the American city, as Social Darwinists argued. However, Strong's call to action reflected the prejudices of his day.*

The city is the nerve center of our civilization. It is also the storm center. The fact, therefore, that it is growing much more rapidly than the whole population is full of significance. . . .

The city has become a serious menace to our civilization, because in it, excepting Mormonism, each of the dangers we have discussed is enhanced, and all are focalized. It has a peculiar attraction for the immigrant. Our fifty principal cities in 1880 contained 39.3 per cent of our entire German population, and 45.8 per cent of the Irish. Our ten larger cities at that time contained only nine per cent of the entire population, but 23 per cent of the foreign. While a little less than one-third of the population of the United States was foreign by birth or parentage, sixty-two per cent of the population of Cincinnati was foreign, eighty-three per cent of Cleveland, sixty-three per cent of Boston, eighty per cent of New York, and ninety-one per cent of Chicago. A census of Massachusetts, taken in 1885, showed that in 65 towns and cities of the state 65.1 per cent of the population was foreign by birth or parentage.

Because our cities are so largely foreign, Romanism finds in them its chief strength.

For the same reason the saloon, together with the intemperance and the liquor power which it represents, is multiplied in the city. East of the Mississippi there was, in 1880, one saloon to every 438 of the population; in Boston, one to every 329; in Cleveland, one to every 192; in Chicago, one to every 179; in New York, one to every 171; in Cincinnati, one to every 124. Of course the demoralizing and pauperizing power of the saloons and their debauching influence in politics increase with their numerical strength.

It is the city where wealth is massed; and here are the tangible evidences of it piled many stories high. Here the sway of Mammon is widest, and his worship the most constant and eager. Here are luxuries gathered—everything that dazzles the eye, or tempts the appetite; here is the most extravagant expenditure. Here, also, is the *congestion* of wealth the severest. Dives and Lazarus are brought face to face; here, in sharp contrast, are the *ennui* of surfeit and the desperation of starvation. The rich are richer, and the poor are poorer, in the city than elsewhere; and, as a rule, the greater the city, the greater are the riches of the rich and the poverty of the poor. Not only does the proportion of the poor increase with the growth of the city, but their condition becomes more wretched. The poor of a city of 8,000 inhabitants are well off compared with many in New York; and there are hardly such depths of woe, such utter and heart-wringing wretchedness in New York as in London. . . .

1. In gathering up the results of the foregoing discussion of these several perils, it should be remarked that to preserve republican institutions requires a *higher average* intelligence and virtue among large populations than among small. The government of 5,000,000 people was a simple thing compared with the government of 50,000,000; and the government of 50,000,000 is a simple thing compared with that of 500,000,000. There are many men who can conduct a small business successfully, who are utterly incapable of managing large interests. In the latter there are multiplied relations whose harmony must be preserved. A mistake is farther reaching. It has, as it were, a longer leverage. This is equally true of the business of government. The man of only average ability and intelligence discharges creditably the duties of mayor in his little town; but he would fail utterly at the head of the state or the nation. If the people are to govern, they must grow more intelligent as the

population and the complications of government increase. And a higher morality is even more essential. As civilization increases, as society becomes more complex, as labor-saving machinery is multiplied and the division of labor becomes more minute, the individual becomes more fractional and dependent. Every savage possesses all the knowledge of the tribe. Throw him upon his own resources, and he is self-sufficient. A civilized man in like circumstances would perish. The savage is independent. Civilize him, and he becomes dependent; the more civilized, the more dependent. And, as men become more dependent on each other, they should be able to rely more implicitly on each other. More complicated and multiplied relations require a more delicate conscience and a stronger sense of justice. And any failure in character or conduct under such conditions is farther reaching and more disastrous in its results.

Is our progress in morals and intelligence at all comparable to the growth of population? The nation's illiteracy has not been discussed, because it is not one of the perils which peculiarly threaten the West; but any one who would calculate our political horoscope must allow it great influence in connection with the baleful stars which are in the ascendant. But the danger which arises from the corruption of popular morals is much greater. The republics of Greece and Rome, and if I mistake not, all the republics that have ever lived and died, were more intelligent at the end than at the beginning; but growing intelligence could not compensate decaying morals. What, then, is our moral progress? Are popular morals as sound as they were twenty years ago? There is, perhaps, no better index of general morality than Sabbath observance; and everybody knows there has been a great increase of Sabbath desecration in twenty years. . . .

2. The fundamental idea of popular government is the distribution of power. It has been the struggle of liberty for ages to wrest power from the hands of one or the few, and lodge it in the hands of the many. We have seen, in the foregoing discussion, that centralized power is rapidly growing. The "boss" makes his bargain, and sells his ten thousand or fifty thousand voters as if they were so many cattle. Centralized wealth is centralized power; and the capitalist and corporation find many ways to control votes. The liquor power controls thousands of votes in every considerable city. The president of the Mormon Church casts, say, sixty thousand votes. The Jesuits, it is said, are all under the command of one man in Washington. The Roman Catholic vote is more or less perfectly controlled by the priests. That means that the Pope can dictate some hundreds of thousands of votes in the United States. Is there anything unrepublican in all this? And we must remember that, if present tendencies continue, these figures will be greatly multiplied in the future. And not only is this immense power lodged in the hand of one man, which in itself is perilous, but it is wielded without the slightest reference to any policy or principle of government, solely in the interests of a church or a business, or for personal ends.

The result of a national election may depend on a single state; the vote of that state may depend on a single city; the vote of that city may depend on a "boss," or a capitalist, or a corporation; or the election may be decided, and the policy of the government may be reversed, by the socialist, or liquor, or Roman Catholic or immigrant vote.

It matters not by what name we call the man who wields this centralized power—whether king, czar, pope, president, capitalist, or boss. Just so far as it is absolute and irresponsible, it is dangerous.

3. These several dangerous elements are singularly netted together, and serve to strengthen each other. It is not necessary to prove that any *one* of them is likely to destroy our national life, in order to show that it is imperiled. A man may die of wounds no one of which is fatal. No soberminded man can look fairly at the facts, and doubt that *together* these perils constitute an array which will seriously endanger our free institutions, if the tendencies which have been pointed out continue; and especially is this true in view of the fact that these perils peculiarly confront the West, where our defense is weakest.

Questions

1. What problems does Strong associate with immigrants and "the liquor power"?

2. What are his greatest fears concerning the city?

3. How does Strong stereotype non-Protestant voters? Why does he assume Protestant voters would act differently?

The Immigrant Experience:
Letters Home (1901–1903)

The American city could be a forbidding place to newcomers. To gauge the spectrum of immigrant experiences, sociologists William I. Thomas (1863–1947) and Florian Znaniecki (1882–1958) undertook a massive research project on The Polish Peasant in Europe and America *(1918). Their work focused on correspondence between immigrants in the United States and family and friends in the old country. Thomas and Znaniecki hoped to demonstrate how city life overwhelmed rural immigrants and led to their "social disorganization."*

SOUTH CHICAGO, *December 6, 1901*

DEAR PARENTS: I send you my lowest bow, as to a father and mother, and I greet you and my brothers with these words: "Praised be Jesus Christus," and I hope in God that you will answer me, "For centuries of centuries. Amen."

And now I wish you, dearest parents, and you also, dearest brother, to meet the Christmas eve and merry holidays in good health and happiness. May God help you in your intentions. Be merry, all of you together. [Health and success; letter received.] I could not answer you at once, for you know that when one comes from work he has no wish to occupy himself with writing [particularly] as I work always at night. . . . I sent you money, 100 roubles, on November 30. I could not send more now, for you know that winter is coming and I must buy clothes. I inform you that Marta has no work yet. She will get work after the holidays, and it may happen that she will marry. . . . I inform you about Jasiek, my brother, that he wrote me a letter from Prussia asking me to take him to America, but he is still too young. Inform me about Antoni, how his health is, for in the spring I will bring him to me. I will send him a ship-ticket, if God grants me health. [Greetings for family and relatives.]

[KONSTANTY BUTKOWSKI]

February 17, 1902

DEAREST PARENTS: . . . I inform you that I have sent a ship-ticket for Antoni. . . . Expect to receive it soon. . . . And remember, Antoni, don't show your papers to anybody, except in places where you must show them. . . . And if you receive the ticket soon, don't wait, but come at once. And if you receive it a week or so before Easter, then don't leave until after the holidays. But after the holidays don't wait; come at once. . . . And send me a telegram from the Castle Garden. You won't pay much and I shall know and will go to the railway-station. Take 15 roubles with you, it will be enough, and change them at once for Prussian money. As to the clothes, take the worst which you have, some three old shirts, that you may have a change on the water. And when you come across the water happily, then throw away all these rags. Bring nothing with you except what you have upon yourself. And don't bring any good shoes either, but everything the worst. As to living, take some dry bread and much sugar, and about half a quart of spirits, and some dry meat. You may take some onions, but don't take any cheese. . . . And be careful in every place about money. Don't talk to any girls on the water. . . . Learn in Bzory when Wojtek will come, for he comes to the same place where I am, so you would have a companion. And about Jan Plonka, if he wants to come, he is not to complain about [reproach] me for in America there are neither Sundays nor holidays; he must go and work. I inform [him] that I shall receive him as my brother. If he wishes he may come. . . .

[Konstanty Butkowski]

November 11 [1902]

Dearest Parents: . . . Now I inform you about Antoni, that he is working in Chicago; it costs 15 cents to go to him. He is boarding, as well as Marta, with acquaintances, with Malewski. He has an easy and clean work, but he earns only enough to live, for he is unable to do heavy work. I see them almost every evening. I go to them. And Marta works in a tailor-shop, but she refuses to listen to me, else she would have been married long ago. So I inform you that I loved her as my own sister, but now I won't talk to her any more, for she refuses to listen. Family remains family only in the first time after coming from home, and later they forget and don't wish any more to acknowledge the familial relations; the American meat inflates them.

I have nothing more to write, except that we are all in good health. More-over, I declare about your letters, give them to somebody else to write, for nei-ther wise nor fool can read such writing. If such writers are to write you may as well not send letters, for I won't read them, only I will throw them into the fire, for I cannot understand. I beg you, describe to me about our country, how things are going on there. And please don't be angry with me for this which I shall write. I write you that it is hard to live alone, so please find some girl for me, but an orderly [honest] one, for in America there is not even one single orderly girl. . . .

Konstanty Butkowski

December 21 [1902]

I, your son, Konstanty Butkowski, inform you, dear parents, about my health. . . . I thank you kindly for your letter, for it was happy. As to the girl, although I don't know her, my companion, who knows her, says that she is stately and pretty. I believe him, as well as you, my parents. For although I don't know her, I ask you, my dear parents, and as you will write me so it will be well. Shall I send her a ship-ticket, or how else shall I do? Ask Mr. and Mrs. Sadowski [her parents], what they will say. And I beg you, dear parents, give them my address and let them write a letter to me, then I shall know with certainty. And write me, please, about her age and about everything which concerns her. I don't need to enumerate; you know yourselves, dear parents. For to send a ship-ticket it is not the same as to send a letter which costs a nickel; what is done cannot be undone. So I beg you once more, as my loving parents, go into this matter and do it well, that there may be no cheating. . . . I shall wait for your letter with great impatience, that I may know what to do. . . .

Konstanty Butkowski

Please inform me, which one is to come, whether the older or the younger one, whether Aleksandra or Stanislawa. Inform me exactly.

June 13 [1902]

Dearest Parents: . . . Konstanty works in the same factory as before and earns $2 a day. I have yet no work, but don't be anxious about me, dear parents . . . for I came to a brother and uncle, not to strangers. If our Lord God gives me health, I shall work enough in America. [News about friends and relatives.] Now I inform you, dear parents, about Wladyslawa Butkowska [cousin]. She lives near us, we see each other every day. She is a doctor's servant. And this doctor has left his wife in Chicago and came [*sic*] to South Chicago. She cooks for him, and she is alone in his house, so people talk about her, that she does not behave well. He pays her $5 a week. I don't know whether it is true or not, but people talk thus because he has left his wife. . . .

[Antoni Butkowski]

Chicago, December 31, 1902

Dear Parents: . . . If Konstanty wrote you to send him a girl answer him that he may send a ship-ticket either to the one from Popów or to the one from Grajewo. Let the one come which is smarter, for he does not know either of them, so send the one which pleases you better. For in America it is so: Let her only know how to prepare for the table, and be beautiful. For in America there is no need of a girl who knows how to spin and to weave. If she knows how to sew, it is well. For if he does not marry he will never make a fortune and will never have anything; he wastes his work and has nothing. And if he marries he will sooner put something aside. For he won't come back any more. In America it is so: Whoever does not intend to return to his country, it is best for him to marry young; then he will sooner have something, for a bachelor in America will never have anything, unless he is particularly self-controlled. [Greetings, wishes, etc.]

ANTONI BUTKOWSKI

SOUTH CHICAGO, April 21, 1903

Now I, Antoni, your son, my dearest parents, and my uncle and the whole family, we inform you that your son Konstanty is no longer alive. He was killed in the foundry [steel-mills]. Now I inform you, dear parents, that he was insured in an association for $1,000. His funeral will cost $300. And the rest which remains, we have the right to receive this money. So now I beg you, dear parents, send an authorization and his birth-certificate to my uncle, Piotr Z., for I am still a minor and cannot appear in an American lawsuit. When he joined his association he insured himself for $1,000 . . . and made a will in your favor, dear parents. But you cannot get it unless you send an authorization to our uncle, for the lawsuit will be here, and it would be difficult for you to get the money [while remaining] in our country, while we shall get it soon and we will send it to you, dear parents. So now, when you receive this letter, send us the papers soon. Only don't listen to stupid people, but ask wise people. . . .

Now I inform you, dear parents, that strange people will write to you letters. Answer each letter, and answer thus, that you commit everything to Piotr Z. For they will try to deceive you, asking to send the authorization to them. But don't listen to anybody . . . only listen to me, as your son; then you will receive money paid for your son and my brother. [Repeats the advice; wishes from the whole family.]

Now I beg you, dear parents, don't grieve. For he is no more, and you won't raise him, and I cannot either. For if you had looked at him, I think your heart would have burst open with sorrow [he was so mutilated]. But in this letter I won't describe anything, how it was with him. It killed him on April 20. In the next letter I shall describe to you everything about the funeral. . . . Well, it is God's will; God has wished thus, and has done it. Only I beg you, dear parents, give for a holy mass, for the sake of his soul. And he will be buried beautifully, on April 22.

[ANTONI BUTKOWSKI]

Questions

1. What are the everyday concerns of Konstanty and his brother Antoni?
2. How does the relationship between Konstanty Butkowski and his parents change over time? Where is this shown in the letters?

3. Does the correspondence reveal more than the sociologists intended? If so, what?

Catharine E. Beecher, "The Christian Family" (1869)

Like her sister Harriet Beecher Stowe, author of Uncle Tom's Cabin, *Catharine E. Beecher (1800–1878) hoped to reach a wide audience through her writings.* The American Woman's Home *was subtitled in part "a guide to the formation and maintenance of economical, healthful, beautiful and Christian homes" and dedicated "to THE WOMEN OF AMERICA, in whose hands rest the real destinies of the republic, as moulded by the early training and preserved amid the maturer influences of home. . . ." Beecher's more famous sister was listed as a coauthor to increase the book's popularity; Catharine did most of the writing.*

It is the aim of this volume to elevate the honor and the remuneration of all employments that sustain the many difficult and varied duties of the family state, and thus to render each department of woman's profession as much desired and respected as are the most honored professions of men.

What, then, is the end designed by the family state which Jesus Christ came into this world to secure?

It is to provide for the training of our race to the highest possible intelligence, virtue, and happiness, by means of the self-sacrificing labors of the wise and good, and this with chief reference to a future immortal existence.

The distinctive feature of the family is self-sacrificing labor of the stronger and wiser members to raise the weaker and more ignorant to equal advantages. The father undergoes toil and self-denial to provide a home, and then the mother becomes a self-sacrificing laborer to train its inmates. The useless, troublesome infant is served in the humblest offices; while both parents unite in training it to an equality with themselves in every advantage. Soon the older children become helpers to raise the younger to a level with their own. When any are sick, those who are well become self-sacrificing ministers. When the parents are old and useless, the children become their self-sacrificing servants.

Thus the discipline of the family state is one of daily self-devotion of the stronger and wiser to elevate and support the weaker members. Nothing could be more contrary to its first principles than for the older and more capable children to combine to secure to themselves the highest advantages, enforcing the drudgeries on the younger, at the sacrifice of their equal culture. . . .

The family state then, is the aptest earthly illustration of the heavenly kingdom, and in it woman is its chief minister. Her great mission is self-denial, in training its members to self-sacrificing labors for the ignorant and weak: if not her own children, then the neglected children of her Father in heaven. She is to rear all under her care to lay up treasures, not on earth, but in heaven. All the pleasures of this life end here; but those who train immortal minds are to reap the fruit of their labor through eternal ages.

To man is appointed the out-door labor—to till the earth, dig the mines, toil in the foundries, traverse the ocean, transport merchandise, labor in manufactories, construct houses, conduct civil, municipal, and state affairs, and all the heavy work, which, most of the day, excludes him from the comforts of a home. But the great stimulus to all these toils, implanted in the heart of every true man, is the desire for a home of his own, and the hopes of paternity. Every man who truly lives for immortality responds to the beatitude, "Children are a heritage from the Lord: blessed is the man that hath his quiver full of them!" The more a father and mother live under the influence of that "immortality which Christ hath brought to light," the more is the blessedness of rearing a family understood and appreciated. Every child trained aright is to dwell forever in exalted bliss with those that gave it life and trained it for heaven.

The blessed privileges of the family state are not confined to those who rear children of their own. Any woman who can earn a livelihood, as every woman should be trained to do, can take a properly qualified female associate, and institute a family of her own, receiving to its heavenly influences the orphan, the sick, the homeless, and the sinful, and by motherly devotion train them to follow the self-denying example of Christ, in educating his earthly children for true happiness in this life and for his eternal home.

And such is the blessedness of aiding to sustain a truly Christian home, that no one comes so near the pattern of the All-perfect One as those who might hold what men call a higher place, and yet humble themselves to the lowest in order to aid in training the young, "not as men-pleasers, but as servants to Christ, with good-will doing service as to the Lord, and not to men." Such are preparing for high places in the kingdom of heaven. "Whosoever will be chiefest among you, let him be your servant."

It is often the case that the true humility of Christ is not understood. It was not in having a low opinion of his own character and claims, but it was in taking a low place in order to raise others to a higher. The worldling seeks to raise himself and family to an equality with others, or, if possible, a superiority to them. The true follower of Christ comes down in order to elevate others.

The maxims and institutions of this world have ever been antagonistic to the teachings and example of Jesus Christ. Men toil for wealth, honor, and power, not as means for raising others to an equality with themselves, but mainly for earthly, selfish advantages. Although the experience of this life shows that children brought up to labor have the fairest chance for a virtuous and prosperous life, and for hope of future eternal blessedness, yet it is the aim of most parents who can do so, to lay up wealth that their children need not labor with the hands as Christ did. And although exhorted by our Lord not to lay up treasure on earth, but rather the imperishable riches which are gained in toiling to train the ignorant and reform the sinful, as yet a large portion of the professed followers of Christ, like his first disciples, are "slow of heart to believe."

Not less have the sacred ministries of the family state been undervalued and warred upon in other directions; for example, the Romish Church has made celibacy a prime virtue, and given its highest honors to those who forsake the family state as ordained by God. Thus came great communities of monks and nuns, shut out from the love and labors of a Christian home; thus, also, came the monkish systems of education, collecting the young in great establishments away from the watch and care of parents, and the healthful and self-sacrificing labors of a home. Thus both religion and education have conspired to degrade the family state.

Still more have civil laws and social customs been opposed to the principles of Jesus Christ. It has ever been assumed that the learned, the rich, and the powerful are not to labor with the hands, as Christ did, and as Paul did when he would "not eat any man's bread for naught, but wrought with labor, not because we have not power" [to live without hand-work,] "but to make ourselves an example." (2 Thess. 3.) . . .

Questions

1. To what extent does Beecher offer a traditional view of women?
2. Where does she broaden or modernize women's role in society?
3. What prejudice does she reveal?

Theodore Dreiser, *Sister Carrie* (1900)

In 1900, Theodore Dreiser (1871–1945) published Sister Carrie, *the story of a small-town Wisconsin girl. Carrie Meeber leaves Columbia City for a factory job in Chicago. She hates the work and eventually becomes a successful (though unhappy) New York actress. The story of an independent woman— and one who lived with men out of wedlock—shocked its turn-of-the-century audience. Worried that the public would reject such a non-Victorian work, the publisher printed only 1,000 copies of* Sister Carrie *and virtually ignored it. The book finally received greater acceptance with a reissue in 1912.*

It was with weak knees and a slight catch in her breathing that she came up to the great shoe company at Adams and Fifth Avenue and entered the elevator. When she stepped out on the fourth floor there was no one at hand, only great aisles of boxes piled to the ceiling. She stood, very much frightened, awaiting some one.

Presently Mr. Brown came up. He did not seem to recognise her.

"What is it you want?" he inquired.

Carrie's heart sank.

"You said I should come this morning to see about work—"

"Oh," he interrupted. "Um—yes. What is your name?"

"Carrie Meeber."

"Yes," said he. "You come with me." . . .

"This is the girl," he said, and turning to Carrie[,] "You go with him." He then returned, and Carrie followed her new superior to a little desk in a corner, which he used as a kind of official centre.

"You've never worked at anything like this before, have you?" he questioned, rather sternly.

"No, sir," she answered.

He seemed rather annoyed at having to bother with such help, but put down her name and then led her across to where a line of girls occupied stools in front of clacking machines. On the shoulder of one of the girls who was punching eye-holes in one piece of the upper, by the aid of the machine, he put his hand.

"You," he said, "show this girl how to do what you're doing. When you get through, come to me."

The girl so addressed rose promptly and gave Carrie her place.

"It isn't hard to do," she said, bending over. "You just take this so, fasten it with this clamp, and start the machine." . . .

The pieces of leather came from the girl at the machine to her right, and were passed to the girl at her left. Carrie saw at once that an average speed was necessary or the work would pile up on her and all those below would be delayed. She had no time to look about, and bent anxiously to her task. The girls at her left and right realised her predicament and feelings, and, in a way, tried to aid her, as much as they dared, by working slower.

At this task she laboured incessantly for some time, finding relief from her own nervous fears and imaginings in the humdrum, mechanical movement of the machine. She felt, as the minutes passed, that the room was not very light. It had a thick odour of fresh leather, but that did not worry her. She felt the eyes of the other help upon her, and troubled lest she was not working fast enough.

Once, when she was fumbling at the little clamp, having made a slight error in setting in the leather, a great hand appeared before her eyes and fastened the clamp for her. It was the foreman. Her heart thumped so that she could scarcely see to go on.

"Start your machine," he said, "start your machine. Don't keep the line waiting."

This recovered her sufficiently and she went excitedly on, hardly breathing until the shadow moved away from behind her. Then she heaved a great breath.

As the morning wore on the room became hotter. She felt the need of a breath of fresh air and a drink of water but did not venture to stir. The stool she sat on was without a back or foot-rest, and she began to feel uncomfortable. She found, after a time, that her back was beginning to ache. She twisted and turned from one position to another slightly different, but it did not ease her for long. She was beginning to weary.

"Stand up, why don't you?" said the girl at her right, without any form of introduction. "They won't care."

Carrie looked at her gratefully. "I guess I will," she said.

She stood up from her stool and worked that way for a while, but it was a more difficult position. Her neck and shoulders ached in bending over.

The spirit of the place impressed itself on her in a rough way. She did not venture to look around, but above the clack of the machine she could hear an occasional remark. She could also note a thing or two out of the side of her eye.

"Did you see Harry last night?" said the girl at her left, addressing her neighbour.

"No."

"You ought to have seen the tie he had on. Gee, but he was a mark."

"S-s-t," said the other girl, bending over her work. The first, silenced, instantly assumed a solemn face. The foreman passed slowly along, eyeing each worker distinctly. The moment he was gone, the conversation was resumed again.

"Say," began the girl at her left, "what jeh think he said?"

"I don't know."

"He said he saw us with Eddie Harris at Martin's last night."

"No!" They both giggled.

A youth with tan-coloured hair, that needed clipping very badly, came shuffling along between the machines, bearing a basket of leather findings under his left arm, and pressed against his stomach. When near Carrie, he stretched out his right hand and gripped one girl under the arm.

"Aw, let me go," she exclaimed angrily. "Duffer."

He only grinned broadly in return.

"Rubber!" he called back as she looked after him. There was nothing of the gallant in him. . . .

Carrie got up and sought her lunch box. She was stiff, a little dizzy, and very thirsty. On the way to the small space portioned off by wood, where all the wraps and lunches were kept, she encountered the foreman, who stared at her hard.

"Well," he said, "did you get along all right?"

"I think so," she replied, very respectfully.

"Um," he replied, for want of something better, and walked on.

Under better material conditions, this kind of work would not have been so bad, but the new socialism which involves pleasant working conditions for employees had not then taken hold upon manufacturing companies.

The place smelled of the oil of the machines and the new leather—a combination which, added to the stale odours of the building, was not pleasant even in cold weather. The floor, though regularly swept every evening, presented a littered surface. Not the slightest provision had been made for the comfort of the employees, the idea being that something was gained by giving them as little and making the work as hard and unremunerative as possible. What we know of foot-rests, swivel-back chairs, dining-rooms for the girls, clean aprons and curling irons supplied free, and a decent cloak room, were unthought of. The washrooms were disagreeable, crude, if not foul places, and the whole atmosphere was sordid. . . .

"Say, Kitty," called one [man] to a girl who was doing a waltz step in a few feet of space near one of the windows, "are you going to the ball with me?"

"Look out, Kitty," called another, "you'll jar your back hair."

"Go on, Rubber," was her only comment.

As Carrie listened to this and much more of similar familiar badinage among the men and girls, she instinctively withdrew into herself. She was not used to this type, and felt that there was something hard and low about it all. She feared that the young boys about would address such remarks to her— boys who . . . seemed uncouth and ridiculous. She made the average feminine distinction between clothes, putting worth, goodness, and distinction in a dress suit, and leaving all the unlovely qualities and those beneath notice in overalls and jumper.

She was glad when the short half hour was over and the wheels began to whirr again. Though wearied, she would be inconspicuous. This illusion ended when another young man passed along the aisle and poked her indifferently in the ribs with his thumb. She turned about, indignation leaping to her eyes, but he had gone on and only once turned to grin. She found it difficult to conquer an inclination to cry.

The girl next to her noticed her state of mind. "Don't you mind," she said. "He's too fresh."

Carrie said nothing, but bent over her work. She felt as though she could hardly endure such a life. Her idea of work had been so entirely different. All during the long afternoon she thought of the city outside and its imposing show, crowds, and fine buildings. Columbia City and the better side of her home life came back. By three o'clock she was sure it must be six, and by four it seemed as if they had forgotten to note the hour and were letting all work overtime. The foreman became a true ogre, prowling constantly about, keeping her tied down to her miserable task. What she heard of the conversation about her only made her feel sure that she did not want to make friends with any of these. When six o'clock came she hurried eagerly away, her arms aching and her limbs stiff from sitting in one position.

As she passed out along the hall after getting her hat, a young machine hand, attracted by her looks, made bold to jest with her.

"Say, Maggie," he called, "if you wait, I'll walk with you."

It was thrown so straight in her direction that she knew who was meant, but never turned to look.

In the crowded elevator, another dusty, toil-stained youth tried to make an impression on her by leering in her face.

One young man, waiting on the walk outside for the appearance of another, grinned at her as she passed.

"Ain't going my way, are you?" he called jocosely.

Carrie turned her face to the west with a subdued heart. As she turned the corner, she saw through the great shiny window the small desk at which she had applied. There were the crowds, hurrying with the same buzz and energy-yielding enthusiasm. She felt a slight relief, but it was only at her escape. She felt ashamed in the face of better dressed girls who went by. She felt as though she should be better served, and her heart revolted.

Questions

1. According to Dreiser, why are there so many women working in such difficult conditions?

2. What does the banter between workers accomplish?

3. How does *Sister Carrie* succeed as social history in ways a factory-inspection report of the era could not?

Henry Adams, *The Education of Henry Adams (on the Columbian Exposition of 1893)* (1918)

Henry Adams (1838–1918) could be forgiven for his air of self-importance. He was, after all, the grandson and great-grandson of presidents. A historian and social critic, Adams dissented from the popular view that progress was wedded to the Industrial Age. In this passage from his autobiography, The Education of Henry Adams *(1918), Adams relates his experience (written, like the rest of the book, in the third person) with modern technology at the Columbian Exposition of 1893.*

The first astonishment became greater every day. That the Exposition should be a natural growth and product of the Northwest offered a step in evolution to startle Darwin; but that it should be anything else seemed an idea more startling still; and even granting it were not—admitting it to be a sort of industrial, speculative growth and product of the Beaux Arts artistically induced to pass the summer on the shore of Lake Michigan—could it be made to seem at home there? Was the American made to seem at home in it? Honestly, he had the air of enjoying it as though it were all his own; he felt it was good; he was proud of it; for the most part, he acted as though he had passed his life in landscape gardening and architectural decoration. If he had not done it himself, he had known how to get it done to suit him, as he knew how to get his wives and daughters dressed at Worth's or Paquin's [designers of the finest women's clothes]. Perhaps he could not do it again; the next time he would want to do it himself and would show his own faults; but for the moment he seemed to have leaped directly from Corinth and Syracuse and Venice, over the heads of London and New York, to impose classical standards on plastic Chicago. Critics had no trouble in criticising the classicism, but all trading cities had always shown trader's taste, and, to the stern purist of religious faith, no art was thinner than Venetian Gothic. All trader's taste smelt of bric-à-brac; Chicago tried at least to give her taste a look of unity.

One sat down to ponder on the steps beneath Richard Hunt's dome almost as deeply as on the steps of Ara Cœli, and much to the same purpose. Here was a breach of continuity—a rupture in historical sequence! Was it real, or only apparent? One's personal universe hung on the answer, for, if the rupture was real and the new American world could take this sharp and conscious twist towards ideals, one's personal friends would come in, at last, as winners in the great American chariot-race for fame. If the people of the Northwest actually knew what was good when they saw it, they would some day talk about Hunt and Richardson [architects], La Farge and St. Gaudens [sculptors], Burnham and McKim, and Stanford White [architects] when their politicians and millionaires were otherwise forgotten. The artists and architects who had done the work offered little encouragement to hope it; they talked freely enough, but not in terms that one cared to quote; and to them the Northwest refused to look artistic. They talked as though they worked only for themselves; as though art, to the Western people, was a stage decoration; a diamond shirt-stud; a paper collar; but possibly the architects of Pæstum and Girgenti [ancient Italian cities] had talked in the same way, and the Greek had said the same thing of Semitic Carthage two thousand years ago.

Jostled by these hopes and doubts, one turned to the exhibits for help, and found it. The industrial schools tried to teach so much and so quickly that the instruction ran to waste. Some millions of other people felt the same helplessness, but few of them were seeking education, and to them helplessness seemed natural and normal, for they had grown up in the habit of thinking a steam-engine or a dynamo as natural as the sun, and expected to understand one as little as the other. For the historian alone the Exposition made a serious effort. Historical exhibits were common, but they never went far enough; none were thoroughly worked out. One of the best was that of the Cunard steamers, but still a student hungry for results found himself obliged to waste a pencil and several sheets of paper trying to calculate exactly when, according to the given increase of power, tonnage, and speed, the growth of the ocean steamer would reach its limits. His figures brought him, he thought, to the year 1927; another generation to spare before force, space, and time should meet. The ocean steamer ran the surest line of triangulation into the future, because it was the nearest of man's products to a unity; railroads taught less because they seemed already finished except for mere increase in number; explosives taught most, but needed a tribe of chemists, physicists, and mathematicians to explain; the dynamo taught least because it had barely reached infancy, and, if its progress was to be constant at the rate of the last ten years, it would result in infinite costly energy within a generation. One lingered long among the dynamos, for they were new, and they gave to history a new phase. Men of science could never understand the ignorance and naïveté of the historian, who, when he came suddenly on a new power, asked naturally what it was; did it pull or did it push? Was it a screw or thrust? Did it flow or vibrate? Was it a wire or a mathematical line? And a score of such questions to which he expected answers and was astonished to get none.

Education ran riot at Chicago, at least for retarded minds which had never faced in concrete form so many matters of which they were ignorant. Men who knew nothing whatever—who had never run a steam-engine, the simplest of forces—who had never put their hands on a lever—had never touched an electric battery—never talked through a telephone, and had not the shadow of a notion what amount of force was meant by a *watt* or an *am-*

père or an *erg,* or any other term of measurement introduced within a hundred years—had no choice but to sit down on the steps and brood as they had never brooded on the benches of Harvard College, either as student or professor, aghast at what they had said and done in all these years, and still more ashamed of the childlike ignorance and babbling futility of the society that let them say and do it. The historical mind can think only in historical processes, and probably this was the first time since historians existed, that any of them had sat down helpless before a mechanical sequence. Before a metaphysical or a theological or a political sequence, most historians had felt helpless, but the single clue to which they had hitherto trusted was the unity of natural force.

Did he himself quite know what he meant? Certainly not! If he had known enough to state his problem, his education would have been complete at once. Chicago asked in 1893 for the first time the question whether the American people knew where they were driving. Adams answered, for one, that he did not know, but would try to find out. On reflecting sufficiently deeply, under the shadow of Richard Hunt's architecture, he decided that the American people probably knew no more than he did; but that they might still be driving or drifting unconsciously to some point in thought, as their solar system was said to be drifting towards some point in space; and that, possibly, if relations enough could be observed, this point might be fixed. Chicago was the first expression of American thought as a unity; one must start there. . . .

Questions

1. Why does the fair's architecture confuse Adams?
2. How does the technology on display overwhelm him?
3. Has this kind of unsettling encounter with modernity been repeated by subsequent generations? In what ways?

Connections Questions

1. Whom do you find the more convincing urban critic, Frederic Howe or Josiah Strong? Why?
2. What might Konstanty Butkowski tell Josiah Strong about city life?
3. Compare the ways in which Catharine Beecher and Theodore Dreiser portray American women. Is one portrait more convincing than the other? Why or why not?

CHAPTER 21

The Progressive Era

Walter Rauschenbusch, "The Church and the Social Movement" (1907)

While serving as the pastor of a Baptist church in New York's Hell's Kitchen, Walter Rauschenbusch (1861–1918) learned firsthand that the poor would not be satisfied with simple exhortations to faith. Rauschenbusch then set out to apply the teachings of the Gospels to contemporary urban life. His writings on the social gospel, like the following selections from Christianity and the Social Crisis *(1907), were those of a Christian socialist. Though more radical politically than most of his contemporaries, Rauschenbusch bears witness to that sense of morality that pervaded the Progressive movement.*

Other organizations may conceivably be indifferent when confronted with the chronic or acute poverty of our cities. The Christian Church cannot. The very name of "Christian" would turn into an indictment if it did not concern itself in the situation in some way.

One answer to the challenge of the Christian spirit has been the organization of institutional church work. A church perhaps organizes a day-nursery or kindergarten; a playground for the children; a meeting-place for young people, or educational facilities for those who are ambitious. It tries to do for people who are living under abnormal conditions what these people under normal conditions ought to do for themselves. This saving helpfulness toward the poor must be distinguished sharply from the money-making efforts of some churches called institutional, which simply run a continuous sacred variety performance.

Confront the Church of Christ with a homeless, playless, joyless, proletarian population, and that is the kind of work to which some Christian spirits will inevitably feel impelled. All honor to me! But it puts a terrible burden on the Church. Institutional work is hard work and costly work. It requires a large plant and an expensive staff. It puts such a strain on the organizing ability and the sympathies of the workers that few can stand it long. The Church by the voluntary gifts and labors of a few here tries to furnish what the entire coöperative community ought to furnish.

Few churches have the resources and leadership to undertake institutional work on a large scale, but most churches in large cities have some institutional features, and all pastors who are at all willing to do it, have institutional work thrust on them. They have to care for the poor. Those of us who passed through the last great industrial depression will never forget the procession of men out of work, out of clothes, out of shoes, and out of hope. They wore down our threshold, and they wore away our hearts. This is the stake of the churches in modern poverty. They are buried at times under a stream of human wreckage. They are turned aside constantly from their more spiritual functions to "serve tables." They have a right, therefore, to inquire who is unloading this burden of poverty and suffering upon them by underpaying, exhausting, and maiming the people. The good Samaritan did not go after the robbers with a shot-gun, but looked after the wounded and helpless man by the wayside. But if hundreds of good Samaritans travelling the same road should find thousands of bruised men groaning to them, they would not be such very good Samaritans if they did not organize a vigilance committee to stop the manufacturing of wounded men. If they did not, presumably the asses who had to lug the wounded to the tavern would have the wisdom to inquire into the causes of their extra work. . . .

In its struggle the working class becomes keenly conscious of the obstacles put in its way by the great institutions of society, the courts, the press, or the Church. It demands not only impartiality, but the kind of sympathy which will condone its mistakes and discern the justice of its cause in spite of the excesses of its followers. When our sympathies are enlisted, we develop a vast faculty for making excuses. If two dogs fight, our own dog is rarely the aggressor. Stealing peaches is a boyish prank when our boy does it, but petty larceny when that dratted boy of our neighbor does it. If the other political party grafts, it is a flagrant shame; if our own party does it, we regret it politely or deny the fact. If Germany annexes a part of Africa, it is brutal aggression; if England does it, she "fulfils her mission of civilization." If the business interests exclude the competition of foreign merchants by a protective tariff, it is a grand national policy; if the trades-unions try to exclude the competition of non-union labor, it is a denial of the right to work and an outrage.

The working class likes to get that kind of sympathy which will take a favorable view of its efforts and its mistakes, and a comprehension of the wrongs under which it suffers. Instead of that the pulpit of late has given its most vigorous interest to the wrongs of those whom militant labor regards as traitors to its cause. It has been more concerned with the fact that some individuals were barred from a job by the unions, than with the fact that the entire wage-working class is debarred from the land, from the tools of production, and from their fair share in the proceeds of production.

It cannot well be denied that there is an increasing alienation between the working class and the churches. That alienation is most complete wherever our industrial development has advanced farthest and has created a distinct class of wage-workers. Several causes have contributed. Many have dropped away because they cannot afford to take their share in the expensive maintenance of a church in a large city. Others because the tone, the spirit, the point of view in the churches, is that of another social class. The commercial and professional classes dominate the spiritual atmosphere in the large city churches. As the workingmen grow more class-conscious, they come to regard the business men as their antagonists and the possessing classes as exploiters who live on their labor, and they resent it when persons belonging to these classes address them with the tone of moral superiority. When ministers handle the labor question, they often seem to the working class partial against them even when the ministers think they are most impartial. Foreign workingmen bring with them the long-standing distrust for the clergy and the Church as tools of oppression which they have learned abroad, and they perpetuate that attitude here. The churches of America suffer for the sins of the churches abroad. The "scientific socialism" imported from older countries through its literature and its advocates is saturated with materialistic philosophy and is apt to create dislike and antagonism for the ideas and institutions of religion.

Thus in spite of the favorable equipment of the Church in America there is imminent danger that the working people will pass from indifference to hostility, from religious enthusiasm to anti-religious bitterness. That would be one of the most unspeakable calamities that could come upon the Church. If we would only take warning by the fate of the churches in Europe, we might avert the desolation that threatens us. We may well be glad that in nearly every city there are a few ministers who are known as the outspoken friends of labor. Their fellowministers may regard them as radicals, lacking in balance, and very likely they are; but in the present situation they are among the most valuable servants of the Church. The workingmen see that there is at least a minority in the Church that champions their cause, and that fact helps to keep their judgment in hopeful suspense about the Church at large. Men who are just as one-sided in favor of capitalism pass as sane and conservative men. If the capitalist class have their court-chaplains, it is only fair that the army of labor should have its army-chaplains who administer the consolations of religion to militant labor.

Thus the Church has a tremendous stake in the social crisis. It may try to maintain an attitude of neutrality, but neither side will permit it. If it is quiescent, it thereby throws its influence on the side of things as they are, and the class which aspires to a fitter place in the organization of society will feel the great spiritual force of the Church as a dead weight against it. If it loses the loyalty and trust of the working class, it loses the very class in which it originated, to which its founders belonged, and which has lifted it to power. If it becomes a religion of the upper classes, it condemns itself to a slow and comfortable death. Protestantism from the outset entered into an intimate alliance with the intelligence and wealth of the city population. As the cities grew in importance since the Reformation, as commerce overshadowed agriculture, and as the business class crowded the feudal aristocracy out of its leading position since the French Revolution, Protestantism throve with the class which had espoused it. It lifted its class, and its class lifted it. . . .

Questions

1. In Rauschenbusch's opinion, why are churches supposed to help the poor?
2. What consequences does Rauschenbusch fear if churches fail to act?
3. Would (and should) the First Amendment interfere with Rauschenbusch's call for an activist faith? Why or why not?
4. How does the religious faith of the Butkowski family (Chapter 20, "The Rise of the City") differ from that of Rauschenbusch?

Jane Addams, *Twenty Years at Hull-House* (1910)

Social reformers found the cities to be filled with problems, not the least of which was garbage. It seemed to accumulate without end in overcrowded working-class and immigrant neighborhoods, and the propensity of horses to produce manure on city streets made matters only worse. Settlement-house pioneer Jane Addams (1860–1935) decided to declare war against garbage in her Hull-House neighborhood on Chicago's near West Side. The undertaking was not the most important in Addams's illustrious career, but it was the kind of commitment to social justice that helped her win a share of the Nobel Peace Prize in 1931.

. . . It is easy for even the most conscientious citizen of Chicago to forget the foul smells of the stockyards and the garbage dumps, when he is living so far from them that he is only occasionally made conscious of their existence, but the residents of a Settlement are perforce constantly surrounded by them. During our first three years on Halsted Street, we had established a small incinerator at Hull-House and we had many times reported the untoward conditions of the ward to the city hall. We had also arranged many talks for the immigrants, pointing out that although a woman may sweep her own doorway in her native village and allow the refuse to innocently decay in the open air and sunshine, in a crowed city quarter, if the garbage is not properly collected and destroyed, a tenement-house mother may see her children sicken and die, and that the immigrants must therefore not only keep their own houses clean, but must also help the authorities to keep the city clean.

Possibly our efforts slightly modified the worst conditions, but they still remained intolerable, and the fourth summer the situation became for me ab-

solutely desperate when I realized in a moment of panic that my delicate little nephew for whom I was guardian could not be with me at Hull-House at
all unless the sickening odors were reduced. I may well be ashamed that
other delicate children who were torn from their families, not into boarding
school but into eternity, had not long before driven me into effective action.
Under the direction of the first man who came as a resident to Hull-House
we began a systematic investigation of the city system of garbage collection,
both as to its efficiency in other wards and its possible connection with the
death rate in the various wards of the city.

The Hull-House Woman's Club had been organized the year before by the
resident kindergartner who had first inaugurated a mothers' meeting. The
members came together, however, in quite a new way that summer when we
discussed with them the high death rate so persistent in our ward. After several club meetings devoted to the subject, despite the fact that the death rate
rose highest in the congested foreign colonies and not in the streets in which
most of the Irish American club women lived, twelve of their number undertook in connection with the residents, to carefully investigate the condition
of the alleys. During August and September the substantiated reports of vio-
lations of the law sent in from Hull-House to the health department were one
thousand and thirty-seven. For the club woman who had finished a long day's
work of washing or ironing followed by the cooking of a hot supper, it would
have been much easier to sit on her doorstep during a summer evening than
to go up and down ill-kept alleys and get into trouble with her neighbors over
the condition of their garbage boxes. It required both civic enterprise and
moral conviction to be willing to do this three evenings a week during the
hottest and most uncomfortable months of the year. Nevertheless, a certain
number of women persisted, as did the residents, and three city inspectors in
succession were transferred from the ward because of unsatisfactory services.
Still the death rate remained high and the condition seemed little improved
throughout the next winter. In sheer desperation, the following spring when
the city contracts were awarded for the removal of garbage, with the backing
of two well-known business men, I put in a bid for the garbage removal of the
nineteenth ward. My paper was thrown out on a technicality but the incident
induced the mayor to appoint me the garbage inspector of the ward.

The salary was a thousand dollars a year, and the loss of that political
"plum" made a great stir among the politicians. The position was no sinecure
whether regarded from the point of view of getting up at six in the morning
to see that the men were early at work; or of following the loaded wagons, un-
easily dropping their contents at intervals, to their dreary destination at the
dump; or of insisting that the contractor must increase the number of his
wagons from nine to thirteen and from thirteen to seventeen, although he assured me that he lost money on every one and that the former inspector had
let him off with seven; or of taking careless landlords into court because they

would not provide the proper garbage receptacles; or of arresting the tenant who tried to make the garbage wagons carry away the contents of his stable.

With the two or three residents who nobly stood by, we set up six of those doleful incinerators which are supposed to burn garbage with the fuel collected in the alley itself. The one factory in town which could utilize old tin cans was a window weight factory, and we deluged that with ten times as many tin cans as it could use—much less would pay for. We made desperate attempts to have the dead animals removed by the contractor who was paid most liberally by the city for that purpose but who, we slowly discovered, always made the police ambulances do the work, delivering the carcasses upon freight cars for shipment to a soap factory in Indiana where they were sold for a good price although the contractor himself was the largest stockholder in the concern. Perhaps our greatest achievement was the discovery of a pavement eighteen inches under the surface in a narrow street, although after it was found we triumphantly discovered a record of its existence in the city archives. The Italians living on the street were much interested but displayed little astonishment, perhaps because they were accustomed to see buried cities exhumed. This pavement became the *casus belli* [cause of war] between myself and the street commissioner when I insisted that its restoration belonged to him, after I had removed the first eight inches of garbage. The matter was finally settled by the mayor himself, who permitted me to drive him to the entrance of the street in what the children called my "garbage phaëton" and who took my side of the controversy.

Questions

1. What was the old way of collecting garbage?
2. Why are conditions so bad in the area around Hull-House?
3. What does Jane Addams accomplish as garbage collector?

Samuel Lipson, Testimony on the Lawrence, Massachusetts, Strike (1912)

Middle-class social reformers of the Progressive Era in time learned what workers had known for generations: factory employment could be both miserable and dangerous. Conditions were so bad in the textile-mill town of Lawrence, Massachusetts, that workers turned to the radical Industrial Workers of the World, which led a successful strike in 1912. Samuel Lipson's testimony before the Socialist congressman Victor L. Berger demonstrates why the textile workers took action.

MR. BERGER. Why did you go on a strike?

MR. LIPSON. I went out on strike because I was unable to make a living for my family.

MR. BERGER. How much wages were you receiving?

MR. LIPSON. My average wage, or the average wage of my trade, is from $9 to $10 a week.

MR. BERGER. What kind of work do you do?

MR. LIPSON. I am a weaver.

MR. BERGER. You are a skilled workman?

MR. LIPSON. Yes, sir; for years.

MR. BERGER. You have been a skilled workman for years and your wages average from $9 to $10 per week?

MR. LIPSON. Yes, sir; that was the average.

MR. BERGER. How many children do you have?

MR. LIPSON. I have four children and a wife.

MR. BERGER. You support a wife and four children from a weekly wage averaging from $9 to $10 per week and you are a skilled workman. Did you have steady work?

MR. LIPSON. Usually the work was steady, but there was times when I used to make from $3 to $4 and $5 per week. We have had to live on $3 per week. We lived on bread and water. . . .

MR. BERGER. How much rent do you pay?

MR. LIPSON. I pay $2.50.

MR. BERGER. Per week?

MR. LIPSON. Yes, sir.

MR. BERGER. You pay $2.50 per week for rent out of $10 weekly wages?

MR. LIPSON. Yes, sir. You asked me whether I supported my family out of $10 per week. Of course we do not use butter at the present time; we use a kind of molasses; we are trying to fool our stomachs with it.

MR. BERGER. It is a bad thing to fool your stomach.

MR. LIPSON.   We know that, but we can not help it. When we go to the store without any money, the storekeeper tells us that he can not sell us anything without the money.

MR. BERGER.   How much were you reduced by reason of the recent cut in the wages?

MR. LIPSON.   From 50 to 65 to 75 cents per week.

MR. BERGER.   How much does a loaf of bread cost in Lawrence?

MR. LIPSON.   Twelve cents; that is what I pay.

MR. BERGER.   The reduction in your wages, according to this, took away five loaves of bread from you every week?

MR. LIPSON.   Yes, sir. When we go into the store now with a dollar and get a peck of potatoes and a few other things, we have no change left out of that dollar. Of course we are living according to what we get. . . .

MR. BERGER.   How many months in the year were you employed?

MR. LIPSON.   I was employed the year through. The company keeps us in the mills no matter whether there is work or not, and sometimes we only go home with $3 or $4 in our envelopes.

MR. BERGER.   Do you do piecework?

MR. LIPSON.   Yes, sir.

MR. BERGER.   What can you tell us about the speeding-up system . . . ?

MR. LIPSON.   The speeding-up system is according to the premium.

MR. BERGER.   They have premiums, also? That is interesting. Kindly give the committee a description of the premium system at Lawrence, Mass.

MR. LIPSON.   The premiums are not alike in all the mills. In some mills they start with $35 and some small change. They get 5 per cent more; and if they come up to it they get 5 per cent more in the month. In other mills, where the machinery runs faster, they are started, say, at $39 per month, and they add 5 per cent per month. When it happens to the weaver to make $44 per month, that means he is getting 10 per cent. It is a heavy month when they get 10 per cent. The loom operatives also get premiums. When a section makes up a certain amount of cloth, they get a certain premium. Therefore they have us to speed up the machinery. If a man can not come up to it he gets fired out. Sometimes one is sick, and sometimes our stomach is empty, because our pay does not always last to the end of the month. When we come to that, we wish it was Saturday, because we usually get our pay on Saturday, but we stay in the mills just the same. They stay there, sick at the loom.

MR. BERGER.   What is the effect, then, of the premium system on the weaker workingman—on the man who can not work as fast as the others?

MR. LIPSON.   The effect upon him is that he is working less. There is no work for him. He has no work; they do not employ him. . . .

MR. BERGER.   You are a member of the strike committee, are you not?

MR. LIPSON.   Yes, sir.

MR. BERGER. Tell us the immediate cause of the strike.

MR. LIPSON. The workers in the American Woolen Co.'s mills had meetings and discussed the question of what can we do to make a living. It was unbearable. In one of our meetings we decided to see the agent of the mill, and one committee went up to see the agent of the mill, and he told them to go back to their machines; he did not want to give them any answer at all. At another one of the mills they were absolutely turned down, and in the Washington mill they were told to go to Boston and see the president of the American Woolen Co., Mr. Wood. When they told us to do that, we sent a special delivery letter to Mr. Wood, telling him about how it is in Lawrence. We expected to get an answer, because it was a special-delivery letter, and we are waiting for that answer still. Well, they were trying to make up two hours, and they tried to speed up the machinery in order to make us do 56 hours work in 54 hours time, and try to cut off the pay at the same time. The question was whether we could make a living. Well, they cut down the wages after they speeded up the machinery, and as they were trying still to speed up the machinery and trying to cut down the wages, we thought we would have to starve.

MR. BERGER. Do you mean to convey by your statement that you were required to do 56 hours work in 54 hours time, because a law was recently passed in Massachusetts cutting down the hours of labor to 54 per week?

MR. LIPSON. Yes, sir.

MR. BERGER. Were you working 56 hours before that new act was passed?

MR. LIPSON. Yes, sir.

MR. BERGER. What effect did this have on the strike?

MR. LIPSON. The people were complaining that it was impossible for them to bear their sufferings any longer, in so many ways.

MR. BERGER. Do you mean that they were required to furnish as much product in 54 hours as in 56 hours?

MR. LIPSON. Yes, sir.

MR. BERGER. And then suffer a cut in wages besides?

MR. LIPSON. Yes, sir. . . .

MR. BERGER. How many of the workers of Lawrence are women and children? How many are men?

MR. LIPSON. I can not tell you about how many, but I can tell you that the majority of them are women and children, and as we are speeding up, these children are doing more work. If they can not do the work, they are fired out. They must do the work that goes from one machine to another, and they must prepare the work for us. If they do not speed up, they are fired out.

MR. BERGER. Do you mean that the children are discharged?

MR. LIPSON. Yes, sir. . . .

MR. BERGER. Do they have any accidents in the factory?

MR. LIPSON.   Yes, sir. . . .

MR. BERGER.   What are the demands of the strikers now?

MR. LIPSON.   The demands are 15 per cent increase in wages, based on 54 hours work per week, and double pay for overtime. The reason I wish to call your attention to the demand for 15 per cent increase is this: These people work sometimes only two or three days in a week. Her father works only three days in a week, and has $2.88 per week for the family, and they absolutely live on bread and water. If you would look at the other children, you would see that they look like skeletons. . . .

MR. BERGER.   What reception did the strikers get from the mill owners?

MR. LIPSON.   I told you before.

MR. BERGER.   I want to know whether you got any other answer. You said Mr. Wood did not answer your letter, and that the foreman simply told the committee to go back to your machines.

MR. LIPSON.   Yes, sir. They said if we did not like it to get out.

MR. BERGER.   Well, you failed to tell us that before, and it is important.

MR. LIPSON.   We are so used to it that I did not mention it. To you these things are new, but to us it is an old story. . . .

Questions

1. How did Samuel Lipson try to extend the family budget?
2. Explain the speeding-up system.
3. What were the causes of the strike in Lawrence?

The Dark Side of Progressivism (1907)

The Ben Ishmael tribe in the Midwest consisted of blacks, whites, and Indians who lived together as nomads; they were 10,000 strong at the turn of the century. The members of the tribe had long been accused of or jailed for prostitution, begging, and vagrancy, among other minor crimes. The state of Indiana found the Ishmaelites trouble enough that the legislature passed a law for the sterilization of inmates. The act was the first of its kind in the nation and showed progressivism at its worst. At least some reformers were willing to invoke science (in this case, eugenics, the study of improving human heredity) for reactionary, racist ends. The threat of such extreme action helped convince the tribe to assimilate into mainstream society.

PREAMBLE.

Whereas, Heredity plays a most important part in the transmission of crime, idiocy and imbecility;

PENAL INSTITUTIONS—SURGICAL OPERATIONS.

Therefore, *Be it enacted by the general assembly of the State of Indiana,* That on and after the passage of this act it shall be compulsory for each and every institution in the state, entrusted with the care of confirmed criminals, idiots, rapists and imbeciles, to appoint upon its staff, in addition to the regular institutional physician, two (2) skilled surgeons of recognized ability, whose duty it shall be, in conjunction with the chief physician of the institution, to examine the mental and physical condition of such inmates as are recommended by the institutional physician and board of managers. If, in the judgment of this committee of experts and the board of managers, procreation is inadvisable and there is no probability of improvement of the mental condition of the inmate, it shall be lawful for the surgeons to perform such operation for the prevention of procreation as shall be decided safest and most effective. But this operation shall not be performed except in cases that have been pronounced unimprovable: *Provided,* That in no case shall the consultation fee be more than three ($3.00) dollars to each expert, to be paid out of the funds appropriated for the maintenance of such institution.

Questions
1. What kind of assumption is made in the statute's preamble?
2. Which types of inmates are considered eligible for sterilization?
3. Does the screening process respect an inmate's human rights?
4. What provision in the statute works against its effective implementation?

Theodore Roosevelt, "The Struggle for Social Justice" (1912)

When Theodore Roosevelt (1858–1919) left the White House in 1908 and went on safari in Africa, a wag commented, "I hope some lion will do his duty." But Roosevelt returned home safely only to be disappointed with the conservative politics of his successor, William Howard Taft (see text p. 576). Roosevelt challenged Taft for the Republican presidential nomination in 1912 and, when he failed, formed his own Progressive party. During the campaign, Roosevelt often spoke on issues of social justice.

Lincoln made his fight on the two great fundamental issues of the right of the people to rule themselves, and not to be ruled by any mere part of the people, and of the vital need that this rule of the people should be exercised for social and industrial justice in a spirit of broad charity and kindliness to all, but with stern insistence that privilege should be eliminated from our industrial life and should be shorn of its power in our political life.

In describing his actions I am using the words which we use at the present day; but they exactly and precisely set forth his position fifty years ago. This position is ours at the present day.

The very rich men whom we mean when we speak of Wall Street have at this crisis shown that they are not loyal to the cause of human rights, human justice, human liberty. The rich man who is a good citizen first of all and a rich man only next, stands on a level with all other good citizens, and the rich man of this type is with us in this contest just as other good citizens, who happen to be wage-workers or retail traders or professional men, are with us. But the rich man who trusts in his riches, the rich man who feels that his wealth entitles him to more than his share of political, social and industrial power, is naturally against us. So likewise the men of little faith, the timid men who fear the people and do not dare trust them, the men who at the bottom of their hearts disbelieve in our whole principle of democratic governmental rule, are also against us. . . .

The representatives of privilege, the men who stand for the special interests and against the rule of the plain people and who distrust the people, care very little for party names.

They oppose us who stand for the cause of progress and of justice. They were accurately described by Lincoln . . . when he said that there had been nothing in politics since the Revolution so congenial to their nature as the position taken by his opponents.

The same thing is true now. Those people are against me because they are against the cause I represent.

These men against whom we stand include the men who desire to exploit the people for their own purposes and to profit financially by the wicked alliance between crooked business and crooked politics. Of course, they include also a large number of worthy and respectable men, who have no improper purpose to serve but who either do not see far into the future, or who are misled as to the facts of the case. Finally, they include those who at this moment represent what Lincoln described as the "old exclusive silk-stocking Whigs—nearly all the Whigs of the nice exclusive sort." . . .

The boss system is based on and thrives by injustice. Wherever you get the boss, wherever you get a Legislature controlled by mercenary politicians, there you will always find that privilege flourishes; there you will always find the great special interests striking hands with the crooked politicians and helping them plunder the people in the interest of both wings of the corrupt alliance.

It is to the interest of every honest man, and perhaps most especially to the interest of the honest big business man, that this alliance shall be broken up, and that we shall have a genuine rule of the people in a spirit of honesty and fair play toward all.

There is far more in this contest than is involved in the momentary victory of any man or any faction.

We are now fighting one phase of the eternal struggle for right and for justice. . . .

As far as we are concerned, the battle is just begun, and we shall go on with it to the end. We hail as our brothers all who contend in any way for the great cause of human rights, for the realization in measurable degree of the doctrines of the brotherhood of man.

We do not for a moment believe that any system of laws, no matter how good, or that any governmental action, can ever take the place of the individual character of the average man and the average woman, which must always in the last analysis be the chief factor in that man's or that woman's success.

But we insist that without just laws and just governmental action the high standard of character of the average American will not suffice to get all that as a Nation we are entitled to.

We must, through the law, make conditions of life more fair, make equality of opportunity more real. We must strive for industrial as well as political democracy.

Every man who fights for the protection of children from excessive toil, for the protection of women from working in factories for too long hours, for the protection, in short, of the workingman and his family so that he may live decently and bring up his children honorably and well—every man who works for any such cause is our fellow worker and we hail him as such.

Remember, that when we work to make this country a better place to live in for those who have been harshly treated by fate, we are also at the same time making it a better place to live in for those who have been well treated by fate.

The great representatives and beneficiaries of privilege, nineteen-twentieths of whom are opposing us with intense animosity, are acting with the utmost short-sightedness from the standpoint of the welfare of their children and their children's children.

We who stand for justice wish to make this country a better place to live in for the man who actually toils, for the wage-worker, for the farmer, for the small business man; and in so striving, we are really defending the cause of the children of those beneficiaries of privilege against what would be fatal action by their fathers. . . .

None of us can really prosper permanently if there are masses among us who are debased and degraded.

The sons of the millionaires will find this a very poor country to live in if men and women who make up the bulk of our ordinary citizenship do not have conditions so shaped that they can lead self-respecting lives on a basis which will permit them to retain their own sense of dignity, to treat their children aright, and to take their part in the life of the community as good citizens.

Exactly as each of us in his private life must stand up for his own rights and yet must respect the rights of others and acknowledge in practical fashion that he is indeed his brother's keeper, so all of us taken collectively, the people as a whole, must feel our obligation to work by governmental action, and in all other ways possible, to make the conditions better for those who are unfairly pressed down in the fierce competition of modern industrial life.

I ask justice for those who in actual life meet with most injustice—and I ask this not only for their sakes but for our own sakes, for the sake of the children and the children's children who are to come after us.

The children of all of us will pay in the future if we do not do justice in the present.

This country will not be a good place for any of us to live in if we do not strive with zeal and efficiency to make it a reasonably good place for all of us to live in.

Nor can our object be obtained save through the genuine control of the people themselves. The people must rule or gradually they will lose all power of being good citizens. The people must control their own destinies or the power of such control will atrophy.

Our cause is the cause of the plain people. It is the cause of social and industrial justice to be achieved by the plain people through the resolute and conscientious use of all the machinery, public and private, State and National, governmental and individual, which is at their command.

This is a great fight in which we are engaged, for it is a fight for human rights, and we who are making it are really making it for every good citizen of this Republic, no matter to what party he may belong.

Questions

1. By Roosevelt's standards, what constitutes a moral rich man?
2. Why does he invoke Abraham Lincoln so often?
3. How does Roosevelt define social justice?

The Progressive Party Platform of 1912

There was nothing ordinary about the Progressive presidential convention held in Chicago during August 1912. The delegates sang "Onward, Christian Soldiers" from the convention floor, Jane Addams seconded the nomination of the candidate, and Theodore Roosevelt delivered his acceptance speech as "A Confession of Faith." The party platform was no less remarkable since it blended Roosevelt's view of the future with a deeply ingrained religious passion.

It is time to set the public welfare in the first place.

THE OLD PARTIES

Political parties exist to secure responsible government and to execute the will of the people.

From these great tasks both of the old parties have turned aside. Instead of instruments to promote the general welfare, they have become the tools of corrupt interests which use them impartially to serve their selfish purposes. Behind the ostensible government sits enthroned an invisible government owing no allegiance and acknowledging no responsibility to the people. . . .

A COVENANT WITH THE PEOPLE

This declaration is our covenant with the people, and we hereby bind the party and its candidates in State and Nation to the pledges made herein.

THE RULE OF THE PEOPLE

The National Progressive party, committed to the principles of government by a self-controlled democracy expressing its will through representatives of the people, pledges itself to secure such alterations in the fundamental law of the several States and the United States as shall insure the representative character of the government.

In particular, the party declares for direct primaries for the nomination of State and National officers; for nationwide preferential primaries for candidates for the presidency; for the direct election of United States Senators by the people; and we urge on the States the policy of the short ballot, with responsibility to the people secured by the initiative, referendum and recall.

AMENDMENT OF CONSTITUTION

The Progressive party, believing that a free people should have the power from time to time to amend their fundamental law so as to adapt it progressively to the changing needs of the people, pledges itself to provide a more easy and expeditious method of amending the Federal Constitution. . . .

EQUAL SUFFRAGE

The Progressive party, believing that no people can justly claim to be a true democracy which denies political rights on account of sex, pledges itself to the task of securing equal suffrage to men and women alike.

CORRUPT PRACTICES

We pledge our party to legislation that will compel strict limitation of all campaign contributions and expenditures, and detailed publicity of both before as well as after primaries and elections.

PUBLICITY AND PUBLIC SERVICE

We pledge our party to legislation compelling the registration of lobbyists; publicity of committee hearings except on foreign affairs, and recording of all votes in committee; and forbidding federal appointees from holding office in State or National political organizations, or taking part as officers or delegates in political conventions for the nomination of elective State or National officials. . . .

SOCIAL AND INDUSTRIAL JUSTICE

The supreme duty of the Nation is the conservation of human resources through an enlightened measure of social and industrial justice. We pledge ourselves to work unceasingly in State and Nation for:

Effective legislation looking to the prevention of industrial accidents, occupational diseases, overwork, involuntary unemployment, and other injurious effects incident to modern industry;

The fixing of minimum safety and health standards for the various occupations, and the exercise of the public authority of State and Nation, including the Federal Control over interstate commerce, and the taxing power, to maintain such standards;

The prohibition of child labor;

Minimum wage standards for working women, to provide a "living wage" in all industrial occupations;

The general prohibition of night work for women and the establishment of an eight hour day for women and young persons;

One day's rest in seven for all wage workers;

The eight hour day in continuous twenty-four-hour industries;

The abolition of the convict contract labor system; substituting a system of prison production for governmental consumption only; and the application of prisoners' earnings to the support of their dependent families;

Publicity as to wages, hours and conditions of labor; full reports upon industrial accidents and diseases; and the opening to public inspection of all tallies, weights, measures and check systems on labor products;

Standards of compensation for death by industrial accident and injury and trade disease which will transfer the burden of lost earnings from the families of working people to the industry, and thus to the community;

The protection of home life against the hazards of sickness, irregular employment and old age through the adoption of a system of social insurance adapted to American use;

The development of the creative labor power of America by lifting the last load of illiteracy from American youth and establishing continuation schools for industrial education under public control and encouraging agricultural education and demonstration in rural schools;

The establishment of industrial research laboratories to put the methods and discoveries of science at the service of American producers;

We favor the organization of the workers, men and women, as a means of protecting their interests and of promoting their progress. . . .

BUSINESS

We believe that true popular government, justice and prosperity go hand in hand, and, so believing, it is our purpose to secure that large measure of general prosperity which is the fruit of legitimate and honest business, fostered by equal justice and by sound progressive laws.

We demand that the test of true prosperity shall be the benefits conferred thereby on all the citizens, not confined to individuals or classes, and that the test of corporate efficiency shall be the ability better to serve the public; that those who profit by control of business affairs shall justify that profit and that control by sharing with the public the fruits thereof.

We therefore demand a strong National regulation of inter-State corporations. The corporation is an essential part of modern business. The concentration of modern business, in some degree, is both inevitable and necessary for national and international business efficiency. But the existing concentration of vast wealth under a corporate system, unguarded and uncontrolled by the Nation, has placed in the hands of a few men enormous, secret, irresponsible power over the daily life of the citizen—a power insufferable in a free Government and certain of abuse.

This power has been abused, in monopoly of National resources, in stock watering, in unfair competition and unfair privileges, and finally in sinister influences on the public agencies of State and Nation. We do not fear commercial power, but we insist that it shall be exercised openly, under publicity, supervision and regulation of the most efficient sort, which will preserve its good while eradicating and preventing its ill.

To that end we urge the establishment of a strong Federal administrative commission of high standing, which shall maintain permanent active supervision over industrial corporations engaged in inter-State commerce, or such of them as are of public importance, doing for them what the Government now does for the National banks, and what is now done for the railroads by the Inter-State Commerce Commission.

Such a commission must enforce the complete publicity of those corporation transactions which are of public interest; must attack unfair competition, false capitalization and special privilege, and by continuous trained watchfulness guard and keep open equally all the highways of American commerce.

Thus the business man will have certain knowledge of the law, and will be able to conduct his business easily in conformity therewith; the investor will find security for his capital; dividends will be rendered more certain, and the savings of the people will be drawn naturally and safely into the channels of trade.

Under such a system of constructive regulation, legitimate business, freed from confusion, uncertainty and fruitless litigation, will develop normally in response to the energy and enterprise of the American business man.

We favor strengthening the Sherman Law by prohibiting agreement to divide territory or limit output; refusing to sell to customers who buy from business rivals; to sell below cost in certain areas while maintaining higher prices in other places; using the power of transportation to aid or injure special business concerns; and other unfair trade practices.

Questions

1. Why would a political party insist on making a covenant with voters? What does this "covenant" suggest about the way Progressives viewed themselves and politics?
2. What does the section on social and industrial justice indicate about the America of 1912?
3. How is business portrayed?

Connections Questions

1. Who would seem likelier to take up the cause of the Lawrence strikers, Walter Rauschenbusch or Jane Addams? Why?
2. How might Rauschenbusch and Addams attack the Indiana eugenics statute?
3. What would Jane Addams find appealing in Theodore Roosevelt's speech on social justice and in the Progressive party's platform?

CHAPTER 22

An Emerging World Power 1877–1914

Grace Service, "Open House Days" for a China Missionary (1905)

China has long fascinated Americans as a market for either souls or products (see text pp. 586–87). Grace (1879–1954) and Robert (1879–1935) Service devoted themselves to the former. The Services were a college-educated couple who in 1905 volunteered to work in China for the Young Men's Christian Association. They spent the rest of their lives in China. It would be the land that welcomed their three sons just as it claimed the life of their infant daughter.

Grace Service's memoirs were edited by her son John, whose career as a China specialist for the State Department fell victim to the witch-hunts of Senator Joseph McCarthy (see Chapter 28 in the text and the reading "Joseph R. McCarthy on Communists in the U.S. Government").

When we left Kiating that September we hired a cargo boat with a high *peng* (a rounded mat roof) and a good wooden floor. The Boy had gone with us as cook to Golden Summit and did so well that we now discharged the dirty cook at Kiating, giving him travel money. The hold of our boat was loaded with loose dried beans which looked to be a clean and non-odorous cargo. We put all our things on the floor level, and the boat was large enough to give plenty of room and, best of all, good head space. Our teacher was with us on the boat and we studied as we traveled. We could even sit at our new desk to study and write. The trip to Chengtu was expected to take about a week.

The floods that summer had caused damage along the river and we saw signs on every hand. Once, walking on the bank, we noticed tangled vines above our heads in tree branches. These were peanut vines that had been washed out of the fields and lodged in the trees. Even at Chengtu the river had covered the big stone bridge outside the South Gate. Close to this place, a big section of the city wall had been undermined (and took many months to repair). But, despite the summer flood, the river was now rather low for that time of the year—and our boat was large. . . .

We were delighted to reach our Chinese home again. A quick check showed that the robbers had taken practically all my table linen as well as some other things. Otherwise all was in good order. A few days of scrubbing, washing windows, hanging clean curtains, and changing shelf and drawer papers made us as clean and fresh as could be. I liked the new desk very much and had it set up in our living room, where it became my special possession and delight. Bob had a large Chinese desk of red bean wood in his study, so he did not need it. My new desk was of what was called "buried nanmu." It had a large flat top. On each side above the table top were six small drawers.

Between these stacks an open space was just right for a row of books. Below on either side were tiers of large drawers. Many and many a letter I wrote on that desk, and many that I received were stowed inside.

That fall we studied, and continued to widen our acquaintances among Chinese. Bob spent much time and thought making plans and establishing contacts with people. An advisory committee was formed as a preliminary step toward the organization of a full-fledged YMCA. Sunday afternoon meetings were held, sometimes at our house, sometimes at the Hodgkins'. . . .

About that time we rented a piece of land at the rear of the Methodist school adjacent to us on the west. It belonged to the mission but was then not needed. It gave us space for two tennis courts with a tea pavilion west of them in the shadow of a high wall. There was also some ground left over for raising vegetables. Eventually we enjoyed many products of our own garden. . . .

When Chinese women called, I had to drop everything. They often came at inopportune times for us, as Chinese meal hours were not the same as ours, and they would stay and stay and stay. To come at ten in the forenoon, or even around noon, and then sit until three in the afternoon was asking a good deal of a hostess, but we had to conform to the habits of the country. A lady often brought a whole train of attendants: perhaps a sister or two, several grown daughters or younger children, and often four or five amahs. The guests sat down to visit, and the servants stood around gazing at everything and being what one might call movable fixtures in the room. It took me a long time to accustom myself to these calls. Gradually I learned the technique, and despite my lack of adequate language could carry them off with some sort of aplomb. I learned the polite phrases, and could fall back on the children and stock questions. Eventually, some of the women became my real friends, so that barriers no longer made such a chasm between us.

All women guests wanted to see our entire house. Most of them, if they expressed any opinion, thought we wasted too much time trying to be clean: clean kitchens and clean floors were no necessity to them. When I visited their homes, I was impressed by the dirty kitchens and their lack of any adequate attention to the floors. Their kitchens were in what we would call sheds. Most of their floors were dingy brick or grimy wood. Frequent expectoration, together with the habit of allowing babies to urinate freely on the floor anywhere and everywhere, made for unhygienic conditions and offensive odors. Cobwebs never seemed to bother Chinese; to this day I have to call servants' attention to them. Upper walls and ceiling spaces seem never to come within range of the Chinese eye; special orders must be given if you want to be sure that high corners will be cleaned. On the other hand, Chinese take great care in polishing the flat top and side surfaces of furniture such as cupboards and sideboards; and a Boy will carefully dust framed pictures every day, sometimes even dusting behind them. . . .

I was busy during these early Chengtu days. Often I rose at 6:30 in the morning to work down my bread. Then there was study, sewing, and general housekeeping. This could include a lot of mold prevention, and packing away all woolens and winter things at the approach of hot weather. Dry cleaners were unheard of, and laundry work demanded much attention and training of servants. It is quite a task to do up men's white summer suits, be they duck, silk, serge, or flannel. I found the Szechwanese to be good washers but poor rinsers. It was my rule to demand ample water for that use. By this means I kept our clothes from taking on that dull, muddy tinge which many housewives regard as one of the prices of living in the Orient.

Late in 1907 the West China Missionary Conference was impending, and I was determined to find a boy who could be wide-awake and efficient. I interviewed several prospects without success. At last a young fellow named Liu Pei-yun appeared. I had never wanted a country boy, because it seemed to me that some education, however little, would hold more potential for training. This boy was the son of a buyer of silk yarn. He could read and write and was an apt pupil in learning the work expected from him. On arrival he knew nothing whatsoever of any foreign furnishings or usages. When I first showed him how to set the table, he asked what the forks were and how they were used! He became a trusted servant, was married in our home, and worked for us from the fall of 1907 until that of 1920. Bob then helped him set up a business for himself in Chengtu. In later years he visited us several times in Shanghai and has always kept up connection with our family. . . .

As the Chinese ladies became less bashful I began to have more callers. Many of them besought me to start some sort of classes for them. They wanted to "learn foreign ways," to knit, crochet, and even to bake the light cakes which they ate in our homes. We were constantly invited to Chinese feasts. Here the procedure is the reverse of our custom. Chinese socializing is done before the meal, and the guests leave directly from the table. This meant that we often sat talking while the very food we were to eat was in preparation. We might hear the fowls squawking as they were chased and killed to be served to us later. The men and women always ate in separate rooms: the men in the main hall or some such public apartment, while we women were relegated to women's bedrooms. I was teaching a few pupils and kept busy in spite of not being well. I still had my attacks of severe pain now and then and was forced to spend a good many days in bed.

Questions

1. What is life like for the Services?
2. How does Grace Service characterize the Chinese people?
3. Why might a Westerner feel superior to the Chinese people in 1907–1908? Do the Services?

Albert Beveridge, "The Command of the Pacific" (1902)

Albert J. Beveridge (1862–1927) was both a politician and a historian. Beveridge offered a polished and comprehensive argument for American imperialism, as he does here concerning the Pacific. Like Theodore Roosevelt and other Progressives, Beveridge saw no contradiction between reform at home and manifest destiny abroad. The Indiana senator gave the following excerpted speech to a San Francisco audience in 1902.

Fellow Americans of California and the Pacific Slope:
The Pacific is the ocean of the future; and the Pacific is yours. The markets of the Orient are the Republic's future commercial salvation; and the Orient's commercial future is yours. Important as other questions are, the one great question that covers seas, and islands, and continents; that will last when other questions have been answered and forgotten; that will determine your present prosperity and the greatness of your children's children in their day, is the mastery of the Pacific and the commercial conquest of the eastern world. . . .

Let us consider the argument of advantage to ourselves, flowing from the Philippines, the Orient and from American mastery of the Pacific. What is the great commercial necessity of the Republic? It is markets—foreign markets. At one time we needed to build up our industries here and for that purpose to save for them our home markets. Protection did that; and to-day our home market is supplied. Now we have invaded the markets of Europe and filled them almost to their capacity with American goods. Our great combinations of capital devoted to manufacturing and transportation compete successfully with foreign manufacturers in their own countries.

But still we have a surplus; and an unsold surplus is commercial peril. Every unsold bushel of wheat reduces the price of every other one of the millions of bushels of wheat produced. If our manufacturers produce more than they can sell, that surplus product causes the mills to shut down until they produce no more than they can sell. And after we supply our own market, after we sell all we can to the markets of Europe, we still have an unsold surplus. If our prosperity continues this must be sold.

Where shall the Republic sell its surplus? Where shall the Pacific coast sell its surplus? And your surplus unsold means your commerce paralyzed, your laboring-men starving. Expansion answers that question. . . .

If it is not true that her possessions help England's commerce, why does not England give them up? Why does not Germany give up her possession in

Northern China? Why is she spending tens of millions of dollars there, building German railways, German docks and vast plants for future German commerce? Why does Russia spend a hundred million dollars of Russian gold building Russian railways through Manchuria and binding that territory, vast in extent as all the states of the Pacific slope combined, to the Russian empire with bands of steel? Why is Japan now preparing to take Manchuria from Russia as she has already taken Formosa from China?

The Philippines do help us in Oriental commerce! They have helped us even now by making the American name known throughout the East, and our commerce with the islands and countries influenced by the Philippines has in two short years leaped from $43,000,000 to $120,000,000.

If an American manufacturer established a great storehouse in London believing that it would help his business and then found his sales in London increasing 300 per cent. in less than three years, would he give away that branch establishment because some theorist told him that branch houses did not help trade and that he could sell as much and more if he shipped direct from his factory to the English purchaser?

And yet this practically is what the Opposition asks the American people to believe about and do with the Philippines. From every English and German possession in the East English and German goods are shipped in bulk and then reshipped as quick orders near at hand call for them. And these possessions influence the entire population of the countries where they are located. . . .

Has the decay of American energy begun with you, men of the West? Who says so is infidel to American character. Answer these slanders of your energy and power, people of the Pacific states—answer them with our ballots! Tell the world that, of all this masterful Nation, none more vital than the men and women who hold aloft the Republic's flag on our Pacific shores!

If we need this Oriental market—and we can not dispose of our surplus without it—what American farmer is willing for us to give the Philippines to America's competitors? What American manufacturer is willing to surrender this permanent commercial advantage to the nations who are striving for those very markets? Yet, that is what the Opposition asks you to do. For if we quit them certainly Germany or England or Japan will take them. . . .

And wherever they [railroads] have gone Chinese commerce has increased, just as our own commerce increases here wherever a railroad goes. And wherever railways go wagon roads branch from them. Thus the methods of modern civilization are weaving a network of modern conditions among this most ancient of peoples. And if China now buys $250,000,000 worth of products from the rest of the world, what will she buy when all this change that is now taking place brings her $400,000,000 as purchasers to the markets of the world? The most conservative experts estimate that China alone will buy at least one thousand million dollars worth of the products of other countries every year. . . .

The Philippines and the Orient are your commercial opportunity. Does our duty as a Nation forbid you to accept it? Does our fitness for the work prevent us from doing it? Or does the Nation's preparedness, the Republic's duty and the commercial necessity of the American people unite in demanding of American statesmanship the holding of the Philippines and the commercial conquest of the Oriental world? . . .

Examine every example of administration of government in the Orient or Africa by a superior power and find the answer to that theory. Come nearer home. Analyze the three years of American administration in Porto [*sic*] Rico—American schools for the humblest, just laws, honest government, prosperous commerce. Now sail for less than a day to the sister island of San [*sic*] Domingo and behold commerce extinguished, justice unknown, government and law a whim, religion degenerated to voodoo rites, and answer whether American administration in Porto Rico, even if it had been without the consent of the governed, is not better for that people than San Domingo's independent savagery.

Let us trust the American people! The most fervent belief in their purity, their power and their destiny is feeble, after all, compared with the reality on which that faith is founded. Great as our fathers were, the citizens of this Republic, on the whole, are greater still to-day, with broader education, loftier outlook. And if this were not so, we should not be worthy of our fathers; for, to do as well as they we must do better. Over the entire Republic the people's common schools increase, churches multiply, culture spreads, the poorest have privileges impossible to the wealthiest fifty years ago. . . .

American soldiers, American teachers, American administrators—all are the instruments of the Nation in discharging the Nation's high duty to the ancient and yet infant people which circumstance has placed in our keeping. If it is said that our duty is to teach the world by example, I ask if our duty ends with that? Does any man's duty to his children end with mere example? Does organized society owe no duty to the orphan and the abandoned save that of example? Why, then, are our schools, our asylums, our benevolent institutions, which force physical and mental training upon the neglected youth of the Republic? And does the parent or does organized society refrain from discharging this duty if the child resists? . . .

Questions

1. What are some of Beveridge's justifications for American imperialism in the Pacific?
2. What assumption does he make concerning Asian markets and the American surplus?
3. How does Beveridge believe that Puerto Rico—and, by implication, the Philippines—will benefit from American control?

Mark Twain, "To the Person Sitting in Darkness" (1901)

Not everyone agreed with Secretary of State John Hay's assessment of the fight with Spain as "a splendid little war." A group of prominent Americans who opposed the acquisition of colonies formed the American Anti-Imperialist League. Among their number was the acclaimed author Mark Twain (1835–1910). Twain ostensibly addressed part of the following essay "To the Person Sitting in Darkness," namely, to what today would be called a person of the Third World.

Twain refers to Joseph Chamberlain, who as colonial secretary for the British government refused to consider South African independence. That intransigence led to the Boer War, which was unfolding at the time of the essay's appearance.

And by and by comes America, and our Master of the Game plays it badly—plays it as Mr. Chamberlain was playing it in South Africa. It was a mistake to do that; also, it was one which was quite unlooked for in a Master who was playing it so well in Cuba. In Cuba, he was playing the usual and regular *American* game, and it was winning, for there is no way to beat it. The Master, contemplating Cuba, said: "Here is an oppressed and friendless little nation which is willing to fight to be free; we go partners, and put up the strength of seventy million sympathizers and the resources of the United States: play!" Nothing but Europe combined could call that hand: and Europe cannot combine on anything. There, in Cuba, he was following our great tradition in a way which made us very proud of him, and proud of the deep dissatisfaction which his play was provoking in continental Europe. Moved by a high inspiration, he threw out those stirring words which proclaimed that forcible annexation would be "criminal aggression"; and in that utterance fired another "shot heard round the world." The memory of that fine saying will be outlived by the remembrance of no act of his but one—that he forgot it within the twelvemonth, and its honorable gospel along with it.

For, presently, came the Philippine temptation. It was strong; it was too strong, and he made that bad mistake: he played the European game, the Chamberlain game. It was a pity; it was a great pity, that error; that one grievous error, that irrevocable error. For it was the very place and time to play the American game again. And at no cost. Rich winnings to be gathered in, too; rich and permanent; indestructible; a fortune transmissible forever to the children of the flag. Not land, not money, not dominion—no, something worth many times more than that dross: our share, the spectacle of a nation of long harrassed and persecuted slaves set free through our influence; our posterity's share, the golden memory of that fair deed. The game was in our hands. If it had been played according to the American rules, Dewey would have sailed away from Manila as soon as he had destroyed the Spanish fleet—after putting up a sign on shore guaranteeing foreign property and life against damage by the Filipinos, and warning the Powers that interference with the emancipated patriots would be regarded as an act unfriendly to the United States. The Powers cannot combine, in even a bad cause, and the sign would not have been molested. . . .

But we played the Chamberlain game, and lost the chance to add another Cuba and another honorable deed to our good record.

The more we examine the mistake, the more clearly we perceive that it is going to be bad for the Business. The Person Sitting in Darkness is almost sure to say: "There is something curious about this—curious and unaccountable. There must be two Americans; one that sets the captive free, and one that takes a once-captive's new freedom away from him, and picks a quarrel with him with nothing to found it on; then kills him to get his land."

The truth is, the Person Sitting in Darkness *is* saying things like that; and for the sake of the Business we must persuade him to look at the Philippine matter in another and healthier way. We must arrange his opinions for him. I believe it can be done; for Mr. Chamberlain has arranged England's opinion of the South African matter, and done it most cleverly and successfully. He presented the facts—some of the facts—and showed those confiding people what the facts meant. He did it statistically, which is a good way. He used the formula: "Twice 2 are 14, and 2 from 9 leaves 35." Figures are effective; figures will convince the elect.

Now, my plan is a still bolder one than Mr. Chamberlain's, though apparently a copy of it. Let us be franker than Mr. Chamberlain; let us audaciously present the whole of the facts, shirking none, then explain them according to Mr. Chamberlain's formula. This daring truthfulness will astonish and dazzle the Person Sitting in Darkness, and he will take the Explanation down before his mental vision has had time to get back into focus. Let us say to him:

"Our case is simple. On the 1st of May, Dewey destroyed the Spanish fleet. This left the Archipelago in the hands of its proper and rightful owners, the Filipino nation. Their army numbered 30,000 men, and they were competent to whip out or starve out the little Spanish garrison; then the people could set up a government of their own devising. Our traditions required that Dewey should now set up his warning sign, and go away. But the Master of the Game happened to think of another plan—the European plan. He acted upon it. This was, to send out an army—ostensibly to help the native patriots put the finishing touch upon their long and plucky struggle for independence, but really to take their land away from them and keep it. That is, in the interest of Progress and Civilization. The plan developed, stage by stage, and quite satisfactorily. We entered into a military alliance with the trusting Filipinos, and they hemmed in Manila on the land side, and by their valuable help the place, with its garrison of 8,000 or 10,000 Spaniards, was captured—a thing which we could not have accomplished unaided at that time. We got their help by—by ingenuity. We knew they were fighting for their independence, and that they had been at it for two years. We knew they supposed that we also were fighting in their worthy cause—just as we had helped the Cubans fight for Cuban independence—and we allowed them to go on thinking so. *Until Manila was ours and we could get along without them.* Then we showed our hand. Of course, they were surprised—that was natural; surprised and disappointed; disappointed and grieved. To them it looked un-American; uncharacteristic; foreign to our established traditions. And this was natural, too; for we were only playing the American Game in public—in private it was the European. It was neatly done, very neatly, and it bewildered them. They could not understand it; for we had been so friendly—so affectionate, even—with those simple-minded patriots! We, our own selves, had brought back out of exile their leader, their hero, their hope, their Washington—Aguinaldo; brought him in a warship, in high honor, under the sacred shelter and hospitality of the flag; brought him back and restored him to his people, and got their moving and eloquent gratitude for it. Yes, we had been so friendly to them, and had heartened them up in so many ways! We had lent them guns and ammunition; advised with them; exchanged pleasant courtesies with them; placed our sick and wounded in their kindly care; intrusted our Spanish prisoners to their humane and honest hands; fought shoulder to shoulder with them against "the common enemy" (our own phrase); praised their mercifulness, praised their fine and honorable conduct; borrowed their trenches, borrowed strong positions which they had previously captured from the Spaniards; petted them, lied to them—officially proclaiming that our land and naval forces came to give them their freedom and displace the bad Spanish Government—fooled them, used them until we needed them no longer; then derided the sucked orange and threw it away. We kept the positions which we had beguiled them of; by and by, we moved a force forward and overlapped patriot ground—a clever thought, for we needed trouble, and this would produce it. A Filipino soldier, crossing the ground, where no one had a right to forbid him, was shot by our sentry. The badgered patriots resented this with arms, without waiting to know whether Aguinaldo, who was absent, would approve or not. Aguinaldo did not approve; but that availed nothing. What we wanted, in the interest of Progress and Civilization, was the Archipelago, unencumbered by patriots struggling for independence; and War was what we needed. We clinched our opportunity. It is Mr. Chamberlain's case over again—at least in its motive and intention; and we played the game as adroitly as he played it himself." . . .

Everything is prosperous, now; everything is just as we should wish it. We have got the Archipelago, and we shall never give it up. Also, we have every reason to hope that we shall have an opportunity before very long to slip out of our congressional contract with Cuba and give her something better in the place of it. It is a rich country, and many of us are already beginning to see that the contract was a sentimental mistake. But now—right now—is the best time to do some profitable rehabilitating work—work that will set us up and make us comfortable, and discourage gossip. We cannot conceal from ourselves that, privately, we are a little troubled about our uniform. It is one of our prides; it is acquainted with honor; it is familiar with great deeds and noble; we love it, we revere it; and so this errand it is on makes us uneasy. And our flag—another pride of ours, our chiefest! We have worshipped it so; and when we have seen it in far lands—glimpsing it unexpectedly in that strange sky, waving its welcome and benediction to us—we have caught our breaths, and uncovered our heads, and couldn't speak, for a moment, for the thought of what it was to us and the great ideals it stood for. Indeed, we *must* do something about these things; it is easily managed. We can have a special one—our states do it: we can have just our usual flag, with the white stripes painted black and the stars replaced by the skull and crossbones.

And we do not need that Civil Commission out there. Having no powers, it has to invent them, and that kind of work cannot be effectively done by just anybody; an expert is required. Mr. Croker can be spared. We do not want the United States represented there, but only the Game.

By help of these suggested amendments, Progress and Civilization in that country can have a boom, and it will take in the Persons who are Sitting in Darkness, and we can resume Business at the old stand.

Questions

1. How does Mark Twain propose to argue the cause of empire?
2. What is his real purpose in recounting recent events?
3. Why does Twain appear to be so cynical?

John Hay, Open Door Notes
(1899, 1900)

Unwilling to make a large military commitment in China, the United States pressed its interests through diplomacy. The following notes from Secretary of State John Hay (1838–1905) compose the Open Door Policy, which remained in force until the triumph of Mao Zedong (Mao Tse-tung) in 1949. Hay's first communication is to Andrew D. White, the American ambassador to Germany. His second is a telegram sent to American embassies and missions in all countries wanting to trade with China.

JOHN HAY TO ANDREW D. WHITE

Department of State, Washington, September 6, 1899

At the time when the Government of the United States was informed by that of Germany that it had leased from His Majesty the Emperor of China the port of Kiao-chao and the adjacent territory in the province of Shantung, assurances were given to the ambassador of the United States at Berlin by the Imperial German minister for foreign affairs that the rights and privileges insured by treaties with China to citizens of the United States would not thereby suffer or be in anywise impaired within the area over which Germany had thus obtained control.

More recently, however, the British Government recognized by a formal agreement with Germany the exclusive right of the latter country to enjoy in said leased area and the contiguous "sphere of influence or interest" certain privileges, more especially those relating to railroads and mining enterprises; but as the exact nature and extent of the rights thus recognized have not been clearly defined, it is possible that serious conflicts of interest may at any time arise not only between British and German subjects within said area, but that the interests of our citizens may also be jeopardized thereby.

Earnestly desirous to remove any cause of irritation and to insure at the same time to the commerce of all nations in China the undoubted benefits which should accrue from a formal recognition by the various powers claiming "spheres of interest" that they shall enjoy perfect equality of treatment for their commerce and navigation within such "spheres," the Government of the United States would be pleased to see His German Majesty's Government give formal assurance, and lend its cooperation in securing like assurances from the other interested powers, that each, within its respective sphere of whatever influence—

First. Will in no way interfere with any treaty port or any vested interest within any so-called "sphere of interest" or leased territory it may have in China.

Second. That the Chinese treaty tariff of the time being shall apply to all merchandise landed or shipped to all such ports as are within said "sphere of interest" (unless they be "free ports"), no matter to what nationality it may belong, and that duties so leviable shall be collected by the Chinese Government.

Third. That it will levy no higher harbor dues on vessels of another nationality frequenting any port in such "sphere" than shall be levied on vessels of its own nationality, and no higher railroad charges over lines built, controlled, or operated within its "sphere" on merchandise belonging to citizens or subjects of other nationality transported through such "sphere" than shall be levied on similar merchandise belonging to its own nationals transported over equal distances.

The liberal policy pursued by His Imperial German Majesty in declaring Kiao-chao a free port and in aiding the Chinese Government in the establishment there of a customhouse are so clearly in line with the proposition which this Government is anxious to see recognized that it entertains the strongest hope that Germany will give its acceptance and hearty support.

The recent ukase of His Majesty the Emperor of Russia declaring the port of Ta-lien-wan open during the whole of the lease under which it is held from China to the merchant ships of all nations, coupled with the categorical assurances made to this Government by His Imperial Majesty's representative at this capital at the same time and since repeated to me by the present Russian ambassador, seem to insure the support of the Emperor to the proposed measure. Our ambassador at the Court of St. Petersburg has in consequence, been instructed to submit it to the Russian Government and to request their early consideration of it. A copy of my instruction on the subject to Mr. Tower is herewith inclosed for your confidential information.

The commercial interests of Great Britain and Japan will be so clearly served by the desired declaration of intentions, and the views of the Governments of these countries as to the desirability of the adopting of measures insuring the benefits of equality of treatment of all foreign trade throughout China are so similar to those entertained by the United States, that their acceptance of the propositions herein outlined and their cooperation in advocating their adoption by the other powers can be confidently expected. I enclose herewith copy of the instruction which I have sent to Mr. Choate on the subject.

In view of the present favorable conditions, you are instructed to submit the above considerations to His Imperial German Majesty's Minister for Foreign Affairs, and to request his early consideration of the subject.

CIRCULAR TELEGRAM TO THE POWERS
COOPERATING IN CHINA

Department of State, Washington, July 3, 1900

In this critical posture of affairs in China it is deemed appropriate to define the attitude of the United States as far as present circumstances permit this to be done. We adhere to the policy initiated by us in 1857 of peace with the Chinese nation, of furtherance of lawful commerce, and of protection of lives and property of our citizens by all means guaranteed under extraterritorial treaty rights and by the law of nations. If wrong be done to our citizens we propose to hold the responsible authors to the uttermost accountability. We regard the condition at Pekin as one of virtual anarchy, whereby power and responsibility are practically devolved upon the local provincial authorities. So long as they are not in overt collusion with rebellion and use their power to protect foreign life and property, we regard them as representing the Chinese people, with whom we seek to remain in peace and friendship. The purpose of the President is, as it has been heretofore, to act concurrently with the other powers; first, in opening up communication with Pekin and rescuing the American officials, missionaries, and other Americans who are in danger; secondly, in affording all possible protection everywhere in China to American life and property; thirdly, in guarding and protecting all legitimate American interests; and fourthly, in aiding to prevent a spread of the disorders to the other provinces of the Empire and a recurrence of such disasters. It is of course too early to forecast the means of attaining this last result; but the policy of the Government of the United States is to seek a solution which may bring about permanent safety and peace to China, preserve Chinese territorial and administrative entity, protect all rights guaranteed to friendly powers by treaty and international law, and safeguard for the world the principle of equal and impartial trade with all parts of the Chinese Empire. . . .

Questions

1. What is the purpose of John Hay's first Open Door Note?
2. How does the second note differ?
3. What does the United States risk in proposing to "preserve Chinese territorial and administrative entity"?

The Roosevelt Corollary to the Monroe Doctrine (1904, 1905)

On domestic issues, Theodore Roosevelt pursued a Square Deal for the American public, but in foreign policy, he preferred to carry a big stick. This could take the form of the Great White Fleet, the muscle-flexing voyage of U.S. battleships around the world in 1907–1908 (see text p. 601), or an addition to the Monroe Doctrine. These two statements by Roosevelt in 1904 and 1905 constitute the Roosevelt Corollary. The United States thus became the "policeman" of the Caribbean, a role it continued to play down to the 1980s in Grenada and Nicaragua (see text p. 897).

ROOSEVELT'S ANNUAL MESSAGE TO CONGRESS, DECEMBER 6, 1904

It is not true that the United States feels any land hunger or entertains any project as regards the other nations of the Western Hemisphere save such as are for their welfare. All that this country desires is to see the neighboring countries stable, orderly, and prosperous. Any country whose people conduct themselves well can count upon our hearty friendship. If a nation shows that it knows how to act with reasonable efficiency and decency in social and political matters, if it keeps order and pays its obligations, it need fear no interference from the United States. Chronic wrong doing, or an impotence which results in a general loosening of the ties of civilized society, may in America, as elsewhere, ultimately require intervention by some civilized nation, and in the Western Hemisphere the adherence of the United States to the Monroe Doctrine may force the United States, however reluctantly, in flagrant cases of such wrong doing or impotence, to the exercise of an international police power. If every country washed by the Caribbean Sea would show the progress in stable and just civilization which with the aid of the Platt amendment Cuba has shown since our troops left the island, and which so many of the republics in both Americas are constantly and brilliantly showing, all question of interference by this Nation with their affairs would be at an end. Our interests and those of our southern neighbors are in reality identical. They have great natural riches, and if within their borders the reign of law and justice obtains, prosperity is sure to come to them. While they thus obey the primary laws of civilized society they may rest assured that they will be treated by us in a spirit of cordial and helpful sympathy. We would interfere with them only in the last resort, and then only if it became evident that their inability or unwillingness to do justice at home and abroad had violated the rights of the United States or had invited foreign aggression to the detriment of the entire body of American nations. It is a mere truism to say that every nation . . . which desires to maintain its freedom, its independence, must ultimately realize that the right of such independence can not be separated from the responsibility of making good use of it.

ROOSEVELT'S ANNUAL MESSAGE TO CONGRESS, DECEMBER 5, 1905

It must be understood that under no circumstances will the United States use the Monroe Doctrine as a cloak for territorial aggression. We desire peace with all the world, but perhaps most of all with the other peoples of the American Continent. There are, of course, limits to the wrongs which any self-respecting nation can endure. It is always possible that wrong actions toward this Nation, or toward citizens of this Nation, in some State unable to keep order among its own people, unable to secure justice from outsiders, and unwilling to do justice to those outsiders who treat it well, may result in our having to take action to protect our rights; but such action will not be taken with a view to territorial aggression, and it will be taken at all only with extreme reluctance and when it has become evident that every other resource has been exhausted.

Moreover, we must make it evident that we do not intend to permit the Monroe Doctrine to be used by any nation on this Continent as a shield to protect it from the consequences of its own misdeeds against foreign nations. If a republic to the south of us commits a tort against a foreign nation, such as an outrage against a citizen of that nation, then the Monroe Doctrine does not force us to interfere to prevent punishment of the tort, save to see that the punishment does not assume the form of territorial occupation. . . . The case is more difficult when it refers to a contractual obligation. Our own Government has always refused to enforce such contractual obligations on behalf of its citizens by an appeal to arms. It is much to be wished that all foreign governments would take the same view. But they do not; and in consequence we are liable at any time to be brought face to face with disagreeable alternatives. On the one hand, this country would certainly decline to go to war to prevent a foreign government from collecting a just debt; on the other hand, it is very inadvisable to permit any foreign power to take possession, even temporarily, of the custom houses of an American Republic in order to enforce the payment of its obligations; for such temporary occupation might turn into a permanent occupation. The only escape from these alternatives may at any time be that we must ourselves undertake to bring about some arrangement by which so much as possible of a just obligation shall be paid. It is far better that this country should put through such an arrangement, rather than allow any foreign country to undertake it. To do so insures the defaulting republic from having to pay debt of an improper character under duress, while it also insures honest creditors of the republic from being passed by in the interest of dishonest or grasping creditors. Moreover, for the United States to take such a position offers the only possible way of insuring us against a clash with some foreign power. The position is, therefore, in the interest of peace as well as in the interest of justice. It is of benefit to our people; it is of benefit to foreign peoples; and most of all it is really of benefit to the people of the country concerned. . . .

Questions

1. Under what circumstances does Roosevelt propose to intervene in the affairs of Caribbean nations?
2. When would he abstain from intervention?
3. What kind of precedent is set with this announcement of "an international police power"?

Connections Questions

1. Imagine a debate on China between Grace Service, Albert Beveridge, and John Hay. What would the biggest points of disagreement be? Would there be any common ground? If so, what?
2. Who makes the stronger case on imperialism, Albert Beveridge or Mark Twain? Why?
3. In what ways could the Open Door Notes and the Roosevelt Corollary antagonize the people they were intended to protect? In light of European and Japanese competition for foreign markets, could the United States have fashioned alternative policies? If so, what kind?

CHAPTER 23

War and the American State 1914–1920

Hervey Allen, *Toward the Flame* (1918)

Poet and novelist Hervey Allen (1888–1949) joined the National Guard following his graduation from the University of Pittsburgh in 1915. Before going to France in 1917, Allen served with the expeditionary force that pursued Pancho Villa (see text p. 618). Although at times disturbing, Allen's account only hints at the horror of a war that claimed the lives of some 14.5 million victims. The following is an excerpt from Allen's wartime diary, Toward the Flame.

Along the edge of these thickets were a number of graves. I was greatly impressed by them. The crosses were well carved out of new wood, and the grave mounds carefully spaded. Here were wreaths of wax flowers, evidently sent from home, and a board giving the epitaph of the deceased, with his rank and honors: "He was a good Christian and fell in France fighting for the Fatherland, *Hier ruht in Gott* [Here he rests in God]." Verily, these seemed to be the same Goths and Vandals who left their graves even in Egypt; unchanged since the days of Rome, and still fighting her civilization, the woods-people against the Latins. Only the illuminating literary curiosity of a Tacitus was lacking to make the inward state of man visible by the delineation of the images of outer things.

We entered some of the dugouts, small, mound-like structures with straw inside. Some of the officers' were larger. There was a little beer garden in the middle of the wood with a chapel and a wreathed cross near by, white stones and twisting "rustic" paths. The railings and booths along these paths were made from roots and branches cleverly bent and woven, and sometimes carved. It reminded me of American "porch furniture" of a certain type. All quite German. Cast-off boots, shell-timers, one or two coats, and shrapnel-bitten helmets lay about with round Boche [an insulting nickname for "German"] hats, "the little round button on top." Picture post-cards and magazines, pistol holsters, and one or two broken rifles completed this cartoon of invasion.

All the litter of material thus left behind was useless. I noticed the pictures of some fat, and rather jolly-looking German girls, and piles of a vast quantity of shells. We looked around thoroughly, but were very wary of traps. I remember making up my mind to make for one of these dugouts in case we were shelled. One always kept a weather eye open.

About all this stuff there was at that time the dire taint of danger. Somehow everything German gave one the creeps. It was connected so intimately with all that was unpleasant, and associated so inevitably with organized fear, that one scarce regarded its owners as men. It seemed *then* as if we were fighting some strange, ruthless, insect-beings from another planet; that we had stumbled upon their nests after smoking them out. One had the same feeling as when waking up at night and realizing that there are rats under the bed.

The captain and I walked along the edge of the wood, encountering our French contingent on the way. They were "at home" in an old German dugout, happily squatted around several small fires, preparing their meal as *they* liked it. After a good deal of difficulty, they had prevailed on our mess sergeant to issue them their rations in bulk so that they could do their own cooking. Such little differences of customs are in reality most profound. Our physical habits were more like the Germans'!

The non-commissioned gas officer picked us up here. He was carrying back the big brass shell for a gas alarm. It gave forth a mellow musical note when touched with a bar of iron or a bayonet. The Germans had used this one themselves for that purpose, so it already had the holes and wire for suspending it. . . .

We moved before it was light, which is very early in summer time in France. The dim columns of men coming out of the woods, the lines of carts and kitchens assembling in the early, gray dawn, all without a light, and generally pretty silently, was always impressive.

In a few minutes we were headed back in the direction from which we had come. There was a full moon, or one nearly so, hanging low in the west. As I jolted along, on legs that seemed more like stilts than limbs with knees, the heavy equipment sagged at every step, and seemed to clink one's teeth together weakly. At last the weariness and the jangle took on a fagged rhythm that for me fell into the comfort of rhyme.

We were beginning to be pretty tired by now and even here needed relief. One no longer got up in the morning full of energy. Hunger, dirt, and strain were telling, and we felt more or less "all in" that day in particular. One was consciously weak.

Nevertheless the country was beautiful; the full moon just sinking in the west looked across the smoking, misty valleys at the rising sun. There was a gorgeous bloody-gold color in the sky, and the woods and fields sparkled deliciously green, looking at a little distance fresh and untouched. But that was only a distant appearance, for this was the country over which two days before the Americans had driven the Germans from one machine gun next to another, and on from crest to crest. A nearer approach showed the snapped tree-trunks, the tossed branches and shell-pitted ground, and at one halt that we made, Nick called me down a little slope to see something.

There was a small spring in a draw beside the road, where two Germans were lying. One was a big, brawny fellow with a brown beard, and the other a mere lad. He looked to be about 14 or 15 with a pathetically childish chin, but he carried potatomasher bombs. They had evidently stopped here to try to fill their canteens, probably both desperate with thirst, when they were overtaken by our men. The young boy must have sheltered himself behind the man while the latter held our fellows back a little. There was a scorched place up the side of the ravine where a hand grenade had exploded, but the big German had been surrounded, and killed by the bayonet right through his chest. His hands were still clutching at the place where the steel had gone through. He was one of the few I ever saw who had been killed by the bayonet. The boy was lying just behind him. His back appeared to have been broken, probably by a blow with the butt of a rifle, and he was contorted into a kind of arch, only his feet and shoulders resting on the ground. It was he who had probably thrown the grenade that had exploded nearby. The little spring had evidently been visited by the wounded, as there were blood and first-aid wrappings about. I refused to have the company water tank filled there. . . .

Questions
1. Describe conditions at the front.
2. How does Allen view the enemy?
3. What does he find at the small spring? What does the scene suggest about the unpredictability of combat?

U.S. Army Mental Tests

American reformers hoped that war would transform society for the better (see text p. 627), but the old prejudice persisted. For example, the Army faced the immense challenge of classifying millions of men for military service. Intelligence testing became an important tool in that undertaking. The tests excerpted here were reprinted in book form in 1920, and for some Americans, measuring intelligence became more than a tool: xenophobes and racists now had a "scientific" argument to back their views.

TEST 2

Get the answers to these examples as quickly as you can.
Use the side of this page to figure on if you need to.

SAMPLES {
1 How many are 5 men and 10 men?...............Answer (**15**)
2 If you walk 4 miles an hour for 3 hours,
     how far do you walk? ....Answer (**12**)

1 How many are 30 men and 7 men? ....Answer (   )

2 If you save $7 a month for 4 months, how much will
   you save? ....Answer (   )
3 If 24 men are divided into squads of 8, how many
   squads will there be?...Answer (   )
4 Mike had 12 cigars. He bought 3 more, and then
   smoked 6. How many cigars did he have left?............Answer (   )
5 A company advanced 5 miles and retreated 3 miles.
   How far was it then from its first position? ....Answer (   )
6 How many hours will it take a truck to go 66 miles at
   the rate of 6 miles an hour? ....Answer (   )
7 How many cigars can you buy for 50 cents at the rate
   of 2 for 5 cents?..Answer (   )
8 A regiment marched 40 miles in five days. The first
   day they marched 9 miles, the second day 6 miles, the
   third 10 miles, the fourth 8 miles. How many miles
   did they march the last day?....................................Answer (   )
9 If you buy two packages of tobacco at 7 cents each and
   a pipe for 65 cents, how much change should you get
   from a two-dollar bill?...Answer (   )
10 If it takes 6 men 3 days to dig a 180-foot drain, how
   many men are needed to dig it in half a day? ....Answer (   )
11 A dealer bought some mules for $800. He sold them
   for $1,000, making $40 on each mule. How many mules
   were there? ....Answer (   )
12 A rectangular bin holds 400 cubic feet of line. If the
   bin is 10 feet long and 5 feet wide, how deep is it?...........Answer (   )
13 A recruit spent one-eighth of his spare change for post
   cards and four times as much for a box of letter paper,
   and then had 90 cents left. How much money did he
   have at first? ....Answer (   )
14 If 3½ tons of coal cost $21, what will 5 1/2 tons cost?........Answer (   )
15 A ship has provisions to last her crew of 500 men
   6 months. How long would it last 1,200 men?..............Answer (   )
16 If a man runs a hundred yards in 10 seconds, how
   many feet does he run in a fifth of a second? ....Answer (   )
17 A U-boat makes 8 miles an hour under water and 15
   miles on the surface. How long will it take to cross a
   100-mile channel, if it has to go two-fifths of the way
   under water? ....Answer (   )
18 If 241 squads of men are to dig 4,097 yards of trench,
   how many yards must be dug by each squad? ....Answer (   )
19 A certain division contains 3,000 artillery, 15,000
   infantry and 1,000 cavalry. If each branch is expanded

proportionately until there are in all 20,900 men, how
many will be added to the artillery? ....Answer (   )

20 A commission house which had already supplied
1,897 barrels of apples to a cantonment delivered the
remainder of its stock to 29 mess halls. Of this
remainder each mess hall received 54 barrels. What
was the total number of barrels supplied? ....Answer (   )

TEST 3

This is a test of common sense. Below are sixteen questions. Three answers are
given to each question. You are to look at the answers carefully; then make a
cross in the square before the best answer to each question, as in the sample:

SAMPLE $\left\{\begin{array}{l}\end{array}\right.$ Why do we use stoves? Because
     □ they look well
     ☒ they keep us warm
     □ they are black

Here the second answer is the best one and is marked with a cross. Begin with
No. 1 and keep on until time is called.

1 Cats are useful animals, because
     □ they catch mice
     □ they are gentle
     □ they are afraid of dogs

2 Why are pencils more commonly carried than fountain pens? Because
     □ they are brightly colored
     □ they are cheaper
     □ they are not so heavy

3 Why is leather used for shoes? Because
     □ it is produced in all countries
     □ it wears well
     □ it is an animal product

4 Why judge a man by what he does rather than what he says? Because
     □ what a man does shows what he really is
     □ it is wrong to tell a lie
     □ a deaf man cannot hear what is said

5 If you were asked what you thought of a person whom you didn't know,
what should you say?
     □ I will go and get acquainted
     □ I think he is all right
     □ I don't know him and can't say

6 Streets are sprinkled in summer
  ☐ to make the air cooler
  ☐ to keep automobiles from skidding
  ☐ to keep down dust
7 Why is wheat better for food than corn? Because
  ☐ it is more nutritious
  ☐ it is more expensive
  ☐ it can be ground finer
8 If a man made a million dollars, he ought to
  ☐ pay off the national debt
  ☐ contribute to various worthy charities
  ☐ give it all to some poor man
9 Why do many persons prefer automobiles to street cars? Because
  ☐ an auto is made of higher grade materials
  ☐ an automobile is more convenient
  ☐ street cars are not as safe
10 The feathers on a bird's wings help him to fly because they
  ☐ make a wide, light surface
  ☐ keep the air off his body
  ☐ keep the wings from cooling off too fast
11 All traffic going one way keeps to the same side of the street because
  ☐ most people are right handed
  ☐ the traffic policeman insists on it
  ☐ it avoids confusion and collisions
12 Why do inventors patent their inventions? Because
  ☐ it gives them control of their inventions
  ☐ it creates a greater demand
  ☐ it is the custom to get patents
13 Freezing water bursts pipes because
  ☐ cold makes the pipes weaker
  ☐ water expands when it freezes
  ☐ the ice stops the flow of water
14 Why are high mountains covered with snow? Because
  ☐ they are near the clouds
  ☐ the sun seldom shines on them
  ☐ the air is cold there
15 If the earth were nearer the sun
  ☐ the stars would disappear
  ☐ our months would be longer
  ☐ the earth would be warmer
16 Why is it colder nearer the poles than nearer the equator? Because
  ☐ the poles are always farther from the sun
  ☐ the sunshine falls obliquely at the poles
  ☐ there is more ice at the poles

Questions

1. What factors might affect test performance?
2. Who is the most likely to test well? Poorly?
3. What do the tests indicate about the state of American education at the time?

Chicago Board of Education, Spelling Book for Grades Four, Five, Six, Seven, Eight (1914)

During the summer of 1917, the Chicago Board of Education discovered that multicultural instruction could run afoul of world affairs. In an effort to make spelling and grammar relevant to at least some of the immigrant population, the board had for some time included the following exercise in its eighth-grade speller. But with the declaration of war in April 1917 (see text p. 618), the board looked like an agent of disloyalty. With people already acting on their own to remove the offensive exercise, the board soon voted to do the same.

SPELLING—EIGHTH GRADE

December 19, 1910
　　　　　　　Note: Dictate to the pupils the following text . . .
　　　　　　　The pupils will be marked on the words in italics. . . .

THE KAISER IN THE MAKING

In the *gymnasium* at Cassel the German *Kaiser* spent three years of his boyhood, a *diligent* but not a *brilliant* pupil, ranking tenth among *seventeen candidates* for the *university*.

Many tales are told of this *period* of his life, and one of them, at least, is *illuminating*.

A *professor*, it is said, wishing to curry favor with his royal pupil, informed him *overnight* of the chapter in Greek that was to be made the *subject* of the next day's lesson.

The young *prince* did what many boys would not have done. As soon as the class room was *opened* on the following morning, he entered and wrote *conspicuously* on the blackboard the *information* that had been given him.

One may say *unhesitatingly* that a boy capable of such an action has the root of a fine *character* in him, *possesses* that *chivalrous* sense of fair play which is the nearest thing to a *religion* that may be looked for at that age, hates *meanness* and *favoritism,* and will, *wherever possible,* expose them. There is in him a *fundamental* bent toward what is clean, manly and aboveboard.

Questions

1. What lessons in character is the exercise intended to convey?
2. Which groups might find this exercise offensive?
3. What does the controversy indicate about the wartime atmosphere in Chicago?

The Home Front: Women Fund-Raisers

As Chapter 23 in the text notes, "Women were the largest group to take advantage of wartime opportunities." Jobs opened up in industry and government service, and women wanting to serve overseas volunteered with the Red Cross and the Young Women's Christian Association. YWCA fund-raising provided a different kind of challenge, as shown in this 1920 state history of wartime welfare campaigns in Iowa.

In the recent struggle there were many active participants who did not shoulder a rifle. A year after the declaration of a state of war a million and a half men were in military service: at that time a million and a half women were engaged in the manufacture of war materials: and as the number in the one class increased, the other force expanded correspondingly. Most of these women were living a life just as novel, just as separated from their previous existence as were the soldiers: and the woman worker was as prone to homesickness and loneliness as was the recruit in the camp. If he needed welfare work and the people furnished it, should she not also be remembered?

The inspector general of the Iowa militia had reported in 1901, on the presence of women in the militia camps, that they were "a nuisance, underfoot, and a detriment to the good work and benefits expected of camp." But, whether a nuisance or not, women were bound to come to the places where the soldiers were—to enjoy a family picnic, to visit the sick in the hospital, or to say a final goodbye before the departure over-seas. Cast alone into a city of barracks, the mother, the sister, or the friend was just as bewildered as was the recruit on his first visit to the neighboring city. If the War Camp Community Service provided for him, should not someone think of her?

Welfare work among soldiers had as one object the preservation of their efficiency by removing the incentives to immorality. But who would guide past temptation in the vicinity of the military camp the girl now suddenly brought into contact with thousands of fighting men?

It was to the Young Women's Christian Association that the welfare of the industrial workers, the women in the camps, and the girls in the cantonment cities was entrusted. The Women's Branch of the Industrial Service Section of the Ordnance Department invited the Association to supervise the recreational activities in these industries. Upon the request of a camp commander the Association was ready to construct a Hostess House for the convenience of women visitors, and safeguards were thrown around the girls by the organization of Patriotic Leagues—an outgrowth of work which had already been done under the Social Morality Committee of this society. . . .

Following the precedent of the Young Men's Christian Association, the women organized a special War Work Council to which was delegated all activities which arose in connection with the war. The first problem was the financing of these various tasks, and it was with this subject that the War Work Council dealt at their first meeting held in New York City on June 7, 1917. It was there resolved that the country should be appealed to for $1,000,000 of which $50,000 would be expended in work abroad.

Although an active campaign was started to obtain $1,000,000, it did not remain the goal. So great was the demand for hostess houses, so insistent the appeal from abroad, that on October 9th a decision was made to place the sum at $4,000,000 of which $1,000,000 would be expended in France and Russia. . . .

How a rural county was organized is illustrated in a report written by Miss Caroline W. Daniels of Independence. "On Nov. 20, 1917, District Y. W. workers from Dubuque called a meeting in the High School Auditorium to organize Buchanan Co. About two dozen women were present. Miss Doris Campbell was chosen Sec-Treas. and I chairman. That afternoon Miss Campbell and I in her car began a tour of the newspaper offices of the county and that evening we had an organization meeting of prospective war leaders for Independence, the county seat. With the consent of the Red Cross officers we used their organization as a fulcrum throughout the county outside the Co. seat. Our method was to drive to every Red Cross group of workers; get permission to explain the need to them while they worked; arrange for some one of their number to take charge of a canvass in their town or township, or region; tell them of their share of the sum asked for from the county (basing this on population); and depart. The same method was used with any other groups we could get access to:—clubs, societies, etc. These groups received us with good will, and took our request as one of the war necessities that must be met, however weary and already over worked they felt. These visits were supplemented by letters, literature, posters, newspaper notices, announcements by townships of returns, etc., etc." . . .

Just as the high school boys were an effective factor in the raising of the fund of the Young Men's Christian Association, so the high school girls contributed to the success of the women's endeavor. Indeed, at Fort Dodge the system was much the same. High school girls were organized on military lines, with a major and two captains. Each captain chose a lieutenant and a corporal from each class. A meeting was held at which time pledge cards, stating the willingness of the girls to give fifty cents a month for ten months, were passed out with instructions to take them home and have them countersigned by their parents. When the cards were returned it was found that $635 had been pledged. More than forty girls of the East High School in Waterloo pledged five dollars each toward the cause. In Washington the high school girls conducted the local campaign and received pledges of more than eight hundred dollars. . . .

Besides apathy and indifference there were in this campaign distinct objections to be overcome. Such was the "dancing girls story." A special article in a Chicago Sunday paper stated that the Young Women's Christian Association planned to bring several hundred girls to Camp Lewis, Washington, and pay them fifteen dollars weekly to dance with the soldiers of the cantonment who were to pay fifteen cents for each dance. In varying forms this story was widely copied and caused some people to hesitate in their giving, although it was immediately declared by campaign officials to be "absolutely false in every detail."

Even in remote rural districts rumors arose. The nature of the reports against which workers had to contend is illustrated by an incident occurring in one Iowa community. After considerable trouble a chairman was found for a township; but "later it was reported to us," states the narrative of the county chairman, "that she changed her mind and telephoned all around the neighborhood warning the women to have nothing to do with the movement as she had discovered (?) that it was all a scheme to collect money for building houses of ill fame for the soldiers of Camp Dodge!!! We bombarded her with publicity material, but got no returns from that township. In less virulent form we ran into this notion a number of times. The work for Red Cross nurses made instant appeal everywhere; but 'Hostess Houses' were either suspected or openly disapproved of. Work to keep safe young girls who flocked to Des Moines met with much criticism from country women who thought 'mothers should look after their own girls' 'that was what they were doing.' "

Questions

1. What kind of general prejudice confronts women involved with the military?

2. Describe the kind of work women fund-raisers do.

3. How were the skills women learned in 1917–1918 applicable to the 1920s and later?

Henry Cabot Lodge, Opposition to the League of Nations (1919)

Woodrow Wilson was slow to realize that domestic politics could threaten his world peace plan. The president erred badly in not appointing any prominent Republicans as delegates to the Paris Conference (see text p. 633). Henry Cabot Lodge (1850–1924) would have been a likely choice as chairman of the Senate Foreign Relations Committee. Instead, Lodge led the opposition with attacks such as the following.

In this draft prepared for a constitution of a league of nations, which is now before the world, there is hardly a clause about the interpretation of which men do not already differ. As it stands there is serious danger that the very nations which sign the constitution of the league will quarrel about the meaning of the various articles before a twelvemonth has passed. It seems to have been very hastily drafted, and the result is crudeness and looseness of expression, unintentional, I hope. There are certainly many doubtful passages and open questions obvious in the articles which can not be settled by individual inference, but which must be made so clear and so distinct that we may all understand the exact meaning of the instrument to which we are asked to set our hands. The language of these articles does not appear to me to have the precision and unmistakable character which a constitution, a treaty, or a law ought to present. The language only too frequently is not the language of laws or statutes. The article concerning mandatories, for example, contains an argument and a statement of existing conditions. Arguments and historical facts have no place in a statute or a treaty. Statutory and legal language must assert and command, not argue and describe. I press this point because there is nothing so vital to the peace of the world as the sanctity of treaties. The suggestion that we can safely sign because we can always violate or abrogate is fatal not only to any league but to peace itself. You can not found world peace upon the cynical "scrap of paper" doctrine so dear to Germany. To whatever instrument the United States sets its hand it must carry out the provisions of that instrument to the last jot and tittle, and observe it absolutely both in letter and in spirit. If this is not done the instrument will become a source of controversy instead of agreement, of dissension instead of harmony. This is all the more essential because it is evident, although not expressly stated, that this league is intended to be indissoluble, for there is no provision for its termination or for the withdrawal of any signatory. We are left to infer that any nation withdrawing from the league exposes itself to penalties and probably to war. Therefore, before we ratify, the terms and language in which the terms are stated must be exact and as precise, as free from any possibility of conflicting interpretations, as it is possible to make them.

The explanation or interpretation of any of these doubtful passages is not sufficient if made by one man, whether that man be the President of the United States, or a Senator, or anyone else. These questions and doubts must be answered and removed by the instrument itself.

It is to be remembered that if there is any dispute about the terms of this constitution there is no court provided that I can find to pass upon differences of opinion as to the terms of the constitution itself. There is no court to fulfill the function which our Supreme Court fulfills. There is provision for tribunals to decide questions submitted for arbitration, but there is no authority to decide differing interpretations as to the terms of the instrument itself.

What I have just said indicates the vast importance of the form and the manner in which the agreements which we are to sign shall be stated. I now come to questions of substance, which seem to me to demand the most careful thought of the entire American people, and particularly of those charged with the responsibility of ratification. We abandon entirely by the proposed constitution the policy laid down by Washington in his Farewell Address and the Monroe doctrine. It is worse than idle, it is not honest, to evade or deny this fact, and every fairminded supporter of this draft plan for a league admits it. I know that some of the ardent advocates of the plan submitted to us regard any suggestion of the importance of the Washington policy as foolish and irrelevant. Perhaps it is. Perhaps the time has come when the policies of Washington should be abandoned; but if we are to cast them aside I think that at least it should be done respectfully and with a sense of gratitude to the great man who formulated them. For nearly a century and a quarter the policies laid down in the Farewell Address have been followed and adhered to by the Government of the United States and by the American people. I doubt if any purely political declaration has ever been observed by any people for so long a time. The principles of the Farewell Address in regard to our foreign relations have been sustained and acted upon by the American people down to the present moment. Washington declared against permanent alliances. He did not close the door on temporary alliances. He did not close the door on temporary alliances for particular purposes. Our entry in the great war just closed was entirely in accord with and violated in no respect the policy laid down by Washington. When we went to war with Germany we made no treaties with the nations engaged in the war against the German Government. The President was so careful in this direction that he did not permit himself ever to refer to the nations by whose side we fought as "allies," but always as "nations associated with us in the war." The attitude recommended by Washington was scrupulously maintained even under the pressure of the great conflict. Now, in the twinkling of an eye, while passion and emotion reign, the Washington policy is to be entirely laid aside and we are to enter upon a permanent and indissoluble alliance. That which we refuse to do in war we are to do in peace, deliberately, coolly, and with no war exigency. Let us not overlook the profound gravity of this step.

Washington was not only a very great man but he was also a very wise man. He looked far into the future and he never omitted human nature from his calculations. He knew well that human nature had not changed fundamentally since mankind had a history. Moreover, he was destitute of any personal ambitions to a degree never equaled by any other very great man known to us. In all the vital questions with which he dealt it was not merely that he thought of his country first and never thought of himself at all. He was so great a man that the fact that this country had produced him was enough of itself to justify the Revolution and our existence as a Nation. Do not think that I overstate this in the fondness of patriotism and with the partiality of one of his countrymen. The opinion I have expressed is the opinion of the world. . . .

That was the opinion of mankind then, and it is the opinion of mankind today, when his statue has been erected in Paris and is about to be erected in London. If we throw aside the political testament of such a man, which has been of living force down to the present instant, because altered circumstances demand it, it is a subject for deep regret and not for rejoicing. . . .

But if we put aside forever the Washington policy in regard to our foreign relations we must always remember that it carries with it the corollary known as the Monroe doctrine. Under the terms of this league draft reported by the committee to the peace conference the Monroe doctrine disappears. It has been our cherished guide and guard for nearly a century. The Monroe doctrine is based on the principle of self-preservation. To say that it is a question of protecting the boundaries, the political integrity, of the American States, is not to state the Monroe doctrine. . . . The real essence of that doctrine is that American questions shall be settled by Americans alone; that the Americas shall be separated from Europe and from the interference of Europe in purely American questions. That is the vital principle of the doctrine. . . .

Questions

1. What most disturbs Lodge about the constitution for the League of Nations?

2. Why does he mention George Washington and the other Founding Fathers?

3. Where is the supposed threat to the Monroe Doctrine and the conduct of American foreign policy?

Calvin Coolidge, The Boston Police Strike (1919)

Americans in 1919 worried over a number of social issues, including labor unrest. Many in the middle class feared that the Bolshevik Revolution was somehow responsible for what seemed to be an unending series of strikes; 4 million workers went on strike that year. Among them were Boston police officers, who had been denied a raise to compensate for wartime inflation. Quite unintentionally, the officers furthered the career of Massachusetts Governor Calvin Coolidge, who made this proclamation on the strike.

The Commonwealth of Massachusetts
By His Excellency Calvin Coolidge, Governor

A PROCLAMATION

There appears to be a misapprehension as to the position of the police of Boston. In the deliberate intention to intimidate and coerce the Government of this Commonwealth a large body of policemen, urging all others to join them, deserted their posts of duty, letting in the enemy. This act of theirs was voluntary, against the advice of their well wishers, long discussed and premeditated, and with the purpose of obstructing the power of the Government to protect its citizens or even to maintain its own existence. Its success meant anarchy. By this act through the operation of the law they dispossessed themselves. They went out of office. They stand as though they had never been appointed.

Other police remained on duty. They are the real heroes of this crisis. The State Guard responded most efficiently. Thousands have volunteered for the Guard and the Militia. Money has been contributed from every walk of life by the hundreds of thousands for the encouragement and relief of these loyal men. These acts have been spontaneous, significant, and decisive. I proposed to support all those who are supporting their own Government with every power which the people have entrusted to me.

There is an obligation, inescapable, no less solemn, to resist all those who do not support the Government. The authority of the Commonwealth cannot

be intimidated or coerced. It cannot be compromised. To place the maintenance of the public security in the hands of a body of men who have attempted to destroy it would be to flout the sovereignty of the laws the people have made. It is my duty to resist any such proposal. Those who would
counsel it join hands with those whose acts have threatened to destroy the
Government. There is no middle ground. Every attempt to prevent the formation of a new police force is a blow at the Government. That way treason
lies. No man has a right to place his own ease or convenience or the opportunity of making money above his duty to the State.

This is the cause of all the people. I call on every citizen to stand by me in
executing the oath of my office by supporting the authority of the Government and resisting all assaults upon it.

Given at the Executive Chamber, in Boston, this twenty-fourth day of September, in the year of our Lord one thousand nine hundred and nineteen, and
of the Independence of the United States of America the one hundred and
forty-fourth.

CALVIN COOLIDGE.

By His Excellency the Governor,
    HERBERT H. BOYNTON
Deputy, Acting Secretary of the Commonwealth

God save the Commonwealth of Massachusetts.

Questions

1. According to Coolidge, do the police have a right to strike? Why or why not?
2. Could Governor Coolidge have found a "middle ground"? Why or why not?
3. How does Coolidge transform a labor dispute into a question of patriotism?

Connections Questions

1. To what extent would the "intelligence" the army sought to measure (see
"Army Mental Tests") have mattered at the front, as detailed by Hervey Allen?
2. Drawing on the documents in this chapter, consider how war transforms society. Especially note its effect on women, minorities, politics, and government.
3. Could a person "patriotically" disagree with Henry Cabot Lodge ("Opposition to the League of Nations") or Calvin Coolidge ("The Boston Police
Strike")? If so, how?

CHAPTER 24

Modern Times: The 1920s

Frederick Lewis Allen, *Only Yesterday* (1931)

Frederick Lewis Allen (1890–1954) wrote Only Yesterday *in 1931. Yet the 1920s, just two years past, were part of a time that no longer existed for Allen and the rest of the nation. From the vantage point of the early Depression years, the complacency that had produced a Warren Harding died on Wall Street in October 1929.*

Back in the early spring of 1919, while Wilson was still at Paris, Samuel G. Blythe, an experienced observer of the political scene, had written in the *Saturday Evening Post* of the temper of the leaders of the Republican Party as they faced the issues of peace:

"You cannot teach an Old Guard new tricks. . . . The Old Guard surrenders but it never dies. Right at this minute, the ancient and archaic Republicans who think they control the destinies of the Republican Party—think they do!—are operating after the manner and style of 1896. The war hasn't made a dent in them. . . . The only way they look is backward." . . .

Consider how perfectly Harding met the requirements. Wilson was a visionary who liked to identify himself with "forward-looking men"; Harding, as Mr. Lowry put it, was as old-fashioned as those wooden Indians which used to stand in front of cigar stores, "a flower of the period before safety razors." Harding believed that statesmanship had come to its apogee in the days of McKinley and Foraker. Wilson was cold; Harding was an affable small-town man, at ease with "folks"; an ideal companion, as one of his friends expressed it, "to play poker with all Saturday night." Wilson had always been difficult of access; Harding was accessible to the last degree. Wilson favored labor, distrusted business men as a class, and talked of "industrial democracy"; Harding looked back with longing eyes to the good old days when the government didn't bother business men with unnecessary regulations, but provided them with fat tariffs and instructed the Department of Justice not to have them on its mind. Wilson was at loggerheads with Congress, and particularly with the Senate; Harding was not only a Senator, but a highly amenable Senator. Wilson had been adept at making enemies; Harding hadn't an enemy in the world. He was genuinely genial. "He had no knobs, he was the same size and smoothness all the way round," wrote Charles Willis Thompson. Wilson thought in terms of the whole world; Harding was for America first. And finally, whereas Wilson wanted America to exert itself nobly, Harding wanted to give it a rest. At Boston, a few weeks before the Convention, he had correctly expressed the growing desire of the people of the country and at the same time had unwittingly added a new word to the language, when he said, "America's present need is not heroics but healing; not nostrums but normalcy; not revolution but restoration; . . . not surgery but serenity." Here was a man whom a country wearied of moral obligations and the hope of the world could take to its heart.

It is credibly reported that the decision in favor of Harding was made by the Republican bosses as early as February, 1920, four months before the Convention. But it was not until four ballots had been taken at the Convention itself—with Wood leading, Lowden second, and Harding fifth—and the wilted delegates had dispersed for the night, that the leaders finally concluded to put Harding over. Harding's political manager, an Ohio boss named Harry M. Daugherty, had predicted that the Convention would be deadlocked and that the nomination would be decided upon by twelve or thirteen men "at two o'clock in the morning in a smoke-filled room." He was precisely right. . . .

On the morning of March 4, 1921—a brilliant morning with a frosty air and a wind which whipped the flags of Washington—Woodrow Wilson, broken and bent and ill, limped from the White House door to a waiting automobile, rode down Pennsylvania Avenue to the Capitol with the stalwart President-elect at his side, and returned to the bitter seclusion of his private house in S Street. Warren Gamaliel Harding was sworn in as President of the United States. The reign of normalcy had begun. . . .

The nation was spiritually tired. Wearied by the excitements of the war and the nervous tension of the Big Red Scare, they hoped for quiet and healing. Sick of Wilson and his talk of America's duty to humanity, callous to political idealism, they hoped for a chance to pursue their private affairs without governmental interference and to forget about public affairs. There might be no such word in the dictionary as normalcy, but normalcy was what they wanted. . . .

Warren Harding had two great assets, and these were already apparent. First, he looked as a President of the United States should. He was superbly handsome. His face and carriage had a Washingtonian nobility and dignity, his eyes were benign; he photographed well and the pictures of him in the rotogravure sections won him affection and respect. And he was the friendliest man who ever had entered the White House. He seemed to like everybody, he wanted to do favors for everybody, he wanted to make everybody happy. His affability was not merely the forced affability of the cold-blooded politician; it was transparently and touchingly genuine. "Neighbor," he had said to Herbert Hoover at their first meeting, during the war, "I want to be helpful." He meant it; and now that he was President, he wanted to be helpful to neighbors from Marion and neighbors from campaign headquarters and to the whole neighborly American public.

His liabilities were not at first so apparent, yet they were disastrously real. Beyond the limited scope of his political experience he was "almost unbelievably ill-informed," as William Allen White put it. His mind was vague and fuzzy. Its quality was revealed in the clogged style of his public addresses, in his choice of turgid and maladroit language ("noninvolvement" in European affairs, "adhesion" to a treaty), and in his frequent attacks of suffix trouble ("normalcy" for normality, "betrothment" for betrothal). It was revealed even more clearly in his helplessness when confronted by questions of policy to which mere good nature could not find the answer. White tells of Harding's coming into the office of one of his secretaries after a day of listening to his advisers wrangling over a tax problem, and crying out: "John, I can't make a damn thing out of this tax problem. I listen to one side and they seem right, and then—God!—I talk to the other side and they seem just as right, and here I am where I started. I know somewhere there is a book that will give me the truth, but, hell, I couldn't read the book. I know somewhere there is an economist who knows the truth, but I don't know where to find him and haven't the sense to know him and trust him when I find him. God! what a job!" His inability to discover for himself the essential facts of a problem and to think it through made him utterly dependent upon subordinates and friends whose mental processes were sharper than his own.

If he had been discriminating in the choice of his friends and advisers, all might have been well. But discrimination had been left out of his equipment. He appointed Charles Evans Hughes and Herbert Hoover and Andrew Mellon to Cabinet positions out of a vague sense that they would provide his administration with the necessary amount of statesmanship, but he was as ready to follow the lead of Daugherty or Fall or Forbes. He had little notion of technical fitness for technical jobs. Offices were plums to him, and he handed them out like a benevolent Santa Claus—beginning with the boys from Marion. He made his brother-in-law Superintendent of Prisons; he not only kept the insignificant Doctor Sawyer, of Sawyer's Sanitarium at Marion, as his personal physician, but bestowed upon him what a White House announcement called a "brigadier-generalcy" (suffix trouble again) and deputed him to study the possible coordination of the health agencies of the government; and for Comptroller of the Currency he selected D. R. Crissinger, a Marion lawyer whose executive banking experience was limited to a few months as president of the National City Bank and Trust Company—of Marion. . . .

And why did he choose such company? The truth was that under his imposing exterior he was just a common small-town man, an "average sensual man," the sort of man who likes nothing better in the world than to be with the old bunch when they gather at Joe's place for an all-Saturday-night session, with waistcoats unbuttoned and cigars between their teeth and an ample supply of bottles and cracked ice at hand. His private life was one of cheap sex episodes; as one reads the confessions of his mistress, who claims that as President he was supporting an illegitimate baby born hardly a year before his election, one is struck by the shabbiness of the whole affair: the clandestine meetings in disreputable hotels, in the Senate Office Building (where Nan Britton believed her child to have been conceived), and even in a coat-closet in the executive offices of the White House itself. (Doubts have been cast upon the truth of the story told in *The President's Daughter*, but is it easy to imagine any one making up out of whole cloth a supposedly autobiographical story compounded of such ignoble adventures?) Even making due allowance for the refracting of Harding's personality through that of Nan Britton, one sees with deadly clarity the essential ordinariness of the man, the commonness of his "Gee, dearie" and "Say, you darling," his being swindled out of a hundred dollars by card sharpers on a train ride, his naïve assurance to Nan, when detectives broke in upon them in a Broadway hotel, that they could not be arrested because it was illegal to detain a Senator while "en route to Washington to serve the people." Warren Harding's ambitious wife had tailored and groomed him into outward respectability and made a man of substance of him; yet even now, after he had reached the White House, the rowdies of the Ohio gang were fundamentally his sort. He had risen above them, he could mingle urbanely with their superiors, but it was in the smoke-filled rooms of the house in H Street that he was really most at home. . . .

Questions

1. What was the popular mood that led Republican leaders to pick Warren Harding?

2. How did Harding win the presidential nomination at the Republican convention?

3. According to Allen, what were Harding's attributes as president? His weaknesses?

4. How reliable is a history written so soon after an event or time? What might make such a work suspect?

Listerine Advertisement (1923)

The success of a consumer society depends in great part on advertising. When the artist Charles Dana Gibson drew his Gibson girls for Life *magazine in the 1890s, he pointed the way for modern advertising. During World War I, the propaganda activities of the Committee on Public Information (see text p. 630) showed again how mass audiences could be swayed by powerful images. This mouthwash ad from 1923 uses elements that have become standard in selling everything from beer to blue jeans.*

Questions

1. What is the role of the dentist in the ad?
2. What are the various reasons given for buying the product?
3. What kind of gender stereotyping is involved in both the artwork and the ad copy?

In his discreet way
he told her

IT had never occurred to her before. But in his discreet, professional way he was able to tell her. And she was sensible enough to be grateful instead of resentful.

In fact, the suggestion he made came to mean a great deal to her.

It brought her greater poise—that feeling of self-assurance that adds to a woman's charm—and, moreover, a new sense of daintiness that she had never been quite so sure of in the past.

* * * * * * * * *

Many people suffer in the same way. Halitosis (the scientific term for unpleasant breath) creeps upon you unawares. Usually you are not able to detect it yourself. And, naturally enough, even your best friends will not tell you.

Fortunately, however, halitosis is usually due to some local condition—often food fermentation in the mouth; something you have eaten; too much smoking. And it may be corrected by the systematic use of Listerine as a mouth wash and gargle.

Dentists know that this well-known antiseptic they have used for half a century, possesses these remarkable properties as a breath deodorant.

Your druggist will supply you. He sells lots of Listerine. It has dozens of other uses as a safe antiseptic. It is particularly valuable, too, at this time of year in combating sore throat. Read the circular that comes with each bottle.—*Lambert Pharmacal Company, Saint Louis, U. S. A.*

For **HALITOSIS**   *use* **LISTERINE**

Advertisement for *The Wanderer* (1926)

"The fact is I am quite happy in a movie, even a bad movie," the novelist Walker Percy admitted. In 1927, 60 million movie patrons most likely would have agreed. For the price of a ticket, a moviegoer could be transported from the Bronx or Mason City to ancient Babylon via scenes, this ad promises, "as convincing as a certified check." Whatever the level of authenticity, The Wanderer helped create a new national culture.

Questions

1. How does the ad draw the reader in?
2. What do the couple pictured at the top suggest?
3. How would a movie like *The Wanderer* homogenize such disparate places as New York City and small-town Iowa?

Grantland Rice, The "Four Horsemen" (1924)

Once they captured the public's imagination, the sports heroes of the 1920s never let go. Jack Dempsey, Red Grange, and Babe Ruth still convey power-ful images some seventy years later. Part of that success is due to the work of sportswriters. When Grantland Rice (1880–1954) wrote about a college foot-ball game, as he did here in 1924, the story concerned far more than the final score. This kind of writing made legends out of Notre Dame coach Knute Rockne and his backfield as it made sports into a kind of secular religion for the American viewing public.

Outlined against a blue-gray October sky, the Four Horsemen rode again. In dramatic lore they are known as Famine, Pestilence, Destruction and Death. These are only aliases. Their real names are Stuhldreher, Miller, Crow-ley and Layden. They formed the crest of the South Bend cyclone before which another fighting Army football team was swept over the precipice at the Polo Grounds yesterday afternoon as 55,000 spectators peered down on the bewildering panorama spread on the green plain below.

A cyclone can't be snared. It may be surrounded, but somewhere it breaks through to keep on going. When the cyclone starts from South Bend, where the candle lights still gleam through the Indiana sycamores, those in the way must take to storm cellars at top speed. Yesterday the cyclone struck again as Notre Dame beat the Army, 13 to 7, with a set of backfield stars that ripped and crashed through a strong Army defense with more speed and power than the warring cadets could meet. . . .

CYCLONE STARTS LIKE ZEPHYR

Rockne's light and tottering line was just as tottering as the Rock of Gibral-tar. It was something more than a match for the Army's great set of forwards, who had earned their fame before. Yet it was not until the second period that the first big thrill of the afternoon set the great crowd into a cheering whirl and brought about the wild flutter of flags that are thrown to the wind in exciting moments. At the game's start Rockne sent in almost entirely a second string cast. The Army got the jump and began to play most of the football. It was the Army attack that made three first downs before Notre Dame had caught its stride. The South Bend cyclone opened like a zephyr.

And then, in the wake of a sudden cheer, out rushed Stuhldreher, Miller, Crowley and Layden, the four star backs who had helped to beat the Army a year ago. Things were to be a trifle different now. After a short opening flurry in the second period, Wood, of the Army, kicked out of bounds on Notre Dame's 20-yard line. The cloud in the west at this point was no larger than a football. There was no sign of a tornado starting. But it happened to be at just this spot that Stuhldreher decided to put on his attack and begin the long and dusty hike.

DYNAMITE GOES OFF

On the first play the fleet Crowley peeled off fifteen yards and the cloud from the west was now beginning to show signs of lightning and thunder. The fleet, powerful Layden got six yards more and then Don Miller added ten. A forward pass from Stuhldreher to Crowley added twelve yards, and a moment later Don Miller ran twenty yards around Army's right wing. He was on his way to glory when Wilson, hurtling across the right of way, nailed him on the 10-yard line and threw him out of bounds. Crowley, Miller and Layden—Miller, Layden and Crowley—one or another, ripping and crashing through, as the Army defense threw everything it had in the way to stop this wild charge that had now come seventy yards. Crowley and Layden added five yards more and then, on a split play, Layden went ten yards across the line as if he had just been fired from the black mouth of a howitzer.

In that second period Notre Dame made eight first downs to the Army's none, which shows the unwavering power of the Western attack that hammered relentlessly and remorselessly without easing up for a second's breath. The Western line was going its full share, led by the crippled Walsh with a broken hand.

But always there was Miller or Crowley or Layden, directed through the right spot by the cool and crafty judgment of Stuhldreher, who picked his plays with the finest possible generalship. The South Bend cyclone had now roared eighty-five yards to a touchdown through one of the strongest defensive teams in the game. The cyclone had struck with too much speed and power to be stopped. It was the preponderance of Western speed that swept the Army back. . . .

ARMY LINE OUTPLAYED

Up to this point the Army had been outplayed by a crushing margin. Notre Dame had put under way four long marches and two of these had yielded touchdowns. Even the stout and experienced Army line was meeting more than it could hold. Notre Dame's brilliant backs had been provided with the finest possible interference, usually led by Stuhldreher, who cut down tackler after tackler by diving at some rival's flying knees. Against this each Army attack had been smothered almost before it got under way. Even the great Wilson, the star from Penn State, one of the great backfield runners of his day and time, rarely had a chance to make any headway through a massed wall of tacklers who were blocking every open route. . . .

The Army brought a fine football team into action, but it was beaten by a faster and smoother team. Rockne's supposedly light, green line was about as heavy as the Army's, and every whit as aggressive. What is even more important, it was faster on its feet, faster in getting around.

It was Western speed and perfect interference that once more brought about Army doom. The Army line couldn't get through fast enough to break up the attacking plays; and once started the bewildering speed and power of the Western backs slashed along for eight, ten and fifteen yards on play after play. And always in front of these offensive drives could be found the whirling form of Stuhldreher, taking the first man out of the play as cleanly as though he had used a hand grenade at close range. This Notre Dame interference was a marvelous thing to look upon.

It formed quickly and came along in unbroken order, always at terrific speed, carried by backs who were as hard to drag down as African buffaloes. On receiving the kickoff, Notre Dame's interference formed something after the manner of the ancient flying wedge, and they drove back up the field with the runner covered for twenty-five and thirty yards at almost every chance. And when a back such as Harry Wilson finds few chances to get started, you can figure upon the defensive strength that is barricading the road. Wilson is one of the hardest backs in the game to suppress, but he found few chances yesterday to show his broken field ability. You can't run through a broken field until you get there.

One strong feature of the Army play was its headlong battle against heavy odds. Even when Notre Dame had scored two touchdowns and was well on its way to a third, the Army fought on with fine spirit until the touchdown chance came at last. And when the chance came Coach McEwan had the play ready for the final march across the line. The Army has a better team than it had last year. So has Notre Dame. We doubt that any team in the country could have beaten Rockne's array yesterday afternoon, East or West. It was a great football team brilliantly directed, a team of speed, power and team play.

The Army has no cause for gloom over its showing. It played first class football against more speed than it could match.

Those who have tackled a cyclone can understand.

Questions

1. How does Rice transform a simple football game?
2. In the process, what does he do to the athlete?
3. How might sportswriting from this era have succeeded as a form of adult education?

Madison Grant, "Closing the Flood-Gates" (1930)

In his work on American nativism, historian John Higham has written of the "Tribal Twenties." Indeed, relations among racial and ethnic groups in the 1920s probably reached their lowest point of all the twentieth century. One of the leading nativists of the time was Madison Grant, a charter member in the Society of Colonial Wars. Grant, however, proved a poor student of the American Revolution. His essay on "the alien in our midst," excerpted here, appeared in 1930, though it maintained its 1920s mindset.

Our Federal Republic has been more fortunate than other modern nations in the exceptional character of its founders. The end of the colonial period was marked by the appearance on the scene of action of an extraordinary group of statesmen. These men were deeply versed in the lessons taught by classical history as well as in the practical application of representative government, which had been slowly evolving in England. Thus equipped, they formulated a written constitution which has been sound enough and elastic enough to stand the strain of 150 years. During this period the nation, organized under its provisions, expanded across the continent and emerged from the scanty resources of the backwoods into one of the great powers of the world. . . .

The Colonists were overwhelmingly Anglo-Saxon and were still more Nordic. Over ninety percent were British, including 82.1 per cent pure English and the balance Scotch and "Scotch-Irish." Over ninety-eight per cent were Nordic, including two and a half per cent Dutch and five and a half per cent German. This does not include the small Huguenot element, which was to a very great extent Nordic. Some, however, if not a majority, of the Pennsylvania Germans were Alpine. The only discordant elements were the Germans in Pennsylvania and small colonies of Portuguese at points on the New England coast, but the last were of little importance. The Founders, however, realized clearly that even these small minorities embodied a potential menace to the unity of the Republic. They realized also that the growth of the Colonial population was so rapid that there was no need of immigration.

Subsequent events have justified these opinions, and it is now known to the well-informed that the population of the United States would be as large as that of the present day, if there had been no immigration whatever. The originally large birth-rate of the native American falls wherever immigrants push in. Immigration means that for each new arrival from across the sea, one American is not born.

The introduction of serf labor to do rough work causes the withdrawal from such manual labor of the native Americans. One hears on every side, as an excuse for bringing in immigrants, that native Americans will not work in the field or in railroad gangs. It is true that they will not work alongside of Negroes or Slovaks or Mexicans, because a mean man makes the job a mean one. In the mountains of the South where there are no Negroes, and in those portions of the Northwest where there are few foreigners, native Americans can be seen today doing all the manual work, as was universally the case two generations ago.

A race that refuses to do manual work and seeks "white collar" jobs, is doomed through its falling birth-rate to replacement by the lower races or classes. In other words, the introduction of immigrants as lowly laborers means a replacement of race. These immigrants drive out the native; they do not mix with him. The Myth of the Melting Pot was the great fallacy of the last generation—fortunately it is utterly discredited today.

If the considered and recorded views of the Founders had prevailed and the nation after the Civil War had not made frantic efforts to "develop a continent" in a single generation and had not imported cheap serf labor for this purpose, the United States would have had today not only a population as large as its present one, but a population that was Nordic and Anglo-Saxon and homogeneous throughout.

Instead of a population homogeneous in race, religion, traditions and aspirations, as was the American nation down to 1840, we have—inserted into the body politic—an immense mass of foreigners, congregated for the most part in the large cities and in the industrial centers. The greater part of these foreigners, even if naturalized, are not in sympathy with American ideals, nor do they either understand or exercise the self-restraint necessary to govern a Republic. Many of these aliens, especially those from Eastern and Southern Europe were drawn from the lowest social strata of their homeland and mistake the liberty they find in America, and the easy-going tolerance of the native American, for an invitation to license and crime.

The closing years of the decade between 1840 and 1850 brought in the first of these foreigners. Germans, fleeing from their fatherland after the collapse of the revolutionary movements, for the most part took up unoccupied lands in the West, although some of them settled in the large cities, notably in St. Louis and Cincinnati. While it cannot be said that they improved the American population either physically or intellectually yet they accepted our form of government and made effort to maintain its traditions.

The Irish, on the other hand, who arrived a few years earlier, settled in the large cities and industrial centers of the North. These Irish were drawn from the submerged and primitive peasantry of South and West Ireland. In race they were partly Mediterranean and partly Nordic mixed with remnants of an aboriginal population. They were, for the most part, day laborers and domestic servants and Catholics. They came into conflict with the native Americans by trying to introduce their church institutions and parochial schools, which were and are regarded as hostile to the public school system of the United States.

When concentrated in large cities these Irish were responsive to the leadership of bosses and were organized in the solid blocs which demoralize our municipal politics. Our republican representative system, coupled with universal suffrage, does not work any too well even in rural districts, but it breaks down utterly in our cities. In recent decades the Irish have advanced somewhat in the social scale, because newcomers, the Poles, Slovaks, and Italians have in turn replaced them in the more menial tasks. . . .

There were few Roman Catholics in the colonies. The Colonial laws were everywhere drastic against Catholics and even in Maryland, which is constantly referred to as a "Catholic colony," the Catholics were in such a great minority that in 1715, they were actually deprived of the franchise by the Protestant majority. John Fiske estimates the number of Roman Catholics at only one-twelfth of the population of Maryland in 1661–1689. The alleged tolerance said to have been exhibited by the Catholics of Maryland cannot be claimed as voluntary on their part for Lord Baltimore received his charter from a Protestant King on the express condition that no religious restrictions against Protestants were to be enacted.

Of their numbers in the United States the Official Catholic Year Book for the year 1928 says: "In 1775 there were only about 23,000 white Catholics in the country, administered to by thirty-four priests, the larger portion living in Maryland and Pennsylvania." In a book published in 1925, under the sanction of M. J. Curley, the Catholic Archbishop of Baltimore, in attempting to estimate the strength of the Catholic population in colonial times, it is stated that in 1790 the total Catholic population of the United States was 35,000 of which about 25,000 were Irish. From this it is obvious that a large proportion of the immigration even from Southern Ireland, and nearly all the immigration from Ulster in colonial times, was Protestant.

Undesirable as was substantially the whole of the immigration of the nineteenth century, it might have been partially Americanized, but, just when that transformation was beginning, two events of great portent happened. One was the exhaustion of free public land open to settlement, and the other was the extension of manufacturing with its call for cheap labor. America entered on a career of industrial development, which, while producing great wealth for a few, transformed whole countrysides and farming villages into factory towns. . . .

Americans were shocked to find what an utterly subordinate place was occupied by the American stock in the opinions of some aliens. An example of this was a poster issued by some thoughtless enthusiast in the Treasury Department in one of the appeals for Liberty Loans. It showed a Howard Chandler Christy girl of pure Nordic type, pointing with pride to a list of names and saying "AMERICANS ALL." Then followed the list:

DuBois	Villotto
Smith	Levy
O'Brien	Turovich
Cejka	Kowalski
Jaucke	Chriczanevicz
Pappandrikopolous	Knutson
Andrassi	Gonzales

The one "American" in that list, so far as he figures at all, is hidden under the sobriquet of "Smith," and there is, we must presume, an implied suggestion that the very beautiful lady is the product of this remarkable melting pot. . . .

Questions

1. How do Grant's ideas differ from those of the Social Darwinists (see text p. 590 and Chapter 19, William Graham Sumner, "The Forgotten Man")?

2. What constitutes Grant's definition of race? How does he define "native Americans"?

3. What groups in the 1920s would have embraced Grant's argument (see text p. 654)? Why?

Marcus Garvey, Editorial
in the *Negro World* (1924)

The Ku Klux Klan presented one view of African-Americans, and Marcus Garvey offered another. The Jamaican-born Garvey (1887–1940) simply reversed the Klan's argument: the United States, not African-Americans, was the problem. The solution appeared in this editorial Garvey wrote in 1924 after the Fourth International Convention of the Negro Peoples of the World. The editorial's rhetoric helped draw 4 million followers to Garvey's Universal Negro Improvement Association.

THE ENEMIES AT WORK

During the whole of the convention and a little prior thereto, the enemies of our cause tried to provoke and confuse our deliberation by the many unpleasant things they systematically published against the Universal Negro Improvement Association. Our enemies in America, especially the Negro Republican politicians of New York, used the general time fuse to explode on our tranquility and thereby destroy the purpose for which we were met, but as is customary, the Universal Negro Improvement Association is always ready for the enemy. They had arranged among themselves to get certain individuals of the Liberian government along with Ernest Lyons, the Liberian Consul-General, in Baltimore, himself a reactionary Negro politician of the old school, to circulate through the Negro press and other agencies such unpleasant news purported to be from Liberia as to create consternation in our ranks and bring about the demoralization that they hoped and calculated for, but as usual, the idiots counted without their hosts. The Universal Negro Improvement Association cannot be destroyed that way, in that it is not only an organization, but is the expression of the spiritual desires of the four hundred million black peoples of the world.

OUR COLONIZATION PROGRAM

As everybody knows, we are preparing to carry out our Liberian colonization program during this and succeeding months. Every arrangement was practically made toward this end. . . . Unfortunately, after all arrangements had been made in this direction, our steamship secured to carry the colonists and all plans laid, these enemies of progress worked in every way to block the carrying out of the plan. For the purpose of deceiving the public and carrying out their obstruction, they tried to make out by the protest that was filed by Ernest Lyons of Baltimore, with the government of Washington, that our Association was of an incendiary character and that it was the intention of the organization to disturb the good relationship that existed between Liberia and other friendly powers. A greater nonsense could not have been advanced by any idiot. What could an organization like the Universal Negro Improvement Association do to destroy the peace of countries that are already established and recognized? . . .

NEGROES DOUBLE-CROSSING

Everybody knows that the hitch in the colonization plan of the Universal Negro Improvement Association in Liberia came about because of double-crossing. The Firestone Rubber and Tire Company, of Ohio, has been spending large sums of money among certain people. The offer, no doubt, was so attractive as to cause certain persons to found the argument to destroy the Universal Negro Improvement Association, so as to favor the Firestone Rubber and Tire Company who, subsequently, got one million acres of Liberian land for actually nothing, to be exploited for rubber and minerals, and in the face of the fact that Liberia is one of the richest rubber countries in the world, an asset that should have been retained for the Liberian people and members of the black race, but now wantonly given over to a white company to be exploited in the interest of white capital, and to create another international complication, as evidenced in the subsequent subjugation of Haiti and the Haitians, after the New York City Bank established itself in Haiti in a similar way as the Firestone Rubber and Tire Company will establish itself in Liberia. Why, every Negro who is doing a little thinking, knows that after the Firestone Rubber and Tire Company gets into Liberia to exploit the one million acres of land, it is only a question of time when the government will be taken out of the hands of the Negroes who rule it, and Liberia will become a white man's country in violation of the constitution of that government as guaranteeing its soil as a home for all Negroes of all climes and nationalities who desire to return to their native land. The thing is so disgraceful that we, ourselves, are ashamed to give full publicity to it, but we do hope that the people of Liberia, who control the government of Liberia, will be speedily informed so that they, through the Senate and House of Representatives, will repudiate the concessions granted to the Firestone Rubber and Tire Company, so as to save their country from eternal spoilation. If the Firestone Rubber and Tire Company should get the concessions in Liberia of one million acres of land, which should have been granted to the Universal Negro Improvement Association for development by Negroes for the good of Negroes, it simply means that in another short while thousands of white men will be sent away from America by the Firestone Rubber and Tire Company to exploit their concessions. These white men going out to colonize, as they generally regard tropical countries, will carry with them the spirit of all other white colonists, superiority over and subjugation of native peoples; hence it will only be a question of time when these gentlemen will change the black population of Liberia into a mongrel race, as they have done in America, [the] West Indies and other tropical countries, and there create another race problem such as is confusing us now in these United States of America. These white gentlemen are not going to allow black men to rule and govern them, so, like China and other places, there will be such complications as to ultimately lead to the abrogation of all native control and government and the setting up of new authority in a country that once belonged to the natives. . . .

MOVE THE LITTLE BARRIERS

So, the little barriers that have been placed in the way by the envious and wicked of our own race can easily be removed if we will get together and work together. Now that the convention has risen, let us redouble our energy everywhere to put the program over. Let us work with our hearts, soul and minds to see that everything is accomplished for the good of the race. We must have our ship in action by next month. At least, we are calculating to have our ship sail out of New York by the 29th of October, laden with the first cargo for the tropics, and to bring back to us tropical fruits and produce, and from thence to sail for Africa, the land of our fathers. Help us make this possible. . . .

With very best wishes for your success, I have the honor to be, Your obedient servant,

Marcus Garvey
President-General
Universal Negro Improvement Association

Questions

1. What does Garvey propose?
2. Why does he consider black Republicans the enemy? What is his purpose in attacking the Firestone Company?
3. How do Garvey's views differ from those of W. E. B. Du Bois (see Chapter 19, W. E. B. Du Bois, "Of Mr. Booker T. Washington")?

Connections Questions

1. Compare the electronic politics of today to the smoke-filled backroom politics of Warren G. Harding's time. How different are they? How similar?

2. Do the ads reprinted in this chapter differ in degree or kind from current advertising? Explain.

3. To what extent, if any, do Madison Grant and Marcus Garvey offer variations on the same argument?

CHAPTER 25

The Great Depression

Stuart Chase, *Prosperity: Fact or Myth* (1929)

Stuart Chase handed in the manuscript for his provocatively titled Prosperity: Fact or Myth *in October 1929, just days before the stock market crash; the book was rushed into print and shipped to bookstores by December. Chase (1888–1985) suggested that much of the prosperity of the 1920s was illusory. In the concluding chapter, he argued that a secure and lasting prosperity awaited the "liberation of the engineer," by which he meant the application of scientific planning principles to economic growth and development.*

BALANCING THE BOOKS

We have let us say an onion. The onion represents the total economic life of the United States at the present time. The heart of the onion is prosperity. How large does it bulk?

First, we must strip off all the states not included in the Middle Atlantic, East North Central, and Pacific states. The National Bureau of Economics finds that by and large these states have not prospered.

Second, in the prosperous belt, we strip off most of the farmers; they have not prospered.

Third, we strip off a large section of the middle class. The small business man, the independent storekeeper, the wholesaler, many professional men and women, have failed to keep income on a par with the new standard of living.

Fourth, we strip off the unemployed. Machinery appears to be displacing factory, railroad, and mining workers—and recently mergers are displacing executives, salesmen and clerks—faster than they can find employment in other fields. The net increase in "technological unemployment" since 1920 exceeds 650,000 men and women.

Fifth, we strip off the coal industry which has been in the doldrums throughout the period.

Sixth, we strip off the textile industry which has been seriously depressed.

Seventh, the boot and shoe industry. Ditto.

Eighth, the leather industry.

Ninth, the shipbuilding industry.

Tenth, the railroad equipment industry.

Eleventh, we strip off the excessive number of businesses which have gone bankrupt during the era.

Twelfth, we strip off those millions of unskilled workers who were teetering on the edge of a bare subsistence in 1922, and by no stretch of the imagination can be called prosperous to-day. The best that can be said is that their position is a little less precarious than it was.

In short only a part of the country has been prosperous, and even in that part are at least 11 soft spots—some of them very unpleasantly soft.

What then remains? . . .

The onion has shrunk, but it has not disappeared. We shall not list all the surviving leaves, but among the significant are:

1. A 20 per cent increase in the national income per capita from 1922 to 1928.
2. A 30 per cent increase in physical production.
3. A 100 per cent increase in the profits of the larger corporations.
4. A housing program expanding faster than population.
5. An increase in average health and longevity.
6. An increase in educational facilities greatly surpassing the growth of population.
7. A per capita increase in savings and insurance.
8. A booming stock market up to October 1929.
9. A 5-hour decline in the average working week.
10. A slowly rising wage scale against a fairly stationary price level.
11. An increasingly fecund, alert and intelligent science of management, resulting primarily in an ever growing productivity per worker. . . .

The trouble with nearly every item on this second list is that while it indicates that we are more prosperous than we were, nothing whatever is said about the *extent of prosperity* from which we started. The base line is missing. If we were barely comfortable in 1922, we ought to be reasonably comfortable to-day. But of course the fact is that some 80 per cent of all American families lived below the budget of health and decency in 1922, and the 20 per cent increase in per capita income since that date, while it has helped to be sure, still leaves probably two-thirds of all families below the line. Unfortunately, too, the 20 per cent cannot all go into intrinsically better food, housing and clothing, but must be applied to appease the clamoring salesmen of the new standard of living with their motor cars, radios, tootsie-rolls, silk stockings, moving pictures, near-fur coats and beauty shoppes. . . .

We have added a little real income and considerable fluff to the totally inadequate distribution of goods and services obtaining in 1922. Is this prosperity in the deeper sense? No. The most that can be said is that the last 7 or 8 years have registered a rate of advance in the direction of a prosperity which may some day be achieved. . . .

A beautiful technique this new science of management; the crowning achievement of prosperity. Given a free hand, it might remake American industry humanly as well as technically. Given a free hand, it might abolish poverty, immeasurably diminish the stresses and strains which have dogged every step of the industrial revolution since the days of [James] Watt. It might flood the nation with essential and even beautiful goods at a fraction of their present cost, raise the curse of Adam, and lay the basis for, if not positively usher in, one of the noblest civilizations which the world has ever seen.

But the hands of management are not free. The technician is constantly undone by the sales department, which floundering in a pecuniary economy, sees no other way—and indeed there is no other way—to maintain capacity than by style changes, annual models, advertising misrepresentation, and high pressure merchandising. He is undone by the vested interests of the owners who demand their pound of flesh in rent, interest and dividends *now*, with no thought for the rounded perfection of engineering principles, and the time which they—and the physical laws which sanction them—demand. Foresters have worked out the technique for a perpetual lumber supply, with annual growth beautifully balanced against annual needs. But private enterprise cannot wait. Tear me down this grove tomorrow—and let the slash burn, and the soil run into the sea—I have a note maturing. So we cut our priceless heritage of forest four times as fast as it grows. In 30 years, at the present rate of exhaustion, it will be all but gone.

Above all, the technician is undone by failure to inaugurate a national system of super-management, whereby production might be articulated to consumptive needs, and the fabulous wastes of excess plants, excess machines, excess overhead costs, uneconomically located industries, cross hauling, jam, tangle and bottlenecks, brought under rational control. That such super-management is not beyond human capacity to operate, the experiences of the Supreme Economic Council during the War, and of the Russian Gosplan [the Soviet State Planning Committee] today, amply demonstrate. What a lordly science of engineering we might have, and to what great human benefit, if industrial anarchy gave way to industrial coördination and socialization in those fields where it logically belongs.

Prosperity in any deeper sense awaits the liberation of the engineer. If the owners will not get off his back—and why should they; they pay him little enough and he fills their safe deposit boxes?—I, for one, would not be sorry to see him combine with the wayfaring man to lift them off. A complicated technical structure should be run by engineers, not hucksters. But the technician is the modern Prometheus in chains.

Questions

1. Why does Chase compare the American economy in the 1920s to an onion?
2. What economic danger signs suggest that prosperity will not last much longer?
3. What does Chase mean when he argues that securing future prosperity depends on the "liberation of the engineer"?

Proposals for Recovery (1930–1931)

The depression hit with such force that the business community was left confused and dispirited. Corporations no less than workers carried the "invisible scar" (see text p. 670) that economic collapse had left behind. Perhaps the problem was a loss of nerve. Maybe a return to prosperity could be sparked by a National Sales Month—or miniature golf. No one really knew.

SNAP OUT OF IT!

Snap out of it! Gloom has reigned long enough. It is time to drop cowardice and exercise courage. Deflation has run an ample course—to carry it much further would mean endless destruction, criminal destruction. The country is sound at the core, sound politically, sound financially, sound industrially, sound commercially. Agricultural prices, too, have been thoroughly deflated, even overdepressed. The nation has its health. It has lost little or none of its real wealth. It is living saner than when everyone was unrestrainedly optimistic. The time has come to cast off our doubts and fears, our hesitancy and timidity, our spasm of "nerves." Summer, the season for holiday-making, is over. The season for fresh planning, new enterprise, hard work, driving force, initiative, concentration on business, is here. Let's go.
    Snap out of it!

NEW BUSINESS WILL ARISE!

*A Storehouse of Facts for Men Who Seek to Utilize
Nation's Latent and Enormous Buying Power—
The Example of Miniature Golf*

By Julius Klein
Assistant Secretary of Commerce

Vigilance and vigor (as one need hardly say) are among the prime essentials of any business victory. Seldom, indeed, is the American business man deficient in the vigor with which he attacks a commercial problem. His energy, his briskness, his whirlwind tactics are proverbial. But such robust vitality is unfortunately not accompanied, in all cases, by a maximum of vigilance—if one includes in that term the painstaking, pertinacious scrutiny of every single fact, every collection of relevant data, that might bear upon his efforts. The value of such study is being realized increasingly—but do we not all know the business man who can be considered only as a mere slap-dash empiricist, with a breezy confidence in hunches and a deep, ingrained dislike of statistical tables and bar-charts?

Yet statistics are quite capable of proving his salvation. His business, in many instances, is dependent absolutely on his knowing commercial trends, economic movements, broad and sweeping social forces. In few decades in all history have such startling changes taken place as those that we have witnessed in the past ten years. A thorough knowledge of those changes may well provide the firmest conceivable basis for encouragement right now. Especially conducive to such optimism are the facts about the steady growth in American income and buying power.

The National Bureau of Economic Research tells us that the total realized income of the people of the continental United States in 1928 was more than $89,000,000,000. And that did not include the income that might be imputed to housewives and householders for services rendered to their families, nor employees' expense accounts, nor the money earned through odd-job employment. That means a per capita income of $740. In the course of a year we are now earning nearly $25,000,000,000 more than we were ten years ago. And when we extend the comparison to 20 years ago, we find that the national income has more than trebled over that period. Even when we make all due allowance for price changes, the increase is very great.

Let us institute, for a moment, a comparison on the basis of "1913 dollars"—that is, dollars having a buying power equivalent to that which they had in 1913. We find that the purchasing power (in such 1913 dollars) of the total wages, salaries, pensions, etc., received by the employees of all American industries was $29,967,000,000 in 1928, as compared with $15,946,000,000 in 1909 and $18,822,000,000 in 1913. The purchasing power, in 1913 dollars, of the average annual earnings of the American wage-worker advanced from $556 in 1909, $594 in 1913, and $550 in 1921 to $705 in 1927 (the most recent year for which a dependable figure is available).

The National Bureau of Economic Research has well said that "the growth in per capita income since 1921 must be regarded as a remarkable phenomenon. The indications are that, in terms of immediate ability to buy goods for consumption purposes, the average American was approximately one-third better off in 1927 than he was in 1921." And the bureau goes on to draw the inevitable conclusions: "Under these circumstances it is not surprising that a tremendous market has developed for furs, automobiles, radios, and other luxuries which were previously beyond the reach of the masses of the population."

More recent, and undeniably significant, is the statement made just the other day by the United States Bureau of Labor Statistics, that the buying power of the dollar expanded more than a tenth in the year that ended June, 1930—and it is nearly a sixth greater than it was four years ago.

These are a few concrete facts (I shall speak later of certain "intangibles") that indicate the rise of new markets for manufacturers and merchants who possess the vision to discern and develop them. . . .

[The] Census of Distribution will throw light on numerous domains of business which have been shrouded hitherto in an almost impenetrable obscurity. When integrated and coordinated with other Census data and relevant facts collected by governmental and able private agencies, these data should make it possible for every business man to evaluate his own position and methods in relation to his competitors, his customers and his sources of supply. From such information, any wide-awake industrialist or merchant can draw concretely useful conclusions as to the dominant commercial currents of a tangible sort.

To be sure, he needs also to be *"en rapport"* with the intangible currents— and this is a bit more difficult. Of one thing, however, he may be very certain: Some of the most potent of those currents spring from the general rise in human standards, attendant upon the growth in income that I mentioned a moment ago.

Customers are constantly displaying more discrimination. They are demanding not alone that an article shall work (that primary pragmatic test)— they are requiring also that it shall possess those intangible but unmistakable factors of distinction and of style.

Good taste among the buying public has been incalculably heightened during this past decade. It has advanced in a rapidly ascending spiral. Any given achievement in the creation of artistic merchandise has enhanced the public receptivity to many others—possibly in unrelated lines. There has been a tremendous stimulation, a restless, eager stirring of what I may call, perhaps, the "mass aesthetic sense."

It is perfectly obvious, of course, that the basic cause of this has been the rise in living standards—the widespread elevation of the scale of creature comforts that prove satisfying to the average man. And we must not be led for a single moment to believe that such standards have suffered any grave, enduring damage through the temporary business recession that had its beginning last October. No—that upward surge is too insistent—the typical desires and aptitudes arising from it have become too ineradicably implanted—to permit of any lasting impairment in this land!

The American people have been traveling, at home and in foreign countries, to a previously inconceivable extent, and their observation has been keen. Travel has been revealing once-unimagined vistas—poignant beauty, arresting design, novel treatment and applications of the articles of common use.

The almost miraculous advance in communication has contributed to this greater sensitiveness to style. Radio descriptions have awakened curiosity— have excited lively interest. A new and fascinating factor has appeared in the radio transmission, even across the broad Atlantic, of pictures of designs of goods that are peculiarly susceptible to style.

Entertainment plays a vital role—no less influential because it is subtle and, in many cases, not immediately perceived. Motion pictures especially (both the purely amusement subjects and the frankly industrial films) have intensified the public consciousness of style.

The Census has disclosed, once more, the seemingly almost irresistible impulse toward urbanization. Our titanic cities are expanding. And in those enormous masses of humanity—with their quick interchanges of ideas, their swirling complexity and immediacy of movement—the influence of style is singularly acute. In the ferment of this urban life, new conceptions are being incessantly produced. Many of these are significant—potentially very valuable—to manufacturers and merchants, if they will keep their eyes open and grasp the opportunities.

We now need, in the city, many things that we once associated only with the seashore or the countryside. This statement may seem strange at first (and I admit quite frankly that its application is restricted), but it is supported by ample facts.

Take, merely as an example, the case of sporting goods of certain types. Let us consider bathing-suits. Not so long ago, these were used almost solely in the open—at the beaches and along our streams. But to-day that condition has been absolutely changed by the building of many splendid urban pools (both indoor and outdoor), adorned with impressive names such as "Plage Biarritz," provided with bronzed lifeguards, and necessitating the wearing of good, attractive bathing-suits. At the old swimming-hole to which we resorted in the days of our youth, we were happy and hilarious in a cheap dingy garment (or maybe none at all)—but that, of course, would never do at the glittering, resplendent "Pompeian Pool" that now allures our patronage. Here we see the creation of a new market, a new demand—and one in which that factor of style-consciousness plays assuredly a potent part.

So, too, with the amazing rise of those miniature golf courses that are springing up by the thousands. The players are the cynosure of many eyes, in near-by structures and on the street. I think there can be no doubt that this new game has stimulated a demand for handsome sports attire on the part of countless persons who would not otherwise have cared so much to garb themselves in gaudy raiment.

Our researchers at the Department of Commerce have estimated that there are now (in the middle of August) no fewer than 25,000 of these bantam-size golf courses in the country, with a value of perhaps $125,000,000 (not including the real estate involved), and by the time this article appears in print there will undoubtedly be thousands more. Think of the market thus created for some rather unusual construction materials—for paints and oils— for electricity—for golf balls and, more especially, for putters! And the end is not in sight. Our Textile Division at Washington is putting forward right now the thoroughly sound idea that, as a protection in inclement weather, these miniature courses need a covering of tent or awning material, which should prove a profitable investment at a cost of from $750 to $3,000 per course. This gives promise of developing a market for millions of dollars' worth of canvas, duck, and metal or wood supports. This entire situation illustrates forcefully the manner in which new businesses may arise unexpectedly and vigorously, in a way to hearten many trades. . . .

NATIONAL SALES MONTH SUGGESTED

H. E. Kranhold, vice-president of Brown & Bigelow, writes suggesting a National Sales Month. He says: "It is estimated that there are five million salesmen in the United States. Suppose it were possible to secure the interest and co-operation of every organization employing salesmen to put on a National Sales Month at the same time. Suppose that each one, through this extra effort, secured two additional orders during the month. Suppose these orders averaged $10. That would mean one hundred million dollars' worth of additional sales. It has been estimated that every dollar in a sale circulates approximately ten times in the course of producing what enters into the manufacture of the goods sold. That would represent, theoretically, a billion dollars. There isn't much question but what, if every organization in the United States did put on a National Sales and a National Buying Month, business immediately would turn for the better. Prosperity does not precede but follows sales."

He suggests December as the most appropriate month, as it is then that "thoughts are turning to Christmas, when retail stores are busy and the result of a big December business would make a happier Christmas for thousands and thousands of people. It would reflect itself in the new year by making business better in January."

Well, can it be organized?

Perhaps Mr. Gifford may see merit in this plan and, with his unique organizing ability, set in motion the machinery necessary for effective action, thus moving business off what Owen D. Young called its "dead center."

Doing nothing leads inevitably to everybody being undone.

Fear is failure—failure of faith.

Questions

1. Why would "snapping out of it" matter?
2. How would a National Sales Month work?
3. Explain how new businesses would have a ripple effect in generating prosperity.

John McCutcheon, "A Wise Economist Asks a Question" (1932)

In a career that spanned forty-three years at the Chicago Tribune, *John T. McCutcheon (1870–1949) demonstrated a rare sense of compassion for a political cartoonist. There is nothing obvious or partisan in his drawing, which may help explain why it won a Pulitzer Prize.*

Questions

1. How does McCutcheon make the man a sympathetic character?
2. Why does he have a squirrel ask the question?
3. What is McCutcheon saying about the American belief in personal responsibility?

Will Rogers, "President Hoover" (1930)

The Depression did nothing to diminish the popularity of radio; if any-thing, it encouraged people to stay at home and turn on free entertainment. Humorist Will Rogers (1879–1935) provided the following view of Herbert Hoover on a broadcast airing April 20, 1930. Listeners who tuned in expect-ing to hear a sendup of the embattled president may have been surprised.

There is Orthodox Quakers and then the modern Quakers. The Orthodox stayed in Philadelphia and the modern ones got out. The further away from Philadelphia they got, the more modern they was. Mr. Hoover's is about the most modern of all of them. They got to Iowa. Of course, there was no California in those days. The motion picture camera hadn't been invented, and then climate was only a condition and not a sales commodity.

Mr. Hoover, he was left an orphan when he was a little boy, at a very early age, and he went to live for a while with an uncle. This uncle lived down in Pawhuska, Indian Territory, now Oklahoma, Pawhuska, Oklahoma. Pawhuska, to give you an idea—now of course maybe you never heard of it—Pawhuska is just fifty-five miles from Claremore, and it is near Tulsa, too, but it is fifty-five miles from Claremore, and he used to come to Claremore. People did from Tulsa, too. Pawhuska and Tulsa people used to come over to Claremore for their mail and to find out what time it was. We had a clock there.

Well, it has always been credited that this splendid association with these fine people that he met down in that country has really molded Mr. Hoover's future character. I mean, I think that is where he got his wonderful charac-ter, was in meeting those people. Just this touch of kind of artistic environ-ment that he got in our country there, that has made him what he is, you know. He wouldn't have developed anything like that if he had stayed any-where else. If he had stayed in Iowa or gone directly to California, he would have just turned out to be another real estate salesman, that is about all he would have been. . . .

The first job he got was in Australia. Well, he thought Australia was too wild a country to get married and take a wife to, that is, a new wife, so he decided to wait until he got to a more civilized place to go before he married. Then he figured, too, that after he got back from Australia, why he wouldn't have to go in debt for the license. So he waited until he finished this job in Aus-tralia, and he got a job in the interior of China. It was quiet and nice and fine there. He got married and went there. China gave him a wonderful reception. They put on the Boxer Rebellion for him when he arrived. They was barri-caded in the town of Zin Zin or Tin Tin, or something like that, or Sen Sen, I don't know the name of it, one of those names, they all sound alike besides

Hongkong. They was barricaded there for a long time, and the Chinamen shot at them for three months. That was for a honeymoon.

He went to South America and Siberia and Africa and Alaska and once in his early days he got as far away from civilization as to do some government surveying in Arkansas. That is my wife's state, I pulled that for her.

Through all these years of travel, Mrs. Hoover stuck right with him and she helped him out in his work. He would think up new places to go, and she would look up the time table and see how to get there. If they stayed two weeks in any one place, why Mr. Hoover joined the Old Settlers Club.

Mrs. Hoover is not only a charming woman but a very brilliant woman. She helped him translate an old book on engineering that was written some four hundred years ago, and nobody knew what the book said, and they figured it out, and of course we don't know whether they figured it out right or not because nobody knows what the book said.

That brings him up to the war in 1914. He was chairman of the American Relief Association, and he helped feed Belgians, and a little later it was found we was worse off than the Belgians, so they brought him home to feed us. He is always feeding somebody. Now he is feeding the Republicans. No Armenian that ever lived can eat more than one of them can.

I always did want to see him elected. I wanted to see how far a competent man could go in politics. It has never been tried before. . . .

Mr. Hoover, you know, he was originally a Democrat himself when he come back. When we was going to run him in 1920, we had him all framed up to run on our side. A lot of people tell you that Mr. Hoover ain't a politician. Well, he ain't a politician in a way, but he is a smart fellow all right, you know. You didn't see him running with the Democrats, did you? No, he liked us all right, but he didn't run with us. He waited until he got on the right side before he run, you know.

The politicians, you know, they have all been against him. That is really what elected him. The minute the people found out the politicians didn't want him, the whole nation said, He is the kind of fellow we want.

Of course, we kid about his commissions and all that, but I tell you in this late Wall Street crisis, I really believe that the way he got all those big men together, really saved a very delicate situation there, and you know there is quite a psychology in getting a lot of big men on commissions with you. You have just got that many more men working with you, you know. Any time you tell a fellow you will put him on some committee or something, he thinks, you know, it kind of makes him do a little better, you know, and I think that is one thing that Mr. Hoover did about that.

Of course, they talk about how everything is getting along and everything. He has only been in a year, and it all depends on what we do the last year. You know, the memory of a voter—you can give him three years of prosperity and then if you give him the last year and he ain't doing very well, a voter just goes to the polls and if he has got a dollar you stay in, and if he ain't got a dollar, you go out, you know. The memory of a voter is about as long as a billy goat. So it is all going to depend on how Mr. Hoover makes out the last year. . . .

You know, when Mr. Coolidge was in and just let everything go along, that was wonderful. Nobody ever asked Coolidge to fix a thing. We just let everything go, and everybody grabbed off what he could and all, never fixed anything. We are great people to go to extremes. We just jump from one thing to another. Now Mr. Hoover is elected and we want him to fix everything. Farm relief—we want him to fix the farmer. Now, the farmer never had relief. You know what I mean. He never had it even under Lincoln, he never had it. But he wants it under Hoover. He thinks Mr. Hoover ought to give him some relief.

Prohibition—they think Mr. Hoover ought to fix prohibition. Well, my goodness, Mr. Hoover can't—I don't know, but if I remember right, the boys had a couple of nips under Calvin's administration, I think they did.

Prosperity—millions of people never had it under nobody and never will have it under anybody, but they all want it under Mr. Hoover.

Women—women in this country, they think Mr. Hoover, my goodness, he ought to come in and wash the dishes, you know, and help take care of the baby or something. They are all wanting something from Mr. Hoover. If the weather is wrong, we blame it on Hoover. So all in all, I believe he is doing a pretty good job, and I only claim one distinction, and that is that I am the only person that I know of that is not on one of his commissions. And so good night.

Questions

1. How does Rogers employ his humor in talking about President Hoover?
2. What is his opinion of Hoover?
3. Why does he seem to have a different opinion of Hoover than most people?

Richard Wright, *American Hunger* (1944)

Like other African-Americans this century, Richard Wright left the rural South in search of opportunity. With the publication of his Chicago-based novel Native Son *in 1940, Wright (1908–1960) became one of the leading American novelists of his generation. For a time in the mid-1930s, Wright was attracted to the Communist party. In this excerpt from his memoir* American Hunger, *the author shows the strengths and weaknesses of communism's appeal.*

One Saturday night, sitting home idle, not caring to visit the girls I had met on my former insurance route, bored with reading, I decided to appear at the John Reed Club in the capacity of an amused spectator. I rode to the Loop and found the number. A dark stairway led upwards; it did not look welcoming. What on earth of importance could transpire in so dingy a place? Through the windows above me I saw vague murals along the walls. I mounted the stairs to a door that was lettered:

The Chicago John Reed Club

I opened it and stepped into the strangest room I had ever seen. Paper and cigarette butts lay on the floor. A few benches ran along the walls, above which were vivid colors depicting colossal figures of workers carrying streaming banners. The mouths of the workers gaped in wild cries; their legs were sprawled over cities. . . .

I sat in a corner and listened while they discussed their magazine, *Left Front*. Were they treating me courteously because I was a Negro? I must let cold reason guide me with these people, I told myself. I was asked to contribute something to the magazine, and I said vaguely that I would consider it. After the meeting I met an Irish girl who worked for an advertising agency, a girl who did social work, a schoolteacher, and the wife of a prominent university professor. I had once worked as a servant for people like these and I was skeptical. I tried to fathom their motives, but I could detect no condescension in them.

I went home full of reflection, probing the sincerity of the strange white people I had met, wondering how they *really* regarded Negroes. I lay on my bed and read the magazines and was amazed to find that there did exist in the world an organized search for the truth of the lives of the oppressed and the isolated. When I had begged bread from the officials, I had wondered dimly if the outcasts could become united in action, thought, and feeling. Now I knew. It was being done in one-sixth of the earth already. The revolutionary words leaped from the printed page and struck me with tremendous force.

It was not the economics of Communism, nor the great power of trade unions, nor the excitement of underground politics that claimed me; my attention was caught by the similarity of the experiences of workers in other lands, by the possibility of uniting scattered but kindred peoples into a whole. My cynicism—which had been my protection against an America that had cast me out—slid from me and, timidly, I began to wonder if a solution of unity was possible. My life as a Negro in America had led me to feel—though my helplessness had made me try to hide it from myself—that the problem of human unity was more important than bread, more important than physical living itself; for I felt that without a common bond uniting men, without a continuous current of shared thought and feeling circulating through the social system, like blood coursing through the body, there could be no living worthy of being called human.

I hungered to share the dominant assumptions of my time and act upon them. I did not want to feel, like an animal in a jungle, that the whole world was alien and hostile. I did not want to make individual war or individual peace. So far I had managed to keep humanly alive through transfusions from books. In my concrete relations with others I had encountered nothing to encourage me to believe in my feelings. It had been by denying what I saw with my eyes, disputing what I felt with my body, that I had managed to keep my identity intact. But it seemed to me that here at least in the realm of revolutionary expression was where Negro experience could find a home, a functioning value and role. Out of the magazines I read came a passionate call for the experiences of the disinherited, and there were none of the same lispings of the missionary in it. It did not say: "Be like us and we will like you, maybe." It said: "If you possess enough courage to speak out what you are, you will find that you are not alone." It urged life to believe in life.

I read on into the night; then, toward dawn, I swung from bed and inserted paper into the typewriter. Feeling for the first time that I could speak to listening ears, I wrote a wild, crude poem in free verse, coining images of black hands playing, working, holding bayonets, stiffening finally in death . . . I read it and felt that in a clumsy way it linked white life with black, merged two streams of common experience.

I heard someone poking about the kitchen.

"Richard, are you ill?" my mother called.

"No. I'm reading." . . .

With my mother standing at my side, lending me her eyes, I stared at a cartoon drawn by a Communist artist; it was the figure of a worker clad in ragged overalls and holding aloft a red banner. The man's eyes bulged; his mouth gaped as wide as his face; his teeth showed; the muscles of his neck were like ropes. Following the man was a horde of nondescript men, women, and children, waving clubs, stones, and pitchforks.

"What are those people going to do?" my mother asked.

"I don't know," I hedged.

"Are these Communist magazines?"

"Yes."

"And do they want people to act like this?"

"Well . . ." I hesitated.

My mother's face showed disgust and moral loathing. She was a gentle woman. Her ideal was Christ upon the cross. How could I tell her that the Communist party wanted her to march in the streets, chanting, singing?

"What do Communists think people are?" she asked.

"They don't quite mean what you see there," I said, fumbling with my words.

"Then what do they mean?"

"This is symbolic," I said.

"Then why don't they speak out what they mean?"

"Maybe they don't know how."

"Then why do they print this stuff?"

"They don't quite know how to appeal to people yet," I admitted, wondering whom I could convince of this if I could not convince my mother.

"That picture's enough to drive a body crazy," she said, dropping the magazine, turning to leave, then pausing at the door.

"You're not getting mixed up with those people?"

"I'm just reading, mama," I dodged.

Questions

1. Why does Wright visit the John Reed Club?
2. What does Wright see as communism's chief attraction?
3. Why does his mother react differently?

Connections Questions

1. Compare the economic arguments in the first two readings of this chapter. How do they differ in assessing economic conditions and the reasons for them?

2. John McCutcheon's cartoon and Will Roger's radio commentary both deal with the Depression. Are their viewpoints similar or different? Why?

3. Would Richard Wright have been sympathetic to the ideas of Marcus Garvey (Chapter 24, "Editorial in the *Negro World*")? Why or why not?

CHAPTER 26

The New Deal 1933–1939

Candidate Attends World Series (1932)

Franklin Roosevelt projected such an image of self-assurance and strength that most Americans either did not realize or did not care that he was severely handicapped from polio. Roosevelt is pictured on the opposite page throwing out the first pitch at Wrigley Field for the third game of the 1932 World Series between the Yankees and Cubs (during which Babe Ruth may or may not have "called" his home run in the fifth inning). The presidential candidate is flanked by Chicago mayor Anton Cermak and son James Roosevelt.

Questions

1. What is FDR hoping to accomplish through his appearance?
2. How is he camouflaging his disability?
3. Why would he choose to appear at this particular event?

Huey Long, *Every Man a King* (1933)

To his supporters, Senator Huey P. Long of Louisiana (see text p. 700) was a saint; to his enemies, he was Satan. Long simply saw himself as "the King-fish." Until an assassin murdered him in 1935, Long and his brand of populism seemed potent enough to threaten FDR's bid for a second term.

Long titled his autobiography Every Man a King. *Following is the plan he said would make it so.*

THE MADDENED FORTUNE HOLDERS AND THEIR INFURIATED PUBLIC PRESS!

The increasing fury with which I have been, and am to be, assailed by reason of the fight and growth of support for limiting the size of fortunes can only be explained by the madness which human nature attaches to the holders of accumulated wealth.

What I have proposed is:—

THE LONG PLAN

1. A capital levy tax on the property owned by any one person of 1% of all over $1,000,000; 2% of all over $2,000,000 etc., until, when it reaches fortunes of over $100,000,000, the government takes all above that figure; which means a limit on the size of any one man's fortune to something like $50,000,000—the balance to go to the government to spread out in its work among all the people.

2. An inheritance tax which does not allow any one person to receive more than $5,000,000 in a lifetime without working for it, all over that amount to go to the government to be spread among the people for its work.

3. An income tax which does not allow any one man to make more than $1,000,000 in one year, exclusive of taxes, the balance to go to the United States for general work among the people.

The foregoing program means all taxes paid by the fortune holders at the top and none by the people at the bottom; the spreading of wealth among all the people and the breaking up of a system of Lords and Slaves in our economic life. It allows the millionaires to have, however, more than they can use for any luxury they can enjoy on earth. But, with such limits, all else can survive.

That the public press should regard my plan and effort as a calamity and me as a menace is no more than should be expected, gauged in the light of past events. . . .

In 1932, the vote for my resolution showed possibly a half dozen other Senators back of it. It grew in the last Congress to nearly twenty Senators. Such growth through one other year will mean the success of a venture, the completion of everything I have undertaken,—the time when I can and will retire from the stress and fury of my public life, maybe as my forties begin,—a contemplation so serene as to appear impossible.

That day will reflect credit on the States whose Senators took the early lead to spread the wealth of the land among all the people.

Then no tear dimmed eyes of a small child will be lifted into the saddened face of a father or mother unable to give it the necessities required by its soul and body for life; then the powerful will be rebuked in the sight of man for holding that which they cannot consume, but which is craved to sustain humanity; the food of the land will feed, the raiment clothe, and the houses shelter all the people; the powerful will be elated by the well being of all, rather than through their greed.

Then, those of us who have pursued that phantom of Jefferson, Jackson, Webster, Theodore Roosevelt and Bryan may hear wafted from their lips in Valhalla:

EVERY MAN A KING

Questions

1. What is Long proposing?
2. Who is most likely to support him?
3. Is Long arguing for reform or revolution? In your answer, consider the status of the rich under the Long Plan.

Eleanor Roosevelt,
"The State's Responsibility for
Fair Working Conditions" (1933)

Although newspaper columnist Westbrook Pegler dismissed Eleanor Roo-
sevelt as "Empress Eleanor," the first lady did not care. She was a longtime so-
cial reformer who would speak her mind and argue for change. In this Scribner's Magazine *piece from 1933, Mrs. Roosevelt (1884–1962) shows that men*
were not the only critics who had an understanding of economic conditions.

No matter how fair employers wish to be, there are always some who will
take advantage of times such as these to lower unnecessarily the standards of
labor, thereby subjecting him to unfair competition. It is necessary to stress
the regulation by law of these unhealthy conditions in industry. It is quite obvious that one cannot depend upon the worker in such times as these to take
care of things in the usual way. Many women, particularly, are not unionized
and even unions have temporarily lowered their standards in order to keep
their people at work. If you face starvation, it is better to accept almost anything than to feel that you and your children are going to be evicted from the
last and the cheapest rooms which you have been able to find and that there
will be no food.

Cut after cut has been accepted by workers in their wages, they have
shared their work by accepting fewer days a week in order that others might
be kept on a few days also, until many of them have fallen far below what I
would consider the normal and proper standard for healthful living. If the future of our country is to be safe and the next generation is to grow up to
healthy and good citizens, it is absolutely necessary to protect the health of our
workers now and at all times.

It has been found, for instance, in Germany, in spite of the depression and
the difficulty in making wages cover good food, that sickness and mortality
rates have been surprisingly low amongst the workers, probably because of
the fact that they have not been obliged to work an unhealthy number of
hours.

Limiting the number of working hours by law has a twofold result. It
spreads the employment, thereby giving more people work, and it protects the
health of the workers. Instead of keeping a few people working a great many
hours and even asking them to share their work with others by working fewer
days, it limits all work to a reasonable number of hours and makes it necessary to employ the number of people required to cover the work.

Refusing to allow people to be paid less than a living wage preserves to us our own market. There is absolutely no use in producing anything if you gradually reduce the number of people able to buy even the cheapest products. The only way to preserve our markets is to pay an adequate wage.

It seems to me that all fair-minded people will realize that it is self-preservation to treat the industrial worker with consideration and fairness at the present time and to uphold the fair employer in his efforts to treat his employees well by preventing unfair competition.

Questions

1. What group is Eleanor Roosevelt attacking?
2. Who is she aligning herself with?
3. What kind of political fallout could such views have for her husband? Should that have been a consideration for her? Why or why not?

Memorial Day Massacre (1937)

Despite support from Washington, organized labor in the 1930s faced a good deal of hostility, some of it violent (see text p. 708). One such incident occurred in Chicago on Memorial Day 1937. The police fired on a strike rally outside a Republic Steel plant; ten people were left dead. Yet this newspaper account affords little sympathy to the victims.

RIOTS BLAMED ON RED CHIEFS

Coroner Moves Today to Seize Mob's Leaders

Impasse Reached in Horner Parley.

Blaming communist agitators in the Committee for Industrial Organization ranks for the Memorial day bloodshed at the Republic Steel corporation plant in South Chicago, Coroner Frank J. Walsh took personal charge of the investigation last night.

The coroner said he is determined to fix the blame for the mob attack on the police who were guarding the company's property rights—an attack which precipitated a riot whose death toll rose yesterday to five.

First Step Toward Punishment.

He will begin that task when the inquest into the deaths opens at 1 P.M. today in the county morgue. The coroner's action is regarded as the first step toward punishment of those who incited the strikers to assail the police with firearms, clubs, and brick-bats in an attempted invasion of the plant.

Coroner Walsh said he had been given definite information that communists inspired the mob.

At the same time communists in John L. Lewis' C.I.O. were flatly charged with responsibility by James L. Mooney, supervising captain, who was in command of the police when the mob attacked.

Capt. Mooney Accuses Reds.

Capt. Mooney said he has been given information that known communists fomented the attack, in which ninety persons other than those killed suffered gunshot wounds and other injuries that sent them to hospitals. Twenty-six of the injured were policemen.

Capt. Mooney said he would present his information to State's Attorney Courtney. This was believed to assure grand jury action leading to punishment of the mob leaders—the same objective as that of Coroner Walsh.

Cites Handbills as Evidence.

The police captain cited inflammatory handbills issued by the Illinois state committee of the communist party as evidence of the communist activities in the riot. These circulars, upholding the rioters, were issued early yesterday, a few hours after the riot.

"The speed with which the handbills were issued, and the accusations they contained," Capt. Mooney said, "show definitely that the communists knew in advance that the workers were going to be led into attacking the police, and that they encouraged the attack."

No Progress at Parley.

A peace conference called by Gov. Horner reached an impasse in the Congress hotel last night when the conferees decided no further progress could be made until an interpretation of certain puzzling provisions of the Wagner labor relations act could be obtained by Robert Pilkington, federal labor conciliator.

When the five hour conference closed just before midnight the governor said another would be held as soon as Pilkington received the required information.

Among those at the meeting were James L. Hyland, western manager of the Republic corporation; Van A. Bittner, regional director of the S. W. O. C.; Martin Durkin, director of the state department of labor; Warren Canaday, assistant United States attorney; and Pilkington.

Bittner to Continue Fight.

After taking leave of the governor Bittner spoke emphatically of the conference.

"Progress made here tonight is not worth a thin dime to anybody," he said. "The company has said that even though a majority vote is taken under the labor relations act it will not sign contracts with the men. The strike will go on until the vote is taken and until the company signs. We will increase picketing at once."

The strike was called by the Steel Workers' Organizing committee of Lewis' C. I. O. against the Republic, Inland, and Youngstown Sheet and Tube companies to win collective bargaining contracts.

Official action did not end with that of Gov. Horner, Coroner Walsh, and Capt. Mooney.

Capt. Thomas Kilroy of the East Chicago police, another commanding officer at the time the mob attacked the bluecoats, announced that sixty seven persons now in custody will be formally charged this morning with conspiracy to commit an illegal act.

This constitutes a felony, Capt. Kilroy said, and is punishable by a maximum penalty of five years in prison and a $2,000 fine.

Thirty four of those against whom the charge is to be leveled are under guard in hospitals, where they are being treated for wounds and injuries suffered in the riot. The others have been removed from hospitals to lockups.

Eight young men and eight girls, who said they are students at the University of Chicago, eluded police guards and joined the ranks of the picketers at the South Chicago plant last night. They carried banners condemning the police for protecting themselves against gunfire, brick-bats, and clubs of the mob. One banner said University of Chicago students are protesting the police action. The spokesman for the professed students said he was Paul Bradley, 20 years old, of New York City.

The Fifth Victim.

At the time the strike began last Wednesday, police agreed to permit the strikers to maintain eight pickets. The arrival of the professed students tripled the number authorized, but no action was taken to halt the picketers.

The fifth victim of the riot was Joseph Rothmund, 47 years old, of 2857 Belmont avenue, a Works Progress administration employee, who had been shot. Rothmund died in the Bridewell hospital.

Two of the previously unidentified dead were identified yesterday.

One was Alfred Causey, 43 years old, 7050 Arizona avenue, a Republic carpenter. He was the father of three children. His widow, Gladys, identified him. She said he recently came here after losing a job with another steel company because of labor activities.

The other was Kenneth Reed, 23 years old, 3921 Deal street, Indiana Harbor, the father of two children. He was an Inland Steel company electrician.

A relative tentatively identified another victim as Sam Popovich, address unknown.

Two men were reported in critical condition in the South Chicago hospital. They were Hilding Anderson, 38 years old, 9804 Avenue D; and Anthony Tagliere, 26, of 615 East 74th street.

Plant Still Working.

The Republic plant, at 115th street and Burley avenue, is still turning out steel despite the strike, which has closed other mills in the Calumet-South Chicago area. It is estimated 22,000 of the 70,000 steel strikers in five states are in this area. Some 1,400 loyal employe[e]s are still working in the Republic's plant.

Some 5,000 strikers and sympathizers met yesterday in Washington park, Indiana Harbor, East Chicago. Speakers were Bittner and Nicholas Fontecchio, who was one of the speakers at the meeting which preceded the riot.

CHICAGOANS LED IN STEEL STRIKE BY OUTSIDERS

Union Organizers Come from Far Points.

Leaders of the steel strike in the Chicago district, whose rabid oratory inflamed the strike mob to fighting pitch before the battle with police at the Republic Steel company plant Sunday, neither live in this area nor are they steel workers.

All are veterans in union organization work. Most of them come from the United Mine Workers of America, which produced John L. Lewis, whose Committee for Industrial Organization is sponsoring the steel strike. All local strike executives are close associates of the beetle-browed Lewis, the labor dictator, who once fought communists in the U. M. W. of A., but now welcomes them with open arms to the C. I. O.

Van A. Bittner is the high mogul of the Steel Workers' Organizing committee in the Great Lakes region. He takes his orders from Philip Murray, the national S. W. O. C. head, and from Lewis. When Lewis speaks, Bittner acts in the territory from Buffalo to the Pacific coast.

Bittner is president of one of the two West Virginia districts of the U. M. W. of A., is a member of the U. M. W. of A. policy committee and sits in on the Appalachian district wage conferences.

Krzycki Is Socialist.

It was after Leo Krzycki's rabble rousing speech that the strike mob marched on the Republic plant Sunday.

He is an old time Socialist from Milwaukee, where he was an under-sherif, former alderman, and unsuccessful candidate for senator.

Born in Poland, Krzycki now is a member of the C. I. O. advisory board, a member of the national executive committee of the Socialist party, and is second in command to Bittner in the western territory of the S. W. O. C.

He called for a world uprising of workers after the bloody civil war in Austria a few years ago. In 1919 he first used his rabble rousing technique to inflame workers in the American Steel and Wire company strike at Waukegan.

Nicholas Fontecchio is the chief commissar for the S. W. O. C. in the Calumet industrial district. He has been an international representative of the U. M. W. of A. for thirty-five years and in 1924 and 1925 led the West Virginia miners in their strike.

Fontecchio and Krzycki were active in the abortive attempt to organize the Fansteel Metallurgical corporation in North Chicago last March.

Two Others from East.

Leo Wisniewski and John Riffe are Fontecchio's assistants. The former, a district representative of the U. M. W. of A. for fourteen years, lives in Fairmount, W. Va., but runs the Gary district for the S. W. O. C. Riffe, a West Virginia officer of the U. M. W. of A., with which he has been connected for ten years, rules the South Chicago district of the S. W. O. C. and lives now at 9233 Huston avenue.

Although not active in the Republic district steel strike, Meyer Adelman became a prominent figure [he weighs 300 pounds] in the Fansteel strike. For his flagrant law flouting activities there he was arrested by Lake county officials. The charges are still pending.

Questions

1. What biases does the story contain?
2. What does the article imply about the strikers' political affiliations?

3. Should the press have the First Amendment right to print such a distorted account? Why or why not?

The Federal Writers' Project: Barre, Vermont

New Deal programs attempted to generate employment in virtually every field from masonry to acting. Some of the most interesting work involved the Federal Writers' Project, which collected folklore and oral histories, among other activities.

A team of FWP writers spent more than a year in Barre, Vermont, interviewing people who made a living from granite. Their stories are filled with the joys and tragedies of anonymous lives.

ALFRED TORNAZZI

Shed-owner Alfred Tornazzi studied sculpture for eight years at the Reale Accademia de Belle Arti di Brera *before coming to the United States. Tornazzi carved the monument he described as his masterpiece around the turn of the century. A statue of a little girl wearing a dress trimmed with delicate eyelet lace, it still stands in a Montpelier cemetery.*

I didn't start operating a shed of my own right away, although I could have. I wanted to learn more of this country, the way the sheds did business. I did carving for a shed in Barre the first year. The second year I went out to our western granite states. I found you could do better, more delicate work with the hard Barre stone, and I learned that it rated high in eastern markets and was quickly becoming known further west, so I decided to settle in or near Barre.

My brother, who had come to this country two years before I did, suggested that we start a shed of our own. It went under the name of Tornazzi Brothers. We've had our ups and downs, but we've made money and we've put out plenty of memorials that we're proud of.

My favorite memorial and what I believe is my masterpiece is one of my very early statues. It's called *The Little Margaret*. It stands in the Green Mount Cemetery in Montpelier. There's a story to that, too. I won't tell the customer's name, although you can easily find out by going to the cemetery and looking at the memorial. This customer wanted me to carve a statue of his little daughter who was dead. I'd never seen the girl. Her family produced a full-length picture of her and asked me to make the statue identical in clothing, posture, et cetera. I said it would be difficult since the picture was a poor one, and faint, but I'd do my best. I completed it, and was justly proud of it. The parents liked it, too. I remember the mother cried and said it looked real. But in spite of their satisfaction, they hated to pay the price agreed upon. I admit it was a steep price, but it was good work, and hard, and they could afford it. Well, the father came to me one day. He pointed to the picture and said, "Look, you promised to make the statue exactly like this picture. You didn't. On the memorial there's a button missing on one shoe. Since they aren't identical you should lower the price." It made me mad. I'd been very careful in carving those shoes; they were those old-fashioned, high-buttoned shoes the girls wore at that time, and since the picture was so dim I'd been careful to make sure of each detail. "They *are* identical," I assured him, and proceeded to prove it. A magnifying glass held over the picture showed that sure enough one button was missing on the shoe. Well, the short of it is the man stopped quibbling and paid the price I'd asked.

Mari Tomasi [conducted interview]

ANTHONY TONELLI

Anthony Tonelli learned the trade of stonecutting in Viggiu, Italy. Silicosis was not an occupational hazard there because the stonecutters worked on marble—softer than granite—in open-air sheds. Tonelli expected to send all his children to college. "At least that will take them away from the sheds," he said, "and after they get out of college they won't want to work with granite. I have planned that."

The life of a stonecutter is fifty years. No more. Every one of them, they all die in their fifties, they are through before that. I am near fifty. I die soon. I expect it. You got to expect it when you work with granite. You can get up any morning and go to work and say to yourself, "I am going to die very soon"; when you see your kids, you can say, "Yes, I am going to leave them soon." And other people are saying, "I am going to retire because I am in my fifties and I want to enjoy life a little," but you say, "I can not retire. I am in the granite business and it will retire me." But I hate like hell to leave my family when I am fifty. Just beginning to live. No children of mine will ever go into the granite sheds. Too much dust. I want them to have fresh air, and good jobs. I don't care what they do, so long as they keep away from the dust of granite.

I have seen big, strong, healthy men come to work. They have laughing eyes, they show they love life, they enjoy themselves. They are good workers. They have strength and knowledge of the job. Skill. And they don't last long. And this keeps up for many years. People grumble. The grumble increases. People lose their heads. I see children with tears in their eyes as they follow the casket to the grave. The big strong men do not last long against stone dust. They die and people cry and the family starves for a while, but all the time I keep saying, "The problem will be solved, this dust will end in the sheds," and they say, "You are a fool, dust will stay here forever, you can't end dust." I laugh now. It is coming to an end but nobody says to me, "You are smart, you tell us years ago that dust problem, this silicosis will be over with." No, I am not smart. I think a lot. I see improvements in every line.

I say the scientists are brilliant. They study when we are not thinking of them. They solve disease when it has killed millions, and they make autos and they get better every year. Look at the children. They get better care. Doctors know more. Why wouldn't they end this big problem of ours? It has caused a lot of suffering. Everybody in the granite business has been sad because of dust, deaths in all families, but now it is near the end. You will see men work longer in the sheds. They will not grow old so fast.

I have gone to work in the morning and after a little while in the shed I couldn't recognize my own body. It was covered from head to foot with dust. Of course we have to breathe that dust in. That is what does it. We give our whole strength, our hearing, our hands, our sight, the eyes, everything we possess to the business. We give our lives, our family, we give everything we have and love, and then what do we get out of it? Just a little money. Granite cutters have always been underpaid. You can't get around it. You go in there and die young. Do you see any of them rich?

You want to know what I do? I am a letterer. I have responsibility. If I cut one little piece from a stone, just when it is nearing completion, that spoils the whole works. It is all destroyed. And I get the gate. I can't take any chances getting drunk with all that at stake. It takes everything I got, everything. After a day in the sheds I am no good for anything, or for anybody. I guess most men wouldn't like it. You got to be strong. How many men can stand it? By the time you become good at your trade, you are ready to die.

John Lynch [conducted interview]

Questions

1. What is work like for stonecutters?
2. What is the greatest danger?
3. Why do people do this kind of work?

Walker Evans, "A Miner's Home: Vicinity Morgantown, West Virginia, July 1935"

The photographer Walker Evans had the ability to take a simple subject and render it profound. Evans (1903–1975) worked periodically for the Farm Security Administration from 1935 to 1938. His assignment was to record poverty in America. The text notes that Evans's work, along with that of such colleagues as Dorothea Lange, Ben Shahn, and Margaret Bourke-White, "permanently shaped the image of the Great Depression."

Questions

1. Describe the scene. Does the boy appear happy?
2. What might be the use of the cardboard advertising on the wall?
3. What is the overall effect of the photograph?

Connections Questions

1. How does the Long Plan compare to the Progressive party platform of 1912? What makes a political idea "radical"?
2. How do the sentiments shown in the newspaper account of the Memorial Day massacre compare to those of Madison Grant (see Chapter 24, "Closing the Flood-Gates")?
3. Consider the ways in which technology—and its limits—shape ideas. How, for example, might a viewer's response change if the photographs of FDR and the boy in this chapter had been in color?

CHAPTER 27

The World at War 1939–1945

The Neutrality Act of 1937

Failure to "make the world safe for democracy" led many Americans to embrace the idea of isolationism in foreign policy. When the Nye Committee on Munitions Manufactures disclosed evidence that weapons makers had earned large profits from World War I, the public demanded protection against any repeats. With the growth of fascism in Europe, Congress moved to keep the United States out of future international conflicts by passing three Neutrality Acts, from 1935 to 1937.

EXPORT OF ARMS, AMMUNITION, AND IMPLEMENTS OF WAR

SECTION 1. (a) Whenever the President shall find that there exists a state of war between, or among, two or more foreign states, the President shall proclaim such fact, and it shall thereafter be unlawful to export, or attempt to export, or cause to be exported, arms, ammunition, or implements of war from any place in the United States to any belligerent state named in such proclamation, or to any neutral state for transshipment to, or for the use of, any such belligerent state.

(b) The President shall, from time to time, by proclamation, extend such embargo upon the export of arms, ammunition, or implements of war to other states as and when they may become involved in such war.

(c) Whenever the President shall find that a state of civil strife exists in a foreign state and that such civil strife is of a magnitude or is being conducted under such conditions that the export of arms, ammunition, or implements of war from the United States to such foreign state would threaten or endanger the peace of the United States, the President shall proclaim such fact, and it shall thereafter be unlawful to export, or attempt to export, or cause to be exported, arms, ammunition, or implements of war from any place in the United States to such foreign state, or to any neutral state for transshipment to, or for the use of, such foreign state.

(d) The President shall, from time to time by proclamation definitely enumerate the arms, ammunition, and implements of war, the export of which is prohibited by this section.

EXPORT OF OTHER ARTICLES AND MATERIALS

SEC. 2. (a) Whenever the President shall have issued a proclamation under the authority of section 1 of this Act and he shall thereafter find that the placing of restrictions on the shipment of certain articles or materials in addition to arms, ammunition, and implements of war from the United States to belligerent states, or to a state wherein civil strife exists, is necessary to promote the security or preserve the peace of the United States or to protect the lives of citizens of the United States, he shall so proclaim, and it shall thereafter be unlawful, for any American vessel to carry such articles or materials to any belligerent state, or to any state wherein civil strife exists, named in such proclamation issued under the authority of section 1 of this Act, or to any neutral state for transshipment to, or for the use of, any such belligerent state or any such state wherein civil strife exists, named in such proclamation issued under the authority of section 1 of this Act, or to any neutral state for transshipment to, or for the use of, any such belligerent state or any such state wherein civil strife exists. The President shall . . . definitely enumerate the articles and materials which it shall be unlawful for American vessels to so transport. . . .

FINANCIAL TRANSACTIONS

SEC. 3. (a) Whenever the President shall have issued a proclamation under the authority of section 1 of this Act, it shall thereafter be unlawful for any person within the United States to purchase, sell, or exchange bonds, securities, or other obligations of the government of any belligerent state or of any state wherein civil strife exists, named in such proclamation, or of any political subdivision of any such state, or of any person acting for or on behalf of the government of any such state, or of any faction or asserted government within any such state wherein civil strife exists, or of any person acting for or on behalf of any faction or asserted government within any such state wherein civil strife exists, issued after the date of such proclamation, or to make any loan or extend any credit to any such government, political subdivision, faction, asserted government, or person: *Provided,* That if the President shall find that such action will serve to protect the commercial or other interests of the United States or its citizens, he may, in his discretion, and to such extent and under such regulations as he may prescribe, except from the operation of his section ordinary commercial credits and short-time obligations in aid of legal transactions and of a character customarily used in normal peacetime commercial transactions. Nothing in this subsection shall be construed to prohibit the solicitation or collection of funds to be used for medical aid and assistance, or for food and clothing to relieve human suffering, when such solicitation or collection of funds is made on behalf of any such government, political subdivision, faction, or asserted government, but all such solicitations and collections of funds shall be subject to the approval of the President and shall be made under such rules and regulations as he shall prescribe. . . .

(c) Whoever shall violate the provisions of this section or of any regulations issued hereunder shall, upon conviction thereof, be fined not more than $50,000 or imprisoned for not more than five years, or both. . . .

EXCEPTIONS—AMERICAN REPUBLICS

SEC. 4. This Act shall not apply to an American republic or republics engaged in war against a non-American state or states, provided the American republic is not cooperating with a non-American state or states in such war.

USE OF AMERICAN PORTS AS BASE OF SUPPLY

SEC. 7. (a) Whenever, during any war in which the United States is neutral, the President, or any person thereunto authorized by him, shall have cause to believe that any vessel, domestic or foreign, whether requiring clearance or not, is about to carry out of a port of the United States, fuel, men, arms, ammunition, implements of war, or other supplies to any warship, tender, or supply ship of a belligerent state, but the evidence is not deemed sufficient to justify forbidding the departure of the vessel as provided for by section 1, title V, chapter 30, of the Act approved June 15, 1917, and if in the President's judgment, such action will serve to maintain peace between the United States and foreign states, or to protect the commercial interests of the United States and its citizens, or to promote the security or neutrality of the United States, he shall have the power and it shall be his duty to require the owner, master, or person in command thereof, before departing from a port of the United States, to give a bond to the United States, with sufficient sureties, in such amount as he shall deem proper, conditioned that the vessel will not deliver the men, or any part of the cargo, to any warship, tender, or supply ship of a belligerent state.

(b) If the President, or any person thereunto authorized by him, shall find that a vessel, domestic or foreign, in a port of the United States, has previously cleared from a port of the United States during such war and delivered its cargo or any part thereof to a warship, tender, or supply ship of a belligerent state, he may prohibit the departure of such vessel during the duration of the war.

TRAVEL ON VESSELS OF BELLIGERENT STATES

SEC. 9. Whenever the President shall have issued a proclamation under the authority of section 1 of this Act it shall thereafter be unlawful for any citizen of the United States to travel on any vessel of the state or states named in such proclamation, except in accordance with such rules and regulations as the President shall prescribe: . . .

ARMING OF AMERICAN MERCHANT VESSELS PROHIBITED

SEC. 10. Whenever the President shall have issued a proclamation under the authority of section 1, it shall thereafter be unlawful, until such proclamation is revoked, for any American vessel engaged in commerce with any belligerent state, or any state wherein civil strife exists, named in such proclamation, to be armed or to carry any armament, arms, ammunition, or implements of war, except small arms and ammunition therefor [for the vessel] which the President may deem necessary.

Questions

1. How is the act designed to keep the United States out of international conflicts?
2. Does it distinguish in any way between aggressors and victims? Why or why not?
3. Does this act identify any U.S. interests in international affairs? If any, what are they?

Franklin D. Roosevelt,
State of the Union Address (1941)

President Roosevelt stated his opposition to isolationism (see text p. 723) more strongly than ever in his State of the Union message to Congress in early 1941. In this speech, he tied Lend-Lease and other international initiatives to his agenda for domestic politics. His concluding comments on the "Four Freedoms" soon became the most famous rationale for American participation in the war. Also contained within them was a striking agenda for a postwar debate both at home and abroad.

I address you, the Members of the Seventy-Seventh Congress, at a moment unprecedented in the history of the Union. I use the word "unprecedented," because at no previous time has American security been as seriously threatened from without as it is today. . . .

What I seek to convey is the historic truth that the United States as a nation has at all times maintained opposition to any attempt to lock us in behind an ancient Chinese wall while the procession of civilization went past. Today, thinking of our children and their children, we oppose enforced isolation for ourselves or for any part of the Americas. . . .

Every realist knows that the democratic way of life is at this moment being directly assailed in every part of the world—assailed either by arms, or by secret spreading of poisonous propaganda by those who seek to destroy unity and promote discord in nations still at peace. During sixteen months this assault has blotted out the whole pattern of democratic life in an appalling number of independent nations, great and small. The assailants are still on the march, threatening other nations, great and small.

Therefore, as your President, performing my constitutional duty to "give to the Congress information of the state of the Union," I find it necessary to report that the future and the safety of our country and of our democracy are overwhelmingly involved in events far beyond our borders.

Armed defense of democratic existence is now being gallantly waged in four continents. If that defense fails, all the population and all the resources of Europe, Asia, Africa and Australia will be dominated by the conquerors. The total of those populations and their resources greatly exceeds the sum total of the population and resources of the whole of the Western Hemisphere—many times over.

In times like these it is immature—and incidentally untrue—for anybody to brag that an unprepared America, single-handed, and with one hand tied behind its back, can hold off the whole world. . . .

A free nation has the right to expect full cooperation from all groups. A free nation has the right to look to the leaders of business, of labor, and of agriculture to take the lead in stimulating effort, not among other groups but within their own groups. The best way of dealing with the few slackers or trouble makers in our midst is, first, to shame them by patriotic example, and, if that fails, to use the sovereignty of government to save government.

As men do not live by bread alone, they do not fight by armaments alone. Those who man our defenses, and those behind them who build our defenses, must have the stamina and courage which come from an unshakable belief in the manner of life which they are defending. The mighty action which we are calling for cannot be based on a disregard of all things worth fighting for. . . .

There is nothing mysterious about the foundations of a healthy and strong democracy. The basic things expected by our people of their political and economic systems are simple. They are: equality of opportunity for youth and for others; jobs for those who can work; security for those who need it; the ending of special privilege for the few; the preservation of civil liberties for all; the enjoyment of the fruits of scientific progress in a wider and constantly rising standard of living.

These are the simple and basic things that must never be lost sight of in the turmoil and unbelievable complexity of our modern world. The inner and abiding strength of our economic and political systems is dependent upon the degree to which they fulfill these expectations.

Many subjects connected with our social economy call for immediate improvement. As examples: We should bring more citizens under the coverage of old age pensions and unemployment insurance. We should widen the opportunities for adequate medical care. We should plan a better system by which persons deserving or needing gainful employment may obtain it.

I have called for personal sacrifice. I am assured of the willingness of almost all Americans to respond to that call. . . .

In the future days, which we seek to make secure, we look forward to a world founded upon four essential human freedoms.

The first is freedom of speech and expression—everywhere in the world.

The second is freedom of every person to worship God in his own way—everywhere in the world.

The third is freedom from want—which, translated into world terms, means economic understandings which will secure to every nation a healthy peace time life for its inhabitants—everywhere in the world.

The fourth is freedom from fear—which, translated into world terms, means a world-wide reduction of armaments to such a point and in such a thorough fashion that no nation will be in a position to commit an act of physical aggression against any neighbor—anywhere in the world.

That is no vision of a distant millenium. It is a definite basis for a kind of world attainable in our own time and generation. That kind of world is the very antithesis of the so-called new order of tyranny which the dictators seek to create with the crash of a bomb.

To that new order we oppose the greater conception—the moral order. A good society is able to face schemes of world domination and foreign revolutions alike without fear.

Since the beginning of our American history we have been engaged in change—in a perpetual peaceful revolution—a revolution which goes on steadily, quietly adjusting itself to changing conditions—without the concentration camp or the quick-lime in the ditch. The world order which we seek is the cooperation of free countries, working together in a friendly, civilized society.

This nation has placed its destiny in the hands and heads and hearts of its millions of free men and women; and its faith in freedom under the guidance of God. Freedom means the supremacy of human rights everywhere. Our support goes to those who struggle to gain those rights or keep them. Our strength is in our unity of purpose.

To that high concept there can be no end save victory.

Questions

1. What "four freedoms" does Roosevelt identify?
2. How does the president link domestic and foreign concerns in the speech?
3. How does he argue against the principles of the Neutrality Acts in favor of an internationalist foreign policy?

Executive Order 9066
"Authorizing the Secretary of War to Prescribe Military Areas" (1942)

After the surprise attack on Pearl Harbor, Americans feared that enemy aliens might attempt espionage and subversion. On February 19, 1942, President Roosevelt issued an executive order authorizing the secretary of war to identify areas of the country where movements of people could be controlled or restricted. This presidential directive evolved into legislation that led to the internment of Japanese and Japanese-Americans living on the West Coast (see text p. 735).

AUTHORIZING THE SECRETARY OF WAR TO PRESCRIBE MILITARY AREAS

WHEREAS the successful prosecution of the war requires every possible protection against espionage and against sabotage to national-defense material, national-defense premises, and national-defense utilities. . . .

NOW, THEREFORE, by virtue of the authority vested in me as President of the United States, and Commander in Chief of the Army and Navy, I hereby authorize and direct the Secretary of War, and the Military Commanders whom he may from time to time designate, whenever he or any designated Commander deems such actions necessary or desirable, to prescribe military areas in such places and of such extent as he or the appropriate Military Commanders may determine, from which any or all persons may be excluded, and with such respect to which, the right of any person to enter, remain in, or leave shall be subject to whatever restrictions the Secretary of War or the appropriate Military Commander may impose in his discretion. The Secretary of War is hereby authorized to provide for residents of any such area who are excluded therefrom, such transportation, food, shelter, and other accommodations as may be necessary, in the judgement of the Secretary of War or the said Military Commander, and until other arrangements are made, to accomplish the purpose of this order. The designation of military areas in any region or locality shall supersede designations of prohibited and restricted areas by the Attorney General under the Proclamations of December 7 and 8, 1941, and shall supersede the responsibility and authority of the Attorney General under the said Proclamations in respect of such prohibited and restricted areas.

I hereby further authorize and direct the Secretary of War and the said Military Commanders to take such other steps as he or the appropriate Military Commander may deem advisable to enforce compliance with the restrictions applicable to each Military area hereinabove authorized to be designated, including the use of Federal troops and other Federal Agencies, with authority to accept assistance of state and local agencies.

I hereby further authorize and direct all Executive Departments, independent establishments and other Federal Agencies, to assist the Secretary of War or the said Military Commanders in carrying out this Executive Order, including the furnishing of medical aid, hospitalization, food, clothing, transportation, use of land, shelter, and other supplies, equipment, utilities, facilities and services.

This order shall not be construed as modifying or limiting in any way the authority heretofore granted under Executive Order No. 8972, dated December 12, 1941, nor shall it be construed as limiting or modifying the duty and responsibility of the Federal Bureau of Investigation, with respect to the investigation of alleged acts of sabotage or the duty and responsibility of the Attorney General and the Department of Justice under the Proclamations of December 7 and 8, 1941, prescribing regulations for the conduct and control of alien enemies, except as such duty and responsibility is superseded by the designation of military areas hereunder.

> *FRANKLIN D. ROOSEVELT*
> The White House
> February 19, 1942.

Questions

1. What specific concerns about national security led to the issuance of Executive Order 9066?

2. Is the order restricting the actions of residents in prescribed military areas specific in identifying individuals or groups? In your opinion, why was it written this way?

3. What limitations does the order place on the secretary of war and others authorized to enforce its provisions?

Norma Yerger Queen, Women on the Home Front (1944)

During World War II, the U.S. Office of War Information gathered information to help shape government policy and to use in wartime propaganda. Norma Yerger Queen of Utah wrote a long letter in response to a request from the office. The letter makes it clear that she knew many Utah women in farm and city families as well as at the military hospital where she worked. She describes both the wartime work experiences of women and the way they and their families viewed women's roles at work and home.

The people of this community all respect women who work regardless of the type of work. Women from the best families & many officers' wives work at our hospital. It is not at all uncommon to meet at evening parties in town women who work in the kitchens or offices of our hospital (Army-Bushnell-large general). The city mayor's wife too works there.

The church disapproves of women working who have small children. The church has a strong influence in our county.

For the canning season in our county men's & women's clubs & the church all recruited vigorously for women for the canneries. . . .

I personally have encouraged officers' wives who have no children to get out and work. Those of us who have done so have been highly respected by the others and we have not lost social standing. In fact many of the social affairs are arranged at our convenience.

Some husbands do not approve of wives working & this has kept home some who do not have small children. Some of the women just do not wish to put forth the effort.

The financial incentive has been the strongest influence among most economic groups but especially among those families who were on relief for many years. Patriotic motivation is sometimes present but sometimes it really is a front for the financial one. A few women work to keep their minds from worrying about sons or husbands in the service.

In this county, the hospital is the chief employer of women. A few go to Ogden (20 miles away) to work in an arsenal, the depot, or the air field. When these Ogden plants first opened quite a few women started to work there, but the long commuting plus the labor at the plants plus their housework proved too much.

Many women thoroughly enjoy working & getting away from the home. They seem to get much more satisfaction out of it than out of housework or bringing up children. Those who quit have done so because of lack of good care for their children, or of inability to do the housework & the job. . . .

I am convinced that if women could work 4 days a week instead of 5½ or 6 that more could take jobs. I found it impossible to work 5½ days & do my housework but when I arranged for 4 days I could manage both. These days one has to do everything—one cannot buy services as formerly. For instance—laundry. I'm lucky. I can send out much of our laundry to the hospital but even so there is a goodly amount that must be done at home—all the ironing of summer dresses is very tiring. I even have to press my husband's trousers—a thing I never did in all my married life. The weekly housecleaning—shoe shining—all things we formerly had done by others. Now we also do home canning. I never in the 14 yrs. of my married life canned 1 jar. Last summer I put up dozens of quarts per instructions of Uncle Sam. I'm only one among many who is now doing a lot of manual labor foreign to our usual custom. I just could not take on all that & an outside job too. It is no fun to eat out—you wait so long for service & the restaurants cannot be immaculately kept—therefore it is more pleasant & quicker to cook & eat at home even after a long day's work. I've talked with the personnel manager at the hospital & he agrees that fewer days a week would be better. The canneries finally took women for as little as 3 hrs. a day.

This is a farming area & many farm wives could not under any arrangements take a war job. They have too much to do at their farm jobs & many now have to go into the fields, run tractors & do other jobs formerly done by men. I marvel at all these women are able to do & feel very inadequate next to them. . . .

Here is the difference between a man working & a woman as seen in our home—while I prepare the evening meal, my husband reads the evening paper. We then do the dishes together after which he reads his medical journal or cogitates over some lecture he is to give or some problem at his lab. I have to make up grocery lists, mend, straighten up a drawer, clean out the ice box, press clothes, put away anything strewn about the house, wash bric a brac, or do several of hundreds of small "woman's work is never done stuff." This consumes from 1 to 2 hrs. each evening after which I'm too weary to read any professional social work literature & think I'm lucky if I can keep up with the daily paper, Time Life or Reader's Digest. All this while my husband is relaxing & resting. When I worked full time, we tried doing the housecleaning together but it just didn't click. He is responsible for introducing penicillin into Bushnell & thus into the army & there were so many visiting brass hats & night conferences he couldn't give even one night a week to the house. Then came a mess of lectures of all kinds of medical meetings—he had to prepare those at home. I got so worn out it was either quit work or do it part time.

This has been a lot of personal experience but I'm sure we are no exception. I thought I was thro[ugh] working in 1938. My husband urged me to help out for the war effort—he's all out for getting the war work done & he agreed to do his share of the housework. He is not lazy but he found we could not do it. I hope this personal experience will help to give you an idea of some of the problems.

Questions

1. According to Norma Yerger Queen, why have women taken jobs during the war? Which reasons are especially important?
2. What practical factors limit women's participation in the labor force? How do they affect women who come from different backgrounds, for example, farms, towns, military bases?
3. How do women's outside jobs affect their home lives? What problems and options does Queen mention?

U.S. Supreme Court,
Smith v. Allwright (1944)

In 1941, Lonnie E. Smith, an African-American citizen, sued S. E. Allwright, an election judge in Harris County (Houston), Texas. Smith asserted he had been denied the right to vote in the Democratic primary because he was not a "white citizen." The Supreme Court agreed to hear the case and overruled lower courts that had relied on a prior Court decision (Grovey v. Townsend) allowing all-white primaries.

The State of Texas by its Constitution and statutes provides that every person, if certain other requirements are met which are not here in issue, qualified by residence in the district or county "shall be deemed a qualified elector." Primary elections for United States Senators, Congressmen and state officers are provided for by Chapters Twelve and Thirteen of the statutes. Under these chapters, the Democratic Party was required to hold the primary which was the occasion of the alleged wrong to petitioned. . . . These nominations are to be made by the qualified voters of the party.

The Democratic Party of Texas is held by the Supreme Court of that state to be a "voluntary association," protected by Section 27 of the Bill of Rights, Art. 1, Constitution of Texas, from interference by the state except that:

"In the interest of fair methods and a fair expression by their members of their preferences in the selection of their nominees, the State may regulate such elections by proper laws."

The Democratic party on May 24, 1932 in a State Convention adopted the following resolution, which has not since been "amended, abrogated, annulled or avoided":

"Be it resolved that all white citizens of the State of Texas who are qualified to vote under the Constitution and laws of the State shall be eligible to membership in the Democratic party and, as such, entitled to participate in its deliberations."

It was by virtue of this resolution that the respondents refused to permit the petitioner to vote.

Texas is free to conduct her elections and limit her electorate as she may deem wise, save only as her action may be affected by the prohibitions of the United States Constitution or in conflict with powers delegated to and exercised by the National Government. The Fourteenth Amendment forbids a state from making or enforcing any law which abridges the privileges or immunities of citizens of the United States and the Fifteenth Amendment specifically interdicts any denial or abridgement by a state of the right of citizens to vote on account of color. . . .

When *Grovey v. Townsend* was written, the Court looked upon the denial of a vote in a primary as a mere refusal by a party of party membership. As the Louisiana statutes for holding primaries are similar to those of Texas, our ruling in *Classic* [another similar case] as to the unitary character of the electoral process calls for a reëxamination as to whether or not the exclusion of Negroes from a Texas party primary was state action.

It may now be taken as a postulate that the right to vote in such a primary for the nomination of candidates without discrimination by the State, like the right to vote in a general election, is a right secured by the Constitution.

We are thus brought to an examination of the qualifications for Democratic primary electors in Texas, to determine whether state action or private action has excluded Negroes from participation.

We think that this statutory system for the selection of party nominees for inclusion on the general election ballot makes the party which is required to follow these legislative directions an agency of the state in so far as it determines the participants in a primary election. The party takes its character as a state agency from the duties imposed upon it by state statutes; the duties do not become matters of private law because they are performed by a political party. . . .

The United States is a constitutional democracy. Its organic law grants to all citizens a right to participate in the choice of elected officials without restriction by any state because of race. This grant to the people of the opportunity for choice is not to be nullified by a state through casting its electoral process in a form which permits a private organization to practice racial discrimination in the election. Constitutional rights would be of little value if they could be thus indirectly denied. . . .

Questions

1. According to the Supreme Court, what limits is Texas bound to observe in arranging its primary elections?
2. Texas argued that the all-white Democratic primary was a *private,* not a public, activity. How did it make this argument? Why did the Court reject it?
3. What influence, if any, might U.S. war aims as stated by President Roosevelt have had on the Supreme Court's decision to hear the case or on the language used in the decision?

Franklin D. Roosevelt
on the Yalta Conference (1945)

The Yalta Conference left the president exhausted and increasingly ill. Roosevelt mostly remained in his cabin on the voyage home across the Atlantic. He met only briefly with Samuel Rosenman, his speechwriter, to review a draft of his address on the Yalta Conference. He delivered that speech to Congress and the American people while sitting down, contrary to his usual practice of standing. This was Roosevelt's last major speech; he died six weeks later, just before the final victory of allied forces in Europe.

I come from the Crimea Conference with a firm belief that we have made a good start on the road to a world of peace.

There were two main purposes in this Crimea Conference. The first was to bring defeat to Germany with the greatest possible speed, and the smallest possible loss of Allied men. That purpose is now being carried out in great force. The German Army, and the German people, are feeling the ever-increasing might of our fighting men and of the Allied armies. Every hour gives us added pride in the heroic advance of our troops in Germany—on German soil—toward a meeting with the gallant Red Army.

The second purpose was to continue to build the foundation for an international accord that would bring order and security after the chaos of the war, that would give some assurance of lasting peace among the Nations of the world.

Toward that goal also, a tremendous stride was made. . . .

When we met at Yalta, in addition to laying our strategic and tactical plans for the complete and final military victory over Germany, there were other problems of vital political consequence.

For instance, first, there were the problems of the occupation and control of Germany—after victory—the complete destruction of her military power, and the assurance that neither the Nazi nor Prussian militarism could again be revived to threaten the peace and the civilization of the world.

Second—again for example—there was the settlement of the few differences that remained among us with respect to the International Security Organization after the Dumbarton Oaks Conference. As you remember, at that time, I said that we had agreed ninety percent. Well, that's a pretty good percentage. I think the other ten percent was ironed out at Yalta.

Third, there were the general political and economic problems common to all of the areas which had been or would be liberated from the Nazi yoke. This is a very special problem. We over here find it difficult to understand the ramifications of many of these problems in foreign lands, but we are trying to.

Fourth, there were the special problems created by a few instances such as Poland and Yugoslavia.

Days were spent in discussing these momentous matters and we argued freely and frankly across the table. But at the end, on every point, unanimous agreement was reached. And more important even than the agreement of words, I may say we achieved a unity of thought and a way of getting along together.

Of course, we know that it was Hitler's hope—and the German war lords'—that we would not agree—that some slight crack might appear in the solid wall of Allied unity, a crack that would give him and his fellow gangsters one last hope of escaping their just doom. That is the objective for which his propaganda machine has been working for many months.

But Hitler has failed. . . .

This time we are not making the mistake of waiting until the end of the war to set up the machinery of peace. This time, as we fight together to win the war finally, we work together to keep it from happening again. . . .

One outstanding example of joint action by the three major Allied powers in the liberated areas was the solution reached on Poland. The whole Polish question was a potential source of trouble in postwar Europe—as it has been sometimes before—and we came to the Conference determined to find a common ground for its solution. And we did—even though everybody does not agree with us, obviously.

Our objective was to help create a strong, independent, and prosperous Nation. That is the thing we must always remember, those words, agreed to by Russia, by Britain, and by the United States: the objective of making Poland a strong, independent, and prosperous Nation, with a government ultimately to be selected by the Polish people themselves.

To achieve that objective, it was necessary to provide for the formation of a new government much more representative than had been possible while Poland was enslaved. There were, as you know, two governments—one in London, one in Lublin—practically in Russia. Accordingly, steps were taken at Yalta to reorganize the existing Provisional Government in Poland on a broader democratic basis, so as to include democratic leaders now in Poland and those abroad. This new, reorganized government will be recognized by all of us as the temporary government of Poland. Poland needs a temporary government in the worst way—an ad interim government, I think is another way of putting it.

However, the new Polish Provisional Government of National Unity will be pledged to holding a free election as soon as possible on the basis of universal suffrage and a secret ballot.

Throughout history, Poland has been the corridor through which attacks on Russia have been made. Twice in this generation, Germany has struck at Russia through this corridor. To insure European security and world peace, a strong and independent Poland is necessary to prevent that from happening again.

The decision with respect to the boundaries of Poland was, frankly, a compromise. I did not agree with all of it, by any means, but we did not go as far as Britain wanted, in certain areas; we did not go as far as Russia wanted, in certain areas; and we did not go as far as I wanted, in certain areas. It *was* a compromise. The decision is one, however, under which the Poles will receive compensation in territory in the North and West in exchange for what they lose by the Curzon Line in the East. The limits of the western border will be permanently fixed in the final Peace Conference. We know, roughly, that it will include—in the new, strong Poland—quite a large slice of what now is called Germany. And it was agreed, also, that the new Poland will have a large and long coast line, and many new harbors. Also, that most of East Prussia will go to Poland. A corner of it will go to Russia. Also, that the anomaly of the Free State of Danzig [now Gdansk] will come to an end; I think Danzig would be a lot better if it were Polish.

It is well known that the people east of the Curzon Line—just for example, here is why I compromised—are predominantly White Russian and Ukrainian—they are not Polish; and a very great majority of the people west of the line are predominantly Polish, except in that part of East Prussia and eastern Germany, which will go to the new Poland. As far back as 1919, representatives of the Allies agreed that the Curzon Line represented a fair boundary between the two peoples. And you must remember, also, that there had not been any Polish government before 1919 for a great many generations.

I am convinced that the agreement on Poland, under the circumstances, is the most hopeful agreement possible for a free, independent, and prosperous Polish state. . . .

The Conference in the Crimea was a turning point—I hope in our history and therefore in the history of the world. There will soon be presented to the Senate of the United States and to the American people a great decision that will determine the fate of the United States—and of the world—for generations to come.

Questions

1. What does FDR believe he accomplished at Yalta?
2. What problems does he acknowledge are still unresolved?
3. Is the speech unduly optimistic? Why or why not?

Connections Questions

1. Was the Neutrality Act of 1937 the right act for the wrong war or just wrong? Discuss.
2. In what ways does Executive Order 9066 violate the spirit of Roosevelt's "Four Freedoms"? Of the reasoning behind the Supreme Court's decision in *Smith v. Allwright*?
3. How successful is FDR in making the results of the Yalta Conference fit into the framework of the "Four Freedoms"?

CHAPTER 28

Cold War America 1945–1960

George Kennan, "The Sources of Soviet Conduct" (1947)

*George Kennan (b. 1904) was a young and ambitious career foreign offi-
cer attached to the American embassy in Moscow. Kennan sent a lengthy
telegram to the State Department in early 1946 warning American policymakers of future Soviet aggression. Those ideas evolved into a position paper
that helped shape the Cold War policy of containment (see text p. 752). Kennan made his views public in July 1947 when, using the pseudonym "X," he
wrote an essay titled "The Sources of Soviet Conduct" for the influential journal* Foreign Affairs.

The political personality of Soviet power as we know it today is the product of ideology and circumstances: ideology inherited by the present Soviet
leaders from the movement in which they had their political origin, and circumstances of the power which they now have exercised for nearly three
decades in Russia. . . .

It is difficult to summarize the set of ideological concepts with which the
Soviet leaders came into power. Marxian ideology, in its Russian-Communist
projection, has always been in process of subtle evolution. The materials on
which it bases itself are extensive and complex. But the outstanding features
of Communist thought as it existed in 1916 may perhaps be summarized as
follows: (a) that the central factor in the life of man, the factor which determines the character of public life and the "physiognomy of society," is the system by which material goods are produced and exchanged; (b) that the capitalist system of production is a nefarious one which inevitably leads to the
exploitation of working class by the capital-owning class and is incapable of developing adequately the economic resources of society or of distributing fairly
the material goods produced by human labor; (c) that capitalism contains the
seeds of its own destruction and must, in view of the inability of the capital-
owning class to adjust itself to economic change, result eventually and in-
escapably in a revolutionary transfer of power to the working class; and (d)
that imperialism, the final phase of capitalism, leads directly to war and revolution.

The rest may be outlined in Lenin's own words: "Unevenness of economic
and political development is the inflexible law of capitalism. It follows from
this that the victory of Socialism may come originally in a few capitalist countries or even in a single capitalist country. The victorious proletariat of that
country, having expropriated the capitalists and having organized Socialist
production at home, would rise against the remaining capitalist world, draw-

ing to itself in the process the oppressed classes of other countries." It must be noted that there was no assumption that capitalism would perish without proletarian revolution. A final push was needed from a revolutionary proletariat movement in order to tip over the tottering structure. But it was regarded as inevitable that sooner or later that push be given. . . .

Now the maintenance of this pattern of Soviet power, namely, the pursuit of unlimited authority domestically, accompanied by the cultivation of the semi-myth of implacable foreign hostility, has gone far to shape the actual machinery of Soviet power as we know it today. Internal organs of administration which did not serve this purpose withered on the vine. Organs which did serve this purpose became vastly swollen. The security of Soviet power came to rest on the iron discipline of the Party, on the severity and ubiquity of the secret police, and on the uncompromising economic monopolism of the state. The "organs of suppression," in which the Soviet leaders had sought security from rival forces, became in large measure the masters of those whom they were designed to serve. Today the major part of the structure of Soviet power is committed to the perfection of the dictatorship and to the maintenance of the concept of Russia as in a state of siege, with the enemy lowering beyond the walls. And the millions of human beings who form that part of the structure of power must defend at all costs this concept of Russia's position, for without it they are themselves superfluous.

As things stand today, the rulers can no longer dream of parting with these organs of suppression. The quest for absolute power, pursued now for nearly three decades with a ruthlessness unparalleled (in scope at least) in modern times, has again produced internally, as it did externally, its own reaction. The excesses of the police apparatus have fanned the potential opposition to the régime into something far greater and more dangerous than it could have been before those excesses began. . . .

II

But we have seen that the Kremlin is under no ideological compulsion to accomplish its purposes in a hurry. Like the Church, it is dealing in ideological concepts which are of long-term validity, and it can afford to be patient. It has no right to risk the existing achievements of the revolution for the sake of vain baubles of the future. The very teachings of Lenin himself require great caution and flexibility in the pursuit of Communist purposes. Again, these precepts are fortified by the lessons of Russian history: of centuries of obscure battles between nomadic forces over the stretches of a vast unfortified plain. Here caution, circumspection, flexibility and deception are the valuable qualities; and their value finds natural appreciation in the Russian or the oriental mind. Thus the Kremlin has no compunction about retreating in the face of superior force. And being under the compulsion of no timetable, it does not get panicky under the necessity for such retreat. Its political action is a fluid stream which moves constantly, wherever it is permitted to move, toward a given goal. Its main concern is to make sure that it has filled every nook and cranny available to it in the basin of world power. But if it finds unassailable barriers in its path, it accepts these philosophically and accommodates itself to them. The main thing is that there should always be pressure, unceasing constant pressure, toward the desired goal. . . .

In these circumstances it is clear that the main element of any United States policy toward the Soviet Union must be that of a long-term, patient but firm and vigilant containment of Russian expansive tendencies. It is important to note, however, that such a policy has nothing to do with outward histrionics: with threats or blustering or superfluous gestures of outward "toughness." . . .

III

In the light of the above, it will be clearly seen that the Soviet pressure against the free institutions of the western world is something that can be contained by the adroit and vigilant application of counter-force at a series of constantly shifting geographical and political points, corresponding to the shifts and manœuvres of Soviet policy, but which cannot be charmed or talked out of existence. . . .

Thus the future of Soviet power may not be by any means as secure as Russian capacity for self-delusion would make it appear to the men in the Kremlin. That they can keep power themselves, they have demonstrated. That they can quietly and easily turn it over to others remains to be proved. Meanwhile, the hardships of their rule and the vicissitudes of international life have taken a heavy toll on the strength and hopes of the great people on whom their power rests. . . . This cannot be proved. And it cannot be disproved: But the possibility remains (and in the opinion of this writer it is a strong one) that Soviet power, like the capitalist world of its conception, bears within it the seeds of its own decay, and that the sprouting of these seeds is well advanced.

IV

It is clear that the United States cannot expect in the foreseeable future to enjoy political intimacy with the Soviet régime. It must continue to regard the Soviet Union as a rival, not a partner, in the political arena. It must continue to expect that Soviet policies will reflect no abstract love of peace and stability, no real faith in the possibility of a permanent happy coexistence of the Socialist and capitalist worlds, but rather a cautious, persistent pressure toward the disruption and weakening of all rival influence and rival power.

Balanced against this are the facts that Russia, as opposed to the western world in general, is still by far the weaker party, that Soviet policy is highly flexible, and that Soviet society may well contain deficiencies which will eventually weaken its own total potential. This would of itself warrant the United States entering with reasonable confidence upon a policy of firm containment, designed to confront the Russians with unalterable counter-force at every point where they show signs of encroaching upon the interests of a peaceful and stable world.

But in actuality the possibilities for American policy are by no means limited to holding the line and hoping for the best. It is entirely possible for the United States to influence by its actions the internal developments, both within Russia and throughout the international Communist movement, by which Russian policy is largely determined. This is not only a question of the modest measure of informational activity which this government can conduct in the Soviet Union and elsewhere, although that, too, is important. It is rather a question of the degree to which the United States can create among the peoples of the world generally the impression of a country which knows what it wants, which is coping successfully with the problems of its internal life and with the responsibilities of a World Power, and which has a spiritual vitality capable of holding its own among the major ideological currents of the time. To the extent that such an impression can be created and maintained, the aims of Russian Communism must appear sterile and quixotic, the hopes and enthusiasm of Moscow's supporters must wane, and added strain must be imposed on the Kremlin's foreign policies. For the palsied decrepitude of the capitalist world is the keystone of Communist philosophy. Even the failure of the United States to experience the early economic depression which the ravens of the Red Square have been predicting with such complacent confidence since hostilities ceased would have deep and important repercussions throughout the Communist world. . . .

It would be an exaggeration to say that American behavior unassisted and alone could exercise a power of life and death over the Communist movement and bring about the early fall of Soviet power in Russia. But the United States has it in its power to increase enormously the strains under which Soviet policy must operate, to force upon the Kremlin a far greater degree of moderation and circumspection than it has had to observe in recent years, and in this way to promote tendencies which must eventually find their outlet in either the break-up or the gradual mellowing of Soviet power. For no mystical, Messianic movement—and particularly not that of the Kremlin—can face frustration indefinitely without eventually adjusting itself in one way or another to the logic of that state of affairs.

Thus the decision will really fall in large measure in this country itself. The issue of Soviet-American relations is in essence a test of the over-all worth of the United States as a nation among nations. To avoid destruction the United States need only measure up to its own best traditions and prove itself worthy of preservation as a great nation. . . .

Questions

1. How much does Soviet communism really have to do with the history Kennan is describing? What role does history play in his analysis?
2. What specific strategies does Kennan propose for carrying out a policy of containment?
3. Would you call this an optimistic view of future U.S.–Soviet relations? Why or why not?

Senator Arthur Vandenberg
on NATO (1949)

By 1948, several European nations had begun planning for their own defense through the Brussels Pact. Senator Arthur Vandenberg (1884–1951) of Michigan, at one time an ardent isolationist, used his position as chairman of the Senate Foreign Relations Committee to include the United States in this new European defense system. The Vandenberg Resolution called for the United States to negotiate with the Brussels Pact signatories to develop a wider defensive arrangement for Western Europe. The outgrowth was the North Atlantic Treaty Organization (see text p. 755). Vandenberg took great pleasure in helping create NATO: "Rarely in our nation's history has such a small egg hatched so quickly into such a large chicken," he wrote in his memoirs. In letters to constituents, he expressed his hopes for NATO.

January 27, 1949

There is no doubt about the fact that it is a "calculated risk" for us to even partially arm the countries of Western Europe. It is also very much of a "calculated risk" if we do *not*. One risk will have to be weighed against the other. You suggest that it will be a safe thing to do "when the economic stability of these countries shall have improved." The basic question we have to settle is whether "economic stability" can precede the creation of a greater sense of physical security. I am inclined to think that "physical security" is a prerequisite to the kind of long-range economic planning which Western Europe requires. The fact remains that the problem is fraught with many hazardous imponderables. I am withholding my own final judgment until I see the precise terms of the treaty under which this new cooperation will be proposed. I think we ought to have wit enough to write it on a basis which is relatively safe. . . .

February 21, 1949

In my opinion, when Mr. Hitler was contemplating World War Two, I believe he would have never launched it if he had had any serious reasons to believe that it might bring him into armed collision with the United States. I think he was sure it would not do so because of our then existing neutrality laws. If an appropriate North Atlantic Pact is written, I think it will exactly reverse this psychology so far as Mr. Stalin is concerned if, as and when he contemplates World War Three. Under such circumstances, I very much doubt whether World War Three happens. . . .

February 22, 1949

I am one of its [the Pact's] authors. I heartily believe in it. I want to give it a maximum chance to help prevent World War Three before it starts. But this requires absolute candor as to what it does and does not promise. I can think of no greater tragedy than to permit our friends in Western Europe to interpret the Pact beyond its actual realities. One reality is that we cannot commit ourselves to automatic war in the future. . . . We are recognizing facts of life as established in the Constitution of the United States. I will go as far as I can within the Constitution. I will not go farther because it would be an imposition upon our own good faith and a false reliance for our friends abroad. I hasten to add that I think we can achieve every essential result for the North Atlantic Pact by staying strictly within the Constitution of the United States and within the Charter of the United Nations. . . .

March 18, 1949

I am glad to know your preliminary reaction to the North Atlantic pact. I agree with you one thousand percent that "this world cannot stand another war." Every effort of my remaining days will be dedicated to this truth. My greatest fear in this connection is that we will somehow drift into another war. . . . If Soviet Russia does start to march it would seem to be completely inevitable that the United States will be the ultimate target and that we shall inevitably be in that war—Pact or no Pact. So it seems to me that our best insurance is to make our position plan in advance. This includes above all else a clear demonstration that our objectives are totally defensive; that we have no goal except peace with honor and justice in a live-and-let-live world.

If you are right and this proposed North Atlantic Pact is "another provocation to another World War" then the Pact ought to be rejected. If I am right in believing that the Pact is our best protection against another World War then the Pact ought to be ratified. Therefore, our current problem is to fully and publicly explore every phase and every angle of the Pact. You may be very sure that I shall insist upon extensive public hearings which will clarify the issue. I want everything ventilated in this connection so that we may reach the wisest possible decision in a situation where we must take a "calculated risk" whichever way the decision goes. . . .

[July 21, 1949]
    Well—as you know we won the big battle [over the North Atlantic Treaty] today by a vote of 82 to 13. . . . It's a great relief to have the battle over—yet I seem to feel a greater responsibility than ever tonight—how will it all work out? At best, it's a calculated risk. But I have a feeling that this day will go down in history as one of the big dates. . . .

Questions

1. According to Senator Vandenberg, what dangers does the United States face in the Cold War?
2. What risks does the United States run by aligning itself so closely with Western Europe? What gains does NATO make possible?
3. What lessons does Vandenberg take from the events preceding World War II? How does he apply them to NATO?

Harry S Truman on Civil Rights (1947)

President Truman's attitude toward civil rights is remarkable for its combination of political pragmatism and honest morality. As he wrote to an old friend and opponent of racial integration: "I am not asking for social equality, because no such thing exists, but I am asking for equality of opportunity for all human beings and, as long as I stay here [in the White House], I am going to continue that fight." That attitude is plain in this speech Truman gave to the National Association for the Advancement of Colored People on June 29, 1947. The site was the Lincoln Memorial, where Martin Luther King, Jr. would deliver his "I Have a Dream" address sixteen years later.

I am happy to be present at the closing session of the 38th Annual Conference of the National Association for the Advancement of Colored People. The occasion of meeting with you here at the Lincoln Memorial affords me the opportunity to congratulate the association upon its effective work for the improvement of our democratic processes.
    I should like to talk to you briefly about civil rights and human freedom. It is my deep conviction that we have reached a turning point in the long history of our country's efforts to guarantee freedom and equality to all our cit-

izens. Recent events in the United States and abroad have made us realize that it is more important today than ever before to insure that all Americans enjoy these rights.

When I say all Americans I mean all Americans.

The civil rights laws written in the early years of our Republic, and the traditions which have been built upon them, are precious to us. Those laws were drawn up with the memory still fresh in men's minds of the tyranny of an absentee government. They were written to protect the citizen against any possible tyrannical act by the new government in this country.

But we cannot be content with a civil liberties program which emphasizes only the need of protection against the possibility of tyranny by the Government.

We cannot stop there.

We must keep moving forward, with new concepts of civil rights to safeguard our heritage. The extension of civil rights today means, not protection of the people *against* the Government, but protection of the people *by* the Government.

We must make the Federal Government a friendly, vigilant defender of the rights and equalities of all Americans. And again I mean all Americans.

As Americans, we believe that every man should be free to live his life as he wishes. He should be limited only by his responsibility to his fellow countrymen. If this freedom is to be more than a dream, each man must be guaranteed equality of opportunity. The only limit to an American's achievement should be his ability, his industry, and his character. These rewards for his effort should be determined only by those truly relevant qualities.

Our immediate task is to remove the last remnants of the barriers which stand between millions of our citizens and their birthright. There is no justifiable reason for discrimination because of ancestry, or religion, or race, or color.

We must not tolerate such limitations on the freedom of any of our people and on their enjoyment of basic rights which every citizen in a truly democratic society must possess.

Every man should have the right to a decent home, the right to an education, the right to adequate medical care, the right to a worthwhile job, the right to an equal share in making the public decisions through the ballot, and the right to a fair trial in a fair court.

We must insure that these rights—on equal terms—are enjoyed by every citizen.

To these principles I pledge my full and continued support.

Many of our people still suffer the indignity of insult, the narrowing fear of intimidation, and, I regret to say, the threat of physical injury and mob violence. Prejudice and intolerance in which these evils are rooted still exist. The conscience of our Nation, and the legal machinery which enforces it, have not yet secured to each citizen full freedom from fear.

We cannot wait another decade or another generation to remedy these evils. We must work, as never before, to cure them now. The aftermath of war and the desire to keep faith with our Nation's historic principles make the need a pressing one.

The support of desperate populations of battle-ravaged countries must be won for the free way of life. We must have them as allies in our continuing struggle for the peaceful solution of the world's problems. Freedom is not an easy lesson to teach, nor an easy cause to sell, to peoples beset by every kind of privation. They may surrender to the false security offered so temptingly by totalitarian regimes unless we can prove the superiority of democracy.

Our case for democracy should be as strong as we can make it. It should rest on practical evidence that we have been able to put our own house in order.

For these compelling reasons, we can no longer afford the luxury of a leisurely attack upon prejudice and discrimination. There is much that State and local governments can do in providing positive safeguards for civil rights. But we cannot, any longer, await the growth of a will to action in the slowest State or the most backward community.

Our National Government must show the way.

This is a difficult and complex undertaking. Federal laws and administrative machineries must be improved and expanded. We must provide the Government with better tools to do the job. As a first step, I appointed an Advisory Committee on Civil Rights last December. Its members, fifteen distinguished private citizens, have been surveying our civil rights difficulties and needs for several months. I am confident that the product of their work will be a sensible and vigorous program for action by all of us.

We must strive to advance civil rights wherever it lies within our power. For example, I have asked the Congress to pass legislation extending basic civil rights to the people of Guam and American Samoa so that these people can share our ideals of freedom and self-government. This step, with others which will follow, is evidence to the rest of the world of our confidence in the ability of all men to build free institutions.

The way ahead is not easy. We shall need all the wisdom, imagination and courage we can muster. We must and shall guarantee the civil rights of all our citizens. Never before has the need been so urgent for skillful and vigorous action to bring us closer to our ideal.

We can reach the goal. When past difficulties faced our Nation we met the challenge with inspiring charters of human rights—the Declaration of Independence, the Constitution, the Bill of Rights, and the Emancipation Proclamation. Today our representatives, and those of other liberty-loving countries on the United Nations Commission on Civil Rights, are preparing an International Bill of Rights. We can be confident that it will be a great landmark in man's long search for freedom since its members consist of such distinguished citizens of the world as Mrs. Franklin D. Roosevelt.

With these noble characters to guide us, and with faith in our hearts, we shall make our land a happier home for our people, a symbol of hope for all men, and a rock of security in a troubled world.

Abraham Lincoln understood as well the ideal which you and I seek today. As this conference closes we would do well to keep in mind his words, when he said,

". . . . if it shall please the Divine Being who determines the destinies of nations, we shall remain a united people, and we will, humbly seeking the Divine Guidance, make their prolonged national existence a source of new benefits to themselves and their successors, and to all classes and conditions of mankind."

Questions

1. What role does President Truman believe the federal government should play in the field of civil rights?
2. What basic rights does Truman make a commitment to protect for all Americans?
3. What steps has the president taken or does he propose to take to advance civil rights in the United States?

Joseph R. McCarthy on Communists in the U.S. Government (1950)

Senator Joseph R. McCarthy (1908–1957) of Wisconsin, who preferred the all-American name Joe, kept a low profile in the Senate through the early years of a term that began in 1947. Figuring that to win reelection in 1952 he would need an issue to bring him national attention, in 1950 he hit on the idea of "communists in government." What began as a campaign issue quickly took on a new life at a time when Americans had grown fearful of communist subversion at home and aggression abroad (see text p. 765). On February 9, 1950, McCarthy tried out his idea in a speech before an audience of Republican women in Wheeling, West Virginia. The senator claimed he had a list of 205 known Communists in the State Department. In this version of the speech (read into the Congressional Record *of February 20, 1950), McCarthy revised the number to 57; a Senate investigating committee later rejected all of his accusations. But McCarthy used his anticommunist crusade to remain in the political spotlight for four years. In 1954, the senator overplayed the issue and became increasingly unpopular. But his name carries on as a term for political extremism.*

The John Service mentioned here is the son of China missionary Grace Service (see Chapter 22, "Open House Days").

Five years after a world war has been won, men's hearts should anticipate a long peace, and men's minds should be free from the heavy weight that comes with war. But this is not such a period—for this is not a period of peace. This is a time of the "cold war." This is a time when all the world is split into two vast, increasingly hostile armed camps—a time of a great armaments race.

Today we can almost physically hear the mutterings and rumblings of an invigorated god of war. You can see it, feel it, and hear it all the way from the hills of Indochina, from the shores of Formosa, right over into the very heart of Europe itself. . . .

[W]e are now engaged in a show-down fight—not the usual war between nations for land areas or other material gains, but a war between two diametrically opposed ideologies.

The great difference between our western Christian world and the atheistic Communist world is not political, ladies and gentlemen, it is moral. . . .

The real, basic difference, however, lies in the religion of immoralism—invented by Marx, preached feverishly by Lenin, and carried to unimaginable extremes by Stalin. This religion of immoralism, if the Red half of the world wins—and well it may—this religion of immoralism will more deeply wound and damage mankind than any conceivable economic or political system.

Karl Marx dismissed God as a hoax, and Lenin and Stalin have added in clear-cut, unmistakable language their resolve that no nation, no people who believe in a God, can exist side by side with their communistic state.

Karl Marx, for example, expelled people from his Communist Party for mentioning such things as justice, humanity, or morality. He called this soulful ravings and sloppy sentimentality.

While Lincoln was a relatively young man in his late thirties, Karl Marx boasted that the Communist specter was haunting Europe. Since that time, hundreds of millions of people and vast areas of the world have fallen under Communist domination. Today, less than 100 years after Lincoln's death, Stalin brags that this Communist specter is not only haunting the world, but is about to completely subjugate it.

Today we are engaged in a final, all-out battle between communistic atheism and Christianity. The modern champions of communism have selected this as the time. And, ladies and gentlemen, the chips are down—they are truly down. . . .

Ladies and gentlemen, can there be anyone here tonight who is so blind as to say that the war is not on? Can there be anyone who fails to realize that the Communist world has said, "The time is now"—and that this is the time for the show-down between the democratic Christian world and the Communist atheistic world?

Unless we face this fact, we shall pay the price that must be paid by those who wait too long.

Six years ago, at the time of the first conference to map out the peace—Dumbarton Oaks—there was within the Soviet orbit 180,000,000 people. Lined up on the antitotalitarian side there were in the world at that time roughly 1,625,000,000 people. Today only 6 years later, there are 800,000,000 people under the absolute domination of Soviet Russia—an increase of over 400 percent. On our side, the figure has shrunk to around 500,000,000. In other words, in less than 6 years the odds have changed from 9 to 1 in our favor to 8 to 5 against us. This indicates the swiftness of the tempo of Communist victories and American defeats in the cold war. As one of our outstanding historical figures once said, "When a great democracy is destroyed, it will not be because of enemies from without, but rather because of enemies from within."

The truth of this statement is becoming terrifyingly clear as we see this country each day losing on every front.

At war's end we were physically the strongest nation on earth and, at least potentially, the most powerful intellectually and morally. Ours could have been the honor of being a beacon in the desert of destruction, a shining living proof that civilization was not yet ready to destroy itself. Unfortunately, we have failed miserably and tragically to arise to the opportunity.

The reason why we find ourselves in a position of impotency is not because our only powerful potential enemy has sent men to invade our shores, but rather because of the traitorous actions of those who have been treated so well by this Nation. It has not been the less fortunate or members of minority groups who have been selling this Nation out, but rather those who have had all the benefits that the wealthiest nation on earth has had to offer—the finest homes, the finest college education, and the finest jobs in Government we can give.

This is glaringly true in the State Department. There the bright young men who are born with silver spoons in their mouths are the ones who have been worst. . . .

When Chiang Kai-shek [Jiang Jieshi] was fighting our war, the State Department had in China a young man named John S. Service. His task, obviously, was not to work for the communization of China. Strangely, however, he sent official reports back to the State Department urging that we torpedo our ally Chiang Kai-shek and stating, in effect, that communism was the best hope of China.

Later, this man—John Service—was picked up by the Federal Bureau of Investigation for turning over to the Communists secret State Department information. Strangely, however, he was never prosecuted. However, Joseph

Grew, the Under Secretary of State, who insisted on his prosecution, was forced to resign. Two days after Grew's successor, Dean Acheson, took over as Under Secretary of State, this man—John Service—who had been picked up by the FBI and who had previously urged that communism was the best hope of China, was not only reinstated in the State Department but promoted. And finally, under Acheson, placed in charge of all placements and promotions.

Today, ladies and gentlemen, this man Service is on his way to represent the State Department and Acheson in Calcutta—by far and away the most important listening post in the Far East. . . .

This, ladies and gentlemen, gives you somewhat of a picture of the type of individuals who have been helping to shape our foreign policy. In my opinion the State Department, which is one of the most important government departments, is thoroughly infested with Communists.

I have in my hand 57 cases of individuals who would appear to be either card carrying members or certainly loyal to the Communist Party, but who nevertheless are still helping to shape our foreign policy.

One thing to remember in discussing the Communists in our Government is that we are not dealing with spies who get 30 pieces of silver to steal the blueprints of a new weapon. We are dealing with a far more sinister type of activity because it permits the enemy to guide and shape our policy. . . .

It is the result of an emotional hang-over and a temporary moral lapse which follows every war. It is the apathy to evil which people who have been subjected to the tremendous evils of war feel. As the people of the world see mass murder, the destruction of defenseless and innocent people, and all of the crime and lack of morals which go with war, they become numb and apathetic. It has always been thus after war.

However, the morals of our people have not been destroyed. They still exist. This cloak of numbness and apathy has only needed a spark to rekindle them. Happily, this spark has finally been supplied.

As you know, very recently the Secretary of State proclaimed his loyalty to a man guilty of what has always been considered as the most abominable of all crimes—of being a traitor to the people who gave him a position of great trust. The Secretary of State in attempting to justify his continued devotion to the man who sold out the Christian world to the atheistic world, referred to Christ's Sermon on the Mount as a justification and reason therefor, and the reaction of the American people to this would have made the heart of Abraham Lincoln happy.

When this pompous diplomat in striped pants, with a phony British accent, proclaimed to the American people that Christ on the Mount endorsed communism, high treason, and betrayal of a sacred trust, the blasphemy was so great that it awakened the dormant indignation of the American people.

He has lighted the spark which is resulting in a moral uprising and will end only when the whole sorry mess of twisted, warped thinkers are swept from the national scene so that we may have a new birth of national honesty and decency in Government.

Questions

1. What do you take the biblical references to mean? Are they appropriate? Why or why not?
2. Given the enemies mentioned, what voters do you think McCarthy is targeting and why?
3. Why was this kind of speech so hard to refute?

Dwight D. Eisenhower, Farewell Address (1961)

During the second Eisenhower administration, it became increasingly clear that science and technology were going to play a crucial role in maintaining America's position in the world order. But what would the elements of that order be, and how would Americans cope with them? The difference between "pure" science and technology and engineering was not clear to the public. Science came under political pressure and ideological scrutiny, whereas technology and engineering seemed to be confined to providing solutions to practical problems. President Eisenhower in his farewell address tried to make clear at least some of the misunderstandings that were bound to arise.

We now stand ten years past the midpoint of a century that has witnessed four major wars among great nations. Three of these involved our own country. Despite these holocausts America is today the strongest, the most influential and most productive nation in the world. Understandably proud of this pre-eminence, we yet realize that America's leadership and prestige depend, not merely upon our unmatched material progress, riches and military strength, but on how we use our power in the interests of world peace and human betterment.

Throughout America's adventure in free government, our basic purposes have been to keep the peace; to foster progress in human achievement, and to enhance liberty, dignity and integrity among people and among nations. To strive for less would be unworthy of a free and religious people. Any failure traceable to arrogance, or our lack of comprehension or readiness to sacrifice would inflict upon us grievous hurt both at home and abroad.

Progress toward these noble goals is persistently threatened by the conflict now engulfing the world. It commands our whole attention, absorbs our very beings. We face a hostile ideology—global in scope, atheistic in character, ruthless in purpose, and insidious in method. Unhappily the danger it poses promises to be of indefinite duration. To meet it successfully, there is called for, not so much the emotional and transitory sacrifices of crisis, but rather those which enable us to carry forward steadily, surely, and without complaint the burdens of a prolonged and complex struggle—with liberty the stake. Only thus shall we remain, despite every provocation, on our charted course toward permanent peace and human betterment. . . .

A vital element in keeping the peace is our military establishment. Our arms must be mighty, ready for instant action, so that no potential aggressor may be tempted to risk his own destruction.

Our military organization today bears little relation to that known by any of my predecessors in peacetime, or indeed by the fighting men of World War II or Korea.

Until the latest of our world conflicts, the United States had no armaments industry. American makers of plowshares could, with time and as required, make swords as well. But now we can no longer risk emergency improvisation of national defense; we have been compelled to create a permanent armaments industry of vast proportions. Added to this, three and a half million men and women are directly engaged in the defense establishment. We annually spend on military security more than the net income of all United States corporations.

This conjunction of an immense military establishment and a large arms industry is new in the American experience. The total influence—economic, political, even spiritual—is felt in every city, every State house, every office of the Federal government. We recognize the imperative need for this development. Yet we must not fail to comprehend its grave implications. Our toil, resources and livelihood are all involved; so is the very structure of our society.

In the councils of government, we must guard against the acquisition of unwarranted influence, whether sought or unsought, by the military-industrial complex. The potential for the disastrous rise of misplaced power exists and will persist.

We must never let the weight of this combination endanger our liberties or democratic processes. We should take nothing for granted. Only an alert and knowledgeable citizenry can compel the proper meshing of the huge industrial and military machinery of defense with our peaceful methods and goals, so that security and liberty may prosper together.

Akin to, and largely responsible for the sweeping changes in our industrial-military posture, has been the technological revolution during recent decades.

In this revolution, research has become central; it also becomes more formalized, complex, and costly. A steadily increasing share is conducted for, by, or at the direction of, the Federal government.

Today, the solitary inventor, tinkering in his shop, has been overshadowed by task forces of scientists in laboratories and testing fields. In the same fashion, the free university, historically the fountainhead of free ideas and scientific discovery, has experienced a revolution in the conduct of research. Partly because of the huge costs involved, a government contract becomes virtually a substitute for intellectual curiosity. For every old blackboard there are now hundreds of new electronic computers.

The prospect of domination of the nation's scholars by Federal employment, project allocations, and the power of money is ever present—and is gravely to be regarded.

Yet, in holding scientific research and discovery in respect, as we should, we must also be alert to the equal and opposite danger that public policy could itself become the captive of a scientific-technological elite.

It is the task of statesmanship to mold, to balance, and to integrate these and other forces, new and old, within the principles of our democratic system—ever aiming toward the supreme goals of our free society.

Another factor in maintaining balance involves the element of time. As we peer into society's future, we—you and I, and our government—must avoid the impulse to live only for today, plundering, for our own ease and convenience, the precious resources of tomorrow. We cannot mortgage the material assets of our grandchildren without risking the loss also of their political and spiritual heritage. We want democracy to survive for all generations to come, not to become the insolvent phantom of tomorrow.

Down the long lane of the history yet to be written America knows that this world of ours, ever growing smaller, must avoid becoming a community of dreadful fear and hate, and be, instead, a proud confederation of mutual trust and respect.

Such a confederation must be one of equals. The weakest must come to the conference table with the same confidence as do we, protected as we are by our moral, economic, and military strength. That table, though scarred by many past frustrations, cannot be abandoned for the certain agony of the battlefield.

Disarmament, with mutual honor and confidence, is a continuing imperative. Together we must learn how to compose differences, not with arms, but with intellect and decent purpose. Because this need is so sharp and apparent I confess that I lay down my official responsibilities in this field with a definite sense of disappointment. As one who has witnessed the horror and the lingering sadness of war—as one who knows that another war could utterly destroy this civilization which has been so slowly and painfully built over thousands of years—I wish I could say tonight that a lasting peace is in sight.

Happily, I can say that war has been avoided. Steady progress toward our ultimate goal has been made. But, so much remains to be done. As a private citizen, I shall never cease to do what little I can to help the world advance along that road. . . .

You and I—my fellow citizens—need to be strong in our faith that all nations, under God, will reach the goal of peace with justice. May we be ever unswerving in devotion to principle, confident but humble with power, diligent in pursuit of the Nation's great goals.

To all the peoples of the world, I once more give expression to America's prayerful and continuing aspiration:

We pray that peoples of all faiths, all races, all nations, may have their great human needs satisfied; that those now denied opportunity shall come to enjoy it to the full; that all who yearn for freedom may experience its spiritual blessings; that those who have freedom will understand, also, its heavy responsibilities; that all who are insensitive to the needs of others will learn charity; that the scourges of poverty, disease and ignorance will be made to disappear from the earth, and that, in the goodness of time, all peoples will come to live together in a peace guaranteed by the binding force of mutual respect and love.

Questions

1. President Eisenhower seems to see a threat to the independence of universities and the sciences as a result of governmental invasion of university laboratories. How does he describe changes in laboratories that would make them subject to such an invasion?

2. His use of the term *military–industrial complex* suggests the potential for a conspiracy against the public interest. How does he relate the military to public and governmental concerns? What role does government play in the development of industrial power?

3. Liberty, the president says, is at stake. From the speech, which institutions seem to be involved? Who is threatening liberty, and what can be done to protect it?

Connections Questions

1. How could Joseph McCarthy find a receptive audience against a presidential administration with a strong anticommunist foreign policy?

2. McCarthyism has often been called a corruption of populism. Do you see any similarities between McCarthy's speech and Luna Kellie's (see Chapter 19, "Stand Up for Nebraska")? If so, what are they?

3. Are the stands taken by Harry Truman on civil rights and Dwight Eisenhower on the military–industrial complex motivated more by politics or conscience? Use background information from the text in framing your answer.

CHAPTER 29

Affluence and Its Contradictions 1945–1965

Nash Motors Advertisement (1945)

War was all-consuming in Europe and Asia but not in the United States, where there had been no combat and relatively light casualties. As World War II neared an end in 1945, many Americans were impatient to see what the future had in store—and what stores would have in the future. Nash Motors offered a hint that May. Such ads helped to set off an era of unprecedented consumption by Americans.

Questions

1. How does the ad balance consumer appeal and patriotism?
2. According to Nash, what appears to be the essence of peace?
3. Given that there were three months of fighting left, was the ad appropriate? Why or why not?

WHEN YOU MEET AGAIN . . .

It will be you again, just you, together again . . .

The road's a ribbon of white in the pale moonlight, and the trees whisper "Everything's going to be all right," and the sound of the wind rushing past is a voice crooning "home, home again, home at last . . ."

Home, at last with the wind and the stars and the girl and the car you've been longing for.

The panel's glow and the wheel in your hands and the feel of her shoulder warm against yours . . . and the lift and power of singing speed and the long, bright beams exploring the night . . . and the deep, sleepy hush of the motor's murmur . . .

All tell you again what you've needed, wanted, waited for . . . you have.

And your heart beats fast for now you know there's *nothing* ahead but the open road and the far-off places where a blue sky rolls to the horizon's edges.

•   •   •

Though here at Nash our entire effort has been devoted to production for war . . . we believe we can look ahead now, think ahead now, to the time when we'll be building cars again, to the time when we'll be making two great new Nash cars designed to be the finest, biggest, most dependable and economical automobiles in their respective fields . . . the new medium-priced Nash Ambassador and the new low-priced Nash "600". And Nash will build these new, advanced cars in numbers three times greater than our 1941 peak. In this way Nash will contribute the jobs, the opportunities, the futures that will help insure the strong, the growing, the prosperous America we owe to those who now work and fight to preserve it.

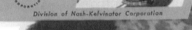

Nash MOTORS

Division of Nash-Kelvinator Corporation

Classifieds from the
Chicago Sunday Tribune (1957)

The 1950s were a transitional decade for American women. Employers were eager to hire (see text p. 784), but the want ads did not promise the same kinds of jobs that men sought. Still, the ads show that notions about work, gender, and worth underwent substantial change at a time when there existed, according to the text, "a significant gap between popular culture and the reality of American lives."

Questions

1. What do the ads stress as benefits?
2. To what extent are these jobs professional?
3. Why would there be separate want-ad sections based on gender?

Executive Secretary
$100 Week

$100 paid weekly to the PRESIDENT'S private secretary. Your own carpeted private office. Average skills nec. as you'll be handling most of your own correspondence. Ability to deal with people important, heavy public contact work involved. FREE at CHICAGO Personnel. 6 E. Randolph [Above Walgreens.] RAndolph 6-2355.

Arrange
Social Functions

Famous college fraternity needs you to take over in their beautiful new national headquarters office. Make arrangements for social functions, send invitations to members, handle enrollments and all convention plans. $70 to start with raise in 30 days for this unusually different position. FREE at LAKE Personnel. 29 E. Madison.
RAndolph 6-4650   11th Fl.

RECEPTION
LITE TYPING

No exp. nec. for this front office reception position. Answer pushbutton phones, greet visitors in beautiful modern office from 9-5. Lt. typing. Sal. high. FREE at LAKE Personnel. 29 E. Madison.
RAndolph 6-4650.   11th Fl.

Reservation
Secretary

Lite steno desired for unique position as secretary in charge of reservations for beautiful hotel. Handle accommodations for important people in the public eye. Poise and ability to deal with people important. Extremely high starting salary. FREE at LAKE Personnel. 29 E. Madison.

RAndolph 6-4650　　　　　　　　11th Fl.

AIRLINE TICKET
SALES GIRL

$305 mo. even during 10 day training period as ticket sales girl with high paying airline. All public contact—no office skills. Single girls receive travel passes for themselves and their families. Absolutely no exp. nec. For details see

| BOULEVARD | 22 W. Madison st. |
| 5th Floor | FInancial 6-3780 |

RECEPTION
WILL TEACH SWBD.

No experience or typing needed to be front office girl in well known commercial art studio. Your nice appearance, friendly manner, interest in public contact qualify. Salary open and high! Vacation this summer! Beginner qualifies. No fee at

| BOULEVARD | 22 W. Madison st. |
| 5th Floor | FInancial 6-3780 |

SECRETARY

Permanent position available for girl to perform secretarial work of a varied nature. Requires person with pleasing personality, experience and ability. Modern air conditioned office located for convenient transportation.

GOSS
PRINTING PRESS CO.
5601 W. 31ST-ST.

BIshop 2-3300　　　　　　　　Ext. 311

SECRETARY
PUBLIC RELATIONS DIR.

Must have good stenographic skills and like to do a variety of work. Age 22-30. Paid vacations, holidays, company cafeteria, and other employee benefits.

ILLINOIS TOOL WORKS
2501 N. Keeler [4200 W.]

SECRETARY
VACATION WITH PAY THIS
SUMMER!

If you're not happy where you are, but don't want to lose your vacation this summer, here's your chance. We need a secretary for a vice president of this advertising agency, one who's neat, accurate taking and transcribing heavy copy dictation on electric typewriter, who can handle details herself, keep her boss on the beam, help out elsewhere in this six-girl office. We're in a spanking new office just a few steps from Van Buren I. C. station. A happy place to work in an expanding organization. Salary starts at $70 per week, but you must work 1 month before vacation starts. We'll test you before hiring—to start at once.

CALL MR. DEAN
WAbash 2-8056

SALES
POSITIONS

HOUSEWIVES

NO
EXPERIENCE
NECESSARY

EARN
EXTRA MONEY
FOR
VACATION

WORK
FULL TIME

PART TIME

SALARY
+ COMMISSION

GOOD EARNINGS

IMMEDIATE
MERCHANDISE
DISCOUNT

APPLY NOW!

GOLDBLATTS

LOOP
STATE AND VAN BUREN

NORTH
4722 N. BROADWAY
3149 N. LINCOLN-AV.

SOUTH
250 PLAZA—PARK FOREST
7975 S. CICERO

Brides! Housewives!

Have You 2 or 3 days to Spare, Each Week?

This part-time job—in a pleasant, air conditioned Michigan avenue office—will take you away from home just enough each week, to sharpen up your interest in your household tasks.

Type of duties in this job? You will alternate chiefly between telephone work and general office work. You'll be working with nice people, and you'll find the days go quickly.

You have your choice of working either 2 or 3 full days [8 hours] each week, but one of the days must be Friday. Also, we have one opening for Sunday work, combined with 2-3 other weekdays.

No previous experience is necessary, but an alert, intelligent attitude and liking for people are important.

If you find this offer appealing—and you're between the ages of 22 and 45 with a high school education—apply Monday through Friday, 9 to 11 a.m. or 1 to 4 p.m.

ROOM 635

CHICAGO TRIBUNE

435 N. Michigan

APPAREL
STORE MANAGER or
DEPT. MGR.
EXPERIENCED for store
at GRAND AND HARLEM

REAL FUTURE FOR AGGRESSIVE LADIES. RTW. MGR. GOOD SALARY, COMMISSIONS. COMPANY BENEFITS AND FUTURE. WILL TRAIN. WRITE FULLY.

Write MDV 397, Tribune

Advertisement for
Green Acres Subdivision (1950)

Green Acres was the place for New Yorkers to be in June 1950, or so developers of this Long Island subdivision hoped. The ad reprinted here was one of countless appeals to turn city people into suburbanites. Most American cities would never be the same because so many of their middle-class residents listened—and left.

A New Home by CHANIN

Six rooms, all on one floor, attached garage, full basement, 34x25, exclusive of laundry space, make this a *complete* home for all the family—comfortable to live in, easy to keep, interesting and inviting to your friends.

Chanin skill of design has given it graciousness and luxury. Rooms are well-proportioned. Friendly entrance vestibule with guest closet, picture windows, front and rear, venetian blinds, china closet with service bar between dining room and kitchen, combination linen closet and laundry hamper, color-harmonized bath with vanitory, medicine cabinet with 14 feet of shelf-room, ceramic tile wainscoting and floor add finish and charm.

The basement easily becomes a recreation or hobby room, a play place for the children.

Chanin precision construction—poured concrete foundation and basement walls, full insulation, weather stripping, copper piping—mean low-cost maintenance. Oil-fired hot water circulating heat provides winter comfort; keeps down fuel bills.

The Hotpoint all-electric kitchen lightens housework. Steel cabinets have 23 square feet of textolite work surfaces. Refrigerator, range, dishwasher, ventilating fan and washing machine (in the basement) all are included in the purchase price.

But more important than details are the experience and integrity of the designer and builder. The Chanin Organization has created more than 6,000 dwelling units. Chanin "know-how" means lasting charm, sturdy lifetime quality.

The purchase price is less than you may think—$14,790 for everything mentioned, plus your choice of several exteriors, 6,000-square foot landscaped plot, sewers, curb, paved street, sidewalk. Veterans pay nothing down. Their 30-year mortgages bear 4 percent interest. Terms to nonveterans are equally attractive.

Compare this house with anything you have seen anywhere near its price range. Compare its location, in a planned, established community, 5 minutes walk from the Valley Stream station, 29 minutes from Penn Station, 17 miles from midtown New York or Brooklyn, near main highways, parkways, schools, churches, stores.

Then walk around Green Acres a bit. Hundreds of other homes, now 8 to 14 years old themselves will tell you that "Chanin-built is well-built" and much more than a phrase. It is a hallmark, a guarantee of building perfection.

Hotpoint appliances used exclusively

BY TRAIN: *Long Island train from Penn Station or Brooklyn to Valley Stream; walk back through park to property. BY CAR: Sunrise Highway to Central Avenue; from Merrick Road or Southern State Parkway, turn on Central Avenue to Sunrise Highway. BY SUBWAY AND BUS: 6th Avenue or 8th Avenue IND train to Parsons Boulevard, Queens. Change to Bee Line's Grant Park bus which passes entrance gates.*

•GREEN ACRES •

"The Planned Residential Community"

SUNRISE HIGHWAY AT CENTRAL AVE., VALLEY STREAM, L. I.

Questions

1. What is the appeal of Green Acres?
2. How does the ad both separate and link the subdivision to the city?
3. Why would New Yorkers be interested in such an ad?

Herbert Gans,
The Urban Villagers (1962)

Just as American metropolitan life as a whole became more segregated in the 1950s and 1960s, urban and suburban residential patterns differed according to class. There were growing "dark ghettoes" as well as white lower-class areas that suffered through the urban crisis.

In contrast to the sense of stifling oppression the dark ghetto engendered, working-class white neighborhoods such as Philadelphia's Kensington and Chicago's Bridgeport gave rise to a tenacious loyalty in their residents. Herbert Gans (b. 1927) found the "urban villagers" of Boston's mostly Italian West End indifferent to the seductions of middle-class suburban culture. So long as they had steady work and were left alone, so long as outsiders—blacks included—did not try to settle in their neighborhood, they were content to remain in the city, living much as their immigrant parents and grandparents had. But Gans's subjects were forced out of their beloved neighborhood when the West End was declared an irredeemable slum and replaced with luxury apartments.

West Enders did not think of their area as a slum and resented the city's description of the area because it cast aspersions on them as slum dwellers. They were not pleased that the apartment buildings were not well kept up outside, but, as long as the landlord kept the building clean, maintained the mechanical system, and did not bother his tenants, they were not seriously disturbed about it. People kept their apartments up-to-date as they could afford to, and most of the ones I saw differed little from lower-middle-class ones in urban and suburban neighborhoods.

Housing is not the same kind of status symbol for the West Enders that it is for middle-class people. They are as concerned about making a good impression on others as anyone else, but the people to be impressed and the ways of impressing them do differ. The people who are entertained in the apartment are intimates. Moreover, they all live in similar circumstances. As a result they evaluate the host not on the basis of his housing, but on his friendliness, his moral qualities, and his ability as a host. Not only are acquaintances and strangers invited less freely to the home than in the middle class, but they are also less important to the West Enders' way of life, and therefore less significant judges of their status. Thus, West Enders, unlike the middle class, do not have to put on as impressive a front for such people. . . .

Whereas most West Enders have no objection to the older suburban towns that surround the Boston city limits, they have little use for the newer suburbs. They described these as too quiet for their tastes, lonely—that is, without street life—and occupied by people concerned only with trying to appear better than they are. West Enders avoid "the country." . . . They do not like its isolation. . . . I was told by one social worker of an experiment some years back to expose West End children to nature by taking them on a trip to Cape Cod. The experiment failed, for the young West Enders found no pleasure in the loneliness of natural surroundings and wanted to get back to the West End as quickly as possible. They were incredulous that anyone could live without people around them. . . .

Many West Enders impressed me as being true urbanites, with empathy for the pace, crowding, and excitement of city life. . . . They are not [cosmopolitan], however; the parts of the city that they use and enjoy are socially, culturally, and physically far different from those frequented by the upper-middle class. . . .

Questions

1. According to Gans, how is home life connected to status for West Enders?
2. Why do West Enders criticize the suburbs?
3. What does Gans mean when he calls West Enders "true urbanites"?

Howell Raines, Interview with Rosa Parks (1977)

Although women often played crucial if underestimated roles in the civil rights movement, Rosa Parks (b. 1913) was truly the mother of the movement. Her refusal to give up her seat on a segregated bus to a white rider set the stage for the nonviolent protest that became so central to the civil rights movement (see text p. 802). Rosa Parks recounted that historic event in an interview with Howell Raines.

I had left my work at the men's alteration shop . . . in the Montgomery Fair department store. . . . I came across the street and looked for a Cleveland Avenue bus that apparently had some seats on it. At that time it was a little hard to get a seat on the bus. . . .

As I got up on the bus and walked to the seat I saw there was only one vacancy that was just back of where it was considered the white section. So this was the seat that I took, next to the aisle, and a man was sitting next to me. Across the aisle there were two women, and there were a few seats at this point in the very front of the bus that was called the white section. . . . And on the third stop there were some people getting on, and at this point all of the front seats were taken. Now in the beginning, at the very first stop I had got on the bus, the back of the bus was filled up with people standing in the aisle and I don't know why this one vacancy that I took was left, because there were quite a few people already standing toward the back of the bus. The third stop is when all the front seats were taken, and this one man was standing and when the driver looked around and saw he was standing, he asked the four of us, the man in the seat with me and the two women across the aisle, to let him have those front seats.

At his first request, didn't any of us move. Then he spoke again and said, "You'd better make it light on yourselves and let me have those seats." At this point, of course, the passenger who would have taken the seat hadn't said anything. In fact, he never did speak to my knowledge. When the three people, the man who was in the seat with me and the two women, stood up and moved into the aisle, I remained where I was. When the driver saw that I was still sitting there, he asked if I was going to stand up. I told him, no, I wasn't. He said, "Well, if you don't stand up, I'm going to have you arrested." I told him to go on and have me arrested.

He got off the bus and came back shortly. A few minutes later, two policemen got on the bus, and they approached me and asked if the driver had asked me to stand up, and I said yes, and they wanted to know why I didn't.

I told them I didn't think I should have to stand up. . . . They placed me under arrest then and had me get in the police car, and I was taken to jail and booked on suspicion. . . . They had to determine whether or not the driver wanted to press charges or swear out a warrant, which he did. Then they took me to jail and I was placed in a cell. In a little while I was taken from the cell, and my picture was made and fingerprints taken. I went back to the cell then, and a few minutes later I was called back again, and when this happened I found out that Mr. E. D. Nixon and Attorney and Mrs. Clifford Durr had come to make bond for me.

Questions

1. What elements of nonviolent protest are evident in Rosa Parks's recollection?
2. Do you think that the fact that Parks was a woman mattered in this event? Why or why not?
3. What does this story indicate about whites in Montgomery and their attitudes—the bus driver and passenger who was supposed to take Parks's seat, for example?

Barnett Newman and Jackson Pollock on Painting

The abstract expressionists Barnett Newman (1905–1970) and Jackson Pollock (1912–1956) were part of an artistic movement little concerned with reassuring a public that had problems with modern art in the 1950s. Newman's and Pollock's views measure the change in American art since the Gilded Age (see text p. 796).

[Newman:] The central issue of painting is the subject-matter. Most people think of subject-matter as what Meyer Schapiro has called "object-matter." It is the "object-matter" that most people want to see in a painting. That is what, for them, makes the painting seem full. For me both the use of objects and the manipulation of areas for the sake of the areas themselves must end up being anecdotal. My subject is anti-anecdotal. An anecdote can be subjective and internal as well as of the external world so that the expression of the biography of self or the intoxicated moment of glowing ecstasy must in the end also become anecdotal. All such painting is essentially episodic which means it calls for a sequel. This must happen if a painting does not give a sensation of wholeness or fulfillment. That is why I have no interest in the episodic or ecstatic, however abstract. . . .

I am always referred to in relation to my color. Yet I know that if I have made a contribution, it is primarily in my drawing. The impressionists changed the way of seeing the world through their kind of drawing; the cubists saw the world anew in their drawing, and I hope that I have contributed a new way of seeing through drawing. Instead of using outlines, instead of making shapes or setting off spaces, my drawings declare the space. Instead of working with the remnants of space, I work with the whole space. . . .

It is full of meaning, but the meaning must come from the seeing, not from the talking. I feel, however, that one of its implications is its assertion of freedom, its denial of dogmatic principles, its repudiation of all dogmatic life. Almost 15 years ago, Harold Rosenberg challenged me to explain what one of my paintings could possibly mean to the world. My answer was that if he and others could read it properly it would mean the end of all state capitalism and totalitarianism. That answer still goes.

[Pollock:] Abstract painting is abstract. It confronts you. There was a reviewer a while back who wrote that my pictures didn't have any beginning or any end. He didn't mean it as a compliment, but it was. It was a fine compliment.

[Pollock:] I've had a period of drawing on canvas in black—with some of my early images coming thru—think the non-objectionists will find them disturbing—and the kids who think it simple to splash a Pollock out.

Questions

1. Why does Newman avoid "object-matter" in his work?
2. What kind of meaning do these artists say their art has?
3. Are Pollock and Newman obliged to make their work understandable to a mass audience? Why or why not?

Connections Questions

1. Using the first three documents, consider how advertising influences people's attitudes about the future.
2. Do the people of Boston's West End have anything in common with Rosa Parks and the African-Americans of Montgomery, Alabama? If so, what?
3. Imagine yourself as a big-city mayor in the 1950s and 1960s. How would you respond to the simultaneous challenges of urban decline and civil rights?

CHAPTER 30

Liberal Reform and Radicalism 1960–1970

Theodore H. White,
"The Television Debates" (1960)

Journalist Theodore H. White believed "the central fact of politics has always been the quality of leadership under the pressure of great forces." White (1915–1986) tested his hypothesis during the presidential campaign of 1960, when the television cameras created their own great pressure during a series of debates between John F. Kennedy and Richard M. Nixon. Kennedy's performance signaled the arrival of electronic, or television, politics.

Television had already demonstrated its primitive power in politics from, at least, the fall of 1952, when, in one broadcast, it had transformed Richard M. Nixon from a negative Vice-Presidential candidate, under attack, into a martyr and an asset to Dwight D. Eisenhower's Presidential campaign. But from 1952 until 1960 television could be used only as an expensive partisan instrument; its time had to be bought and paid for by political parties for their own candidates. The audiences such partisan broadcasts assembled, like the audiences at political rallies, were audiences of the convinced—of convinced Republicans for Republican candidates, of convinced Democrats for Democratic candidates. Generally, the most effective political broadcast could assemble hardly more than half the audience of the commercial show that it replaced. This was why so many candidates and their television advisers sought two-minute or five-minute spots tacked on to the major programs that engaged the nation's fancy; the general audience would not tune out a hostile candidate if he appeared for only two or three minutes, and thus a candidate, using TV "spots" had a much better chance of reaching the members of the opposition party and the "independents," whom he must lure to listen to and then vote for him. The 1960 idea of a "debate," in which both major candidates would appear simultaneously, thus promised to bring both Democrats and Republicans together in the same viewing audience for the first time. Some optimists thought the debates would at least double the exposure of both candidates. How much more they would do than "double" the exposure no one, in the summer of 1960, dreamed. . . .

By mid-September all had been arranged. There would be four debates—on September 26th, October 7th, October 13th and October 21st. The first would be produced by CBS out of Chicago, the second by NBC out of Washington, the third by ABC out of New York and Los Angeles and the fourth, again by ABC, out of New York.

In the event, when all was over, the audience exceeded the wildest fancies and claims of the television networks. Each individual broadcast averaged an audience set at a low of 65,000,000 and a high of 70,000,000. The greatest previous audience in television history had been for the climactic game of the 1959 World Series, when an estimated 90,000,000 Americans had tuned in to watch the White Sox play the Dodgers. When, finally, figures were assembled for all four debates, the total audience for the television debates on the Presidency exceeded even this figure.

All this, of course, was far in the future when, on Sunday, September 25th, 1960, John F. Kennedy arrived in Chicago from Cleveland, Ohio, to stay at the Ambassador East Hotel, and Richard M. Nixon came from Washington, D.C., to stop at the Pick-Congress Hotel, to prepare, each in his own way, for the confrontation.

Kennedy's preparation was marked by his typical attention to organization and his air of casual self-possession; the man behaves, in any crisis, as if it consisted only of a sequence of necessary things to be done that will become complicated if emotions intrude. His personal Brain Trust of three had arrived and assembled at the Knickerbocker Hotel in Chicago on Sunday, the day before. The chief of these three was, of course, Ted Sorensen; with Sorensen was Richard Goodwin, a twenty-eight-year-old lawyer, an elongated elfin man with a capacity for fact and reasoning that had made him Number One man only two years before at the Harvard Law School; and Mike Feldman, a burly and impressive man, a one-time instructor of law at the University of Pennsylvania, later a highly successful businessman, who had abandoned business to follow Kennedy's star as Chief of the Senator's Legislative Research. With them, they had brought the portable Kennedy campaign research library—a Sears Roebuck foot locker of documents—and now, for a twenty-four-hour session at the Knickerbocker Hotel, stretching around the clock, they operated like young men at college cramming for an exam. When they had finished, they had prepared fifteen pages of copy boiling down into twelve or thirteen subject areas the relevant facts and probable questions they thought the correspondents on the panel, or Mr. Nixon, might raise. All three had worked with Kennedy closely for years. They knew that as a member of the House and the Senate Committees on Labor he was fully familiar with all the issues that might arise on domestic policy (the subject of the first debate) and that it was necessary to fix in his mind, not the issues or understanding, but only the latest data. . . .

Several who were present remember the performance as vividly as those who were present at the Hyannisport meeting in October, 1959. The candidate lay on his bed in a white, open-necked T shirt and army suntan pants, and fired questions at his intimates. He held in his hand the fact cards that Goodwin and Feldman had prepared for him during the afternoon, and as he finished each, he sent it spinning off the bed to the floor. Finally, at about 6:30, he rose from his bed and decided to have dinner. He ate what is called "a splendid dinner" all by himself in his room, then emerged in a white shirt and dark-gray suit, called for a stop watch and proceeded to the old converted sports arena that is now CBS Station WBBM at McClurg Court in Chicago, to face his rival for the Presidency of the United States.

Richard M. Nixon had preceded him to the studio. Nixon had spent the day in solitude without companions in the loneliness of his room at the Pick-Congress. The Vice-President was tired; the drive of campaigning in the previous two weeks had caused him to lose another five pounds since he had left the hospital; his TV advisers had urged that he arrive in Chicago on Saturday and have a full day of rest before he went on the air on Monday, but they had been unable to get through to him, and had not even been able to reach his press secretary, Herbert Klein. Mr. Nixon thus arrived in Chicago late on Sunday evening, unbriefed on the magnitude of the trial he was approaching; on Monday he spoke during the morning to the United Brotherhood of Carpenters and Joiners, an appearance his TV advisers considered a misfortune— the Brotherhood was a hostile union audience, whose negative reaction, they knew, would psychologically disturb their contender.

When Nixon returned to his hotel from the Brotherhood appearance at 12:30, he became incommunicado while his frantic TV technicians tried to reach him or brief him on the setting of the debate, the staging, the problems he might encounter. The Vice-President received one visitor for five minutes that afternoon in his suite, and he received one long telephone call—from Henry Cabot Lodge, who, reportedly, urged him to be careful to erase the "assassin image" when he went on the air. For the rest, the Vice-President was alone, in consultation with no one. Finally, as he emerged from the hotel to drive through Chicago traffic to the studio, one TV adviser was permitted to ride with him and hastily brief him in the ten-minute drive. The adviser urged that the Vice-President come out swinging—that this was a contest, a fight, and that Kennedy must be jolted at the first exchange. The Vice-President was of another mind, however—and wondered whether the suggestion had originated with his adviser or with someone else, like Frank Stanton, President of CBS, who, said the Vice-President, only wanted a good show. Thus they arrived at the studio; as Nixon got out, he struck his knee again—a nasty crack— on the edge of the automobile door, just as he had on his first accident to the knee at Greensboro, North Carolina. An observer reports that his face went all "white and pasty" but that he quickly recovered and entered the studio. . . .

Mr. Nixon's advisers and representatives, understandably nervous since they could not communicate with their principal, had made the best preparation they could. They had earlier requested that both candidates talk from a lectern, standing—and Kennedy had agreed. They had asked several days earlier that the two candidates be seated farther apart from each other than originally planned—and that had been agreed on too. Now, on the day of the debate, they paid meticulous attention to each detail. They were worried about the deep eye shadows in Nixon's face and they requested and adjusted two tiny spotlights ("inkies" in television parlance) to shine directly into his eye wells and illuminate the darkness there; they asked that a table be placed in front of the moderator, and this was agreed to also; they requested that no shots be taken of Nixon's left profile during the debate; and this was also agreed to.

The Kennedy advisers had no requests; they seemed as cocky and confident as their chief.

Nixon entered the studio about an hour before air time and inspected the setting, let himself be televised on an interior camera briefly for the inspection of his advisers, then paced moodily about in the back of the studio. He beckoned the producer to him at one point as he paced and asked as a personal favor that he not be on camera if he happened to be mopping sweat from his face. (That night, contrary to most reports, Nixon was wearing no theatrical make-up. In order to tone down his dark beard stubble on the screen, an adviser had applied only a light coating of "Lazy Shave," a pancake make-up with which a man who has heavy afternoon beard growth may powder his face to conceal the growth.) . . .

"Good evening," said Howard K. Smith, the gray and handsome moderator. "The television and radio stations of the United States . . . are proud to provide for a discussion of issues in the current political campaign by the two major candidates for the Presidency. The candidates need no introduction. . . ."

And they were on air, before seventy million Americans.

Questions

1. By 1960, how important had television become in national politics?
2. What problems does candidate Nixon experience going into the debate that might have affected viewers' perception of his performance?
3. Are televised debates a fair and accurate measure of a candidate's abilities? Why or why not?

John F. Kennedy,
Inaugural Address (1961)

President Kennedy's inaugural address is best known for his call to national self-sacrifice: "Ask not what your country can do for you—ask what you can do for your country." It was the sort of broad appeal for which he was famous. The call to national sacrifice thus included efforts, as he put it, to "explore the stars, conquer the deserts, eradicate disease, tap the ocean depths, and encourage the arts and commerce." In more concrete terms, sacrifice meant everything from prevailing in the space race to joining the new President's Council on Physical Fitness; it could inspire people to devote themselves to humanitarian work in the Peace Corps or to train for counterinsurgency.

The address also showed clearly Kennedy's devotion to foreign policy. The new president affirmed the western alliance, warned off the Soviets, and appealed to the Third World, which, only then emerging from its colonial past, was the prime object of superpower competition.

We observe today not a victory of party but a celebration of freedom—symbolizing an end as well as a beginning—signifying renewal as well as change. For I have sworn before you and Almighty God the same solemn oath our forebears prescribed nearly a century and three quarters ago.

The world is very different now. For man holds in his mortal hands the power to abolish all forms of human poverty and all forms of human life. And yet the same revolutionary beliefs for which our forebears fought are still at issue around the globe—the belief that the rights of man come not from the generosity of the state but from the hand of God.

We dare not forget today that we are the heirs of that first revolution. Let the word go forth from this time and place, to friend and foe alike, that the torch has been passed to a new generation of Americans—born in this century, tempered by war, disciplined by a hard and bitter peace, proud of our ancient heritage—and unwilling to witness or permit the slow undoing of those human rights to which this nation has always been committed, and to which we are committed today at home and around the world.

Let every nation know, whether it wishes us well or ill, that we shall bear any burden, meet any hardship, support any friend, oppose any foe, to assure the survival and the success of liberty.

This we pledge and more.

To those allies whose cultural and spiritual origins we share, we pledge the loyalty of faithful friends. United, there is little we cannot do in a host of co-operative ventures. Divided, there is little we can do—for we do not meet a powerful challenge at odds and split asunder.

To those new states whom we welcome to the ranks of the free, we pledge our word that one form of colonial control shall not have passed away merely to be replaced by a far more iron tyranny. We shall not always expect to find them supporting our view. But we shall always hope to find them strongly supporting their own freedom—and to remember that in the past, those who foolishly sought power by riding the back of the tiger ended up inside.

To those peoples in the huts and villages of half the globe struggling to break the bonds of mass misery, we pledge our best efforts to help them help themselves . . . not because the Communists may be doing it, not because we seek their votes, but because it is right. If a free society cannot help the many who are poor, it cannot save the few who are rich. . . .

Finally, to those nations who would make themselves our adversary, we offer not a pledge but a request: that both sides begin anew the quest for peace, before the dark powers of destruction unleashed by science engulf all humanity in planned or accidental self-destruction.

We dare not tempt them with weakness. For only when our arms are sufficient beyond doubt can we be certain beyond doubt that they will never be employed. . . .

In the long history of the world, only a few generations have been granted the role of defending freedom in its hour of maximum danger. I do not shrink from this responsibility—I welcome it.

Questions

1. President Kennedy begins his speech with appeals to the "revolutionary beliefs for which our forebears fought." How can these beliefs be used to fight the Cold War in the Third World?

2. What parts of the address are aimed at the communist superpowers, and what is Kennedy's posture toward them?

3. Kennedy is asking Americans to sacrifice for American ideals. How does he promise to live up to those ideals himself?

Martin Luther King, Jr.,
Letter from
Birmingham City Jail (1963)

In April and May of 1963, the Reverend Martin Luther King, Jr. and the Southern Christian Leadership Conference led a series of mass protests in Birmingham, Alabama. On Good Friday, April 12, King allowed himself to be arrested and jailed for leading a demonstration. He explained his actions and ideas about nonviolence in the now famous "Letter from Birmingham City Jail" addressed to other members of the clergy.

My dear Fellow Clergymen,

While confined here in the Birmingham city jail, I came across your recent statement calling our present activities "unwise and untimely." Seldom, if ever, do I pause to answer criticism of my work and ideas. If I sought to answer all of the criticisms that cross my desk, my secretaries would be engaged in little else in the course of the day, and I would have no time for constructive work. But since I feel that you are men of genuine good will and your criticisms are sincerely set forth, I would like to answer your statement in what I hope will be patient and reasonable terms.

I think I should give the reason for my being in Birmingham, since you have been influenced by the argument of "outsiders coming in." I have the honor of serving as president of the Southern Christian Leadership Conference, an organization operating in every southern state, with headquarters in Atlanta, Georgia. We have some eighty-five affiliate organizations all across the South—one being the Alabama Christian Movement for Human Rights. Whenever necessary and possible we share staff, educational and financial resources with our affiliates. Several months ago our local affiliate here in Birmingham invited us to be on call to engage in a nonviolent direct-action program if such were deemed necessary. We readily consented and when the hour came we lived up to our promises. So I am here, along with several members of my staff, because we were invited here. I am here because I have basic organizational ties here. . . .

In any nonviolent campaign there are four basic steps: (1) collection of the facts to determine whether injustices are alive, (2) negotiation, (3) self-purification, and (4) direct action. We have gone through all of these steps in Birmingham. There can be no gainsaying of the fact that racial injustice engulfs this community.

Birmingham is probably the most thoroughly segregated city in the United States. Its ugly record of police brutality is known in every section of this country. Its injust treatment of Negroes in the courts is a notorious reality. There have been more unsolved bombings of Negro homes and churches in Birmingham than any city in this nation. These are the hard, brutal and un-believable facts. On the basis of these conditions Negro leaders sought to ne-gotiate with the city fathers. But the political leaders consistently refused to engage in good faith negotiation.

Then came the opportunity last September to talk with some of the lead-ers of the economic community. In these negotiating sessions certain promises were made by the merchants—such as the promise to remove the humiliat-ing racial signs from the stores. On the basis of these promises Rev. Shut-tlesworth and the leaders of the Alabama Christian Movement for Human Rights agreed to call a moratorium on any type of demonstrations. As the weeks and months unfolded we realized that we were the victims of a broken promise. The signs remained. Like so many experiences of the past we were confronted with blasted hopes, and the dark shadow of a deep disappointment settled upon us. So we had no alternative except that of preparing for direct action, whereby we would present our very bodies as a means of laying our case before the conscience of the local and national community. We were not unmindful of the difficulties involved. So we decided to go through a process of self-purification. We started having workshops on nonviolence and repeatedly asked ourselves the questions, "Are you able to accept blows with-out retaliating?" "Are you able to endure the ordeals of jail?" We decided to set our direct-action program around the Easter season, realizing that with the exception of Christmas, this was the largest shopping period of the year.

You may well ask, "Why direct action? Why sit-ins, marches, etc.? Isn't ne-gotiation a better path?" You are exactly right in your call for negotiation. In-deed, this is the purpose of direct action. Nonviolent direct action seeks to create such a crisis and establish such creative tension that a community that has constantly refused to negotiate is forced to confront the issue. It seeks so to dramatize the issue that it can no longer be ignored. . . . So the purpose of the direct action is to create a situation so crisis-packed that it will inevitably open the door to negotiation. We, therefore, concur with you in your call for negotiation. Too long has our beloved Southland been bogged down in the tragic attempt to live in monologue rather than dialogue.

My friends, I must say to you that we have not made a single gain in civil rights without determined legal and nonviolent pressure. History is the long and tragic story of the fact that privileged groups seldom give up their privi-leges voluntarily. Individuals may see the moral light and voluntarily give up their unjust posture; but as Reinhold Niebuhr has reminded us, groups are more immoral than individuals.

We know through painful experience that freedom is never voluntarily given by the oppressor; it must be demanded by the oppressed. Frankly, I have never yet engaged in a direct action movement that was "well-timed," according to the timetable of those who have not suffered unduly from the disease of segregation. For years now I have heard the words "Wait!" It rings in the ear of every Negro with a piercing familiarity. This "Wait" has almost always meant "Never." . . . We must come to see with the distinguished jurist of yesterday that "justice too long delayed is justice denied." We have waited for more than 340 years for our constitutional and God-given rights. The nations of Asia and Africa are moving with jetlike speed toward the goal of political independence, and we still creep at horse and buggy pace toward the gaining of a cup of coffee at a lunch counter. I guess it is easy for those who have never felt the stinging darts of segregation to say, "Wait." But when you have seen vicious mobs lynch your mothers and fathers at will and drown your sisters and brothers at whim; when you have seen hate-filled policemen curse, kick, brutalize and even kill your black brothers and sisters with impunity; when you see the vast majority of your twenty million Negro brothers smothering in an airtight cage of poverty in the midst of an affluent society; when you suddenly find your tongue twisted and your speech stammering as you seek to explain to your six-year-old daughter why she can't go to the public amusement park that has just been advertised on television, and see tears welling up in her little eyes when she is told that Funtown is closed to colored children, and see the depressing clouds of inferiority begin to form in her little mental sky, and see her begin to distort her little personality by unconsciously developing a bitterness toward white people; when you have to concoct an answer for a five-year-old son asking in agonizing pathos: "Daddy, why do white people treat colored people so mean?"; when you take a cross-country drive and find it necessary to sleep night after night in the uncomfortable corners of your automobile because no motel will accept you; when you are humiliated day in and day out by nagging signs reading "white" and "colored"; when your first name becomes "nigger" and your middle name becomes "boy" (however old you are) and your last name becomes "John," and when your wife and mother are never given the respected title "Mrs."; when you are harried by day and haunted by night by the fact that you are a Negro, living constantly at tiptoe stance, never quite knowing what to expect next, and plagued with inner fears and outer resentments; when you are forever fighting a degenerating sense of "nobodiness"; then you will understand why we find it difficult to wait. There comes a time when the cup of endurance runs over, and men are no longer willing to be plunged into an abyss of injustice where they experience the blackness of corroding despair. I hope, sirs, you can understand our legitimate and unavoidable impatience. . . .

We must come to see that human progress never rolls in on wheels of inevitability. It comes through the tireless efforts and persistent work of men willing to be co-workers with God, and without this hard work time itself becomes an ally of the forces of social stagnation. We must use time creatively, and forever realize that the time is always ripe to do right. Now is the time to make real the promise of democracy, and transform our pending national elegy into a creative psalm of brotherhood. Now is the time to lift our national policy from the quicksand of racial injustice to the solid rock of human dignity.

You spoke of our activity in Birmingham as extreme. At first I was rather disappointed that fellow clergymen would see my nonviolent efforts as those of the extremist. I started thinking about the fact that I stand in the middle of two opposing forces in the Negro community. One is a force of complacency made up of Negroes who, as a result of long years of oppression, have been so completely drained of self-respect and a sense of "somebodiness" that they have adjusted to segregation, and, of a few Negroes in the middle class who, because of a degree of academic and economic security, and because at points they profit by segregation, have unconsciously become insensitive to the problems of the masses. The other force is one of bitterness and hatred, and comes perilously close to advocating violence. It is expressed in the various black nationalist groups that are springing up over the nation, the largest and best known being Elijah Muhammad's Muslim movement. This movement is nourished by the contemporary frustration over the continued existence of racial discrimination. It is made up of people who have lost faith in America, who have absolutely repudiated Christianity, and who have concluded that the white man is an incorrigible"devil." I have tried to stand between these two forces, saying that we need not follow the "do-nothingism" of the complacent or the hatred and despair of the black nationalist. There is the more excellent way of love and nonviolent protest. I'm grateful to God that, through the Negro church, the dimension of nonviolence entered our struggle. If this philosophy had not emerged, I am convinced that by now many streets of the South would be flowing with floods of blood. And I am further convinced that if our white brothers dismiss as "rabble-rousers" and "outside agitators" those of us who are working through the channels of nonviolent direct action and refuse to support our nonviolent efforts, millions of Negroes, out of frustration and despair, will seek solace and security in black nationalist ideologies, a development that will lead inevitably to a frightening racial nightmare.

Oppressed people cannot remain oppressed forever. The urge for freedom will eventually come. This is what happened to the American Negro. Something within has reminded him of his birthright of freedom; something without has reminded him that he can gain it. . . .

In spite of my shattered dreams of the past, I came to Birmingham with the hope that the white religious leadership of this community would see the justice of our cause, and with deep moral concern, serve as the channel through which our just grievances would get to the power structure. I had hoped that each of you would understand. But again I have been disappointed. I have heard numerous religious leaders of the South call upon their worshippers to comply with a desegregation decision because it is the *law,* but I have longed to hear white ministers say, "Follow this decree because integration is morally *right* and the Negro is your brother." In the midst of blatant injustice inflicted upon the Negro, I have watched white churches stand on the sideline and merely mouth pious irrelevancies and sanctimonious trivialities. In the midst of a mighty struggle to rid our nation of racial and economic injustice, I have heard so many ministers say, "Those are social issues with which the gospel has no real concern," and I have watched so many churches commit themselves to a completely otherworldly religion which made a strange distinction between body and soul, the sacred and the secular. . . .

I'm sorry that I can't join you in your praise for the police department.

It is true that they have been rather disciplined in their public handling of the demonstrators. In this sense they have been rather publicly "nonviolent." But for what purpose? To preserve the evil system of segregation. Over the last few years I have consistently preached that nonviolence demands that the means we use must be as pure as the ends we seek. So I have tried to make it clear that it is wrong to use immoral means to attain moral ends. But now I must affirm that it is just as wrong, or even more so, to use moral means to preserve immoral ends. Maybe Mr. Connor and his policemen have been rather publicly nonviolent, as Chief Pritchett was in Albany, Georgia, but they have used the moral means of nonviolence to maintain the immoral end of flagrant racial injustice. T.S. Eliot has said that there is no greater treason than to do the right deed for the wrong reason.

I wish you had commended the Negro sit-inners and demonstrators of Birmingham for their sublime courage, their willingness to suffer and their amazing discipline in the midst of the most inhuman provocation. . . .

One day the South will know that when these disinherited children of God sat down at lunch counters they were in reality standing up for the best in the American dream and the most sacred values in our Judeo-Christian heritage, and thusly, carrying our whole nation back to those great wells of democracy which were dug deep by the Founding Fathers in the formulation of the Constitution and the Declaration of Independence. . . .

I hope this letter finds you strong in the faith. I also hope that circumstances will soon make it possible for me to meet each of you, not as an integrationist or a civil rights leader, but as a fellow clergyman and a Christian brother. Let us all hope that the dark clouds of racial prejudice will soon pass away and the deep fog of misunderstanding will be lifted from our fear-drenched communities and in some not too distant tomorrow the radiant stars of love and brotherhood will shine over our great nation with all of their scintillating beauty.

Yours for the cause of Peace and Brotherhood,
Martin Luther King, Jr.

Questions

1. What does this letter indicate about the tenets of Reverend King's philosophy of nonviolence?
2. What is King's attitude toward moderate members of the white clergy? How does he hope to alter the position of his white colleagues?
3. Do you find the overall tone of the letter to be optimistic or pessimistic? What evidence can you cite to support your conclusion? What does this tell you about the civil rights movement in 1963?

Michael Harrington,
The Other America (1962)

Like Walter Rauschenbusch (see Chapter 21, "The Church and the Social Movement"), Michael Harrington found that religious conviction led to social action. When he belonged to the Catholic Worker Movement, Harrington (1928–1989) learned to see Christ even in "the pathetic, shambling, shivering creature who would wander in off the streets." Where others saw only prosperity, Harrington focused attention on the "millions who are poor in the United States [and who] tend to become increasingly invisible."

The United States in the sixties contains an affluent society within its borders. Millions and tens of millions enjoy the highest standard of life the world has ever known. This blessing is mixed. It is built upon a peculiarly distorted economy, one that often proliferates pseudo-needs rather than satisfying human needs. For some, it has resulted in a sense of spiritual emptiness, of alienation. Yet a man would be a fool to prefer hunger to satiety, and the material gains at least open up the possibility of a rich and full existence.

At the same time, the United States contains an underdeveloped nation, a culture of poverty. Its inhabitants do not suffer the extreme privation of the peasants of Asia or the tribesmen of Africa, yet the mechanism of the misery is similar. They are beyond history, beyond progress, sunk in a paralyzing, maiming routine. . . .

In this summary chapter, I hope I can supply at least some of the material for such a vision. Let us try to understand the other America as a whole, to see its perspective for the future if it is left alone, to realize the responsibility and the potential for ending this nation in our midst.

But, when all is said and done, the decisive moment occurs after all the sociology and the description is in. There is really no such thing as "the material for a vision." After one reads the facts, either there are anger and shame, or there are not. And, as usual, the fate of the poor hangs upon the decision of the better-off. If this anger and shame are not forthcoming, someone can write a book about the other America a generation from now and it will be the same, or worse.

I

Perhaps the most important analytic point to have emerged in this description of the other America is the fact that poverty in America forms a culture, a way of life and feeling, that it makes a whole. It is crucial to generalize this idea, for it profoundly affects how one moves to destroy poverty. . . .

To realize this is to see that there are some tens of millions of Americans who are beyond the welfare state. Some of them are simply not covered by social legislation: they are omitted from Social Security and from minimum wage. Others are covered, but since they are so poor they do not know how to take advantage of the opportunities, or else their coverage is so inadequate as not to make a difference.

The welfare state was designed during that great burst of social creativity that took place in the 1930's. As previously noted its structure corresponds to the needs of those who played the most important role in building it: the middle third, the organized workers, the forces of urban liberalism, and so on. At the worst, there is "socialism for the rich and free enterprise for the poor," as when the huge corporation farms are the main beneficiaries of the farm program while the poor farmers get practically nothing; or when public funds are directed to aid in the construction of luxury housing while the slums are left to themselves (or become more dense as space is created for the well-off).

So there is the fundamental paradox of the welfare state: that it is not built for the desperate, but for those who are already capable of helping themselves. As long as the illusion persists that the poor are merrily freeloading on the public dole, so long will the other America continue unthreatened. The truth, it must be understood, is the exact opposite. The poor get less out of the welfare state than any group in America. . . .

In short, being poor is not one aspect of a person's life in this country; it is his life. Taken as a whole, poverty is a culture. Taken on the family level, it has the same quality. These are people who lack education and skill, who have bad health, poor housing, low levels of aspiration and high levels of mental distress. They are, in the language of sociology, "multiproblem" families. Each disability is the more intense because it exists within a web of disabilities. And if one problem is solved, and the others are left constant, there is little gain.

One might translate these facts into the moralistic language so dear to those who would condemn the poor for their faults. The other Americans are those who live at a level of life beneath moral choice, who are so submerged in their poverty that one cannot begin to talk about free choice. The point is not to make them wards of the state. Rather, society must help them before they can help themselves.

Questions

1. Why is Harrington critical of the American economy?
2. What does he say are the limits of the welfare state?
3. How does poverty define a person's life?

The Consequences of Termination for the Menominees of Wisconsin (1965)

Congress in the 1950s endorsed a new policy for native Americans. It was termination, to end "the legal standing of native tribes and move their members off reservations and into cities" [see text p. 800]. But what looked good in Washington did not necessarily work for people like the Menominees of Wisconsin. A Menominee advocacy group helped win reversal of the policy in 1965. Before the decade was out, other native American protests would grow increasingly controversial.

Senator Watkins badly wanted our termination. He was firmly convinced that factors such as our status as Reservation Indians, our tribal ownership of land, and our tax exemption were blocking our initiative, our freedom, and our development of private enterprise. He wished to see us rapidly assimilated into the mainstream of American society—as tax paying, hard working, "emancipated" citizens. . . .

One June 20, 1953, [Utah Senator Arthur V.] Watkins spoke for 45 minutes to our General Council. He told us that Congress had already decided on terminating us, and that at most we could have three years before our "affairs would be turned over to us"—and that we would not receive our per capitas until *after* termination.

After he left, our Council had the opportunity to vote on the "principle of termination!" Some opportunity! What little understanding we had of what termination would mean! The vote was 169 to 5 in favor of the "principle of termination." A mere 5 percent of the 3,200 Menominee people participated in this vote. Most of our people chose to be absent from the meeting in order to express their negative reaction to termination. Many who did vote affirmatively that day believed that termination was coming from Congress whether the Menominee liked it or not. Others thought that they were voting *only* in favor of receiving their per capitas. . . .

We then set about preparing a termination plan, which the BIA subsequently emasculated, and we received word that Senator Watkins was pressing ahead with his *own* termination bill. *Another* general council meeting was called, one which is seldom mentioned, but at which the Menominee voted 197 to 0 to *oppose and reject* termination. But our feelings did not matter—and although the Watkins bill met a temporary defeat on technical grounds in the House in late 1953, Senator Watkins re-introduced it in 1954.

We became convinced that there was *no* alternative to accepting termination. Therefore, all we pleaded for was adequate time to plan this sudden and revolutionary change in our lives! On June 17, 1954, the Menominee Termination Act was signed into law by President Eisenhower. . . .

Termination represented a gigantic and revolutionary *forced* change in the traditional Menominee way of life. Congress expected us to replace our Indian way of life with a complicated corporate style of living. Congress expected immediate Menominee assimilation of non-Indian culture, values, and life styles. . . .

The immediate effect of termination on our tribe was the loss of most of our hundred-year-old treaty rights, protections, and services. No amount of explanation or imagination prior to termination could have prepared us for the shock of what these losses meant.

Congress withdrew its trusteeship of our lands, transferring to MEI [Menominee Enterprises, Inc., the corporation which was to supervise Menominee holdings after termination] the responsibility for protecting these lands, our greatest assets. As we shall explain, far from being able to preserve our land, MEI has been forced to sell it. And because our land is now being sold to non-Menominee, termination is doing to us what allotment has done to other Indian tribes.

Congress also extinguished our ancient system of tribal "ownership" of land (under which no individual had separate title to his home) and transferred title to MEI. Consequently, we individual Menominee suddenly discovered that we would be forced to buy from MEI the land which had always been considered our own, and to pay title to our homesites. Thus began the tragic process of our corporation "feeding off" our people.

We Menominee lost our right to tax exemption. Both MEI and individual Menominee found themselves saddled with tax burdens particularly crushing to a small tribe struggling to develop economically.

BIA health, education and utility services ceased. We lost all medical and dental care within the Reservation. Both our reservation and hospital were closed because they failed to meet state standards. Individual Menominee were forced to pay for electricity and water that they previously received at no cost. Our county found it had to renovate at high cost its substandard sewerage system.

Finally, with termination and the closing of our tribal rolls, our children born since 1954 have been legally deprived of their birthright as Menominee Indians. Like all other Menominee, they have lost their entitlement to United States Government benefits and services to Indians. . . . The only major Menominee treaty right which the government has allowed us to retain has been our hunting and fishing right. Wisconsin had tried to deprive us of this right, but in 1968, after costly litigation, the United States Supreme Court ruled that this treaty right had "survived" termination. . . .

We hope you can appreciate the magnitude of these treaty losses to us. Visualize a situation similar to ours happening in one of your home states. Imagine the outrage of the people in one of your own communities if Congress should attempt to terminate their basic property, inheritance, and civil rights. . . .

Today Menominee County is the poorest county in Wisconsin. It has the highest birthrate in the state and ranks at or near the bottom of Wisconsin counties in income, housing, property value, education, employment, sanitation and health. The most recent figures available (1967) show that the annual income of nearly 80 percent of our families falls below the federal poverty level of $3,000. The per capita annual income of our wage earners in 1965 was estimated at $881, the lowest in the state. . . .

We have told a story which is very tragic, yet it is a true story of the Menominee people since termination. We have told how termination has meant the loss of treaty benefits, has pushed our already poor community further into the depths of poverty, forced our sale of assets, and denied us a democratic community.

DRUMS COMMITTEE, *Menominee*

Questions

1. Who wanted termination for the Menominees and why?
2. What were the consequences of the policy?

3. How can a society protect a minority group like the Menominees with such different cultural traditions?

Connections Questions

1. Using the first two documents, consider how a candidate's image and rhetoric are conveyed by television. Is there cause for concern? Why or why not?

2. To what extent, if any, does Michael Harrington's treatment of poverty in the 1960s apply to the 1990s?

3. How can social change take place without incurring widespread backlash? Frame your answer with reference to the final three documents in this section.

CHAPTER 31

Vietnam
and America
1954–1975

Ho Chi Minh, Vietnam's Declaration
of Independence (1945)

After surviving for centuries under foreign domination, Vietnam declared
itself independent in 1945 and hoped to chart its own course in a postcolonial
world. The chief architect of this independence movement was Ho Chi Minh
(1890–1969), who had adopted communism as his governing philosophy dur-
ing travels to Russia and France. On V-J Day, September 2, 1945, Ho spoke
to his people while conveying a message to a much wider audience.

All men are created equal: they are endowed by their Creator with certain
unalienable Rights: among these are Life, Liberty, and the pursuit of Happiness.

This immortal statement was made in the Declaration of Independence of
the United States of America in 1776. In a broader sense, this means: All the
peoples on the earth are equal from birth, all the peoples have a right to live,
to be happy and free.

The Declaration of the French Revolution made in 1791 on the Rights of
Man and the Citizen also states: "All men are born free and with equal rights,
and must always remain free and have equal rights."

Those are undeniable truths.

Nevertheless, for more than eighty years, the French imperialist, abusing
the standard of Liberty, Equality, and Fraternity, have violated our Fatherland
and oppressed our fellow citizens. They have acted contrary to the ideals of
humanity and justice.

In the field of politics, they have deprived our people of every democratic
liberty.

They have enforced inhuman laws: they have set up three distinct political regimes in the North, the Center, and the South of Vietnam in order to
wreck our national unity and prevent our people from being united.

They have built more prisons than schools. They have mercilessly slain
our patriots; they have drowned our uprisings in rivers of blood.

They have fettered public opinion; they have practiced obscurantism
against our people.

To weaken our race they have forced us to use opium and alcohol.

In the field of economics, they have fleeced us to the backbone, impover-
ished our people and devastated our land.

They have robbed us of our rice fields, our mines, our forests, and our raw
materials. They have monopolized the issuing of bank notes and the export
trade.

They have invented numerous unjustifiable taxes and reduced our people, especially our peasantry, to a state of extreme poverty.

They have hampered the prospering of our national bourgeoisie; they have mercilessly exploited our workers.

In the autumn of 1940, when the Japanese fascists violated Indochina's territory to establish new bases in their fight against the Allies, the French imperialists went down on their bended knees and handed over our country to them.

Thus, from that date, our people were subjected to the double yoke of the French and the Japanese. Their sufferings and miseries increased. The result was that, from the end of last year to the beginning of this year, from Quang Tri Province to the North of Vietnam, more than two million of our fellow citizens died from starvation. On March 9 [1945], the French troops were disarmed by the Japanese. The French colonialists either fled or surrendered, showing that not only were they incapable of "protecting" us, but that, in the span of five years, they had twice sold our country to the Japanese.

On several occasions before March 9, the Vietminh League urged the French to ally themselves with it against the Japanese. Instead of agreeing to this proposal, the French colonialists so intensified their terrorist activities against the Vietminh members that before fleeing they massacred a great number of our political prisoners detained at Yen Bay and Cao Bang.

Notwithstanding all this, our fellow citizens have always manifested toward the French a tolerant and humane attitude. Even after the Japanese Putsch of March, 1945, the Vietminh League helped many Frenchmen to cross the frontier, rescued some of them from Japanese jails, and protected French lives and property.

From the autumn of 1940, our country had in fact ceased to be a French colony and had become a Japanese possession.

After the Japanese had surrendered to the Allies, our whole people rose to regain our national sovereignty and to found the Democratic Republic of Vietnam.

The truth is that we have wrested our independence from the Japanese and not from the French.

The French have fled, the Japanese have capitulated. Emperor Bao Dai has abdicated. Our people have broken the chains which for nearly a century have fettered them and have won independence for the Fatherland. Our people at the same time have overthrown the monarchic regime that has reigned supreme for dozens of centuries. In its place has been established the present Democratic Republic.

For these reasons, we, members of the Provisional Government, representing the whole Vietnamese people, declare that from now on we break off all relations of a colonial character with France, we repeal all the international obligation that France has so far subscribed to on behalf of Vietnam, and we abolish all the special rights the French have unlawfully acquired in our Fatherland.

The whole Vietnamese people, animated by a common purpose, are determined to fight to the bitter end against any attempt by the French colonialists to reconquer their country.

We are convinced that the Allied nations, which at Teheran and San Francisco have acknowledged the principles of self-determination and equality of nations, will not refuse to acknowledge the independence of Vietnam.

A people who have courageously opposed French domination for more than eighty years, a people who have fought side by side with the Allies against the fascists during these last years, such a people must be free and independent.

For these reasons, we, members of the Provisional Government of the Democratic Republic of Vietnam, solemnly declare to the world that Vietnam has the right to be a free and independent country—and in fact it is so already. The entire Vietnamese people are determined to mobilize all their physical and mental strength, to sacrifice their lives and property in order to safeguard their independence and liberty.

Questions

1. How does Ho Chi Minh make a direct appeal to the United States to support independence for Vietnam? How accurate is his comparison of the American colonies in 1776 to Vietnam in 1945?

2. What specific charges does Ho level against France to justify his call for an independent Vietnam?

3. Why does Ho expect the Western nations to turn against one of their own to support him and the Vietnamese people?

The Gulf of Tonkin Resolution (1964)

President Johnson claimed that the Gulf of Tonkin Resolution reflected a public consensus in favor of his Vietnam policy. Yet his administration refused to explain exactly what had happened in the gulf, which suggests Johnson knew there was no real consensus. Moreover, the resolution was a congressional surrender of its constitutional right to declare war. Oregon senator Wayne Morse, one of only two dissenters in all of Congress, warned against this "historic mistake" that effectively subverted the Constitution. But the resolution passed, and Johnson conducted the war largely on his terms.

SECTION 1. Whereas naval units of the Communist regime in Vietnam, in violation of the principles of the Charter of the United Nations and of international law, have deliberately and repeatedly attacked the United States naval vessels present in international waters, and have thereby created a serious threat to international peace;

Whereas these attacks are part of a deliberate and systematic campaign of aggression that the Communist regime in North Vietnam has been waging against its neighbors and the nations joined with them in the collective defense of their freedom;

Whereas the United States is assisting the peoples of southeast Asia to protect their political freedom and has not territorial, military or political ambitions in that area, but desires only that these peoples should be left in peace to work out their own destinies in their own way: Now, therefore, be it:

Resolved by the Senate and House of Representatives of the United States of America in Congress assembled, That the Congress approves and supports the determination of the President, as Commander in Chief, to take all necessary measures to repel any armed attack against the forces of the United States and to prevent further aggression.

SEC. 2. The United States regards as vital to its national interests and to world peace the maintenance of international peace and security in southeast Asia. . . . The United States is, therefore, prepared, as the President determines, to take all necessary steps, including the use of armed force, to assist any member or protocol state of the Southeast Asia Collective Defense Treaty requesting assistance in defense of its freedom.

SEC. 3. This resolution shall expire when the President shall determine that the peace and security of the area is reasonably assured. . . .

Questions

1. What are the North Vietnamese accused of?
2. According to the resolution, what are the American interests in the region?
3. How does the resolution grant a free hand to the president?

Students for a Democratic Society, *Port Huron Statement* (1962)

The Students for a Democratic Society (SDS) played a leading role in the youth movement. In 1962, Al Haber and Tom Hayden, two University of Michigan activists, organized the founding meeting of SDS, which was held at a United Auto Workers retreat in Port Huron, Michigan. The students approved the following manifesto.

INTRODUCTION: AGENDA FOR A GENERATION

We are people of this generation, bred in at least modest comfort, housed now in universities, looking uncomfortably to the world we inherit.

When we were kids the United States was the wealthiest and strongest country in the world; the only one with the atom bomb, the least scarred by modern war, an initiator of the United Nations that we thought would distribute Western influence throughout the world. Freedom and equality for each individual, government of, by, and for the people—these American values we found good, principles by which we could live as men. Many of us began maturing in complacency.

As we grew, however, our comfort was penetrated by events too troubling to dismiss. First, the permeating and victimizing fact of human degradation, symbolized by the Southern struggle against racial bigotry, compelled most of us from silence to activism. Second, the enclosing fact of the Cold War, symbolized by the presence of the Bomb, brought awareness that we ourselves, and our friends, and millions of abstract "others" we knew more directly because of our common peril, might die at any time. We might deliberately ignore, or avoid, or fail to feel all other human problems, but not these two, for these were too immediate and crushing in their impact, too challenging in the demand that we as individuals take the responsibility for encounter and resolution.

While these and other problems either directly oppressed us or rankled our consciences and became our own subjective concerns, we began to see complicated and disturbing paradoxes in our surrounding America. The declaration "all men are created equal . . ." rang hollow before the facts of Negro life in the South and the big cities of the North. The proclaimed peaceful intentions of the United States contradicted its economic and military investments in the Cold War status quo. . . .

Not only did tarnish appear on our image of American virtue, not only did disillusion occur when the hypocrisy of American ideals was discovered, but we began to sense that what we had originally seen as the American Golden Age was actually the decline of an era. The worldwide outbreak of revolution against colonialism and imperialism, the entrenchment of totalitarian states, the menace of war, overpopulation, international disorder, supertechnology—these trends were testing the tenacity of our own commitment to democracy and freedom and our abilities to visualize their application to a world in upheaval.

Our work is guided by the sense that we may be the last generation in the experiment with living. But we are a minority—the vast majority of our people regard the temporary equilibriums of our society and world as eternally-functional parts. In this is perhaps the outstanding paradox: we ourselves are imbued with urgency, yet the message of our society is that there is no viable alternative to the present. Beneath the reassuring tones of the politicians, beneath the common opinion that America will "muddle through," beneath the stagnation of those who have closed their minds to the future, is the pervading feeling that there simply are no alternatives, that our times have witnessed the exhaustion not only of Utopias, but of any new departures as well. Feeling the press of complexity upon the emptiness of life, people are fearful of the thought that at any moment things might be thrust out of control. They fear change itself, since change might smash whatever invisible framework seems to hold back chaos for them now. For most Americans, all crusades are suspect, threatening. The fact that each individual sees apathy in his fellows perpetuates the common reluctance to organize for change. The dominant institutions are complex enough to blunt the minds of their potential critics, and entrenched enough to swiftly dissipate or entirely repel the energies of protest and reform, thus limiting human expectancies. Then, too, we are a materially improved society, and by our own improvements we seem to have weakened the case for further change. . . .

The search for truly democratic alternatives to the present, and a commitment to social experimentation with them, is a worthy and fulfilling human enterprise, one which moves us and, we hope, others today. On such a basis do we offer this document of our convictions and analysis: as an effort in understanding and changing the conditions of humanity in the late twentieth century, an effort rooted in the ancient, still unfulfilled conception of man attaining determining influence over his circumstances of life.

VALUES

Making values explicit—an initial task in establishing alternatives—is an activity that has been devalued and corrupted. The conventional moral terms of the age, the politician moralities—"free world," "people's democracies"— reflect realities poorly, if at all, and seem to function more as ruling myths than as descriptive principles. But neither has our experience in the universities brought us moral enlightenment. Our professors and administrators sacrifice controversy to public relations; their curriculums change more slowly than the living events of the world; their skills and silence are purchased by investors in the arms race; passion is called unscholastic. The questions we might want raised—what is really important? can we live in a different and better way? if we wanted to change society, how would we do it?—are not thought to be questions of a "fruitful, empirical nature," and thus are brushed aside. . . .

Men have unrealized potential for self-cultivation, self-direction, self-understanding, and creativity. It is this potential that we regard as crucial and to which we appeal, not to the human potentiality for violence, unreason, and submission to authority. The goal of man and society should be human independence: a concern not with image of popularity but with finding a meaning in life that is personally authentic; a quality of mind not compulsively driven by a sense of powerlessness, nor one which unthinkingly adopts status values, nor one which represses all threats to its habits, but one which has full, spontaneous access to present and past experiences, one which easily unites the fragmented parts of personal history, one which openly faces problems which are troubling and unresolved; one with an intuitive awareness of possibilities, an active sense of curiosity, an ability and willingness to learn.

This kind of independence does not mean egotistic individualism—the object is not to have one's way so much as it is to have a way that is one's own. Nor do we deify man—we merely have faith in his potential.

Human relationships should involve fraternity and honesty. Human interdependence is contemporary fact; human brotherhood must be willed, however, as a condition of future survival and as the most appropriate form of social relations. Personal links between man and man are needed, especially to go beyond the partial and fragmentary bonds of function that bind men only as worker to worker, employer to employee, teacher to student, American to Russian. . . .

We would replace power rooted in possession, privilege, or circumstance by power and uniqueness rooted in love, reflectiveness, reason, and creativity. As a *social system* we seek the establishment of a democracy of individual participation, governed by two central aims: that the individual share in those social decisions determining the quality and direction of his life; that society be organized to encourage independence in men and provide the media for their common participation. . . .

Questions

1. What indictments does the *Port Huron Statement* bring against mainstream American society? How valid are they?
2. What does the statement say about generational differences?
3. What is the statement's position on civil rights? academia?

Lynda Van Devanter, *Home Before Morning: The Story of an Army Nurse in Vietnam* (1983)

Many of the young men and women who volunteered for Vietnam were answering President Kennedy's call to national service. Lynda Van Devanter, fresh out of nursing school, believed that going to Vietnam was the right thing to do. During her time "in country," Van Devanter saw her views change dramatically: she came to resent President Nixon and the American policymakers who promoted the war; detested the "Saigon warriors" who pushed papers in the safety of their offices but never entered the field of fire; and hated the "lily-livered" South Vietnamese troops who gave too little support to the American forces. But what hurt her most was the reception she received on her return home to "the world." Van Devanter discovered that many Americans did not want to be reminded of the war.

When the soldiers of World War II came home, they were met by brass bands, ticker-tape parades, and people so thankful for their service that even those who had never heard a shot fired in anger were treated with respect. It was a time when words like honor, glory, and duty held some value, a time when a returning GI was viewed with esteem so high it bordered on awe. To be a veteran was to be seen as a person of courage, a champion of democracy, an ideal against which all citizens could measure themselves. If you had answered your country's call, you were a hero. And in those days, heroes were plentiful.

But somewhere between 1945 and 1970, words like bravery, sacrifice, and valor had gone out of vogue. . . . When I returned to my country in June of 1970, I began to learn a very bitter lesson. The values with which I had been raised had changed; in the eyes of most Americans, the military services had no more heroes, merely babykillers, misfits, and fools. I was certain that I was neither a babykiller nor a misfit. Maybe I was a fool. . . .

Perhaps if I hadn't expected anything at all when I returned to the States, I would not have been disappointed. Maybe I would have been contented simply to be on American soil. Maybe all of us who arrived at Travis Air Force Base on June 16 had unrealistic expectations.

But we didn't ask for a brass band. We didn't ask for a parade. We didn't even ask for much of a thank you. All we wanted was some transportation to San Francisco International Airport so we could hop connecting flights to get home to our families. We gave the Army a year of our lives, a year with more difficulties than most Americans face in fifty years. The least the Army could have done was to give us a ride.

At Travis we were herded onto buses and driven to the Oakland Army Terminal where they dumped us around 5 A.M. with a "so long, suckers" from the driver and a feeling that we were no more than warm bodies who had outlived their usefulness. Unfortunately, San Francisco International was at least twenty miles away. Since most of us had to get flights from there, wouldn't it have been logical to drop us at the airport? Or was I expecting too much out of the Army when I asked it to be logical?

I checked into commercial buses and taxis, but none were running. There was a transit strike on, and it was nearly impossible to get public transportation of any kind. So I hung one of my suitcases from my left shoulder, hefted my duffel bag onto my right shoulder, grabbed my overnight case with my left hand and my purse with my right, and struggling under the weight, walked out to the highway, where I stuck out my thumb and waited. I was no stranger to hitchhiking. It was the only way to get around in Vietnam. Back in 'Nam, I would usually stand on the flight line in my fatigues, combat boots, jungle hat, pigtails, and a smile. Getting a ride there was a cinch. In fact, planes would sometimes reach the end of the runway, then return to offer me a lift.

But hitchhiking in the real world, I was quickly finding out, was nowhere near as easy—especially if you were wearing a uniform. The cars whizzed past me during rush hour, while I patiently waited for a good Samaritan to stop. A few drivers gave me the finger. I tried to ignore them. Some slowed long enough to yell obscenities. One threw a carton of trash and another nearly hit me with a half-empty can of soda. Finally, two guys stopped in a red and yellow Volkswagen bus. The one on the passenger side opened his door. I ran to the car, dragging the duffel bag and other luggage behind me. I was hot, tired, and dirty.

"Going anywhere near the airport?" I asked.

"Sure am," the guy said. He had long brown hair, blue eyes framed by wire-rimmed glasses, and a full curly beard. There was patches on his jeans and a peace sign on his T-shirt. His relaxed, easy smile was deceptive.

I smiled back and lifted my duffel bag to put it inside the van. But the guy slammed the door shut. "We're going past the airport, sucker, but we don't take Army pigs." He spit on me, I was stunned. . . .

[The driver] floored the accelerator and they both laughed uncontrollably as the VW spun its wheels for a few seconds, throwing dirt and stones back at me before it roared away. The drivers of other passing cars also laughed.

I looked down at my chest. On top of my nametag sat a big glob of brownish-colored saliva. I couldn't touch it. I didn't have the energy to wipe it away. Instead, I watched as it ran down my name tag and over a button before it was absorbed into the green material of my uniform.

I wasn't angry, just confused. I wanted to know why. Why would he spit on me? What had I done to him? To either of them? It might have been simple to say I had gone to war and they blamed me for killing innocent people, but didn't they understand that I didn't want this war any more than the most vocal of peace marchers? Didn't they realize that those of us who had seen the war firsthand were probably more antiwar than they were? That we had seen friends suffer and die? That we had seen children destroyed? That we had seen futures crushed?

Were they that naive?

Or were they merely insensitive creeps who used the excuse of my uniform to vent their hostility toward all people?

I waited a few more hours, holding my thumb out until I thought my arm would fall off. After awhile, I stopped watching people as they hurled their insults. I had begun noticing the people who didn't scream as they drove by. I soon realized they all had something in common. It was what I eventually came to refer to as "the look." It was a combination of surprise at seeing a woman in uniform, and hatred for what they assumed I represented. Most of them never bothered to try to conceal it. "The look" would start around the eyes, as if they were peering right through me. Their faces would harden into stone. I was a pariah, a nonperson so low that they believed they could squash me underfoot. . . .

While I stood there alone, I almost wished I was back in 'Nam. At least there you expected some people to hate you. That was a war. But here, in the United States, I guess I wanted everything to be wonderful. I thought that life would be different, that there would be no more pain. No more death. No more sorrow. It was all going to be good again. It had to be good again. I had had enough of fighting, and hatred, and bitterness.

Around 10:30 A.M., when I had given up hope and was sitting on my duffel bag . . . an old black man in a beat up '58 Chevy stopped and got out of his car. He walked with a limp and leaned forward as if he couldn't stand straight.

His clothes were frayed and his face deeply lined. He ran his bony fingers through his gray-black hair, then shook his head and smiled. "I don't know where you're going, little girl," he said. "But I been by here four times since early morning and you ain't got a ride yet. I can't let you spend your whole life on this road." He was only headed for the other side of Oakland, but he said he'd rather go out of his way than see me stranded. He even carried my duffel bag to the trunk. As we drove south on 101, I didn't say much other than thank you, but my disillusionment was obvious.

"People ain't all bad, little girl," he said. "It's just some folks are crazy mixed up these days. You keep in mind that it's gotta get better, cause it can't get any worse."

Questions

1. What does Lynda Van Devanter believe had changed between 1945 and 1970?
2. Why was Van Devanter so surprised at the "welcome" she received? Why did she wish she were back in Vietnam instead?
3. How could this kind of reception affect veterans readjusting to civilian life?

Eleanor Wimbish,
A Mother Remembers Her Son
at "the Wall" (1984)

The Vietnam Veterans Memorial commemorates all the men and women who served in Vietnam as well as the 58,000 who died during the war. In this letter from Mrs. Eleanor Wimbish to her son Billy at "the Wall," a mother expresses both grief and love for her child who did not come home from the war. Sergeant William R. Stocks died in Vietnam on February 13, 1969, at age twenty-one years. Billy's mother has sent him more than two dozen letters at the Wall.

Dear Bill,

Today is February 13, 1984. I came to this black wall again to see and touch your name, and as I do I wonder if anyone ever stops to realize that next to your name, on this black wall, is your mother's heart. A heart broken 15 years ago today, when you lost your life in Vietnam.

And as I look at your name, William R. Stocks, I think of how many, many times I used to wonder how scared and homesick you must have been in that strange country called Vietnam. And if and how it might have changed you, for you were the most happy-go-lucky kid in the world, hardly ever sad or unhappy. And until the day I die, I will see you as you laughed at me, even when I was very mad at you, and the next thing I knew, we were laughing together.

But on the past New Year's Day, I had my answer. I talked by phone to a friend of yours from Michigan, who spent your last Christmas and the last four months of your life with you. Jim told me how you died, for he was there and saw the helicopter crash. He told me how you had flown your quota and had not been scheduled to fly that day. How the regular pilot was unable to fly, and had been replaced by someone with less experience. How they did not know the exact cause of the crash. How it was either hit by enemy fire, or they hit a pole or something unknown. How the blades went through the chopper and hit you. How you lived about a half hour, but were unconscious and therefore did not suffer.

He said how your jobs were like sitting ducks. They would send you men out to draw the enemy into the open and *then* they would send in the big guns and planes to take over. Meantime, death came to so many of you.

He told me how, after a while over there, instead of a yellow streak, the men got a mean streak down their backs. Each day the streak got bigger and the men became meaner. Everyone but *you*, Bill. He said how you stayed the same, happy-go-lucky guy that you were when you arrived in Vietnam. How your warmth and friendliness drew the guys to you. How your [lieutenant] gave you the nickname of "Spanky," and soon your group, Jim included, were all known as "Spanky's gang." How when you died it made it so much harder on them for you were their moral support. And he said how you of all people should never have been the one to die.

Oh, God, how it hurts to write this. But I must face it and then put it to rest. I know that after Jim talked to me, he must have relived it all over again and suffered so. Before I hung up the phone I told Jim I loved him. Loved him for just being your close friend, and for sharing the last days of your life with you, and for being there with you when you died. How lucky you were to have him for a friend, and how lucky he was to have had you.

Later that same day I received a phone call from a mother in Billings, Montana. She had lost her daughter, her only child, a year ago. She needed someone to talk to for no one would let her talk about the tragedy. She said she had seen me on [television] on New Year's Eve, after the Christmas letter I wrote to you and left at this memorial had drawn newspaper and television attention. She said she had been thinking about me all day, and just had to talk to me. She talked to me of her pain, and seemingly needed me to help her with it. I cried with this heartbroken mother, and after I hung up the phone, I laid my head down and cried as hard for her. Here was a mother calling me for help with her pain over the loss of her child, a grown daughter. And as I sobbed I thought, how can I help her with her pain when I have never completely been able to cope with my own?

They tell me the letters I write to you and leave here at this memorial are waking others up to the fact that there is still much pain left, after all these years, from the Vietnam War.

But this I know, I would rather to have had you for 21 years, and all the pain that goes with losing you, than never to have had you at all.

Mom

Questions

1. There was a great camaraderie between soldiers in Vietnam. How does Billy's mother realize this?
2. How has Eleanor Wimbish helped other parents who have lost children? What does she think of this new role?
3. How has "the Wall" helped families come to terms with the loss of loved ones?

Connections Questions

1. Would it have been possible for Presidents Truman and Eisenhower to work with Ho Chi Minh? Why or why not?
2. How does the *Port Huron Statement* compare as a call to arms to *Common Sense* (see Chapter 6), or the Declaration of Independence (see the Documents section of text)? What are its strengths? Its weaknesses?
3. To what extent are the experiences of Lynda Van Devanter and Eleanor Wimbish similar? Different?

CHAPTER 32

The Lean Years:
1969–1980

Daniel Patrick Moynihan, "Memorandum for the President" (1970)

Daniel Patrick Moynihan served in both Democratic and Republican administrations during the 1960s. As a domestic adviser to Richard Nixon in 1970, Moynihan (b. 1927) urged a racial policy of "benign neglect." The memorandum reprinted here quickly became controversial when it was leaked to the press in March 1970. Moynihan's work showed yet again that race is a divisive social and political issue for Americans.

Following is the text of a "Memorandum for the President" by Daniel P. Moynihan, counselor to President Nixon, on the position of Negroes:

As the new year begins, it occurs to me that you might find useful a general assessment of the position of Negroes at the end of the first year of your Administration, and of the decade in which their position has been the central domestic political issue.

In quantitative terms, which are reliable, the American Negro is making extraordinary progress. In political terms, somewhat less reliable, this would also appear to be true. In each case, however, there would seem to be countercurrents that pose a serious threat to the welfare of the blacks and the stability of the society, white and black.

1. Employment and Income

The nineteen-sixties saw the great breakthrough for blacks. A third (32 per cent) of all families of Negro and other races earned $8,000 or more in 1968 compared, in constant dollars, with 15 per cent in 1960.

The South is still a problem. Slightly more than half (52 per cent) of the Negro population lived in the South in 1969. There, only 19 per cent of families of Negro and other races earned over $8,000.

Young Negro families are achieving income parity with young white families. Outside the South, young husband-wife Negro families have 99 per cent of the income of whites! For families headed by a male age 25 to 34 the proportion was 87 per cent. Thus, it may be this ancient gap is finally closing.

Income reflects employment, and this changed dramatically in the nineteen-sixties. Blacks continued to have twice the unemployment rates of whites, but these were down for both groups. In 1969, the rate for married men of Negro and other races was only 2.5 per cent. Teenagers, on the other hand, continued their appalling rates: 24.4 per cent in 1969.

Black occupations improved dramatically. The number of professional and technical employees doubled in the period 1960–68. This was two and a half times the increase for whites. In 1969, Negro and other races provided 10 per cent of the other-than-college teachers. This is roughly their proportion of the population (11 per cent).

2. Education

In 1968, 19 per cent of Negro children 3 and 4 years old were enrolled in school, compared to 15 per cent of white children. Forty-five per cent of Negroes 18 and 19 years old were in school, almost the equal of the white proportion of 51 per cent. Negro college enrollment rose 85 per cent between 1964 and 1968, by which time there were 434,000 Negro college students. (The total full-time university population of Great Britain is 200,000.)

Educational achievement should not be exaggerated. Only 16 per cent of Negro high school seniors have verbal test scores at or above grade level. But blacks are staying in school.

3. Female-Headed Families

This problem does not get better, it gets worse. In 1969, the proportion of husband-wife families of Negro and other races declined once again, this time to 68.7 per cent. The illegitimacy ratio rose once again, this time to 29.4 per cent of all live births. (The white ratio rose more sharply, but was still only 4.9 per cent.)

Increasingly, the problem of Negro poverty is the problem of the female-headed family. In 1968, 56 per cent of Negro families with income under $3,000 were female-headed. In 1968, for the first time, the number of poor Negro children in female-headed families (2,241,000) was greater than the number in male-headed families (1,947,000). . . .

5. Social Alienation

With no real evidence, I would nonetheless suggest that a great deal of the crime, the fire-setting, the rampant school violence and other such phenomena in the black community have become quasi-politicized. Hatred—revenge—against whites is now an acceptable excuse for doing what might have been done anyway. This is bad news for any society, especially when it takes forms which the Black Panthers seem to have adopted.

This social alienation among the black lower classes is matched, and probably enhanced, by a virulent form of anti-white feeling among portions of the large and prosperous black middle class. It would be difficult to overestimate the degree to which young, well-educated blacks detest white America.

6. The Nixon Administration

As you have candidly acknowledged, the relation of the Administration to the black population is a problem. I think it ought also to be acknowledged that we are a long way from solving it. During the past year, intense efforts have been made by the Administration to develop programs that will be of help to the blacks. I dare say, as much or more time and attention goes into this effort in this Administration than any in history. But little has come of it. There has been a great deal of political ineptness in some departments, and you have been the loser.

I don't know what you can do about this. Perhaps nothing. But I do have four suggestions.

First. Sometime early in the year, I would gather together the Administration officials who are most involved with these matters and talk out the subject a bit. There really is a need for a more coherent Administration approach to a number of issues. (Which I can list for you, if you like.)

Second. The time may have come when the issue of race could benefit from a period of "benign neglect." The subject has been too much talked about. The forum has been too much taken over to hysterics, paranoids and boodlers on all sides. We may need a period in which Negro progress continues and racial rhetoric fades. The Administration can help bring this about by paying close attention to such progress—as we are doing—while seeking to avoid situations in which extremists of either race are given opportunities for martyrdom, heroics, histrionics or whatever. Greater attention to Indians, Mexican-Americans and Puerto Ricans would be useful. A tendency to ignore provocations from groups such as the Black Panthers might also be useful. (The Panthers were apparently almost defunct until the Chicago police raided one of their headquarters and transformed them into culture heroes for the white—and black—middle class. You perhaps did not note on the society page of yesterday's Times that Mrs. Leonard Bernstein gave a cocktail party on Wednesday to raise money for the Panthers. Mrs. W. Vincent Astor was among the guests. Mrs. Peter Duchin, "the rich blonde wife of the orchestra leader," was thrilled. "I've never met a Panther," she said. "This is a first for me.") . . .

Fourth. There is a silent black majority as well as a white one. It is mostly working class, as against lower middle class. It is politically moderate (on issues other than racial equality) and shares most of the concerns of its white counterpart. This group has been generally ignored by the Government and the media. The more recognition we can give to it, the better off we shall all be. (I would take it, for example, that Ambassador [Jerome H.] Holland is a natural leader of this segment of the black community. There are others like him.)

Questions
1. What does Moynihan mean by "benign neglect"?
2. What advances in race relations does he note? What problems?
3. Given the text of the memorandum, why did it generate controversy?

White House Conversations (1972)

On June 17, 1972, seven men were arrested for a break-in at the headquarters of the Democratic National Committee in the Watergate hotel and office complex in Washington, D.C. The arrests led to revelations that forced Richard Nixon to resign his presidency on August 9, 1974.

Nixon had arranged to have all conversations in the Oval Office taped secretly, in part because he wanted the tapes to use in writing a history of his administration. When one of his junior aides told a congressional committee about the existence of the tapes, the Watergate investigation focused exclusively on this source (see text p. 867). Nixon fiercely resisted pressure to release the tapes—he knew they would provide the "smoking gun," the incontrovertible evidence that he had committed several crimes, including the suppression of evidence and the obstruction of justice by ordering officials in the White House, the CIA, and the FBI to participate in the cover-up.

The first conversation excerpted here took place six days after the break-in. The president met with H. R. Haldeman, his chief of staff, to discuss the early progress of the FBI's investigation of the event. The second conversation is with John Dean, the White House counsel (the official lawyer to the president). Reference is also made to former U.S. Attorney General John Mitchell, campaign director of the Committee to Re-Elect the President (CREEP); John Ehrlichman, the domestic affairs assistant to the president; and E. Howard

Hunt and G. Gordon Liddy, former CIA agents and private security consultants to the Nixon White House.

June 23, 1972

HALDEMAN: Now, on the investigation, you know the Democratic break-in thing, we're back in the problem area because the FBI is not under control, because [Director Patrick] Gray doesn't exactly know how to control it and they have—their investigation is now leading into some productive areas. . . . They've been able to trace the money—not through the money itself—but through the bank sources—the banker. And it goes in some directions we don't want it to go. Ah, also there have been some [other] things—like an informant came in off the street to the FBI in Miami who was a photographer or has a friend who is a photographer who developed some films through this guy [Bernard] Barker and the films had pictures of Democratic National Committee letterhead documents and things. So it's things like that that are filtering in. . . . [John] Mitchell came up with yesterday, and John Dean analyzed very carefully last night and concludes, concurs now with Mitchell's recommendation that the only way to solve this . . . is for us to have [CIA Assistant Director Vernon] Walters call Pat Gray and just say, "Stay to hell out of this—this is ah, [our] business here. We don't want you to go any further on it." That's not an unusual development, and ah, that would take care of it.

PRESIDENT: What about Pat Gray—you mean Pat Gray doesn't want to?

HALDEMAN: Pat does want to. He doesn't know how to, and he doesn't have any basis for doing it. Given this, he will then have the basis. He'll call [FBI Assistant Director] Mark Felt in, and the two of them—and Mark Felt wants to cooperate because he's ambitious—

PRESIDENT: Yeah.

HALDEMAN: He'll call him in and say, "We've got the signal from across the river to put the hold on this." And that will fit rather well because the FBI agents who are working the case, at this point, feel that's what it is.

PRESIDENT: This is CIA? They've traced the money? Who'd they trace it to? . . .

HALDEMAN: Ken Dahlberg.

PRESIDENT: Who the hell is Ken Dahlberg?

HALDEMAN: He gave $25,000 in Minnesota and, ah, the check went directly to this guy Barker.

PRESIDENT: It isn't from the Committee though, from [Maurice] Stans?

HALDEMAN: Yeah. It is. It's directly traceable and there's some more through some Texas people that went to the Mexican bank which can also be traced to the Mexican bank—they'll get their names today.

PRESIDENT: Well, I mean, there's no way—I'm just thinking if they don't cooperate, what do they say? That they were approached by the Cubans? That's what Dahlberg has to say, the Texans too.

HALDEMAN: Well, if they will. But then we're relying on more and more people all the time. That's the problem and they'll [the FBI] . . . stop if we could take this other route.

PRESIDENT: All right.

HALDEMAN: [Mitchell and Dean] say the only way to do that is from White House instructions. And it's got to be to [CIA Director Richard] Helms and to—ah, what's his name? . . . Walters. . . . And the proposal would be that . . . [John] Ehrlichman and I call them in, and say, ah—

PRESIDENT: All right, fine. How do you call him in—I mean you just—well, we protected Helms from one hell of a lot of things.

HALDEMAN: That's what Ehrlichman says.

PRESIDENT: Of course; this [Howard] Hunt [business]. That will uncover a lot of things. You open that scab there's a hell of a lot of things and we just feel that it would be very detrimental to have this thing go any further. This involves these Cubans, Hunt, and a lot of hanky-panky that we have nothing to do with ourselves. Well, what the hell, did Mitchell know about this?

HALDEMAN: I think so. I don't think he knew the details, but I think he knew.

PRESIDENT: He didn't know how it was going to be handled though—with Dahlberg and the Texans and so forth? Well who was the asshole that did? Is it [G. Gordon] Liddy? Is that the fellow? He must be a little nuts!

HALDEMAN: He is.

PRESIDENT: I mean he just isn't well screwed on, is he? Is that the problem?

HALDEMAN: No, but he was under pressure, apparently, to get more information, and as he got more pressure, he pushed the people harder.

PRESIDENT: Pressure from Mitchell?

HALDEMAN: Apparently. . . .

PRESIDENT: All right, fine, I understand it all. We won't second-guess Mitchell and the rest. Thank God it wasn't [special White House counsel Charles] Colson.

HALDEMAN: The FBI interviewed Colson yesterday. They determined that would be a good thing to do. To have him take an interrogation, which he did, and the FBI guys working the case concluded that there were one or two possibilities—one, that this was a White House (they don't think that there is anything at the Election Committee); they think it was either a White House operation and they had some obscure reasons for it—non-political, or it was a—Cuban [operation] and [involved] the CIA. And after the interrogation of Colson yesterday, they concluded it was not the White House, but are now convinced it is a CIA thing, so the CIA turnoff would—

PRESIDENT: Well, not sure of their analysis, I'm not going to get that involved. I'm (unintelligible).

HALDEMAN: No, sir, we don't want you to.

PRESIDENT: You call them in.

HALDEMAN: Good deal.

PRESIDENT: Play it tough. That's the way they play it and that's the way we are going to play it. . . .

PRESIDENT: O.K. . . . Just say (unintelligible) very bad to have this fellow Hunt, ah, he knows too damned much. . . . If it gets out that this is all involved, the Cuba thing, it would be a fiasco. It would make the CIA look bad, it's going to make Hunt look bad, and it is likely to blow the whole Bay of Pigs thing which we think would be very unfortunate—both for CIA, and for the country, at this time, and for American foreign policy. Just tell him to lay off. Don't you [think] so?

HALDEMAN: Yep. That's the basis to do it on. Just leave it at that. . . .

September 15, 1972

PRESIDENT: We are all in it together. This is a war. We take a few shots and it will be over. We will give them a few shots and it will be over. Don't worry. I wouldn't want to be on the other side right now. Would you?

DEAN: Along that line, one of the things I've tried to do, I have begun to keep notes on a lot of people who are emerging as less than our friends because this will be over some day and we shouldn't forget the way some of them have treated us.

PRESIDENT: I want the most comprehensive notes on all those who tried to do us in. They didn't have to do it. If we had had a very close election and they were playing the other side I would understand this. No—they were doing this quite deliberately and they are asking for it and they are going to get it. We have not used the power in this first four years, as you know. . . . We have not used the Bureau, and we have not used the Justice Department, but things are going to change now. And they are either going to do it right or go.

DEAN: What an exciting prospect.

PRESIDENT: Thanks. It has to be done. We have been (adjective deleted) fools for us to come into this election campaign, and not do anything with regard to the Democratic Senators who are running, et cetera. And who the hell are they after? They are after us. It is absolutely ridiculous. It is not going to be that way anymore.

Questions

1. According to these transcripts, how much did President Nixon know about the financial and security operations of his reelection campaign?

2. What did Nixon know on June 23, 1972, concerning the Watergate break-in and related matters? What evidence do the transcripts provide that Nixon ordered the CIA and the FBI to participate in the cover-up?

3. Do the transcripts reveal other matters that Nixon might not have wanted made public or that might have affected public respect for government?

William Serrin,
Homestead (1992)

Homestead, Pennsylvania, was a hardscrabble community that owed much of its existence to the steel industry. The Homestead Works opened in 1881 and remained in operation for the next 105 years. William Serrin found the story of the people, place, and industry so compelling that he left the New York Times *to write it.*

II

The town government continued to face enormous problems. The borough's deficit increased from $30,000 in 1989 to $300,000 in 1990, and the population continued to fall. It was 4,179 in the 1990 census, down 17.9 percent from 5,092 in 1980. In 1988, the corporation sold the Homestead Works to the Park Corporation for $14 million—$2.5 million for the land and $11.5 million for the equipment and machinery. Soon, demolition crews arrived, and one by one the old mills came down. For a time, Mayor Simko continued to believe that the Valley Machine Shop would be purchased from Park and reopened, but the letter of intent that he had been expecting the day we had toured the works had not come through. The investors said that reopening the mill would not be feasible, in view of the depressed condition of the steel industry. . . .

The corporation's interest in steel continued to shrink. In early 1991, its steel operations became an independent subsidiary. In May, its stock was split into two—one for energy, one for steel—and the steel stock was dropped from the Dow Jones Industrial Average and replaced by the stock of the Walt Disney Company.

By this time, the national union's membership had dropped to 490,000, one-third of the 1.4 million who had belonged in 1979. In 1991, a plan to organize white-collar workers was announced, and a woman organizer with substantial experience in the field was hired. But the effort failed. . . .

IV

Most of the men who lost their jobs when the mill went down accepted their fate and settled in, living on part-time work or on pensions. Many had trouble sleeping and finding things to do with the time on their hands. They dropped children or grandchildren off at school, helped around the house, worked on the lawn. After a time, their wives and children got used to having them around. Sometimes the men drove down by the works and watched the demolition crews taking it down. The men would have reunions at one of the firehouses or social clubs, but those were not much fun. One by one they stopped going, and soon no one planned reunions anymore.

"I still think about that damn place," Bob Krovocheck said. He had worked in the mill for thirty-eight years and was fifty-six years old when he lost his job. His highest pay was twenty-seven thousand dollars in 1985. He tried working as a janitor for four dollars an hour, but he was overweight and had bad knees, and the work was too demanding, so he had to quit. His wife had been seriously injured in an automobile accident on the Pennsylvania Turnpike in 1981, and he spent much of his time taking care of her. They lived on his pension of $1,100 a month, $876 after taxes and medical deductions.

Krovocheck missed the mill enormously. "I dream about it every once in a while," he said. "I miss going to work, being around the guys, the eight-hour turn, the routine. I miss the money, too. It was a good living. I wasn't living from payday to payday. It's funny. I remember that every once in a while one of us in the mill would say, 'Let's get our pension and get out of here.' But pensioneering ain't all that great, especially if you've got somebody sick you're taking care of.

"During the day, I take care of the wife, get the meals, keep the house halfway decent. It ain't like she would keep it. I do the cooking and laundry. I read quite a bit. I go up the street and have a couple of beers. I go to the store and get the groceries. I come home and make supper. I watch TV. I go to bed. I get rather depressed, especially when I drive up past where we worked, the structural mill. I'm okay, if you want to call me okay." . . .

Ray McGuire, a repairman, had worked in the mill for thirty-six years and had taken only two sick days. He got a pension of $1,000 a month and caught on as an electrician, going from one shop to another, wherever he was needed. Sometimes a temporary agency found him work, or else he would hear of something himself. He worked for a while at the machine company that now occupied part of the old Mesta Machine plant. One day he had to go to the Homestead Works to pick up some tools. "I went to the exact place where I worked, and I got so nauseated I thought I was going to throw up," he said. "I thought: 'I worked here. What are you people doing to this place? What are you doing to my cranes?' And then I thought: 'Wait a minute. This wasn't my place. These weren't my cranes.' But that's the way I thought—that it was my place." He lived in Pleasant Hills, not far from Homestead, but he no longer went to Homestead at night. He was afraid of crime there, and besides, he got despondent when he went to Homestead, even when he just drove through the town. "The place looks like a morgue," he said.

Bob Todd, a craneman and grievance man, was unemployed for a year. Then he was called to the Edgar Thomson Works, where he got a job as a safety man in the slab mill, making seventeen thousand dollars a year. It was not as much as he had been making at Homestead, but it was a job. About two hundred Homestead workers were given jobs there, and another few dozen were hired by the Irvin Works.

Bill Brennan, a millwright, had worked in the mill for thirty-nine years and was sixty-four when he retired on his pension of $775 a month after deductions. He also got Social Security, and his house was paid for. His father had worked at the Homestead Works, and so had his three brothers. In 1984, when he had a heart-bypass operation, he was on sick leave for six months. His heart was now okay, though he had to take three pills a day. When he went back into the mill after his bypass, the other millwrights carried him, hid him out, for six months—they did the heavy work that he had done and did not tell the supervisors. He would pick up a sledgehammer or a big crescent wrench, and the others would take it from him and tell him to go somewhere, get lost, and they would do the job. "I miss guys like that, good working people," he said.

Bobby Schneider, a roller, got a part-time job tending bar at the Slovak Club in Munhall. He had worked in the mill for thirty-one years and had earned $35,000 in his best year. The bartender's job wasn't much, though it got him out of the house and gave him something to do. He lived on a pension check of $1,077 a month after deductions. His wife worked as a secretary in a real-estate company. His section of the last beam rolled at the Homestead Works was still in the trunk of his car, four years after the mill went down. He had intended to shine it up and put it in the house, but he never got around to it. His two pals, Red Hrabic and Jimmie Sherlock, both lived on pensions of about $900 a month and were doing okay. The three of them met at Hess's Bar in Hunkie Hollow almost every afternoon at about four, or maybe at the Slovak Club, in Munhall, if Schneider was tending bar there.

There was much crying in Homestead. Men and women often went to wakes and funerals, for there were many deaths among the men from the works. I knew or heard of three dozen men who died or committed suicide. That's a lot of men gone, and at an early age, too. I think that many of them died because the mill closed, though I can't prove it. But it's a lot of dead guys, isn't it?

There was one man I never got out of my mind—Rich Locher, the hooker from Number Two Structural who had denounced the government's retraining programs at the meeting with the two men in the pinstripe suits from Senator Heinz's staff. I had planned to meet with Locher, but time passed, and I was busy. One winter day, preparing for a trip to Homestead, I wrote down his telephone number, thinking I would go see him. When I got to Homestead, I ran into Mike Stout, the former grievance man. When I told him that I was going to call Locher, he said: "Don't bother. Locher is dead. He finished the retraining program but couldn't get a nursing job, so he took a gun and killed himself—shot half his head away, in his garage." Stout continued with his paperwork and did not look up. One more death was not much to him. He knew too many stories like this.

I liked Locher. He was a good man. He had a temper and often used profane language, but don't many of us? He was an excellent father and husband, and he probably deserved more out of life than to take two brief vacations at hot trailer parks in Virginia and go out to eat once a month at McDonald's or Long John Silver's, to lose his job as a craneman and not get a job as a nurse. One more thing. Locher was right about the training programs. They were bullshit.

Questions

1. How does the plant's closing affect community institutions?
2. Why does the mill exert such an influence on its ex-workers?
3. What program is supposed to help unemployed steelworkers get back into the economy? Why is Serrin so critical of it?

Gloria Steinem, Statement in Support of the Equal Rights Amendment (1970)

In 1972, Gloria Steinem (b. 1934) and other journalists founded Ms. *magazine, which became the most successful mass-circulation feminist publication. She is an acknowledged leader of the modern feminist movement. Her testimony to the Senate Subcommittee on Constitutional Amendments, given in support of the Equal Rights Amendment, includes the major tenets of the feminist position.*

The truth is that all our problems stem from the same sex based myths. We may appear before you as white radicals or the middle-aged middle class or black soul sisters, but we are all sisters in fighting against these outdated myths. Like racial myths, they have been reflected in our laws. Let me list a few.

That women are biologically inferior to men. In fact, an equally good case can be made for the reverse. Women live longer than men, even when the men are not subject to business pressures. Women survived Nazi concentration camps better, keep cooler heads in emergencies currently studied by disaster-researchers, are protected against heart attacks by their female sex hormones, and are so much more durable at every stage of life that nature must conceive 20 to 50 percent more males in order to keep the balance going.

Man's hunting activities are forever being pointed to as tribal proof of superiority. But while he was hunting, women built houses, tilled the fields, developed animal husbandry, and perfected language. Men, being all alone in the bush, often developed into a creature as strong as women, fleeter of foot, but not very bright.

However, I don't want to prove the superiority of one sex to another. That would only be repeating a male mistake. English scientists once definitively proved, after all, that the English were descended from the angels, while the Irish were descended from the apes; it was the rationale for England's domination of Ireland for more than a century. The point is that science is used to support current myth and economics almost as much as the church was.

What we do know is that the difference between two races or two sexes is much smaller than the differences to be found within each group. Therefore, in spite of the slide show on female inferiorities that I understand was shown to you yesterday, the law makes much more sense when it treats individuals, not groups bundled together by some condition of birth. . . .

Another myth, that women are already treated equally in this society. I am sure there has been ample testimony to prove that equal pay for equal work, equal chance for advancement, and equal training or encouragement is obscenely scarce in every field, even those—like food and fashion industries—that are supposedly "feminine."

A deeper result of social and legal injustice, however, is what sociologists refer to as "Internalized Aggression." Victims of aggression absorb the myth of their own inferiority, and come to believe that their group is in fact second class. Even when they themselves realize they are not second class, they may still think their group is, thus the tendency to be the only Jew in the club, the only black woman on the block, the only woman in the office.

Women suffer this second class treatment from the moment they are born. They are expected to be, rather than achieve, to function biologically rather than learn. A brother, whatever his intellect, is more likely to get the family's encouragement and education money, while girls are often pressured to conceal ambition and intelligence, to "Uncle Tom."

I interviewed a New York public school teacher who told me about a black teenager's desire to be a doctor. With all the barriers in mind, she suggested kindly that he be a veterinarian instead.

The same day, a high school teacher mentioned a girl who wanted to be a doctor. The teacher said, "How about a nurse?"

Teachers, parents, and the Supreme Court may exude a protective, well-meaning rationale, but limiting the individual's ambition is doing no one a favor. Certainly not this country; it needs all the talent it can get.

Another myth, that American women hold great economic power. Fifty-one percent of all shareholders in this country are women. That is a favorite male-chauvinist statistic. However, the number of shares they hold is so small that the total is only 18 percent of all the shares. Even those holdings are often controlled by men.

Similarly, only 5 percent of all the people in the country who receive $10,000 a year or more, earned or otherwise, are women. And that includes the famous rich widows.

The constantly repeated myth of our economic power seems less testimony to our real power than to the resentment of what little power we do have.

Another myth, that children must have full-time mothers. American mothers spend more time with their homes and children than those of any other society we know about. In the past, joint families, servants, a prevalent system in which grandparents raised the children, or family field work in the agrarian systems—all these factors contributed more to child care than the labor-saving devices of which we are so proud.

The truth is that most American children seem to be suffering from too much mother, and too little father. Part of the program of Women's Liberation is a return of fathers to their children. If laws permit women equal work and pay opportunities, men will then be relieved of their role as sole breadwinner. Fewer ulcers, fewer hours of meaningless work, equal responsibility for his own children: these are a few of the reasons that Women's Liberation is Men's Liberation too. . . .

When black people leave their 19th century roles, they are feared. When women dare to leave theirs, they are ridiculed. We understand this; we accept the burden of ridicule. It won't keep us quiet anymore.

Similarly, it shouldn't deceive male observers into thinking that this is somehow a joke. We are 51 percent of the population; we are essentially united on these issues across boundaries of class or race or age; and we may well end by changing this society more than the civil rights movement. That is an apt parallel. We, too, have our right wing and left wing, our separatists, gradualists, and Uncle Toms. But we are changing our own consciousness, and that of the country. Engels noted the relationship of the authoritarian, nuclear family to capitalism; the father as capitalist, the mother as means of production, and the children as labor. He said the family would change as the economic system did, and that seems to have happened, whether we want to admit it or not. Women's bodies will no longer be owned by the state for the production of workers and soldiers; birth control and abortion are facts of everyday life. The new family is an egalitarian family.

Gunnar Myrdal noted 30 years ago the parallel between women and Negroes in this country. Both suffered from such restricting social myths as: smaller brains, passive natures, inability to govern themselves (and certainly not white men), sex objects only, childlike natures, special skills, and the like. When evaluating a general statement about women, it might be valuable to substitute "black people" for "women"—just to test the prejudice at work.

And it might be valuable to do this constitutionally as well. Neither group is going to be content as a cheap labor pool anymore. And neither is going to be content without full constitutional rights. . . .

Women are not more moral than men. We are only uncorrupted by power. But we do not want to imitate men, to join this country as it is, and I think our very participation will change it. Perhaps women elected leaders—and there will be many of them—will not be so likely to dominate black people or yellow people or men; anybody who looks different from us.

After all, we won't have our masculinity to prove.

Questions

1. What comparisons does Gloria Steinem make between women and African-Americans?

2. What arguments involving the family does Steinem indicate are used by ERA opponents? How does she counter them?

3. According to Steinem, in what ways do men and women differ? How is this significant?

Phyllis Schlafly, *The Power of the Positive Woman* (1977)

By the late 1970s, many Americans had grown frustrated with what seemed to be a constant litany of social criticism. Increasingly, they were attracted to views such as those expressed by conservative activist Phyllis Schlafly (b. 1924). For Schlafly and others, the problem was the critics, not society. In the following excerpt, Schlafly outlines what she thinks the women's movement should entail.

The women's liberationists and their dupes who try to tell each other that the sexual drive of men and women is really the same, and that it is only societal restraints that inhibit women from an equal desire, an equal enjoyment, and an equal freedom from the consequences, are doomed to frustration forever. It just isn't so, and pretending cannot make it so. The differences are not a woman's weakness but her strength. . . .

The Positive Woman recognizes the fact that, when it comes to sex, women are simply not the equal of men. The sexual drive of men is much stronger than that of women. That is how the human race was designed in order that it might perpetuate itself. The other side of the coin is that it is easier for women to control their sexual appetites. A Positive Woman cannot defeat a man in a wrestling or boxing match, but she can motivate him, inspire him, encourage him, teach him, restrain him, reward him, and have power over him that he can never achieve over her with all his muscle. How or whether a Positive Woman uses her power is determined solely by the way she alone defines her goals and develops her skills.

The differences between men and women are also emotional and psychological. Without woman's innate maternal instinct, the human race would have died out centuries ago. There is nothing so helpless in all earthly life as the newborn infant. It will die within hours if not cared for. Even in the most primitive, uneducated societies, women have always cared for their newborn babies. They didn't need any schooling to teach them how. They didn't need any welfare workers to tell them it is their social obligation. Even in societies to whom such concepts as "ought," "social responsibility," and "compassion for the helpless" were unknown, mothers cared for their new babies.

Why? Because caring for a baby serves the natural maternal need of a woman. Although not nearly so total as the baby's need, the woman's need is nonetheless real.

The overriding psychological need of a woman is to love something alive. A baby fulfills this need in the lives of most women. If a baby is not available to fill that need, women search for a baby-substitute. This is the reason why women have traditionally gone into teaching and nursing careers. They are doing what comes naturally to the female psyche. The schoolchild or the patient of any age provides an outlet for a woman to express her natural maternal need.

This maternal need in women is the reason why mothers whose children have grown up and flown from the nest are sometimes cut loose from their psychological moorings. The maternal need in women can show itself in love for grandchildren, nieces, nephews, or even neighbors' children. The maternal need in some women has even manifested itself in an extraordinary affection lavished on a dog, cat, or a parakeet.

This is not to say that every woman must have a baby in order to be fulfilled. But it is to say that fulfillment for most women involves expressing their natural maternal urge by loving and caring for someone. . . .

The Positive Woman finds somebody on whom she can lavish her maternal love so that it doesn't well up inside her and cause psychological frustrations. Surely no woman is so isolated by geography or insulated by spirit that she cannot find someone worthy of her maternal love. All persons, men and women, gain by sharing something of themselves with their fellow humans, but women profit most of all because it is part of their very nature. . . .

Most women's organizations, recognizing the preference of most women to avoid hard-driving competition, handle the matter of succession of officers by the device of a nominating committee. This eliminates the unpleasantness and the tension of a competitive confrontation every year or two. Many women's organizations customarily use a prayer attributed to Mary, Queen of Scots, which is an excellent analysis by a woman of women's faults:

Keep us, O God, from pettiness; let us be large in thought, in word, in deed. Let us be done with fault-finding and leave off self-seeking. . . . Grant that we may realize it is the little things that create differences, that in the big things of life we are at one. . . .

Questions

1. Why does Phyllis Schlafly refer to psychology?
2. How does Schlafly compare to reformers such as Frances Willard (Chapter 19, "Woman and Temperance") and Jane Addams (Chapter 21, "Twenty Years at Hull-House")?
3. Does she see men and women as true equals? Why or why not?

Connections Questions

1. What is it about the Watergate tapes that has so damaged the American presidency?

2. What is the human component behind the term *deindustrialization*? Use "Homestead" in your response.

3. Construct a debate on feminism between Gloria Steinem and Phyllis Schlafly. What, if any, points would they agree on? To broaden the debate, you might include such figures as Abigail Adams (Chapter 7, "Abigail and John Adams Debate the Rights of Women"), Elizabeth Cady Stanton (Chapter 12, Seneca Falls Resolutions), Frances Willard (Chapter 19, "Woman and Temperance"), and Jane Addams (Chapter 21, "Twenty Years at Hull-House"). Is there a consensus on what constitutes feminism?

CHAPTER 33

A New Domestic and World Order 1981 to the Present

Ronald Reagan, *An American Life* (1990)

Although Ronald Reagan (b. 1911) at times seemed to treat public office as another acting role (see text p. 892), he did possess firmly grounded political views that were the product of his upbringing. These excerpts from Reagan's autobiography, An American Life, *describe both his youth in Dixon, Illinois, and his perceptions of the effect government had on townspeople caught up in the Great Depression. These experiences helped shape his views on the role of government in society.*

Later in life I learned that, compared with some of the folks who lived in Dixon, our family was "poor." But I didn't know that when I was growing up. And I never thought of our family as disadvantaged. Only later did the government decide that it had to tell people they were poor.

We always rented our home and never had enough money for luxuries. But I don't remember suffering because of that. Although my mother sometimes took in sewing to supplement my dad's wages and I grew up wearing my brother's clothes and shoes after he'd outgrown them, we always had enough to eat and Nelle was forever finding people who were worse off then we were and going out of her way to help them.

In those days, our main meal—dinner—was at noon and frequently consisted of a dish my mother called "oatmeal meat." She'd cook a batch of oatmeal and mix it with hamburger (I suspect the relative portions of each may have varied according to our current economic status), then serve it with some gravy she'd made while cooking the hamburger.

I remember the first time she brought a plate of oatmeal meat to the table. There was a thick, round patty buried in gravy that I'd never seen before. I bit into it. It was moist and meaty, the most wonderful thing I'd ever eaten. Of course, I didn't realize oatmeal meat was born of poverty.

Nowadays, I bet doctors would say it was healthy for us, too.

Dixon straddles the Rock River, a stretch of blue-green water flanked by wooded hills and limestone cliffs that meanders through the farmland of northwestern Illinois on its way to the Mississippi.

The river, which was often called the "Hudson of the West," was my playground during some of the happiest moments of my life. During the winter, it froze and became a skating rink as wide as two football fields and as long as I wanted to make it. In the summer, I swam and fished in the river and ventured as far as I dared on overnight canoe trips through the Rock River Valley, pretending with playmates to be a nineteenth-century explorer.

In my hand-me-down overalls, I hiked the hills and cliffs above the river, tried (unsuccessfully) to trap muskrats at the river's edge, and played "Cowboys and Indians" on hillsides above the river.

When we first moved to Dixon, we lived on the south side of the river. When we could afford it, we moved across the river to a larger house on the north side. As I look back on those days in Dixon, I think my life was as sweet and idyllic as it could be, as close as I could imagine for a young boy to the world created by Mark Twain in *The Adventures of Tom Sawyer.* . . .

For a twenty-one-year-old fresh out of college, broadcasting the Big Ten games was like a dream, and as the end of the season approached, I prayed the people at WOC would offer me a permanent job. But after the final game, Pete told me the station didn't have an opening. He said if something came up, he'd call me, but with the Depression growing worse daily, he sounded as if there wasn't much hope.

Once again, disappointed and frustrated, I headed for home.

Back in Dixon, Jack [Reagan's father] reminded me that while I'd been talking about forward passes and quarterback sneaks, events a lot more important than football games had been occurring: Franklin D. Roosevelt had been elected the thirty-second president of the United States by a landslide and Jack predicted he would pull America out of its tailspin.

There weren't many Democrats in Dixon and Jack was probably the most outspoken of them, never missing a chance to speak up for the working man or sing the praises of Roosevelt.

I had become a Democrat, by birth, I suppose, and a few months after my twenty-first birthday, I cast my first vote for Roosevelt and the full Democratic ticket. And, like Jack—and millions of other Americans—I soon idolized FDR. He'd entered the White House facing a national emergency as grim as any the country has ever faced and, acting quickly, he had implemented a plan of action to deal with the crisis.

During his Fireside Chats, his strong, gentle, confident voice resonated across the nation with an eloquence that brought comfort and resilience to a nation caught up in a storm and reassured us that we could lick any problem. I will never forget him for that.

With his alphabet soup of federal agencies, FDR in many ways set in motion the forces that later sought to create big government and bring a form of veiled socialism to America. But I think that many people forget Roosevelt ran for president on a platform dedicated to reducing waste and fat in government. He called for cutting federal spending by twenty-five percent, eliminating useless boards and commissions and returning to states and communities powers that had been wrongfully seized by the federal government. If he had not been distracted by war, I think he would have resisted the relentless expansion of the federal government that followed him. One of his sons, Franklin Roosevelt, Jr., often told me that his father had said many times his welfare and relief programs during the Depression were meant only as emergency, stopgap measures to cope with a crisis, not the seeds of what others later tried to turn into a permanent welfare state. Government giveaway programs, FDR said, "destroy the human spirit," and he was right. As smart as he was, though, I suspect even FDR didn't realize that once you created a bureaucracy, it took on a life of its own. It was almost impossible to close down a bureaucracy once it had been created.

After FDR's election, Jack, as one of the few Democrats in town, was appointed to implement some of the new federal relief programs in Dixon. It removed him from the ranks of the unemployed and also gave me my first opportunity to watch government in action.

As administrator of federal relief programs, Jack shared a small office in Dixon with the County Supervisor of Poor. Every week, people who had lost their jobs came to the office to pick up sacks of flour, potatoes, and other food and pieces of scrip they could exchange for groceries at stores in town.

Occasionally, I dropped into the office to wait for Jack before we walked home together. I was shocked to see the fathers of many of my schoolmates waiting in line for handouts—men I had known most of my life, who had had jobs I'd thought were as permanent as the city itself.

Jack knew that accepting handouts was tough on the dignity of the men and came up with a plan to help them recover some of it. He began leaving home early in the morning and making rounds of the county, asking if anyone had odd jobs available, then, if they did, persuaded the people to let him find somebody to do the work. The next week when the men came in for their handouts, Jack offered the work he'd found to those who'd been out of work the longest.

I'll never forget the faces of these men when Jack told them their turn had come up for a job: They brightened like a burst of neon, and when they left Dad's office, I swear the men were standing a little taller. They wanted *work*, not handouts.

Not long after that, Jack told several men he had found a week's work for them. They responded to this news with a rustling of feet. Eventually, one broke the silence and said: "Jack, the last time you got me some work, the people at the relief office took my family off welfare; they said I had a job and even though it was temporary, I wasn't eligible for relief anymore. I just can't afford to take another job."

Later on, thanks again to his party connections, Jack was placed in charge of the Works Progress Administration office in Dixon. The WPA was one of the most productive elements of FDR's alphabet soup of agencies because it put people to work building roads, bridges, and other projects. Like Jack's informal program, it gave men and women a chance to make some money along with the satisfaction of knowing they *earned* it. But just as Jack got the program up and running, there was a decline in the number of people applying for work on the projects. Since he knew there hadn't been a cure for unemployment in Dixon, he began asking questions and discovered the federal welfare workers were telling able-bodied men in Dixon that they shouldn't take the WPA jobs because they were being taken care of and didn't need help from the WPA.

After a while, Jack couldn't get any of his projects going; he couldn't get enough men sprung from the welfare giveaway program. I wasn't sophisticated enough to realize what I learned later: The first rule of a bureaucracy is to protect the bureaucracy. If the people running the welfare program had let their clientele find other ways of making a living, that would have reduced their importance and their budget.

Questions

1. What political values does President Reagan take from growing up in a small town?
2. How do his observations on the Depression compare to those in Chapters 25 and 26 of the text?
3. Was the world of 1920s and 1930s America relevant to social problems a half-century later? Why or why not?

George Gilder, *Wealth and Poverty* (1981)

In Wealth and Poverty, *a book that strongly influenced the Reagan administration, the conservative theorist George Gilder argued that it was the immoral and irresponsible behavior of the poor themselves rather than any structural defects in the economy that perpetuated poverty in the United States. Gilder echoed long-held American beliefs about the individual as moral agent.*

The only dependable route from poverty is always work, family, and faith. The first principle is that in order to move up, the poor must not only work, they must work harder than the classes above them. Every previous generation of the lower class has made such efforts. But the current poor, white even more than black, are refusing to work hard. Irwin Garfinkel and Robert Haveman, authors of the ingenious and sophisticated study of what they call *Earnings Capacity Utilization Rates*, have calculated the degree to which various income groups use their opportunities—how hard they work outside the home. This study shows that, for several understandable reasons, the current poor work substantially less, for fewer hours and weeks a year, and earn less in proportion to their age, education, and other credentials (even *after* correcting the figures for unemployment, disability, and presumed discrimination) than either their predecessors in American cities or those now above them on the income scale. (The study was made at the federally funded Institute for Research on Poverty at the University of Wisconsin and used data from the census and the Michigan longitudinal survey.) The findings lend important confirmation to the growing body of evidence that work effort is the crucial unmeasured variable in American productivity and income distribution, and that current welfare and other subsidy programs substantially reduce work. The poor choose leisure not because of moral weakness, but because they are paid to do so.

A program to lift by transfers and preferences the incomes of less diligent groups is politically divisive—and very unlikely—because it incurs the bitter resistance of the real working class. In addition, such an effort breaks the psychological link between effort and reward, which is crucial to long-run upward mobility. Because effective work consists not in merely fulfilling the requirements of labor contracts, but in "putting out" with alertness and emotional commitment, workers have to understand and feel deeply that what they are given depends on what they give—that they must supply work in order to demand goods. Parents and schools must inculcate this idea in their children both by instruction and example. Nothing is more deadly to achievement than the belief that effort will not be rewarded, that the world is a bleak and discriminatory place in which only the predatory and the specially preferred can get ahead. Such a view in the home discourages the work effort in school that shapes earnings capacity afterward. As with so many aspects of human performance, work effort begins in family experiences, and its sources can be best explored through an examination of family structure.

Indeed, after work the second principle of upward mobility is the maintenance of monogamous marriage and family. Adjusting for discrimination against women and for child-care responsibilities, the Wisconsin study indicates that married men work between two and one-third and four times harder than married women, and more than twice as hard as female family heads. The work effort of married men increases with their age, credentials, education, job experience, and birth of children, while the work effort of married women steadily declines. Most important in judging the impact of marriage, husbands work 50 percent harder than bachelors of comparable age, education, and skills.

The effect of marriage, thus, is to increase the work effort of men by about half. Since men have higher earnings capacity to begin with, and since the female capacity-utilization figures would be even lower without an adjustment for discrimination, it is manifest that the maintenance of families is the key factor in reducing poverty.

Once a family is headed by a woman, it is almost impossible for it to greatly raise its income even if the woman is highly educated and trained and she hires day-care or domestic help. Her family responsibilities and distractions tend to prevent her from the kind of all-out commitment that is necessary for the full use of earning power. Few women with children make earning money the top priority in their lives.

A married man, on the other hand, is spurred by the claims of family to channel his otherwise disruptive male aggressions into his performance as a provider for a wife and children. These sexual differences alone, which manifest themselves in all societies known to anthropology, dictate that the first priority of any serious program against poverty is to strengthen the male role in poor families. . . .

The short-sighted outlook of poverty stems largely from the breakdown of family responsibilities among fathers. The lives of the poor, all too often, are governed by the rhythms of tension and release that characterize the sexual experience of young single men. Because female sexuality, as it evolved over the millennia, is psychologically rooted in the bearing and nurturing of children, women have long horizons within their very bodies, glimpses of eternity within their wombs. Civilized society is dependent upon the submission of the short-term sexuality of young men to the extended maternal horizons of women. This is what happens in monogamous marriage; the man disciplines his sexuality and extends it into the future through the womb of a woman. The woman gives him access to his children, otherwise forever denied him; and he gives her the product of his labor, otherwise dissipated on temporary pleasures. The woman gives him a unique link to the future and a vision of it; he gives her faithfulness and a commitment to a lifetime of hard work. If work effort is the first principle of overcoming poverty, marriage is the prime source of upwardly mobile work.

It is love that changes the short horizons of youth and poverty into the long horizons of marriage and career. When marriages fail, the man often returns to the more primitive rhythms of singleness. On the average, his income drops by one-third and he shows a far higher propensity for drink, drugs, and crime. But when marriages in general hold firm and men in general love and support their children, Banfield's lower-class style changes into middle-class futurity.

The key to the intractable poverty of the hardcore American poor is the dominance of single and separated men in poor communities. Black "unrelated individuals" are not much more likely to be in poverty than white ones. The problem is neither race nor matriarchy in any meaningful sense. It is familial anarchy among the concentrated poor of the inner city, in which flamboyant and impulsive youths rather than responsible men provide the themes of aspiration. The result is that male sexual rhythms tend to prevail, and boys are brought up without authoritative fathers in the home to instill in them the values of responsible paternity: the discipline and love of children and the dependable performance of the provider role. "If she wants me, *she'll* pay," one young stud assured me in prison, and perhaps, in the welfare culture, she can and will. Thus the pattern is extended into future generations.

Questions

1. What does Gilder see as the primary cause of poverty?
2. What does he see as the solution to the problem?
3. Why would Gilder's ideas have appealed so strongly to Ronald Reagan?

Oliver North, Testimony before Congress (1987)

Lieutenant Colonel Oliver North (b. 1943) was a principal figure in the Iran-Contra scandal that broke in 1986 (see text p. 894). North was accused of using the profits from the secret sale of arms to Iran to provide aid to the Contra guerrillas in Nicaragua. Testifying before the House–Senate investigative committee, North depicted himself as a loyal soldier carrying out the wishes of his superiors to the best of his ability. He contrasted his own patriotic devotion to the "fickle, vacillating, unpredictable, on-again off-again" policies of the legislators who were scrutinizing his actions.

As you all know by now, my name is Oliver North, Lieutenant Colonel, United States Marine Corps. My best friend is my wife Betsy, to whom I have been married for 19 years, and with whom I have had four wonderful children, aged 18, 16, 11 and 6.

I came to the National Security Council six years ago to work in the administration of a great president. As a staff member, I came to understand his goals and his desires. I admired his policies, his strength, and his ability to bring our country together. I observed the President to be a leader who cared deeply about people, and who believed that the interests of our country were advanced by recognizing that ours is a nation at risk and a dangerous world, and acting accordingly. He tried, and in my opinion succeeded, in advancing the cause of world peace by strengthening our country, by acting to restore and sustain democracy throughout the world, and by having the courage to take decisive action when needed. . . .

I worked hard on the political military strategy restoring and sustaining democracy in Central America and in particular, El Salvador. We sought to achieve the democratic outcome in Nicaragua that this administration still supports, which involved keeping the contras together in both body and soul. We made efforts to open a new relationship with Iran, and recover our hostages. We worked on the development of a concerted policy regarding terrorists and terrorism and a capability for dealing in a concerted manner with that threat. . . .

There were many problems. I believed that we worked as hard as we could to solve them, and sometimes we succeeded, and sometimes we failed, but at least we tried, and I want to tell you that I, for one, will never regret having tried.

I believe that this is a strange process that you are putting me and others through. Apparently, the President has chosen not to assert his prerogatives, and you have been permitted to make the rules. You called before you the officials of the Executive Branch. You put them under oath for what must be collectively thousands of hours of testimony. You dissect that testimony to find inconsistencies and declare some to be truthful and others to be liars. You make the rulings as to what is proper and what is not proper. You put the testimony which you think is helpful to your goal up before the people and leave others out. It's sort of like a baseball game in which you are both the player and the umpire. It's a game in which you call the balls and strikes and where you determine who is out and who is safe. And in the end you determine the score and declare yourselves the winner.

From where I sit, it is not the fairest process. One thing is, I think, for certain—that you will not investigate yourselves in this matter. There is not much chance that you will conclude at the end of these hearings that the Boland Amendments and the frequent policy changes therefore were unwise or that your restrictions should not have been imposed on the Executive Branch. You are not likely to conclude that the Administration acted properly by trying to sustain the freedom fighters in Nicaragua when they were abandoned, and you are not likely to conclude by commending the President of the United States who tried constantly to recover our citizens and achieve an opening that is strategically vital—Iran. I would not be frank with you if I did not admit that the last several months have been difficult for me and my family. It has been difficult to be on the front pages of every newspaper in the land day after day, to be the lead story on national television day after day, to be photographed thousands of times by bands of photographers who chase us around since November just because my name arose at the hearings. It is difficult to be caught in the middle of a constitutional struggle between the Executive and legislative branches over who will formulate and direct the foreign policy of this nation. It is difficult to be vilified by people in and out of this body, some who have proclaimed that I am guilty of criminal conduct even before they heard me. . . . And, as I indicated yesterday, I think it was insensitive of this committee to place before the cameras my home address at a time when my family and I are under 24-hour armed guard by over a dozen government agents of the naval Investigative Service because of fear that terrorists will seek revenge for my official acts and carry out their announced intentions to kill me.

It is also difficult to comprehend that my work at the NSC—all of which was approved and carried out in the best interests of our country—has led to two massive parallel investigations staffed by over 200 people. It is mind-boggling to me that one of those investigations is criminal and that some here have attempted to criminalize policy differences between co-equal branches of government and the Executive's conduct of foreign affairs.

I believe it is inevitable that the Congress will in the end blame the Executive Branch, but I suggest to you that it is Congress which must accept at least some of the blame in the Nicaraguan freedom fighters' matter. Plain and simple, the Congress is to blame because of the fickle, vacillating, unpredictable, on-again off-again policy toward the Nicaraguan Democratic Resistance—the so-called Contras. . . .

Armies need food and consistent help. They need a flow of money, of arms, clothing and medical supplies. The Congress of the United States allowed the executive to encourage them, to do battle, and then abandoned them. The Congress of the United States left soldiers in the field unsupported and vulnerable to their communist enemies. When the executive branch did everything possible within the law to prevent them from being wiped out by Moscow's surrogates in Havana and Managua, you then had the investigation to blame the problem on the executive branch; It does not make sense to me.

In my opinion, these hearings have caused serious damage to our national interests. Our adversaries laugh at us and our friends recoil in horror. I suppose it would be one thing if the intelligence committees wanted to hear all of this in private and thereafter pass laws which in the view of Congress make for better policies or better functioning of government. But, to hold them publicly for the whole world to see strikes me as very harmful. Not only does it embarrass our friends and allies with whom we have worked, many of whom have helped us in various programs, but must also make them very wary of helping us again.

I believe that these hearings, perhaps unintentionally so, have revealed matters of great secrecy in the operation of our government. And sources and methods of intelligence activities have clearly been revealed to the detriment of our security. . . .

I don't mind telling you that I'm angry that what some have attempted to do to me and my family [sic]. I believe that the committee hearings will show that you have struck some blows. But, I am going to walk from here with my head high and my shoulders straight because I am proud of what we accomplished. I am proud of the efforts that we made, and I am proud of the fight that we fought. I am proud of serving the administration of a great president. . . . In closing, Mr. Chairman, and I thank you for this opportunity, I would just simply like to thank the tens of thousands of Americans who have communicated their support, encouragement and prayers for me and my family in this difficult time. Thank you, sir.

Questions

1. How does Oliver North justify his role in the Iran-Contra affair?
2. Why does North maintain that congressional scrutiny of decisions by the executive branch of government is unwise and unjustified?
3. Why do you think many Americans were persuaded by Colonel North's defense of his actions? Are you persuaded by his arguments? Why or why not?

Proposition 187 (1994)

Anxiety over immigration often occurs during periods of economic stress, and California in the early and mid-1990s was no exception. As a bulwark of the military-industrial complex, the state may have suffered more than any other from the end of the Cold War. The "peace dividend" there seemed to be a combination of high unemployment and taxes.

Such was the environment in 1994, when Californians passed Proposition 187. The referendum sought to deny government services to illegal immigrants. Ironically, many legal immigrants who were politically conservative turned against the Republican party for supporting the measure.

SECTION 1. Findings and Declaration.

The People of California find and declare as follows:

That they have suffered and are suffering economic hardship caused by the presence of illegal aliens in this state.

That they have suffered and are suffering personal injury and damage caused by the criminal conduct of illegal aliens in this state.

That they have a right to the protection of their government from any person or persons entering this country unlawfully.

Therefore, the People of California declare their intention to provide for cooperation between their agencies of state and local government with the federal government, and to establish a system of required notification by and between such agencies to prevent illegal aliens in the United States from receiving benefits or public services in the State of California.

SECTION 2. Manufacture, Distribution or Sale of False Citizenship or Resident Alien Documents: Crime and Punishment.

Section 113 is added to the Penal Code, to read:

113. Any person who manufactures, distributes or sells false documents to conceal the true citizenship or resident alien status of another person is guilty of a felony, and shall be punished by imprisonment in the state prison for five years or by a fine of seventy-five thousand dollars ($75,000). . . .

SECTION 5. Exclusion of Illegal Aliens from Public Social Services.

Section 10001.5 is added to the Welfare and Institutions Code, to read:

10001.5.(a) In order to carry out the intention of the People of California that only citizens of the United States and aliens lawfully admitted to the United States may receive the benefits of public social services and to ensure that all persons employed in the providing of those services shall diligently protect public funds from misuse, the provisions of this section are adopted.

(b) A Person shall not receive any public social services to which he or she may be otherwise entitled until the legal status of that person has been verified as one of the following:

(1) A citizen of the United States.

(2) An alien lawfully admitted as a permanent resident.

(3) An alien lawfully admitted for a temporary period of time.

(c) If any public entity in this state to whom a person has applied for public social services determines or reasonably suspects, based upon the information provided to it, that the person is an alien in the United States in violation of federal law, the following procedures shall be followed by the public entity:

(1) The entity shall not provide the person with benefits or services.

(2) The entity shall, in writing, notify the person of his or her apparent illegal immigration status, and that the person must either obtain legal status or leave the United States.

(3) The entity shall also notify the State Director of Social Services, the Attorney General of California, and the United States Immigration and Naturalization Service of the apparent illegal status, and shall provide any additional information that may be requested by any other public entity.

SECTION 6. Exclusion of Illegal Aliens from Publicly-Funded Health Care.

Chapter 1.3 (commencing with Section 130) is added to Part 1 of Division 1 of the Health and Safety Code, to read:

Chapter 1.3. Publicly-Funded Health Care Services

130. (a) In order to carry out the intention of the People of California that, excepting emergency medical care as required by federal law, only citizens of the United States and aliens lawfully admitted to the United States may receive the benefits of publicly-funded health care, and to ensure that all persons employed in the providing of those services shall diligently protect public funds from misuse, the provisions of this section are adopted.

(b) A person shall not receive any health care services from a publicly-funded health care facility to which he or she is otherwise entitled until the legal status of that person has been verified as one of the following:

(1) A citizen of the United States.

(2) An alien lawfully admitted as a permanent resident.

(3) An alien lawfully admitted for a temporary period of time.

(c) If any publicly-funded health care facility in this state from whom a person seeks health care services, other than emergency medical care as required by federal law, determines or reasonably suspects, based upon the information provided to it, that the person is an alien in the United States in violation of federal law, the following procedures shall be followed by the facility:

(1) The facility shall not provide the person with services.

(2) The facility shall, in writing, notify the person of his or her apparent illegal immigration status, and that the person must either obtain legal status or leave the United States.

(3) The facility shall also notify the State Director of Health Services, the Attorney General of California, and the United States Immigration and Naturalization Service of the apparent illegal status, and shall provide any additional information that may be requested by any other public entity. . . .

SECTION 7. Exclusion of Illegal Aliens from Public Elementary and Secondary Schools.

Section 48215 is added to the Education Code, to read:

48215. (a) No public elementary or secondary school shall admit, or permit the attendance of, any child who is not a citizen of the United States, an alien lawfully admitted as a permanent resident, or a person who is otherwise authorized under federal law to be present in the United States. . . .

Questions

1. To what extent are these findings and declarations convincing? What, if any, facts are missing?

2. Which provisions appear reasonable and which appear unfair? Why?

3. Imagine writing a state referendum on immigration. How would it compare to Proposition 187?

Alvin Toffler,
"The Electronic Cottage" (1980)

As the historian Frederick Jackson Turner suggested, Americans are forever looking to the frontier—and the better future that may accompany it. The critic and futurist Alvin Toffler fits into that tradition. Toffler sees the communications revolution of the second half of the twentieth century as the third great wave of change in human history, following agriculture and the Industrial Revolution. The frontier is cyberspace, and changes ushered in by the computer, Toffler believes, promise a great future if developed correctly. Here Toffler discusses how the Third Wave will make work once again a cottage industry.

THE HOME-CENTERED SOCIETY

If the electronic cottage were to spread, a chain of consequences of great importance would flow through society. Many of these consequences would please the most ardent environmentalist or techno-rebel, while at the same time opening new options for business entrepreneurship.

Community Impact: Work at home involving any sizeable fraction of the population could mean greater community stability—a goal that now seems beyond our reach in many high-change regions. If employees can perform some or all of their work tasks at home, they do not have to move every time they change jobs, as many are compelled to do today. They can simply plug into a different computer.

This implies less forced mobility, less stress on the individual, fewer transient human relationships, and greater participation in community life. Today when a family moves into a community, suspecting that it will be moving out again in a year or two, its members are markedly reluctant to join neighborhood organizations, to make deep friendships, to engage in local politics, and to commit themselves to community life generally. The electronic cottage could help restore a sense of community belonging, and touch off a renaissance among voluntary organizations like churches, women's groups, lodges, clubs, athletic and youth organizations. The electronic cottage could mean more of what sociologists, with their love of German jargon, call *gemeinschaft*.

Environmental Impact: The transfer of work, or any part of it, into the home could not only reduce energy requirements . . . but could also lead to energy decentralization. Instead of requiring highly concentrated amounts of energy in a few high-rise offices or sprawling factory complexes, and therefore requiring highly centralized energy generation, the electronic cottage system would spread out energy demand and thus make it easier to use solar, wind, and other alternative energy technologies. Small-scale energy generation units in each home could substitute for at least some of the centralized energy now required. This implies a decline in pollution as well, for two reasons: first, the switch to renewable energy sources on a small-scale basis eliminates the need for high-polluting fuels, and second, it means smaller releases of highly concentrated pollutants that overload the environment at a few critical locations.

Economic Impact: Some businesses would shrink in such a system, and others proliferate or grow. Clearly, the electronics and computer and communications industries would flourish. By contrast, the oil companies, the auto industry, and commercial real estate developers would be hurt. A whole new group of small-scale computer stores and information services would spring up; the postal service, by contrast, would shrink. Papermakers would do less well; most service industries and white-collar industries would benefit. . . .

Psychological Impact: The picture of a work world that is increasingly dependent upon abstract symbols conjures up an overcerebral work environment that is alien to us and, at one level, more impersonal than at present. But at a different level, work at home suggests a deepening of face-to-face and emotional relationships in both the home and the neighborhood. Rather than a world of purely vicarious human relationships, with an electric screen interposed between the individual and the rest of humanity, as imagined in many science fiction stories, one can postulate a world divided into two sets of human relationships—one real, the other vicarious—with different rules and roles in each. . . .

Certainly not everyone can or will (or will want to) work at home. Certainly we face a conflict over pay scales and opportunity cost. What happens to the society when an increased amount of human interaction on the job is vicarious while face-to-face, emotion-to-emotion interaction intensifies in the home? What about cities? What happens to the unemployment figures? What, in fact, do we mean by the terms "employment" and "unemployment" in such a system? It would be naïve to dismiss such questions and problems.

But if there are unanswered questions and possibly painful difficulties, there are also new possibilities. The leap to a new system of production is likely to render irrelevant many of the most intractable problems of the passing era. The misery of feudal toil, for example, could not be alleviated within the system of feudal agriculture. It was not eliminated by peasant revolts, by altruistic nobles, or by religious utopians. Toil remained miserable until it was altered entirely by the arrival of the factory system, with its own strikingly different drawbacks.

In turn, the characteristic problems of industrial society—from unemployment to grinding monotony on the job, to overspecialization, to the callous treatment of the individual, to low wages—may, despite the best intentions and promises of job enlargers, trade unions, benign employers, or revolutionary workers' parties, be wholly unresolvable within the framework of the Second Wave production system. If such problems have remained for 300 years, under both capitalist and socialist arrangements, there is cause to think they may be inherent in the mode of production.

The leap to a new production system, in both manufacturing and the white-collar sector, and the possible breakthrough to the electronic cottage, promise to change all the existing terms of debate, making obsolete most of the issues over which men and women today argue, struggle, and sometimes die.

We cannot today know if, in fact, the electronic cottage will become the norm of the future. Nevertheless, it is worth recognizing that if as few as 10 to 20 percent of the work force as presently defined were to make this historic transfer over the next 20 to 30 years, our entire economy, our cities, our family structure, our values, and even our politics would be altered almost beyond our recognition.

It is a possibility—a plausibility, perhaps—to be pondered. . . .

Questions

1. What is the great appeal of this kind of look at the future?
2. What, if any, downside does Toffler see to this new arrangement?
3. What problems might working at home involve that Toffler ignores? What advantages are there to working outside the home?

Connections Questions

1. Compare the ideas of George Gilder to William Graham Sumner (see Chapter 19, "The Forgotten Man"). Are there major differences? Is Gilder outdated, or was Sumner ahead of his time as a social critic? Explain.
2. Is Proposition 187 a rehashing of the ideas of Madison Grant (see Chapter 24, "Closing the Flood-Gates") or something else? How so?
3. What is the inherent appeal in the ideas of Ronald Reagan and Alvin Toffler? Will that popularity carry over into the next century? Why or why not?

ACKNOWLEDGMENTS

CHAPTER 16

"Carl Schurz, Report on Conditions in the South." U.S. Congress, Senate, 39th Cong. 1st session (1865). Excerpts taken from Doc. No. 2, pp. 1–5, 8, 36–39, 41–44.

"The Mississippi Black Codes (1865)." Excerpts taken from *Laws of Mississippi* (1865), pp. 82 ff.

"Thaddeus Stevens on Black Suffrage and Land Redistribution (1867)." Excerpt taken from *Congressional Globe,* January 3, 1867, p. 252; March 19, 1867, p. 203.

"The Rise and Fall of Northern Support for Reconstruction (1868, 1874)." Cartoons by Thomas Nast, "This is a White Man's Government," from *Harper's Weekly,* September 5, 1868 and "Colored Rule in a Reconstructed State," from *Harper's Weekly,* March 14, 1874. Art courtesy of Research Libraries, New York Public Library.

Excerpt taken from *A Fool's Errand, By One of the Fools* [Albion W. Tourgee]. (New York: Fords, Howard, & Hulbert, 1878), pp. 182–192.

"Republicanism vs. Grantism (1872)." Excerpt taken from *Charles Sumner: His Complete Works* (Lee and Shepard, 1900; reprint New York: Negro University Press, 1969), vol. 20, pp. 83–171.

CHAPTER 17

"Our First Winter on the Prairie." Taken from *A Son of the Middle Border* by Hamlin Garland, (1920), pp. 85–98. Reprinted with the permission of Macmillan, a division of Simon & Schuster.

Excerpt taken from *A Century of Dishonor* by Helen Hunt Jackson. First published by Harper & Brothers, 1881; reprinted by Harper & Row, 1965, pp. 338–342. By permission of the publisher.

"The Chinese Exclusion Act (1882)." Taken from *Statutes at Large,* vol. 22, pp. 58ff.

"Hetch Hetchy Valley." Excerpt taken from *The Mountains of California* by John Muir. Published by Houghton Mifflin Company (1917), vol. 2, pp. 278–290. Reprinted by permission.

"Farmer Green's Reaper." Excerpt taken from *History of the Grange Movement; or, The Farmer's War against Monopolies* by Edward Winslow Martin. (Chicago: National Publishing Company, 1874), pp. 339–346.

CHAPTER 18

"Philip Danforth Armour Testifies before the U.S. Senate (1889)." Taken from *Armour and His Times* by Harper Leech and John Charles Carroll. (New York: D. Appleton-Century, 1938), pp. 193–196.

Rocco Corresca. "The Biography of a Bootblack." Taken from *Workers Speak: Self Portraits* edited by Leon Stein and Philip Taft, 1902–1906; reprint, New York: Arno and New York Times, 1971, pp. 83–87.

Anonymous (A Black Domestic), "More Slavery at the South." First published in *The Independent* 72, January 25, 1912, pp. 196–200. Reprinted in *Women in the American Economy: A Documentary History, 1675 to 1929* by Elliott Brownlee and Mary M. Brownlee, published by Yale University Press, 1976, pp. 244–249.

"The Principles of Scientific Management (1911)." Excerpt taken from *Scientific Management* by Frederick Winslow Taylor. Published by Harper & Row, 1947; reprint Westport, Conn.: Greenwood Press, 1972, pp. 58–57.

Terence V. Powderly, "The Army of the Unemployed" Excerpt taken from *The Labor Movement: The Problems of Today* edited by George E. McNeill (1971), pp. 577–584. Reprinted by permission of Augustus M. Kelley Publishers. Originally published by A. M. Bridgeman & Company (Boston) & M. W. Hazen Co. (New York), 1887.

CHAPTER 19

"The Forgotten Man." Originally presented by William Graham Summer in an address to the Brooklyn Historical Society in 1883. Reprinted in *The Forgotten Man and Other Essays* edited by Albert Galloway Keller, Yale University Press (1919).

"Women and Temperance." Speech delivered by Frances E. Willard in 1876. Published in *Women and Temperance or, The Work and Workers of the Woman's Christian Temperance Union* by Frances E. Willard, 1883. Reprinted by Arno Press (1972), pp. 452–457.

Luna Kellie, "Stand Up for Nebraska." Taken from *Prairie Populist: The Memoirs of Luna Kellie* edited by Jane Taylor Nelson, pp. 127–132. Copyright © 1992 by the University of Iowa Press. Reprinted by permission of the publisher. Originally published in *Alliance Independent,* January 11, 1894.

Ida B. Wells, "Lynching at the Curve." Taken from *Crusade for Justice: The Autobiography of Ida B. Wells* edited by Alfreda M. Duster, pp. 47–51. Copyright © 1970 by The University of Chicago Press. Reprinted by permission of the publisher.

Excerpt taken from *The Souls of Black Folk* by W. E. B. Du Bois, Penguin Books (1989), pp. 36–50. Originally published by A.C. McClurg, 1903.

CHAPTER 20

"The City Beautiful." Excerpt taken from *The City: The Hope of Democracy* by Frederic C. Howe, University of Washington Press (1967), pp. 239–245. Originally published by Charles Scribner's Sons, 1905.

Josiah Strong, "The Dangers of Cities (1886)." Excerpts taken from *Our Country* edited by Jurgen Herbst. Published by Harvard University Press (1963), pp. 171–174, 176, 183–185.

"The Immigrant Experience: Letters Home (1901–1903)." Letters from Konstanty and Antoni Butkowski to their parents, December 6, 1901–April 21, 1903. Reprinted in *The Polish Peasant in Europe and America,* 2 volumes, by William I. Thomas and Florian Anaiecki, Dover Publications, Inc. (1958). This is an unabridged unaltered reproduction of the second edition originally published by Alfred A. Knopf (1927).

"The Christian Family." Excerpt taken from *The American Woman's Home or, Principles of Domestic Science* by Catharine E. Beecher and Harriet Beecher Stowe. Copyright © 1975 Stowe Day Foundation. Published by Library of Victorian Culture, an imprint of The American Life Foundation 1979, pp. 17–22. Originally published by J. B. Ford & Company, 1869. Reprinted by permission of the Stowe Day Foundation/Harriet Beecher Stowe, Center, Hartford, CT.

Excerpt taken from *Sister Carrie* by Theodore Dreiser, in Bantam Books, a division of Bantam Doubleday Dell Publishing Group, Inc. (1958), pp. 28–33. Originally published by Doubleday, Page & Company, 1900.

"On the Columbian Exposition of 1893." Excerpt taken from *The Education of Henry Adams* by Henry Adams, Modern Library (1931), pp. 340–343. Originally published by the Massachusetts Historical Society (1918).

CHAPTER 21

"The Church and the Social Movement (1907)." Excerpts taken from *Christianity and the Social Crisis* by Walter Rauschenbusch. Published by Macmillan, 1912, pp. 304–305, 328–331. Courtesy of Carl Rauschenbush, age 95, (Walter's last surviving child).

Excerpt from *Twenty Years at Hull House: With Autobiographical Notes* by Jane Addams, New American Library, n.d., pp. 200–204. Originally published by Phillips Publishing Company (1910).

Samuel Lipson, "Testimony on the Lawrence, Massachusetts Strike." Excerpt taken from *Hearings on House Resolutions 409 and 433, The Strike at Lawrence, Mass.,* 62nd Congress, 2nd session (1912). H. Doc. 671, pp. 32–36. U.S. Congress, House Committee on Rules.

"The Dark Side of Progressivism." Excerpt taken from *Laws of the State of Indiana* (1907), pp. 377–378.

Theodore Roosevelt, "The Struggle for Social Justice." Excerpt taken from *Progressive Principles: Selections from Addresses Made during the Presidential Campaign of 1912* edited by Elmer H. Youngman (New York: Progressive National Service, 1913), pp. 199–207.

"The Progressive Party Platform of 1912." Taken from *National Party Platforms 1840–1964* by Kirk H. Porter and Donald Bruce Johnson, comps., University of Illinois Press, 1966, pp. 175–178. Reprinted by permission.

CHAPTER 22

"Open House Days" for a China Missionary (1905). Excerpt taken from *Golden Inches: The China Memoir of Grace Service* edited by John S. Service, pp. 67–75. Copyright © 1989 by the Regents of the University of California. Reprinted by permission of the University of California Press.

"The Command of the Pacific (1902)." Excerpts taken from *The Meaning of the Times and Other Speeches* by Albert J. Beveridge, Books for Libraries Press (1968), pp. 188, 190–197. Originally published by Bobbs-Merrill (1908).

Mark Twain, "To the Person Sitting in the Darkness (1901)." Excerpt taken from *Mark Twain: Collected Tales, Sketches, Speeches, and Essays, 1891–1910.* Published by Library of America, a division of Literary Classics of U.S., Inc. (1992), pp. 465–473.

John Hay, "Open Door Notes (1899, 1900)." Excerpt taken from *Documents of American History,* 10th edition edited by Henry Steele Commager and Milton Cantor. Published by Prentice Hall (1988), vol. 2, pp. 9–11. Letter from John Hay to Andrew D. White, September 6, 1899; and JH circular letter to the powers cooperating in China, July 3, 1900.

"The Roosevelt Corollary to the Monroe Doctrine (1904, 1905)." Excerpts taken from *A Compilation of the Messages and Papers of the Presidents* edited by James D. Richardson, vol. 10, pp. 831–832; vol. 14, pp. 6944ff. Theodore Roosevelt. Fourth annual message to Congress, December 6, 1904 and his fifth annual message to Congress, December 5, 1905.

CHAPTER 23

Excerpts from *Toward the Flame: A War Diary* by Hervey Allen. Copyright © 1926, 1934 by Hervey Allen. Copyright © 1954, 1962 by Ann Andrews Allen. Published by the University of Pittsburgh Press (1968), pp. 111–119. Originally published by Henry Holt & Company, (1926). Reprinted by permission of Henry Holt & Company, Inc.

"U.S. Army Mental Tests." Tests 2 and 3 from *Army Mental Tests* by Clarence S. Yoakum and Robert M. Yerkes, pp. 206–209. Copyright © 1920 by Henry Holt & Company, Inc. Published with the authorization of the War Department.

Chicago Board of Education, *Spelling Book for Grades Four, Five, Six, Seven, Eight* (1914).

"The Home Front: Women Fund-Raisers." Excerpts taken from "The Campaign of the Young Women's Christian Association," in *Welfare Campaigns in Iowa* by Marcus L. Hansen. Published by the State Historical Society of Iowa, 1920, pp. 100–103, 105–106, 108, 111–112. Reprinted by permission of the publisher.

"Opposition to the League of Nations." Taken from *The Senate and the League of Nations* by Henry Cabot Lodge. Published by Charles Scribner's Sons, 1925, pp. 227–233. This speech was given by Henry Cabot Lodge to the U.S. Senate, February 28, 1919.

"The Boston Police Strike." Taken from *Have Faith in Massachusetts: A Collection of Speeches and Messages,* 2nd edition by Calvin Coolidge. Published by Houghton Mifflin Company, Inc., 1919, pp. 225–227.

CHAPTER 24

Excerpts taken from *Only Yesterday: An Informal History of the Nineteen-Twenties* by Frederick Lewis Allen. Copyright © 1931 by Frederick Lewis Allen. Copyright renewed 1959 by Agnes Rogers Allen. Reprinted by permission of HarperCollins Publishers, Inc.

Listerine Advertisement (1932). *"In his discreet way he told her."* Courtesy of Warner Lambert Company, the owner of the trademark LISTERINE™ and the copyrighted material in the ad. All rights reserved.

"The Wanderer" still. Copyright © by Universal City Studios, Inc. Courtesy of MCA Publishing Rights, a division of MCA Inc. All Rights Reserved.

"Closing the Flood-Gates." Excerpt taken from *The Alien in Our Midst or, Selling Our Birthright for a Mess of Pottage: The Written Voices of a Number of Americans (Present and Former) on Immigration and Its Results* edited by Madison Grant and Charles Steward Davison. (New York: Galton Publishing Company, 1930), pp. 13–21.

"Editorial in the *Negro World.*" Taken from *Negro World,* September 2, 1924. Reprinted courtesy of The Marcus Garvey & UNIA Papers Project, African Studies Center, University of California, Los Angeles.

CHAPTER 25

Excerpts taken from *Prosperity: Fact or Myth* by Stuart Chase. Published by C. Boni, 1929, pp. 173–177, 186–188.

Proposals for Recovery (1930–1931). Taken from "Fact and Comment" by B.C. Forbes in *Forbes,* September 15, 1930, p.11; "New Business Will Arise!" by Julius Klein in *Forbes,* September 15, 1930, pp. 15–17; "National Sales Month Suggested," in "Fact and Comment" by B.C. Forbes, October 15, 1931, p. 10. Reprinted by permission of *Forbes* magazine. © Forbes, Inc., 1930.

John T. McCutcheon cartoon. "A Wise Economist Asks a Question (1932)." © Tribune Media Services, Inc. All Rights Reserved. Reprinted with permission.

"President Hoover." As broadcast on E.R. Squibb & Sons, April 20, 1930. From the Archives of the Will Rogers Museum of Oklahoma. Reprinted by permission.

Excerpt taken from *American Hunger* by Richard Wright. Copyright © 1944 by Richard Wright. Copyright © 1977 by Ellen Wright. Reprinted by permission of HarperCollins Publishers, Inc.

CHAPTER 26

"Candidate Attends World Series." Photo reproduction courtesy of the Joseph M. Jacobs Collection of Rooseveltiana, Special Collection. The University Library, The University of Illinois at Chicago.

Huey Long. Taken from *Every Man a King: The Autobiography of Huey P. Long* by Huey Long. Published by Quadrangle Books (1964), pp. 338–340. First published by National Book Company (1933).

Eleanor Roosevelt. "The State's Responsibility for Fair Working Conditions." Taken from *Scribner's Magazine,* March 1933, p. 140. Copyright 1933 by Charles Scribner's Sons; copyright renewed © 1961 by Charles Scribner's Sons. Reprinted with the permission of Scribner, a division of Simon & Schuster.

"Memorial Day Massacre." Reprinted from "Riots Blamed on Red Chiefs: Coroner Moves Today to Seize Mob's Leaders," and "Chicagoans Led in Steel Strike by Outsiders: Union Organizers Come from Far Points," in the *Chicago Daily Tribune,* June 1, 1937. Copyrighted © Chicago Tribune Company. All rights reserved. Used with permission.

"The Federal Writres' Project: Barre, Vermont." Excerpts from "Alfred Tornazzi" interview conducted by Marie Tomasi and "Anthony Tonelli" interview conducted by John Lynch as reprinted in *First Person America* edited by Ann Banks. Published by W.W. Norton & Company, Inc. 1991, pp. 101–102, 104–105. By permission of the author.

"A Miner's Home: Vicinity Morgantown, West Virginia, July 1935." Photograph by Walker Evans. From *Walker Evans: Photographs for the Farm Security Administration, 1935–1938.* Published by Da Capo Press, 1973. Courtesy of the Farm Security Administration Collection, Library of Congress.

CHAPTER 27

"The Neutrality Act of 1937." Taken from *Statues at Large*, volume 50, p. 121 (United States).

Franklin D. Roosevelt, "State of the Union Address." Taken from *The Public Papers and Addresses of Franklin D. Roosevelt, 1937*, edited by Samuel I. Rosenman. Published by Macmillan, 1941, pp. 406–411.

Executive Order 9066, "Authorizing the Secretary of War to Prescribe Military Areas." Taken from the 7 *Federal Register*, no. 38, p. 1407 (February 25, 1942).

Norma Yerger Queen, "Women on the Home Front." From the Office of War Information, 1944.

U.S. Supreme Court, *Smith v. Allwright*. 321 U.S. 649 (1944).

Franklin D. Roosevelt on the Yalta Conference. Taken from *The Public Papers and Addresses of Franklin D. Roosevelt, 1944–1945* edited by Samuel I. Rosenman. Published by Harper & Bros. 1950, pp. 571–586.

CHAPTER 28

George Kennan, "The Sources of Soviet Conduct." Taken from *Foreign Affairs*, July 1947, pp. 566–582. Copyright © 1947 by The Council on Foreign Relations, Inc. Reprinted by permission of *Foreign Affairs*.

Senator Arthur Vandenberg on NATO. Excerpts taken from *The Private Papers of Senator Vandenberg* edited by Arthur H. Vandenberg, Jr. with the collaboration of Joe Alex Morris. Copyright © 1952 by Arthur Vandenberg, Jr. © renewed 1980. Reprinted by permission of Houghton Mifflin Company. All rights reserved.

Harry S. Truman on Civil Rights. Excerpt taken from *Public Papers of the Presidents of the United States: Harry S. Truman, 1947*. (Washington, D.C.: U.S. Government Printing Office, 1963), pp. 311–313.

Joseph R. McCarthy on Communists in the U.S. Government (1950). Excerpt taken from *Congressional Record*, 81st Congress, 2nd Session, 1950, vol. 96, pt. 2, pp. 1954–1957.

Dwight D. Eisenhower, Farewell Address (1961). Taken from *Public Papers of the Presidents of the United States: Dwight D. Eisenhower, 1960–1961*. (Washington, D.C.: U.S. Government Printing Office, 1961), pp. 1035–1040.

CHAPTER 29

Advertisement for Green Acres Subdivision. From *The New York Times*, June 25, 1950, sec. 8, p. 6.

Excerpt taken from *The Urban Villagers* by Herbert J. Gans, pp. 20–23. Copyright © 1962 by The Free Press. Copyright © 1982 by Herbert J. Gans. Reprinted with the permission of The Free Press, a division of Simon & Schuster.

Howell Raines, "Interview with Rosa Parks." Excerpt taken from *My Soul is Rested: The Story of the Civil Rights Movement in the Deep South* by Howell Raimes, pp. 40–41. Copyright © 1977 by Howell Raines. Reprinted by permission of The Putnam Publishing Group.

Barnett Newman and Jackson Pollock on Painting. Excerpts taken from (1) an interview with Barnett Newman by Dorothy Seckler, "Frontiers in Space," *Art in America*, vol. 50, no. 2 (Summer 1962), pp. 86–87; (2) "Unframed Space" in "The Talk of the Town" from *The New Yorker*, August 5, 1950, p. 16; and (3) an unpublished letter from Jackson Pollock to Alfonso Ossorio and Edward Dragon, June 7, 1951. All three in Los Angeles Country Museum of Art, *New School: The First Generation—Paintings of the 1940's and 1950's* (a catalogue of the exhibition with statements by the artists and critics), edited by Maurice Tuchman (July 16–August 1, 1965), Lytton Gallery), pp. 23–25. New Yorker piece: © 1950 The New Yorker Magazine, Inc. Reprinted by permission. All rights reserved. Quotation in Pollock letter to Ossorio and Dragon (1951): © 1998 Pollock-Krasner Foundation/Artists Rights Society (ARS), New York. By permission of ARS.

CHAPTER 30

"The Television Debates." Excerpt taken from *The Making of the President, 1960* by Theodore H. White. Copyright © 1961 by Theodord H. White. Published by Atheneum, a division of Simon & Schuster, pp. 279–287. Reprinted with the permission of the publisher.

John F. Kennedy, "Inaugural Address." Taken from *Public Papers of the Presidents of the United States: John F. Kennedy, 1961.* (Washington, D.C.: U.S. Government Printing Office, 1962), pp. 1–3.

Martin Luther King, Jr. "Letter from Birmingham City Jail" (1963). Taken from *A Testament of Hope: The Essential Writings of Martin Luther King, Jr.* edited by James Melvin Washington. Published by HarperCollins, 1991, pp. 289–302. Reprinted by arrangement with The Heirs to the Estate of Martin Luther King, Jr. c/o The Writers House, Inc. as agent for the proprietor. Copyright © 1963 by Martin Luther King, Jr.: Copyright renewed 1991 by Coretta Scott King.

Michael Harrington. Excerpt taken from *The Other America: Poverty in the United States* by Michael Harrington, pp. 158–162. Copyright © 1962, 1969, 1981 by Michael Harrington. Reprinted with the permission of Simon & Schuster.

"The Consequences of Termination for the Menominees of Wisconsin." Excerpts taken from *Native American Testimony: A Chronicle of Indian–White Relations from Prophecy to the Present, 1492–1992* edited by Peter Nabokov. Published by Viking Penguin 1991, pp. 344–347. DRUMS Committee, Menominee, chronology from

DRUMS testimony, Hearings on Senate Concurrent Resolution Number 26, Senate Committee on Interior and Insular Affairs, July 21, 1971.

CHAPTER 31

Ho Chi Minh, "Vietnam's Declaration of Independence (1945)." Taken from *Ho Chi Minh: Selected Writings, 1920–1969* by Ho Chi Minh. Published by Foreign Languages Publishing House, 1977, pp. 53–56. Reprinted in *Ho Chi Minh Selected Writings* (The Gioi Publishers, 1994.) Reprinted by permission.

"The Gulf of Tonkin Resolution (1964)." Taken from *Department of State Bulletin*, August 29, 1964, p. 268.

Students for a Democratic Society, "The Port Huron Statement (1962)." Reprinted by permission of Senator Tom Hayden. A copy of the third printing is available in the Labadie Collection, Hatcher Graduate Library, University of Michigan.

Excerpt taken from *Home Before Morning: The Story of an Army Nurse in Vietnam* by Lynda Van Devanter, with Christopher Morgan. Published by Beaufort Books, 1983, pp. 209–212.

Eleanor Wimbish, "A Mother Remembers Her Son at 'The Wall' " (1984). Excerpt taken from *Dear America: Letters Home from Vietnam* edited by Bernard Edelman for the New York Vietnam Veterans Memorial Commission. Published by W. W. Norton & Company, 1985, pp. 299–300. Reprinted by permission of the author.

CHAPTER 32

Daniel Patrick Moynihan, "Memorandum for the President" (1970). Taken from "Text of the Moynihan Memorandum on the Status of Negroes." *The New York Times*, March 1, 1970. Copyright © 1970 The New York Times Company. Reprinted by permission.

"White House Conversations (1972)." Excerpt taken from U.S. Congress, House, *Hearings before the Committee on the Judiciary*, 93rd Congress, 2nd session, 1974. White House transcripts of conversations between H. R. Haldeman and Richard Nixon in the Oval Office of the President, June 23, 1972.

Excerpt taken from *Homestead: The Glory and Tragedy of an American Steel Town* by William Serrin. Copyright © 1992 by William Serrin. Reprinted by permission of Times, Books, a division of Random House, Inc.

Excerpt taken from *The Power of the Positive Woman* by Phyllis Schlafly. Copyright © 1977 by Phyllis Schlafly. Reprinted by permission of Arlington House, Inc., a division of Crown Publishers, Inc.

CHAPTER 33

Ronald Reagan. Excerpts taken from *An American Life* by Ronald Reagan, pp. 27–29, 66–69. Copyright © 1990 by Ronald W. Reagan. Reprinted with the permission of Simon & Schuster.

George Gilder. Excerpt taken from *Wealth and Poverty* by George Gilder, pp. 68–71. Copyright © 1981 by George Gilder. Reprinted by permission of Georges Borchardt, Inc. on behalf of the author.

Oliver North, "Testimony before Congress." Taken from *Joint Hearings before the Senate Select Committee on Secret Military Assistance to Iran and the Nicaraguan Opposition and the House Select Committee to Investigate Covert Arms Transactions with Iran,* 100th Congress, 1st. session, pt. 1, 1987.

"Proposition 187." *California Voter Information: Proposition 187, Text of Proposed Law.* California Secretary of State's Office.

Alvin Toffler, "The Electronic Cottage." Excerpt taken from *The Third Wave* by Alvin Toffler. Copyright © 1980 by Alvin Toffler. Reprinted by permission of William Morrow & Company, Inc.